Adobe **Premiere Pro**

2024 Release

Classroom in a Book®
The official training workbook from Adobe

Maxim Jago

Adobe Premiere Pro Classroom in a Book® 2024 Release

Writer: Maxim Jago
Adobe Press Executive Editor: Laura Norman
Sponsoring Editor: Anshul Sharma
Development Editor: Victor Gavenda
Adobe Press Production Editor: Tracey Croom
Technical Reviewer: Jarle Leirpoll
Keystroke Reviewer: Megan Ahearn
Copyeditor: Linda Laflamme
Proofreader: Kim Wimpsett
Compositor: Kim Scott, Bumpy Design
Indexer: James Minkin
Cover Illustration: Fanny Texier, behance.net/fannytexier
Interior Designer: Mimi Heft

ISBN-13: 978-0-13-831856-7

ISBN-10:   0-13-831856-5

WHERE ARE THE LESSON FILES?

Purchase of this Classroom in a Book in any format gives you access to the lesson files you'll need to complete the exercises in the book.

1   Go to *peachpit.com/PremiereProCIB2024*.

2   Sign in or create a new account.

3   Click Submit.

> ● **Note:** If you encounter problems registering your product or accessing the lesson files or web edition, go to *peachpit.com/support* for assistance.

4   Answer the questions as proof of purchase.

5   The lesson files can be accessed through the Registered Products tab on your Account page.

6   Click the Access Bonus Content link below the title of your product to proceed to the download page. Click the lesson file links to download them to your computer.

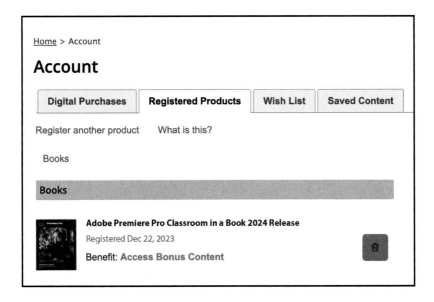

> ● **Note:** If you purchased a digital product directly from *peachpit.com*, your product will already be registered. Look for the Access Bonus Content link on the Registered Products tab in your account.

Important!

The video clips and other media files provided with this book are practice files, provided for your personal, educational use in these lessons only. You are not authorized to use these files commercially or to publish, share, or distribute them in any form without written permission from Adobe Inc., and the individual copyright holders of the various items. Do not share videos created with these lesson files publicly. This includes, but is not limited to, distribution via social media or online video services including YouTube and Vimeo. You will find a complete copyright statement on the copyright page at the beginning of this book.

Thanks to Patrick Cannell for the music "Ambient Heavens," copyright © 2015 by Patrick Cannell.

Thanks to Patrick Cannell for the music "Cooking Montage," copyright © 2015 by Patrick Cannell.

Thanks to Luisa Winters at MidAtlanticDrones.com for Valley Of Fire footage, copyright © 2019 Maxim Jago.

Footage from *Andrea Sweeney NYC*, copyright © 2015 by Maxim Jago.

Footage from *Laura in the Snow*, copyright © 2015 by Maxim Jago.

Footage from *Theft Unexpected*, copyright © 2014 by Maxim Jago.

Footage from *She*, copyright © 2017 by Maxim Jago.

ACKNOWLEDGMENTS

Producing effective learning materials for such an advanced technology is a team effort. Friends, colleagues, fellow filmmakers, and technology experts have all contributed to this book. There are too many names to mention, but let's say this: I have often joked that in Britain we don't say "awesome." Instead, we say "perfectly acceptable." On this occasion, "perfectly acceptable" simply isn't enough. Rather, I will have to say our British equivalent of "super awesome." Those people who make this world better by sharing, nurturing, caring, showing, telling, demonstrating, making, and helping are all definitely "much more than acceptable."

Everything on these pages was inspected by a team of experienced editors who checked and corrected typos, spelling errors, naming errors, false attributions, suspect grammar, unhelpful phrasing, and inconsistent descriptions. This wonderful team didn't just highlight text that needed correcting. They offered positive alternatives that I could simply agree to and so, in a literal sense, this book is the product of many people's contributions. I'd like to thank the teams at Peachpit and Adobe Press, who made it possible to produce such a beautifully finessed work.

As each draft lesson was completed, the most amazing and highly experienced Victor Gavenda checked over the text to make sure it was ideally accessible for learners, and all references to the technology were reviewed by the remarkable media technology expert Jarle Leirpoll, who has an incredible depth of knowledge of Premiere Pro. I tip my hat to Linda Laflamme for reviewing the copy and spotting things we would otherwise have completely missed. Tracey Croom kept us all on-track, Kim Scott and Kim Wimpsett take the credit for the beautiful layout you see before you, and Megan Ahearn has the enviable title of Keystroker—checking each and every step in the exercises presented here to make sure everything happens just as expected.

Some of the content of this book is derived from material originally written by the world-renowned media trainer Richard Harrington. The original table of contents was worked out by the two of us, and a substantial amount of the content remains unchanged or is significantly informed by his original work.

Finally, let's not forget Adobe. The passion and enthusiasm demonstrated by those wonderful individuals, who are so committed to creatives like you and me, qualifies as "the most acceptable of all." They are, indeed, extraordinarily awesome!

—Maxim Jago

CONTENTS

GETTING STARTED

Adobe Premiere Pro, the essential video-editing application for professionals and video enthusiasts, is an incredibly scalable, efficient, and flexible video-editing system. It supports a broad range of video, audio, and image formats. Premiere Pro lets you work faster and more creatively without converting your media. The complete set of powerful and exclusive tools lets you overcome any editorial, production, and workflow challenges to deliver the high-quality work you demand.

Adobe has developed a user experience that is intuitive, flexible, and efficient, with unified design elements that match across multiple applications, making it easier to explore and discover new workflows.

About Classroom in a Book

Adobe Premiere Pro Classroom in a Book 2024 Release is part of the official training series for Adobe. The lessons are designed so that you can learn at your own pace. If you're new to Premiere Pro, you'll learn the fundamental concepts and features you'll use to create projects. This book also teaches many advanced features, including tips and techniques for using the latest version of this software.

The lessons in this edition include opportunities for hands-on practice using features such as chroma keying, dynamic trimming, color correction, media management, audio and video effects, audio mixing, and captioning. You'll also learn how to create files for the web and social media with Adobe Media Encoder. Premiere Pro is available for both macOS and Windows and uses the same project files on both platforms.

Prerequisites

Before following the exercises in the *Adobe Premiere Pro Classroom in a Book 2024 Release,* make sure your system is set up correctly and that you've installed the required software and hardware. You can view updated system requirements here:

helpx.adobe.com/premiere-pro/system-requirements.html

You should have a working knowledge of your computer and operating system. For example, you should know how to use the mouse or trackpad and standard menus and commands and also how to open, save, and close files. You should also feel comfortable navigating folders and copying files between folders. If you need to review these techniques, see the support pages for your macOS or Windows system.

It's not necessary to have a working knowledge of video concepts and terminology. If you come across a term you're not familiar with, consult the glossary at the end of the book.

Installing Premiere Pro

You must purchase an Adobe Creative Cloud subscription, or obtain a trial version, separately from this book. For system requirements and complete instructions on installing the software, visit *helpx.adobe.com/support*. You can purchase Adobe Creative Cloud by visiting *adobe.com/creativecloud*. Follow the on-screen instructions. In addition to Premiere Pro, you may want to install Photoshop, After Effects, and Audition. Adobe Media Encoder is installed automatically when you install Premiere Pro. These are all included with the full Adobe Creative Cloud license.

Selecting audio hardware

Premiere Pro has preferences to choose the audio hardware to use for playback and recording. This is useful because you may want the audio for your editing projects to come through professional studio monitors while other system sounds come through smaller or built-in computer monitors.

When you open Premiere Pro for the first time, you may need to select the audio hardware to use before playback will work. Access the Audio Hardware preferences in Premiere Pro > Settings > Audio Hardware (macOS) or Edit > Preferences > Audio Hardware (Windows).

There are advanced options for configuring audio hardware, but you'll generally just need to choose the System Default Input and System Default Output. With the System Default options selected, Premiere Pro can automatically switch to your system audio selection if you change it—for example, if you plug headphones in.

Optimizing performance

Editing video places high demands on your computer processor and memory. A more powerful computer will make your editing experience faster and more efficient, which translates to a more fluid and enjoyable creative experience—that is, more creative flow.

Premiere Pro takes advantage of multicore processors (CPUs) and multiprocessor systems. The faster the processors and the more CPU cores there are, the better the performance you'll experience.

The minimum system memory is 8 GB, and 16 GB or more is recommended for High-Definition (HD) media; 32 GB or higher is recommended for Ultra-High-Definition (UHD, or 4K) media.

The speed of the storage drives you use for video playback is also a factor. A dedicated fast storage drive is recommended for your media. A RAID disk array or fast solid-state drive for your media files is strongly recommended, particularly if you're working with high-resolution or high data-rate RAW media content. Storing your media files and program files on the same hard drive can affect performance. Keep your media files on a separate disk, if possible, for speed and easier media management.

Premiere Pro can harness the power of your computer's graphics hardware, or *graphics processing unit* (GPU), to improve playback performance. GPU acceleration provides a significant performance improvement, and most video cards with at least 2 GB of dedicated video memory (VRAM) will work, but 4 GB VRAM or more is recommended. You will find information about hardware and software requirements on the Adobe website at *helpx.adobe.com/premiere-pro/system-requirements.html*.

Online content

Your purchase of this Classroom in a Book includes online materials provided by way of your Account page on *peachpit.com*.

Lesson files

To work through the projects in this book, you will need to download the lesson files by following the instructions.

Web Edition

The Web Edition is an online interactive version of the book providing an enhanced learning experience. Your Web Edition can be accessed from any device with a connection to the internet, and it contains the following:

- The complete text of the book
- Hours of instructional video keyed to the text
- Interactive quizzes

Accessing the lesson files and Web Edition

Note: If you encounter problems registering your product or accessing the lesson files or web edition, go to *peachpit.com/support* for assistance.

You must register your purchase on *peachpit.com* to access the online content.

1　Go to *peachpit.com/PremiereProCIB2024*.

2　Sign in, or create a new account.

3　On the "Register a Product" page, the ISBN for this title should be pre-populated into the ISBN box. Click Submit.

4　Answer the question as proof of purchase.

5　The lesson files can be accessed from the Registered Products tab on your Account page. Click the Access Bonus Content link below the title of your product to proceed to the download page. Click the lesson file link(s) to download them to your computer.

Note: If you purchased a digital product directly from *peachpit.com*, your product will already be registered. Look for the Access Bonus Content link on the Registered Products tab in your account.

The Web Edition can be accessed from the Digital Purchases tab on your Account page. Click the Launch link to access the product.

Bonus material

This book has so much great material that we couldn't fit it all in the printed pages, so we placed these items on *peachpit.com*:

* Lesson 17, "Managing Your Projects"

* A glossary of common technical terms used in video production and editing

You will find this lesson on your account page (Lessons & Update Files tab) once you register your book, as described in "Accessing the lesson files and Web Edition."

Using the lesson files

Tip: If you don't have a dedicated storage location for your video files, placing the lesson files on your computer's desktop will make them easy to find and work with.

The lessons in this book use the downloadable lesson files, including video clips, audio files, photos, and image files created in Photoshop and Illustrator. Some lessons use files from other lessons, so you'll need to keep the entire collection of lesson assets on your storage drive as you work through the book. You will need about 7 GB of storage space for the lesson files.

Relinking the lesson files

The Premiere Pro projects included with the lesson files have links to specific media files. Because you are copying the files to a new location, you may need to update those links when you open projects for the first time.

If you open a project and Premiere Pro is unable to find a linked media file, the Link Media dialog box may open, inviting you to relink offline files. If this happens, select an offline clip on the list and click the Locate button. A file browser panel will appear.

Locate your copy of the Lessons folder using the navigator on the left, and click Search. Premiere Pro will locate the media file inside the Lessons folder. To hide all other files, making it easy to select the correct one, select the option to display only exact name matches.

Premiere Pro displays the last known file path and filename and the currently selected file path and file name at the top of the panel for reference. Select the file, and click OK.

The option to relink other files is enabled by default, so once you've located one file, the rest should reconnect automatically. For more information about relocating offline media files, see Lesson 17 (if you have the print version of this book, see "Bonus material" later in this section).

How to use these lessons

The lessons in this book include step-by-step instructions. Each lesson stands alone, but many build on previous lessons. For this reason, the best way to learn from this book is to proceed through the lessons one after another.

The lessons teach you new skills in the order you might normally use them. The lessons begin with acquiring media files such as video, audio, and graphics; and they go on to creating a rough-cut sequence, adding effects, sweetening the audio, and ultimately exporting the project.

Many pages contain additional "sidebar" information boxes that explain a particular technology or offer alternative workflows. It's not necessary to read these additional boxes, or follow the workflows, to learn Premiere Pro, but you may find them interesting and helpful as they will deepen your understanding and often provide additional context.

By the end of these lessons, you'll have a good understanding of the complete end-to-end video post-production workflow, with the specific skills you need to edit on your own.

As you explore the skills described in this book, you may find it helpful to review earlier lessons you have already completed and to practice the fundamental editing techniques regularly. The later advanced workflows build on fundamental principles introduced early on, and if you take a few moments to recap earlier lessons, it makes it easier to discover the common principles that apply. The more you practice, the faster you will build your confidence as an editor.

The focus of this book is on the technical skills editors use every day to produce film, television, and social media videos. Taking time to try different ways of achieving results can help to expand your artistic skills. As you learn new technical skills, watch videos created by experienced editors with a critical eye and see if you can recognize the technical workflow they employed. More often than not, the most impactful techniques are the simplest, once you know the workflow.

Practice makes perfect!

Additional resources

Adobe Premiere Pro Classroom in a Book 2024 Release is not meant to replace documentation that comes with the program or to be a comprehensive reference for every feature. Only the commands and options used in the lessons are explained in this book. For comprehensive information about program features and tutorials, refer to the following resources, which you can reach by choosing commands from the Premiere Pro Help menu.

Adobe Premiere Pro Learn and Support: *helpx.adobe.com/premiere-pro.html* is where you can find and browse Help and Support content on Adobe.com. You can also reach that page by choosing Help > Premiere Pro Help or by pressing F1. On the Learn & Support page, click User Guide for documentation on individual features or visit *helpx.adobe.com/premiere-pro/user-guide.html.*

Premiere Pro tutorials: For a wide range of interactive tutorials on Adobe Premiere Pro features that you can follow in the app, choose Help > Premiere Pro In-App Tutorials. For online tutorials, choose Help > Premiere Pro Online Tutorials or visit *helpx.adobe.com/premiere-pro/tutorials.html.* You can also access tutorials from the Home screen by clicking Learn. A different set of tutorials is provided inside Premiere Pro in the Learn panel.

Premiere Pro blog: *blog.adobe.com/en/topics/premiere-pro* brings you tutorials, product news, and inspirational articles about using Premiere Pro.

Creative Cloud tutorials: For inspiration, key techniques, cross-application workflows, and updates on new features, go to the Creative Cloud tutorials page, *helpx.adobe.com/creative-cloud/tutorials.html,* and click the link for Premiere Pro.

Adobe Community: Tap into peer-to-peer discussions, questions, and answers on Adobe products at the Adobe Support Community page at *community.adobe.com.* Click the Premiere Pro link to visit the Premiere Pro community.

Adobe Creative Cloud Discover: This online resource offers thoughtful articles on design and design issues, a gallery showcasing the work of top-notch designers and artists, tutorials, and more. Check it out at *creativecloud.adobe.com/discover.*

Resources for educators: *adobe.com/education* and *edex.adobe.com* offer a treasure trove of information for instructors who teach classes on Adobe software. Find solutions for education at all levels, including free curricula that use an integrated approach to teaching Adobe software. These curricula can be used to prepare for the Adobe Certified Professional exams. To learn more about the exams, visit *edex.adobe.com/adobe-certified-professional/exams.*

Adobe Premiere Pro product home page: *adobe.com/products/premiere* has more information about the features and functionality of the application.

1 TOURING ADOBE PREMIERE PRO

Lesson overview

In this lesson, you'll learn how to do the following:

- Perform nonlinear editing.

- Understand the standard digital video workflow.

- Enhance the workflow with high-level features.

- Explore workspaces.

- Customize workspaces.

- Set keyboard shortcuts.

 This lesson will take about 75 minutes to complete. To get the lesson files used in this chapter, download them from the web page for this book at *peachpit.com/PremiereProCIB2024*. For more information, see "Accessing the lesson files and Web Edition" in the "Getting Started" section at the beginning of this book. Store the files on your computer in a convenient location.

Adobe Premiere Pro is a video-editing system that supports the latest technology and cameras with powerful tools that are intuitive to use and that integrate perfectly with almost every video acquisition source and delivery standard.

Starting the lesson

There is always great demand for high-quality video content. Today's video producers and editors work in a fast-changing landscape of old and new technologies. Despite rapid change in camera systems and the video creation and distribution landscape—particularly with the expansion of social media platforms, generative artificial intelligence (AI) technologies, and increased marketing production values—the goal of great video editing remains unchanged: You want to take your source footage and shape it, guided by your original vision, so that you can effectively communicate with your audience.

In Adobe Premiere Pro, you'll find a powerful and intuitive video-editing system that supports the latest technology and cameras with flexible tools that are easy to use. These tools integrate perfectly with almost every type of media and support a wide range of third-party plug-ins and other post-production tools.

In this lesson, you'll begin by reviewing the essential post-production workflow that most editors follow, and then you'll learn about the main components of the Premiere Pro interface and how to create custom workspaces.

Performing nonlinear editing in Premiere Pro

Premiere Pro is a *nonlinear editor* (NLE). Like a word processing application, Premiere Pro lets you place, replace, and move video, audio, and images anywhere you want in your final edited work. You don't need to make adjustments in a particular order; you can change any part of your project at any time—that's the nonlinear part of an NLE.

You'll combine multiple pieces of media, called *clips*, to create a *sequence*. You can edit any part of the sequence in any order and then change the contents or move clips so that they play earlier or later. You can blend layers of video together, change the image size, adjust the colors, add special effects, adjust the audio mix, and more.

You can combine multiple sequences and jump to any moment in a video clip or sequence without needing to fast-forward or rewind. In Premiere Pro, organizing the clips you're working with is like organizing files on your computer.

Premiere Pro supports many media file formats, including XDCAM, XAVC, DPX, DVCProHD, QuickTime (including Apple ProRes), AVCHD (including AVCCAM and NXCAM), AVC-Intra, DNxHR, and Canon XF. RAW video formats are supported, including media from RED, ARRI, Sony, Canon, and Blackmagic cameras, as well as Apple ProRes RAW and multiple 360° video, DSLR video, and phone camera formats.

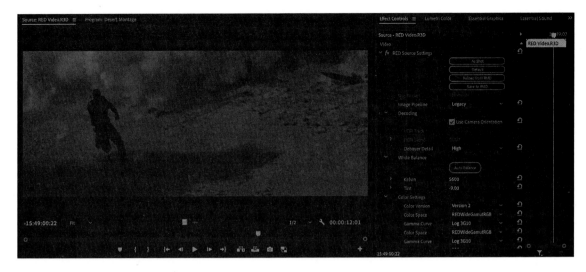

Premiere Pro features native support for RAW media from RED cameras, with settings to control the way the media is interpreted.

Using the standard digital video workflow

As you gain editing experience, you'll develop your own preferences for the order in which to work on the different aspects of your project. Each stage of post-production requires a particular kind of attention and different tools. Also, some projects call for more time spent on one stage than another.

Whether you skip through some stages with a quick mental check or spend hours (even days!) dedicated to perfecting an aspect of your project, you'll almost certainly go through the following steps:

1   **Acquire your media:** This can mean recording original footage, creating new animated content, selecting stock media, using generative AI to create new media, or gathering a variety of assets for a project.

2   **Ingest the video to your editing storage:** Premiere Pro can read media files (like video files from a camera) directly, usually with no need for conversion. Be sure to back up your files to a second location because storage drives sometimes physically fail unexpectedly. For video editing, use fast storage for smooth play-back of your media files.

3   **Organize your clips:** Your project may have a lot of video content to choose from. Invest the time to organize clips into special folders in your project called *bins*—a term taken from the days of editing celluloid film. Organized strips of film would be stored in large cloth-lined bins to allow quick access for the editor. You can add color labels and other information as metadata (metadata is addi-tional information about the clips or media files) to help keep things organized.

4 **Create a sequence:** In the Timeline panel, selectively combine the parts of the video and audio clips that you want into a sequence. A *sequence* is your complete edited video.

5 **Add transitions:** Place special transition effects between sequence clips, add video effects, and create composite visuals by placing clips on multiple layers (called *tracks* in the Timeline panel).

6 **Create or import titles, graphics, and captions:** Add them to your sequence to help tell the story.

7 **Adjust the audio mix:** Adjust the volume of your audio clips to get the mix just right, and use transitions and effects on your audio clips to improve the sound.

8 **Output:** Export your finished project to a file.

Premiere Pro supports each of these steps with industry-leading tools. A large community of creative and technical professionals is waiting to share their experience and support your development as an editor.

Enhancing the workflow with Premiere Pro

Premiere Pro has easy-to-use tools for video-editing beginners. It also has advanced tools for manipulating, adjusting, and fine-tuning your projects.

You may not make use of all the following features in your first few video projects. However, as your experience and understanding of nonlinear editing grows, you'll want to expand your capabilities.

It's beyond the scope of one book to cover all of the expansive creative tools and capabilities of Premiere Pro. Still, this book will enable you to fully post-produce professional projects and get you ready to take your skills to the next level.

The following topics will be covered:

- **Advanced audio editing:** Learn to use the advanced audio effects and editing tools in Premiere Pro. As well as producing a soundtrack mix, you can clean up noisy audio, reduce reverb, make sample-level edits, apply multiple audio effects to audio clips or whole tracks, and use state-of-the-art Virtual Studio Technology (VST) plug-ins.

- **Color correction and grading:** Correct and enhance the look of your footage with advanced color-correction filters, accessed via a dedicated color correction and grading panel. You can make secondary color-correction selections that allow you to adjust isolated colors, adjust selected areas of an image to improve the composition, and automatically match the colors in two images.

- **Keyframe controls:** Premiere Pro gives you precise control over the timing of visual and motion effects without using a separate compositing or motion graphics application. Keyframes use a standard interface design; if you learn to use them in Premiere Pro, you'll know how to use them in all Adobe Creative Cloud products in which they're available.

- **Broad hardware support:** Choose from a wide range of compatible input and output hardware. Premiere Pro system specifications range from low-cost desktop computers and laptops for video editing up to high-performance work-stations that can easily edit high-definition (HD), 4K, 8K, 3D stereoscopic, and 360° video.

- **GPU acceleration:** The Mercury Playback Engine operates in two modes: one that uses only software running in the central processing unit (CPU) for playback and one that uses graphics processing unit (GPU) acceleration for enhanced playback performance. GPU acceleration mode requires graphics hardware that meets minimum specifications in your workstation. See *helpx.adobe.com/premiere-pro/system-requirements.html* for a list of recom-mended graphics cards. Most modern cards with a minimum of 2 GB of dedi-cated video memory will work.

- **Multicamera editing:** You can quickly and easily edit productions shot with multiple cameras. Multiple camera sources are displayed in a split view, and you can choose a camera view by clicking the appropriate screen or using a short-cut key. You can automatically sync multiple camera angles based on clip audio or timecode.

- **Project management:** View, delete, move, search for, and reorganize clips and bins. Consolidate your projects by copying just the media used in sequences to a single location, and then reclaim storage space by deleting unused media files.

- **Metadata:** Premiere Pro supports Adobe XMP, which stores additional informa-tion about media as metadata that multiple applications can access. You can use this metadata to locate clips or communicate important information, such as preferred takes or copyright notices.

- **Creating titles:** Create titles and graphics with the Essential Graphics panel. You can also use graphics created in almost any suitable software. For instance, you can import Adobe Photoshop files as flattened images or as separate layers that you can combine or animate selectively. You also can use Adobe After Effects motion graphics templates.

- **Advanced trimming:** Make precise adjustments to the start and end timing of clips in sequences using dedicated trimming tools. Premiere Pro provides quick, simple trimming keyboard shortcuts, as well as advanced on-screen trimming tools to make complex timing adjustments to multiple clips.

- **Reframing visual elements:** Perhaps you are delivering widescreen, vertical, and square video versions of your content. You can adjust and perfect the composi-tion for every type of output manually or automatically.

- **Media encoding:** Export your sequence to create a media file that is perfect for your needs using simplified Quick Export presets or details settings. Use the advanced features of Adobe Media Encoder to create copies of your finished sequence in multiple formats, based on presets or your own detailed specifications. You can apply color adjustments, timing changes, and information overlays during export, as well as upload media to social media platforms in a single step.

- **360° video for VR headsets:** Edit and post-produce 360° video footage using a special VR Video display mode that lets you see specific regions of the picture, or view both your video and your edited clips via a VR headset, allowing a more natural and intuitive editing experience. Dedicated visual effects that meet the unique demands of 360° video are available.

Expanding the workflow

Although you can work with Premiere Pro as a stand-alone application, it is also a team player. Premiere Pro is part of Adobe Creative Cloud, which means you have access to several other specialized tools.

Understanding the way these software components work together will improve your efficiency and give you more creative freedom.

Including other applications in the editing workflow

Premiere Pro is a versatile video and audio post-production tool, but it's just one component of Adobe Creative Cloud—a complete print, web, and video environment that includes video-focused software for the following:

- High-end 3D motion effects creation

- Complex text animation generation

- Layered graphics production

- Vector artwork creation

- Audio production

To incorporate one or more of these features into a production, you can use other components of Adobe Creative Cloud. The software set has everything you need to produce advanced, professionally finished videos.

Here's a brief description of the other components:

- **Adobe Express:** All-in-one design, photo, and video tool to make content creation easy.

- **Adobe Premiere Rush:** Intuitive mobile and desktop video editing tool that can produce projects compatible with Premiere Pro (for advanced finishing).

- **After Effects:** The popular tool of choice for motion graphics, animation, and visual effects artists.

- **Adobe Character Animator:** A tool for creating advanced animation with natural movement for 2D puppets using your webcam for face and body movement tracking.

- **Adobe Photoshop:** The industry-standard image-editing and graphics-creation product. You can work with photos and video to prepare them for your project.

- **Adobe Audition:** The powerful and intuitive system for audio editing, audio cleanup and sweetening, music creation and adjustment, and multitrack mix creation.

- **Adobe Illustrator:** Professional vector graphics-creation software for print, video, and the web.

- **Adobe Media Encoder:** A tool that allows you to process files to produce content for any screen directly from Premiere Pro, After Effects, and Audition.

- **Adobe Dynamic Link:** A cross-product technology that enables you to work in real time with media, compositions, and sequences shared between After Effects, Audition, and Premiere Pro.

Exploring the Adobe Creative Cloud video workflow

Your Premiere Pro and Creative Cloud workflow will vary depending on the needs of each project. Here are a few scenarios:

- Use Photoshop to touch up and apply effects to still images and layered image compositions from a digital camera, a scanner, or a video clip. Then use them as source media in Premiere Pro. Changes made in Photoshop update in Premiere Pro.

- Send clips directly from the Premiere Pro timeline to Adobe Audition for professional audio cleanup and sweetening. Changes made in Audition update in Premiere Pro.

- Send an entire Premiere Pro sequence to Adobe Audition to complete a professional audio mix, including compatible effects and level adjustments; the session can contain video so you can compose and adjust levels in Audition based on the action.

- Using Dynamic Link, include video compositions from After Effects in Premiere Pro projects. Apply special effects, add animation, and add visual elements in After Effects. Adjustments made in After Effects appear in Premiere Pro immediately.

- Use After Effects to create motion graphics templates that are directly editable in Premiere Pro. Dedicated controls allow specific types of changes to be made while retaining the original look and feel of the template.

- Use Adobe Media Encoder to export video projects in multiple resolutions and codecs for display on websites, display via social media, or archiving. You can use the built-in presets, effects, and social media support to upload directly from Premiere Pro to social media platforms.

Naturally, most of this book focuses on workflows involving only Premiere Pro. However, sidebars will explain ways to include Adobe Creative Cloud components in your workflows for additional effects work and finishing.

Touring the Premiere Pro interface

● **Note:** To ensure that the tools function and the defaults are set exactly as described in this lesson, reset the Premiere Pro preferences by holding Option (macOS) or Alt (Windows) while launching the application and then clicking Continue in the Reset Options dialog box.

It's helpful to begin by getting familiar with the editing interface so you can recognize the tools as you work with them in the following lessons. To make it easier for you to customize the user interface, Premiere Pro includes *workspaces*. Workspaces quickly position the various panels and tools onscreen in ways that are helpful for particular activities, such as editing, special effects work, or audio mixing.

You'll begin by taking a brief tour of the Editing workspace. In most of the exercises in this book, you'll use a Premiere Pro project from this book's companion DVD (or downloaded lesson files if you are using the eBook). Before you continue, make sure you've copied all the lesson folders and contents to your computer storage.

Next, launch Premiere Pro. The Home screen appears.

The first few times you launch Premiere Pro, the Home screen shows links to online training videos that will help you get started.

If you have opened projects previously, a list will appear in the middle of the Home screen. You can hover the pointer over a recent item to see the project file location in a pop-up window.

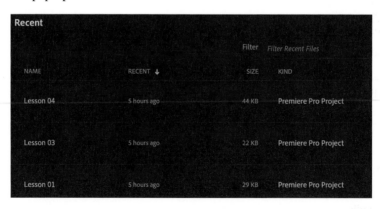

A Premiere Pro project file contains all your creative decisions for a project, links (referred to as *clips*) to your selected media files, sequences made by combining those clips, special effects settings, and more. Premiere Pro project files have the filename extension .prproj.

Lesson 01.prproj

Whenever you work in Premiere Pro, you will be making adjustments to a project file. You need to create a new project file or open an existing one to use Premiere Pro.

There are a few important buttons on the Home screen, some of which look like text but can actually be clicked (look out for text that works as a button in the Premiere Pro interface):

- **Home:** Takes you back to this screen.

- **Learn:** Displays multiple tutorials to help you get up to speed with Premiere Pro.

- **New Project:** Creates a new project file. It's a good idea to choose a name that will be easy to identify later (in other words, avoid using the name New Project).

- **Open Project:** Click this to open an existing project by browsing for the project file. You can also double-click an existing project file in the macOS Finder or Windows Explorer to open it in Premiere Pro.

- **New Team Project:** Creates a new collaborative project using the Adobe Team Project service. Team Projects are beyond the scope of this book but use the same tools and editing techniques that you will learn here—just collaboratively.

- **Open Team Project:** Opens the Manage Team Projects dialog box to allow you to select an existing Team Project to work on.

- **Open Premiere Rush Project:** Opens an existing Premiere Rush project in Premiere Pro. Any projects you created with Premiere Rush will be available here, as long as you used the same Adobe ID as for Premiere Pro.

Try opening an existing Premiere Pro project:

1 Click Open Project.

2 In the file navigation dialog box that appears, navigate to the Lessons folder; then double-click the Lesson 01.prproj project file to open the first lesson. Leave the file open for the next exercise.

After you open an existing project file, the Link Media dialog box may open, asking where a particular media file is. This will occasionally happen when the original media files are saved on a storage device (or drive letter) different from the one you're using. You'll need to tell Premiere Pro where the file is.

Note: If you are using a version of Premiere Pro later than the one used in making this book, when you open the Lesson 01.prproj file, an alert may ask you to save it in a new format. Updating the format of the file won't interfere with working through the exercises, so click OK.

In the Link Media box that prompts you to link the media file, you'll see a list of missing items, with the first already highlighted. Click Locate, at the bottom right.

At the top of the Locate File dialog box you'll see Last Path (that's the last known location for the file) and Path (that's the current location you have browsed to).

Using the folders on the left, navigate to the Lessons/Assets folder, and click Search at the bottom right. Premiere Pro will locate the missing file and highlight it on the right side of the window. Select the file, and click OK. Premiere Pro will remember this location for other missing files and relink them automatically without your needing to link each one individually.

To learn more about managing media, see the online bonus chapter "Managing Your Projects."

Hands-On: Editing your first video

● **Note:** It's best to copy all the lesson assets to your computer storage and leave them there until you complete this book; some lessons reuse assets from previous lessons.

The first series of exercises walks you through editing a simple video. You'll get hands-on experience using the principal features of Premiere Pro.

Because you are going to make changes to the project file, you'll start by saving a new version. Then to ensure the steps described here match your screen, you'll reset the Premiere Pro user interface to its default configuration. After that, you'll learn about the main editing tools and user interface features in Premiere Pro.

1   With Lesson 01.prproj open in Premiere Pro, choose File > Save As. Save a copy of the project with the name **Lesson 01 Working.prproj**.

2   By default, Premiere Pro opens in the Learning workspace. We're going to dive right in to editing using the Editing workspace: Choose Window > Workspaces > Editing to make sure the Editing workspace is selected (see "Exploring workspaces" for more information on workspaces).

3   Choose Window > Workspaces > Reset To Saved Layout to reset the workspace to the default settings.

● **Note:** Unlike most other panels, the Timeline panel does not include its own name in its heading. Instead, the name of the current sequence is shown. In this case, it's Desert Montage.

This project contains a number of video clips. Some have already been edited into a sequence in the Timeline panel (for more information about panels, see "Exploring workspaces").

Let's add some more clips to the sequence.

4   Along the top edge of the Timeline panel, named Desert Montage in this project, notice the horizontal bar with a series of numbers—the *time ruler.* The blue playhead control connected to the time ruler works the same way as the playhead when viewing video files in a player. Try clicking a location on the time ruler—the playhead jumps to the time you click.

5   Place the playhead to the far left of the Timeline panel time ruler.

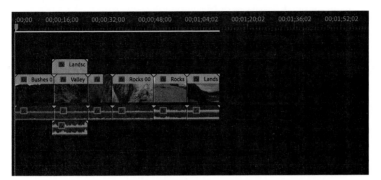

6   Press the spacebar to play the current sequence. The Program Monitor (top-right corner of the Premiere Pro interface) displays the contents of the sequence.

In the lower-left corner of the Premiere Pro interface, you will find the Project panel, which contains clips and other assets associated with the current project. The panel name includes the current project name, Project: Lesson 01 Working.

The lower-left corner of the Project panel holds a series of buttons that you use to select different ways of viewing the contents of the panel.

7   Click the Icon View  button if it's not already selected.

Icon view makes it easier to identify clips based on their contents.

8 Drag the clip named Bushes 001 from the Project panel to the end of the existing series of clips already in the Timeline panel. Be sure to drag it by the thumbnail image and not the clip name.

If you line up the new clip with an existing clip, you'll notice the new clip jumps into position, exactly aligning with the end of the existing clip. If this does not happen, snapping is turned off in the Timeline panel. Click the Snap In Timeline 🔲 button at the upper-left corner of the Timeline panel to turn it on 🔲.

9 Scroll down in the Project panel and find several more clips of your choice to add to the sequence. Drag each one into the sequence.

At any time, you can review your sequence by positioning the Timeline playhead at the beginning of the sequence (at its left end) and using the spacebar to start and stop playback.

10 When you have finished adding several clips to the sequence, play through it to see the result.

You can place the Timeline playhead anywhere and play from that moment.

There is one item you will not be able to drag from the Project panel into the sequence: the sequence itself, called Desert Montage.

The Project panel displays both clips and sequences. You can have as many sequences as you like in a project, and they are identifiable by the icon in the lower-right corner of the clip thumbnail 🔲 (in Icon view or in Freeform View) or the item icon in List view 🔳.

Congratulations! You edited a sequence!

Tip: The Reset To Saved Layout command displays a keyboard shortcut in the menu. Many tasks can be performed using keyboard shortcuts, including choosing workspaces. If you're using a computer with a non-U.S. keyboard, the shortcuts available to you might use different keys from the ones shown here. See "Using and setting keyboard shortcuts" later in this lesson for more information.

Exploring workspaces

The Premiere Pro interface is divided into *panels*. Each panel has a particular purpose. For example, the Effects panel lists all the effects available for you to apply to clips, while the Effect Controls panel gives you access to the settings for those effects.

A *workspace* is a preset arrangement of panels, organized to make particular tasks easier. There's one for editing, another for working on audio, and another for making color adjustments, for example.

Every panel is accessible from the Window menu, but workspaces are a quicker way to access several panels at once and have them laid out exactly as you need them.

Before you begin, make sure you're using the default Editing workspace by choosing Window > Workspaces > Editing. Then, to reset the Editing workspace, choose Window > Workspaces > Reset To Saved Layout.

The name of your current project is displayed at the top of the Premiere Pro interface.

At the top left of the interface, the Home button 🏠 opens the Home screen, allowing you to quickly open a recent project or create a new one.

Next to the Home button, the words *Import*, *Edit*, and *Export* are all buttons you can click; these floating words are examples of an elegant design feature you'll discover in a number of areas in Premiere Pro. The buttons switch the interface between these three important modes.

For now, stay in the Edit mode—you will learn about the other modes in later lessons.

At the top right of the interface, the Workspaces menu ▣ gives quick access to several workspaces for particular tasks. You'll use some of these workspaces as you progress through these lessons. For now, make sure Editing is selected.

▶ **Tip:** In the Workspaces menu, choose Show Workspace Label to display the name of the current workspace next to the menu.

If you're new to nonlinear editing, the default Editing workspace might look like a lot of new buttons and menus to learn. Don't panic. Things become simpler when you know what the buttons are for. The interface is designed to make video editing easy, so commonly used controls are immediately accessible.

Workspaces consist of particular panels positioned and sized helpfully. You can save space by gathering several panels into a *panel group*. The names of all the panels in the group are displayed across the top. Click a panel name to bring that panel to the "front" of the group.

When many panels are combined, there may not be enough space to display all their names. If this is the case, a list of all the panels in the group becomes available. Click the chevron in the upper-right corner of the panel group to access a particular panel.

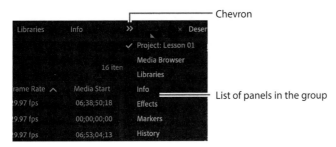

You can display any panel by choosing it from the Window menu, so if you can't locate a panel, just look there.

The principal elements are shown here.

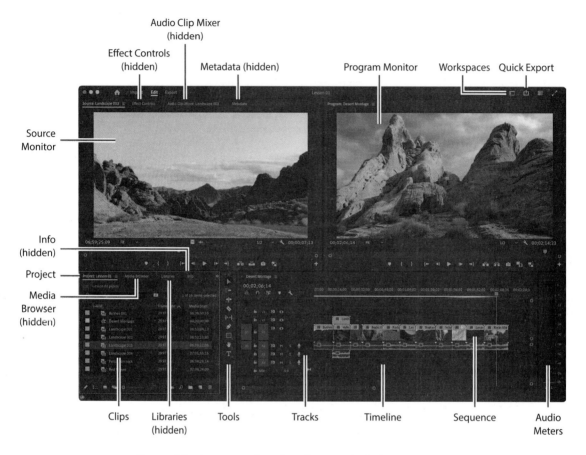

Some of the important interface elements include:

- **Project panel:** This is where you organize your clips (these are the links to your media files), sequences, and graphics in *bins*. Bins are similar to folders—you can place one bin inside another for more advanced organization of your project.

- **Timeline panel:** This is where you'll do most of your creative work. You view and work on *sequences* (the term for video clips edited together) in the Timeline panel. One feature of sequences is that you can *nest* them (place one sequence inside another sequence). Combining sequences this way, you can break up a production into manageable chunks or create unique special effects.

- **Tracks:** You can layer—or *composite*—video clips, images, graphics, and titles on an unlimited number of tracks. Video and graphic clips on upper video tracks cover whatever is directly below them on the timeline. Therefore, you need to give clips on higher tracks some form of transparency or reduce their size if you want clips on lower tracks to show.

- **Monitors:** Use the Source Monitor (on the left) to view and select parts of clips (your original footage). To view a clip in the Source Monitor, double-click its icon in the Project panel, or drag it into the Source Monitor. The Program Monitor (on the right) shows the contents of your current sequence, displayed in the Timeline panel.

- **Media Browser:** This panel allows you to browse your storage to choose media to import into your project. Like Import mode, the Media Browser is especially useful for camera media and RAW files because it allows you to preview the files before importing. You can use Import mode to import, too, but the Media Browser has additional options to help you stay organized.

- **Libraries:** This panel gives access to assets that you can share between projects, such as custom Lumetri color Looks, Motion Graphics templates, graphics, and shared libraries. For more information, go to *helpx.adobe.com/premiere-pro/ using/creative-cloud-libraries.html.*

- **Effects panel:** This panel contains most of the effects you will use in your sequences, including video and audio effects and transitions. Effects are grouped by type to make them easier to find, and there's a search box at the top of the panel. Once applied, the controls for these effects are displayed in the Effect Controls panel.

- **Effect Controls panel:** This panel displays the controls for any effects applied to a clip you select in a sequence or open in the Source Monitor. If you select a visual clip in the Timeline panel, Motion, Opacity, and Time Remapping adjustment controls are automatically available. Most effect settings can be adjusted over time.

- **Audio Clip Mixer:** This panel is based on audio production studio hardware, with volume sliders and pan controls. There is one set of controls for each audio track on the timeline. The adjustments you make are applied to audio clips. There's also an Audio Track Mixer for applying audio adjustments to tracks rather than to clips.

- **Tools panel:** Each icon in this panel gives access to a tool that performs a specific function in the Timeline panel or the Program Monitor. You'll use and learn more about many of these tools in upcoming lessons. The Selection tool is context-sensitive, which means it changes function depending on where you click. If your pointer doesn't work as you expect, check to see you have the right tool selected.

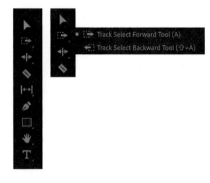

Several tools have a small triangle icon, indicating a menu of additional tools. Click and hold one of these tools to see the menu of options.

- **Info panel:** The Info panel displays information about any item you select in the Project panel or any clip or transition you select in a sequence.

- **History panel:** This panel tracks the steps you take and lets you easily undo a series of changes. When you select a previous step, all steps that followed it are also undone.

- **Quick Export:** This button ▣ in the upper-right corner gives fast access to popular media file export options for sharing your work.

Most panels display their name at the top. When a panel is grouped with other panels, the name is underlined when you select it. The currently active panel is outlined in blue. Most panels have a menu next to their name ▤ with options particular to that panel; this important menu is simply called the *panel menu*. For example, the Project panel menu provides options for the Project panel.

Using the Learning workspace

Although other workspaces are intended to facilitate a particular creative activity, the Learning workspace is an exception. This workspace includes the Learn panel, which offers tutorials to help you build familiarity with the Premiere Pro interface and learn important skills.

You will find the tutorials complement the exercises in this book well, and you may find it helpful to practice first with this book and then explore the relevant tutorials to reinforce the lessons you have learned.

Customizing a workspace

In addition to choosing between the default workspaces, you can adjust the position and location of panels to create a workspace that works best for you. You can create multiple custom workspaces for different tasks.

• As you change the size of a panel or panel group, other panels change size to compensate.

• Every panel within a panel group is accessible by clicking its name.

• All panels are movable—you can drag a panel from one group to another.

• You can drag a panel out of a group to become a separate floating panel.

• You can double-click the name of any panel to toggle it between full screen and its original size.

In this exercise, you'll adjust some panels and save a customized workspace.

1 In the Project panel, double-click the icon for the clip Valley 001 to open it in the Source Monitor.

2 Position your pointer on the vertical divider between the Source Monitor and the Program Monitor. The pointer will change to a double-headed arrow ⬌ when it's in the right position. Drag left and right to change the sizes of those panels. You can choose to have different sizes for your video displays, which is useful at different stages of post-production.

3 Now place the pointer on the horizontal divider between the Program Monitor and the Timeline panel. The pointer will change when it's in the right position. Drag up and down to change the sizes of these panels.

4 Click the name of the Media Browser (at its top), and drag it to the middle of the Source Monitor until a blue rectangle appears (the *drop zone*—displayed as a center highlight). Release the Media Browser to dock it in that panel group.

5 Drag the Effects panel (which is grouped with the Project panel by default) by its name to a point just inside the right edge of its current panel group until a blue trapezoid-shaped area (the drop zone) is highlighted.

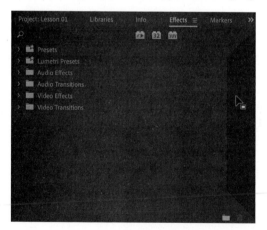

6 Release the Effects panel; it is now alone in its own panel group. Remember, if you can't see the Effects panel, you can choose it from the Window menu.

When you drag a panel by its name, a drop zone is displayed. If the highlighted drop zone is a rectangle, the panel will go into the selected panel group as an additional tab when it's dropped. If the drop zone is a trapezoid, it will create a new panel group. If the drop zone is green, you'll create a new panel group that is the full length or width of the Premiere Pro interface.

You can also pull panels into their own floating windows.

7 Command-drag (macOS)/Ctrl-drag (Windows) the Source Monitor out of its panel group.

8 Drop the Source Monitor anywhere, creating a floating panel. You can resize the panel by dragging a corner or a side.

▶ **Tip:** You may need to resize some panels to see all of their controls.

● **Note:** You can save changes to new workspaces you have created. When you do, resetting to default will restore the most recently saved version of the workspace.

As you gain experience, you might want to create and save the layout of your panels as a customized workspace. To do so at any time, choose Window > Workspaces > Save As New Workspace. Type a name, and click OK.

9 Now, to return to a recognizable starting point, choose Window > Workspaces > Editing. Then, to reset the Editing workspace, choose Window > Workspaces > Reset To Saved Layout.

Introducing preferences

The more you edit video, the more you'll want to customize Premiere Pro to match your specific needs. Premiere Pro has several types of settings. For example, panel menus ☰, which are accessible by clicking the menu button next to a panel name, have options that relate to each panel, while individual clips in a sequence have settings you can access by right-clicking them.

The panel name, displayed at the top of each panel, is often referred to as the *panel tab*. This is the area of a panel you use to move the panel, almost like a handle you can grab the panel by.

There are also application-wide user preferences, which are grouped into a single dialog box for easy access. These don't change from project to project. Preferences will be covered in depth as they relate to the individual lessons in this book. Let's look at an example.

● **Note:** You can change the font size for List view in the Project panel by choosing Font Size from the panel menu and then choosing Small, Medium (Default), Large, or Extra Large from the submenu.

Note: When you open the Preferences dialog box, it's not too important which category you choose from the menu first, as you can always quickly switch to another.

1 Choose Premiere Pro > Settings > Appearance (macOS) or Edit > Preferences > Appearance (Windows).

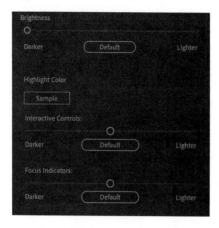

2 Drag the Brightness slider to the right to suit your preference.

The default brightness is a dark gray to help you see colors correctly (human perception of color is influenced by surrounding colors). There are additional options for controlling the brightness of interface highlights.

3 Experiment with the Interactive Controls and Focus Indicators sliders. The difference in the brightness of the onscreen sample is subtle, but adjusting these sliders can make quite a big difference to your editing experience.

4 Set all three settings to Default by clicking the Default buttons when you have finished experimenting.

5 Switch to the Auto Save preferences by clicking Auto Save on the left.

Note: Premiere Pro allows you to open multiple projects at the same time. For this reason, you'll see options for "project(s)" rather than just "project."

Imagine if you had worked for hours and then there was a power outage. If you hadn't saved recently, you'd have lost a lot of work. With the Auto Save options, you can decide how often you would like Premiere Pro to save an automated backup of your project file and how many versions you would like to keep in total. Auto Save backups automatically have the date and time they were created added to the filename.

Project files are small relative to media files, so you can usually increase the number of project versions without impacting system performance.

You'll notice there's an option to save a backup project to Creative Cloud.

This option creates an additional backup of your project file in your Creative Cloud Files folder. If you suffer a total system failure while working, you can log in to any Premiere Pro editing system with your Adobe ID to access the backup project file and quickly continue working. For this to work, you also have to make sure that you have backups—preferably multiple backups—of all your media files.

6   Click Cancel to close the Preferences dialog box without applying any changes.

Using and setting keyboard shortcuts

Premiere Pro makes extensive use of keyboard shortcuts. Once you know them, these are usually faster and easier than clicking an item in a menu or hunting down an item in a panel. Several keyboard shortcuts are shared universally by nonlinear editing systems. The spacebar, for example, starts and stops playback—this even works on some websites.

Some standard keyboard shortcuts come from celluloid film-editing traditions. The I and O keys, for example, are used to set In and Out points for footage and sequences: These special marks indicate the start and end of a desired section and were originally drawn on celluloid directly.

Many shortcuts are available, but not all are assigned a key by default. This allows flexibility when setting up your editing system.

1   Choose Premiere Pro > Keyboard Shortcuts (macOS) or Edit > Keyboard Shortcuts (Windows).

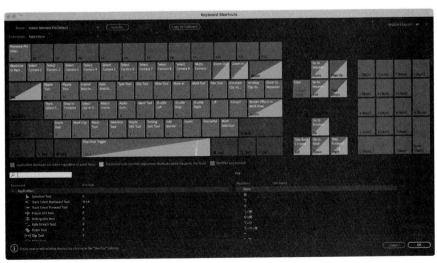

It can be a little daunting to see the number of keyboard shortcuts available, but by the end of this book you will recognize most of the options displayed here. Some keyboard shortcuts are specific to individual panels.

2 You can use the Commands menu at the top of the dialog box to choose the name of a panel to create or edit shortcuts for that panel. By default, the dialog box shows application-wide shortcuts.

Specialized keyboards are available with color-coded keys that have shortcuts printed on them. These make it easier to remember commonly used shortcuts.

3 When you open the Keyboard Shortcuts settings, the search box is automatically active to help you find a particular shortcut. Click outside of the search box (to deselect it), and try pressing Command (macOS) or Ctrl (Windows).

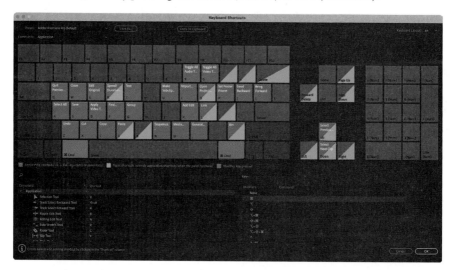

The keyboard shortcut display updates to show the results of combining the modifier key with the character keys. Notice there are many keys without short-cuts assigned when you use a modifier key. These are available for you to assign your own shortcuts.

4 Now try combinations of modifier keys including Shift+Option (macOS) or Shift+Alt (Windows). You can set keyboard shortcuts with any combination of modifier keys.

If you press a character key, or character and modifier key combination, that particular shortcut information is displayed.

The list at the bottom left of the Keyboard Shortcuts dialog box includes every option you can assign to a key—it's a long list, so use the search box at the top to help you find the option you want.

5 To change a keyboard shortcut:

- Having found an option you would like to assign to a key, drag it from the list onto the key you would like to use in the upper part of the dialog box. If you hold modifier keys while performing this operation, they'll be included in the shortcut. You can also drag a key from the virtual keyboard onto an option.

- To remove a shortcut, click the key, and choose Clear at the lower-right corner.

6 For now, click Cancel.

Moving, backing up, and syncing user settings

User settings include a number of important options. The defaults work well in most cases, but it's likely you'll want to make a few adjustments over time. For example, you might prefer the interface to be brighter than the default.

Premiere Pro includes the option to share your user settings between multiple computers: When installing Premiere Pro, you will enter your Adobe ID to confirm your software license. You can use the same ID to store your user settings in Creative Cloud, allowing you to synchronize and update them from any installation of Premiere Pro.

You can sync your user settings while working with Premiere Pro by choosing Premiere Pro > Sync Settings > Sync Settings Now (macOS) or File > Sync Settings > Sync Settings Now (Windows).

If a dialog box appears asking if you would like to save changes you have made, click Yes.

Review questions

1 Why is Premiere Pro considered a nonlinear editor?

2 Describe the basic video-editing workflow.

3 What is the Media Browser used for?

4 Can you save a customized workspace?

5 What is the purpose of the Source Monitor and the Program Monitor?

6 How can you drag a panel to its own floating panel?

Review answers

1 Premiere Pro lets you place video clips, audio clips, and graphics anywhere in a sequence; rearrange items already in a sequence; add transitions; apply effects; and do any number of other video-editing steps in any order that suits you. You're not tied to a particular line of action.

2 Transfer media to your computer; create a sequence by combining video, audio, and still-image clips in the Timeline panel; make color correction adjustments; add effects and transitions; add text and graphics; mix your audio; and export the finished product as a video file.

3 The Media Browser allows you to browse and import media files without having to open an external file browser. It's particularly useful when you're working with video camera footage because it allows you to easily preview footage.

4 Yes. You can save any customized workspace by choosing Window > Workspaces > Save As New Workspace.

5 You can view and select part of your original footage in the Source Monitor and use the Program Monitor to view the contents of the current sequence displayed in the Timeline panel.

6 Drag the name of the panel while holding down Command (macOS) or Ctrl (Windows).

2 SETTING UP A PROJECT

Lesson overview

In this lesson, you'll learn how to do the following:

- Choose project settings.
- Choose video rendering and playback settings.
- Choose video and audio display settings.
- Create scratch disks.
- Use sequence presets.
- Customize sequence settings.

 This lesson will take about 60 minutes to complete. You will not need any of the lesson files.

Before you begin editing, you'll learn how to create a new project and choose sequence settings that tell Premiere Pro how to play your video and audio clips.

Starting the lesson

If you're not yet familiar with video and audio technology, you might find all the options a little overwhelming. Luckily, Adobe Premiere Pro gives you easy shortcuts to get started. Plus, the principles of video and sound reproduction are the same no matter what kind of project you're creating.

It's just a question of knowing what you want to do. To help you plan and manage your projects, this lesson contains information about formats and video technology. You may decide to revisit this lesson later, as your familiarity with Premiere Pro and nonlinear video editing develops. You don't need to understand all of these concepts to edit videos.

In practice, you're unlikely to make changes to the default settings when creating a new project, but it's helpful to know what the options mean.

A Premiere Pro project file stores links to all the video, graphic, and sound files you have imported.

Lesson 01.prproj

Each item is displayed in the Project panel as a clip. The name *clip* originally described a section of celluloid film (lengths of film were literally clipped to separate them from a roll), but these days the term refers to any item in the project, regardless of the type of media. You could have an audio clip or an image sequence clip, for example.

● **Note:** Premiere Pro project files are identical on macOS and Windows. Apart from a small number of differences in menu layouts, the user experience is the same on both operating systems too.

Clips displayed in the Project panel appear to be media files, but they are actually only links to those files. It's helpful to understand that a clip displayed in the Project panel and the media file it links to are two separate things. For example, you can delete one without affecting the other (more on this later).

When working on a project, you will create at least one *sequence*—that is, a series of clips that play, one after another, sometimes overlapping, with special effects, titles, and sound, to form your completed creative work. While editing, you will choose which parts of your clips to use and in which order they'll play.

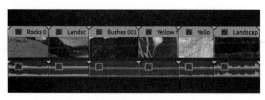

The beauty of nonlinear editing with Premiere Pro is that you can change your mind about almost anything, at any time.

Premiere Pro project files have the file extension *.prproj.*

Starting a new project is straightforward. You create a new project file, import media, choose a sequence preset, and start editing. The first three of these steps can be completed all at once!

When you create a new project, you can choose to automatically create a sequence with settings that match your media. You can also create one or more sequences later. Whichever method you choose, your sequence(s) will have playback settings (such as frame rate and frame size).

It's important to understand how the sequence settings change the way Premiere Pro plays your video and audio clips (all clips are automatically adjusted, if necessary, to match the sequence settings). If you decide to configure sequence settings manually, you can speed up the process by using a preset to choose the settings and then make adjustments, if necessary, for your particular project.

Even if you create a sequence automatically based on your media, it's helpful to understand all of the settings because you may discover you need to adjust one or more options for a particular project.

You need to know the kind of video and audio your camera records because your sequence settings will usually be based on your source footage to minimize conversion during playback. Sequence settings presets are named after delivery standards like Broadcast, HD, Social, and UHD. Still, you'll want to choose an option that is as close as possible to your original media, leaving any conversion to the final output stage.

In this lesson, you'll learn how to create a new Premiere Pro project and choose sequence settings. You'll also learn about different kinds of audio tracks and what preview files are.

About seconds and frames

When a camera records video, it captures a series of still images of the action. When it captures enough images each second, the result looks like moving video during playback. Each picture is called a *frame*, and the number of frames each second is usually called the *frames per second* (fps) or the recording or playback *frame rate*.

The fps will vary depending on your camera/video format and settings. It could be any number, including 23.976, 24, 25, 29.97, 30, 50, or 59.94. Most cameras allow you to choose between more than one frame rate and more than one frame size. It's important to know the recording settings for your media so you can be sure you have selected the correct playback options in Premiere Pro

Creating a project

Let's begin by creating a new project.

1 Launch Premiere Pro. The Home screen appears. Click the magnifying glass at the top right of the Home screen to open a multipurpose Search screen. If you enter text into the text box at the top of the screen, Premiere Pro will list the names of previously opened project files and tutorials from Adobe Premiere Pro Learn & Support that contain the text. You must be connected to the internet to access the tutorials.

- **What's new:** Next to the magnifying glass is a gift box icon. Click this to display a list of significant features in the Premiere Pro version you are using.

- **User button:** Next to the gift box icon is a thumbnail of your Adobe ID profile picture. If you just signed up, this may be a generic thumbnail. Click the button to manage your Creative Cloud account online.

2 Click New Project to open Premiere Pro in Import mode, with project creation options displayed.

The dialog box that appears serves two purposes.

Set project name   Set project file location   Thumbnail size   Display grid or list   Search   Media to import

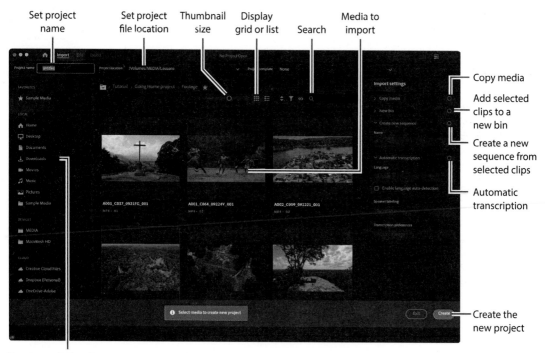

Browse media locations

While you work on an existing project, this is the screen you'll use to browse and import media. You can also create a new project and sequence here, which is what you're going to do next.

On the left side, you can browse the various storage locations on your system. When you select a location, media files stored there will appear in the middle section of the screen. By default, sample media is displayed.

You can change the size of thumbnails and switch between displaying thumbnails in a grid or a list of items using the controls at the top.

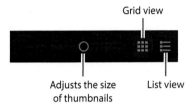

Grid view

Adjusts the size
of thumbnails

List view

On the right side, there are four options you can select to speed up project creation:

*   **Copy Media:** Copies of the media files you have selected will be placed in the location of your choice. Premiere Pro will then use these copies in your project, not the original files. This can be useful if you are adding media from external drives or camera cards that you might remove later.

*   **New Bin:** In a project, clips can be organized in containers that work a lot like folders, called *bins*. With this option toggled on, a bin will be added to the project automatically with selected clips placed inside it.

*   **Create New Sequence:** Automatically create a sequence with settings that match the first clip you select (for more information on sequence settings, see "Setting up a sequence" later in the lesson).

*   **Automatic Transcription:** Automatically transcribe clips to allow Text-Based Editing techniques and fast caption creation.

For now, you'll create a new project and sequence with just three clips so you can explore the important settings relating to project sequence setup.

3   Click in the Project Name box, and name your new project **First Project**.

4   Click the Project Location menu and click Choose Location. Browse to the Lessons folder and click Choose to establish this folder as the location for the new project.

> ● **Note:** When choosing a location for future project files, you may want to choose a recently used location from the Project Location menu.

5 From the list of storage locations on the left side of the interface, select the location for the Lessons folder, and then, in the middle of the window, browse to the folder Lessons/Assets/Video And Audio Files/Theft Unexpected. Make sure the display is set to Grid View so you can view the clip thumbnails.

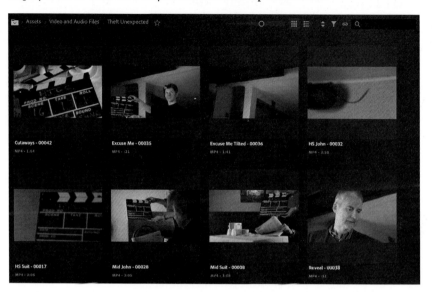

6 Click the Excuse Me – 00035 clip once to select it. Notice you can hover over thumbnails in the grid view to see a preview of their contents.

When you select the clip, Premiere Pro highlights it in blue and adds it to a collection at the bottom of the window.

7 Single-click the clip HS John - 00032 and the clip Mid Suit - 00008. Notice all three clips are highlighted in blue and displayed in the collection at the bottom of the window.

You have now selected three clips to include in your new project. It's not necessary to select media while creating a project, but it can speed up the process, particularly if you are working on a simple project with few clips.

8 On the right side of the window, in the Import Settings area, make sure Copy Media, New Bin, and Automatic Transcription are toggled off. Make sure Create New Sequence is toggled on.

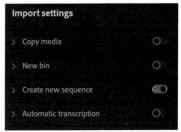

9 Click Create to create your new project.

You just created a project with three clips already added along with a sequence, ready and waiting for you to begin editing.

10 Until now, you have been selecting and resetting workspaces using the Window menu, but there's a handy shortcut: In the upper-right corner, click the Workspaces menu 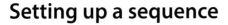 and choose Editing. This opens and positions several interface elements that are commonly used when editing.

11 To ensure you are viewing the default version of the Editing workspace, open the Workspaces menu again, and choose Reset To Saved Layout.

12 This is probably a good time to save your work. Choose File > Save.

Setting up a sequence

In your Premiere Pro project, you will create a sequence (or several sequences) into which you'll place video clips, audio clips, and graphics. A *sequence* is an item that appears in your project, a little like an empty bucket that you will fill with clips. Just like media files, sequences have a frame rate (frames per second) and frame size (image resolution). If a clip has a frame rate or frame size that doesn't match the sequence settings, it's converted during playback. This automatic process of adapting all clips in a sequence to match the sequence settings (if necessary) is called *conforming.*

Each sequence in your project can have different settings. You'll generally want to choose settings that match your original media as precisely as possible to minimize conforming during playback. Matching the settings reduces the work your system must do to play your clips, improving playback performance and maximizing image quality.

If you're editing a project with mixed-format media, you may have to choose which media to match with your sequence settings. You can mix formats easily, but because playback performance improves when the clips match the sequence settings, you'll often choose settings that match the majority of your media files.

If the first clip you add to a sequence does not match the settings of your sequence, Premiere Pro checks if you would like to change the sequence settings automatically to match it.

When you're starting out in video editing, you may find the number of available file types, codecs, and formats a little overwhelming. Premiere Pro can work natively with a wide range of video and audio formats and codecs and will often play mismatched formats smoothly.

However, when Premiere Pro has to adjust video for playback because of mismatched sequence settings, your editing system must work harder to play the video, and this will impact real-time performance (you might experience more dropped frames that make the playback appear to freeze occasionally). It's worth taking the time before you start editing to make sure the sequence settings closely match your original media files.

The essential factors for video formats are always the same: the number of frames per second, the frame size (the number of pixels in the picture horizontally and vertically), and the audio format (Stereo, Mono, or 5.1 Surround Sound). If you were to turn your sequence into a media file without applying a conversion to it, then the frame rate, audio format, frame size, and so on for the new file would all match whichever settings you chose when you created the sequence.

When you output your sequence to a file, you can choose any format you like (for more on exporting, see Lesson 16, "Exporting Frames, Clips, and Sequences").

Creating a sequence that automatically matches your source

If you're not sure what sequence settings you should choose, don't worry. Premiere Pro can create a sequence based on your clip. In fact, you have already made a sequence this way, while creating your project.

You can also automatically create a new sequence with matching settings in the Project panel. At the bottom of the Project panel, you'll find the New Item menu ⬛. You may need to resize the panel to see the icon. Use this menu to create new items for your project, including sequences, captions, and color mattes (full-screen color graphics useful for backgrounds).

To automatically create a sequence with format settings that match your media, drag any clip (or multiple clips, or even a whole bin) in the Project panel onto the

New Item menu. A new sequence will be created with the same name as the first clip selected, as well as a matching frame size and frame rate.

You can also select one or more clips, right-click the selection, and choose New Sequence From Clip.

Using this method, you can be confident your sequence settings will work with your media. If the Timeline panel is empty, you can also drag a clip (or multiple clips) into it to create a sequence with matching settings.

Choosing the correct preset

If you know exactly the settings you need for a new sequence, you can configure the sequence settings precisely. If you're not so sure, you can begin with a preset.

1   Click the New Item menu ▣ at the lower-right corner of the Project panel now and choose Sequence.

The New Sequence dialog box has four tabs: Sequence Presets, Settings, Tracks, and VR Video.

▶ **Tip:** You can also press the keyboard shortcut Command+N (macOS) or Ctrl+N (Windows) to open the New Sequence dialog box.

Note: The Preset Description area on the right side of the Sequence Presets tab often describes the kind of camera used to capture media in this format.

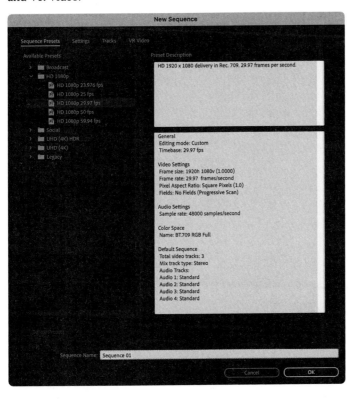

When you choose a preset, Premiere Pro applies several settings that control the way video clips will be displayed when added to the sequence. After choosing a preset, you can adjust these settings on the Settings tab if necessary.

You'll find a wide range of preset configuration options for the most commonly used media formats, grouped based on delivery formats. There are also several legacy presets used by previous versions of Premiere Pro.

You can click the disclosure triangle to see specific formats in a group. These are typically designed around frame rates and frame sizes. Let's look at an example.

2 Click the disclosure triangle next to the group HD 1080p.

You can now see five options based on frame rates, all with the same frame size. Remember that video cameras can often shoot video using multiple frame rates.

3 Select the HD 1080p 29.97 fps preset by clicking its name.

For this sequence, use the default settings. Take a moment to familiarize yourself with the description displayed on the right.

● **Note:** The name Sequence 01 is the default name given to sequences created when you use Import mode. To change it, expand the Create New Sequence setting and enter a new name in the Name field.

4 Click in the Sequence Name box, and name your sequence **First Sequence**.

5 Click OK to create the sequence.

You now have two sequences in the Project panel, Sequence 01 and First Sequence, and they have confusingly similar names! Even with a simple project of this kind, it's clear that staying organized is important.

6 Choose File > Save.

Congratulations! You have made a new project with Premiere Pro.

Codecs and formats

Codec is a shortening of the words *coder* and *decoder*. It's the way video and audio information is stored and replayed.

A file used to store video and/or audio, such as QuickTime MOV, MP4, or MXF, is a *container* that can contain one of many different video and audio codec configurations.

The media file is referred to as the *wrapper*, and the video and audio inside the file, stored using a codec, are sometimes referred to as the *essence*.

If you output your finished sequence to a file, you'll choose a format, a file type, and a codec.

The word *format* has multiple meanings depending on the context.

A format is a frame rate, frame size, audio sample rate, and so on. The word is also used to describe a type of media file or a collection of settings that incorporate both the visual and sound settings and the type of codec used, and its configuration.

For clarity, in this book we tend to use the word *format* to describe the frame rate, frame size, audio sample rate, and so on.

Customizing sequence settings

Once you've selected the sequence preset that most closely matches your source video, you may want to adjust the settings to meet a particular delivery requirement or in-house workflow. Let's take a look at those settings.

1 Choose File > New > Sequence.

2 Choose the HD 1080p 29.97 fps preset again by clicking its name. This lets you view the settings while reading about them.

   Premiere Pro will automatically conform footage you add to your timeline so that it matches your sequence settings, giving you a standard frame rate and frame size, regardless of the original clip format. This makes the sequence settings a critical part of your project configuration.

3 Click Settings at the top of the dialog box.

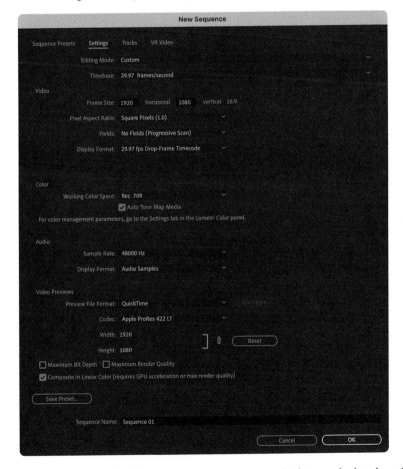

Tip: You created a new sequence using the File menu this time. There are often several ways to achieve the same goal in Premiere Pro.

Tip: If you wanted to produce a square video for social media, you could change the frame size to 1080x1080 (or any other square resolution). To access the Frame Size options, use the Editing Mode menu to choose Custom.

You chose a 29.97 fps (frames per second) preset, which is used when broadcasting NTSC video on traditional TV networks.

Creating a sequence preset

Although the standard presets usually work, you may sometimes need to create a custom preset. To do so quickly, first choose a sequence preset that matches your media closely, and then make custom selections in the Settings and Tracks areas of the New Sequence dialog box. Having adjusted the settings, you can save your custom preset for future use by clicking the Save Preset button near the bottom of the Settings area.

When you save a preset, you can give your customized sequence settings preset a name in the Save Sequence Preset dialog box, add notes if you want, and click OK. The preset will appear in a Custom folder with the other sequence presets.

4 If your media matches the selected preset, it's not necessary to change the settings. Take a moment to look at each setting in the New Sequence dialog box to build familiarity with the choices required to configure a sequence.

The new sequence you are creating is intended for online distribution only, so change the Timebase to **30 frames/second** to accurately measure playback speed.

Maximum Bit Depth and Maximum Render Quality sequence settings

When you're editing with GPU acceleration (that's when dedicated computer graphics hardware performs some of the visual effects rendering and playback), advanced algorithms are used, and effects that support it always render in 32-bit color—which is very high quality.

When working without GPU acceleration, you can enable Maximum Bit Depth, and Premiere Pro will render effects at the maximum quality possible. For many effects, this means 32-bit floating-point color, which allows for trillions of color combinations. This is the best possible quality for your effects but is more work for your computer, so you may get lower performance in real-time playback (unwanted video freezing during playback).

If you enable the Maximum Render Quality option or if you have GPU acceleration enabled in the project's settings, Premiere Pro uses a more advanced system for *transforms* (those are visual adjustments such as scaling, rotation, and repositioning). Without this option, you might see minor artifacts or noise in the picture when you perform transforms.

Both of these options can be turned off or on at any time, so you can edit without them to maximize performance and then enable them in the export settings when you output your finished work. Even with both options enabled you can use real-time effects and expect reasonable performance from Premiere Pro.

For a more detailed explanation of these settings, see:
blog.frame.io/2021/06/07/premiere-pro-max-render-quality-max-bit-depth.

The Editing Mode menu can be used to limit the options available to settings that best match specific types of media. Some options will make several menus unavailable to help avoid choosing incompatible options. For complete flexibility, keep the menu set to Custom.

5 Click the Tracks tab to view those settings. You'll explore these in the next step.

Understanding audio track types

When you add a video or audio clip to a sequence, you'll always put it on a *track* in the Timeline panel. Tracks are horizontal areas in the Timeline panel that hold clips in a particular position in time.

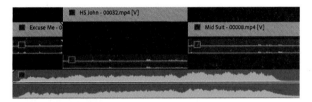

There is more than one video track, and video clips placed on an upper track will appear in front of clips on a lower track. For example, if you have text or a graphic on your second video track and a video clip on your first video track (below it), you'll see the graphic in front of the video.

The Tracks tab in the New Sequence dialog box allows you to preselect the track types for the new sequence. You can add or remove tracks at any time while editing, so these options are perhaps most useful when creating a custom sequence preset with names already assigned to audio tracks.

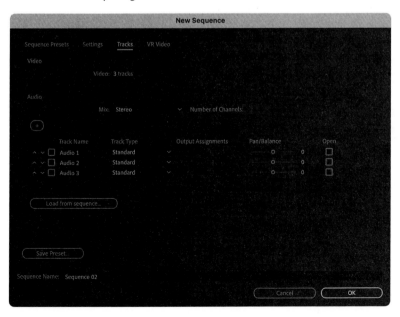

All audio tracks are played at the same time to create a combined audio mix. To create a mix, simply position your audio clips on different tracks, lined up in time. Narration, sound bites, sound effects, and music can be organized by putting them on different tracks. You can also rename tracks, making it easier to find your way around more complex sequences.

Premiere Pro lets you specify how many video and audio tracks will be included when the new sequence is created. The setting you choose from the Audio > Mix menu configures the sequence audio mix output your sequence will produce. This can be Stereo, 5.1, Multichannel, or Mono. You can't change this setting later, so choose carefully when creating a new sequence. For now, leave this set to Stereo (the default).

An audio track can be one of several types. Each track type is designed for a specific type of audio clip. When you choose a particular track type from the menu in the Track Type column, Premiere Pro shows the right controls to make adjustments to the sound, based on the number of audio channels in the track. For example, stereo clips need different controls than 5.1 surround-sound clips.

The types of audio tracks are:

- **Standard:** These tracks are for both mono and stereo audio clips.

- **5.1:** These tracks are for audio clips with 5.1 audio (the kind used for surround-sound mixes).

- **Adaptive:** Adaptive tracks are for mono, stereo, or multichannel audio and give you precise control over the output routing for each audio channel. For example, you could decide the track audio channel 3 should be output to your mix in channel 5. This workflow is used for multilingual TV, where precise control of audio channels is used at the point of transmission.

- **Mono:** This track type will accept only mono audio clips.

The Submix options available in the Track Type menu are used in advanced audio mixing workflows that are beyond the scope of this book.

You can't accidentally put an audio clip on the wrong kind of track. Premiere Pro makes sure clips go to the right kind of track. In fact, when you add a clip to a sequence, Premiere Pro will automatically create the right kind of track if one doesn't exist already.

You'll explore audio more in Lesson 10, "Editing and Mixing Audio." For now, click Cancel to close the New Sequence dialog box.

Exploring the Project Settings dialog box

Now that you have created a new project and added sequences and clips, let's explore the important options available in the Project Settings dialog box.

Choose File > Project Settings > General to open the Project Settings dialog box for your current project.

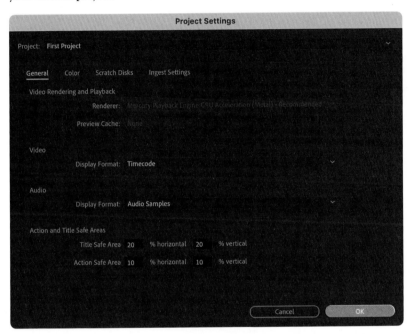

You can modify any of these settings at any time, so don't worry about getting things wrong.

Choose video rendering and playback settings

While you're working creatively with video clips in your sequences, it's likely you will apply some visual effects to adjust the appearance of your footage. Some special effects can be played immediately, combining your original video with the effect and displaying the results as soon as you click Play. When this happens, it's called *real-time playback*.

Real-time playback is desirable because it means you can watch the results of your creative choices right away, staying in your creative flow without waiting.

If you use lots of effects on a clip or if you use effects that are not designed for real-time playback, your computer may not be able to display the results at the full frame rate. Premiere Pro will attempt to display your video clips, combined with the special effects, but it may not show every single frame each second. When this happens, it's described as *dropping* frames.

Premiere Pro displays colored lines along the top of the Timeline panel, where you build sequences, to tell you when extra work is required to play back your video. No line, a green line, or a yellow line means Premiere Pro expects to be able to play without dropping frames. A red line means Premiere Pro expects to drop frames when playing that section of the sequence.

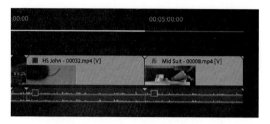

Note: A red line at the top of the Timeline panel doesn't mean frames definitely will be dropped. It just means visual adjustments aren't accelerated, so on a less powerful machine dropped frames are more likely.

If you can't see every frame when you play your sequence, it's okay! It won't affect the final results. When you're done editing and you output your finished sequence, it'll be full quality, with all the frames intact (more on this in Lesson 16).

Real-time playback can make a difference to your editing experience and your ability to preview the effects you apply with confidence. If frames are being dropped, there is a simple solution: preview rendering.

When you render, Premiere Pro creates new media files that look like the results of your effects work and then plays back those files in place of the original footage. The rendered preview is a regular video file, so playback is at reasonable quality and full frame rate, without your computer having to do any extra work.

You render effects in a sequence by choosing a render command from the Sequence menu.

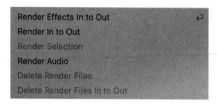

Tip: Many menu items display a keyboard shortcut on the right. In this case, the shortcut for Render Effects In To Out is Return (macOS) or Enter (Windows).

What do *rendering* and *real time* mean?

Rendering visual effects is a little like producing an artist's rendering with a pencil. Drawing an image takes up paper and time—both of which are limited resources.

When you render a section of a sequence, it takes time, and a new media file is created.

For example, imagine you have a piece of video that is too dark. You add a visual effect to make it brighter, but the video-editing system you are using is unable to both play the original video and make it brighter at the same time. In this situation, you'd have your system render the effect, creating a new temporary video file that looks like the original video combined with the visual effect that makes it brighter.

When your edited sequence plays, sections that are rendered display the newly rendered video file instead of the original clip (or clips). The process is invisible and seamless. In this example, the rendered file would look like the original video file but brighter.

When the part of your sequence with the brightened clip has finished playing, your system invisibly and seamlessly switches back from playing that preview file to playing the other original video files in the sequence.

Rendering takes up extra media storage space, and it takes time. Also, because you're viewing a new video file that is a copy of your original media, there might be some minor loss of quality. Once a section of your sequence is rendered, you will be able to preview the results of your effect smoothly with the Playback Resolution set to Full.

Real-time playback, by contrast, is immediate! When using a real-time effect, your system plays the original video clip combined with the effect right away, without waiting for the effect to render. The only limitation with real-time performance is that the amount you can do without rendering depends on how powerful your system is. More effects require more work to play back, for example. You can dramatically improve real-time performance by using the right kind of graphics card (see the sidebar "The Mercury Playback Engine"). Plus, you'll need to use effects that are designed for GPU acceleration (not all effects are).

Back in the Project Settings dialog box, in the Video Rendering And Playback settings on the General tab, if the Renderer menu is available, it means more than one option is available.

The menu has two types of settings you will choose between:

- **Mercury Playback Engine GPU Acceleration:** If you choose this rendering option, Premiere Pro will send many playback tasks to the graphics hardware on your computer, giving you lots of real-time effects and smooth preview playback of mixed formats in your sequences. You may see an option to use CUDA, OpenCL, or Metal for GPU acceleration, depending on your graphics hardware and your operating system. Performance can vary, and some graphics hardware configurations allow multiple types of acceleration, so you may need to experiment to find the best option for your system. On macOS, you will only be able to use Metal. Some advanced system GPU configurations also allow you to choose a persistent Preview Cache in Premiere Pro to improve playback. You'll want to experiment with this option for optimum playback performance.

- **Mercury Playback Engine Software Only:** This mode will still usually give acceptable performance. If your system does not have graphics hardware that can be used for GPU acceleration, only this option will be available, and you won't be able to open the Renderer menu.

You will almost certainly want to choose GPU acceleration and benefit from the additional performance if you can. However, if you experience performance or stability issues using GPU acceleration, choose the Software Only option in this menu. You can change these options at any time—including in the middle of working on a project.

Choose a GPU option now, if it's available.

The Mercury Playback Engine

The Mercury Playback Engine, which decodes and displays video files in Premiere Pro, has three main features.

- **Playback performance:** Premiere Pro plays back video files efficiently, even when working with video formats that are difficult to play back, such as H.264, H.265, or AVCHD. If you're filming with a DSLR camera or phone camera, for example, chances are your media is recorded using the H.264 codec. Thanks to the Mercury Playback Engine, you'll find that these files play back smoothly. If your GPU supports hardware acceleration (see CUDA, OpenCL, Apple Metal, and Intel graphics support), you can improve playback performance by enabling hardware-accelerated decoding in the Premiere Pro Media Preferences.

- **64-bit and multithreading:** Premiere Pro can use all the random-access memory (RAM) on your computer. This is particularly useful when you're working with high-definition or ultra-high-definition video (for example, 4K and above). The Mercury Playback Engine is multithreaded, which means it uses all the CPU cores in your computer. The more powerful your computer is, the higher the performance you'll see in Premiere Pro.

- **CUDA, OpenCL, Apple Metal, and Intel graphics support:** If you have the right graphics hardware, Premiere Pro can send some of the work for playing back video to the graphics card, rather than putting the entire processing burden on the CPU in your computer. The results are even better performance and responsiveness when working with sequences, and many special effects will play in real time, without dropping frames.

For more information about supported graphics cards, see:
helpx.adobe.com/premiere-pro/system-requirements.html.

Choosing the video and audio display formats

The next two areas of the General tab in the Project Settings dialog box allow you to choose how Premiere Pro should display time for your video and audio clips.

In most cases, you'll want the default options: From the Video Display Format menu, choose Timecode, and from the Audio Display Format menu, choose Audio Samples. These settings don't change the way Premiere Pro plays video or audio clips, only the way time measurement is displayed—and you can change the settings at any time.

The Video Display Format menu

There are four options for Video Display Format. The correct choice for a given project largely depends on whether you are working with video or celluloid film as your source material. It's rare to produce content using film, so if you are not sure, choose Timecode.

The choices are as follows:

- **Timecode:** This is the default option. Timecode is a universal system for counting hours, minutes, seconds, and individual frames of video. The same system is used by cameras, professional video recorders, and nonlinear editing systems around the world.

- **Feet + Frames 16mm or Feet + Frames 35mm:** This is used if your source files are captured from celluloid film and you intend to give your editing decisions to a lab so it can cut the original negative.

- **Frames:** This option counts the number of frames of video. This is sometimes used for animation projects.

For now, leave the menu set to Timecode.

The Audio Display Format menu

For audio files, time can be displayed as samples or milliseconds.

The choices are as follows:

- **Audio Samples:** When digital audio is recorded, the sound level (technically, the air pressure level) captured by the microphone is sampled thousands of times a second. In the case of most professional video cameras, this happens 48,000 times per second. When playing clips and sequences, you can choose to display (and edit) audio time as hours, minutes, seconds, and *frames*, or as hours, minutes, seconds, and *samples*.

- **Milliseconds:** With this mode chosen, audio time can be displayed as hours, minutes, seconds, and *thousandths of a second* instead of samples.

By default, you can zoom the Timeline panel enough to view individual clip segment frames. However, you can easily switch to showing the audio display format instead. This powerful feature lets you make the tiniest adjustments to your audio.

For now, leave the Audio Display Format option set to Audio Samples.

Action and Title Safe areas

When creating projects intended for home TVs, you'll probably need to compensate for the way TVs crop the edge of the picture to produce a clean edge.

Traditionally, there are two areas to be concerned with:

- **Action Safe:** The image area that might be cropped on most TVs; keep important image content inside this area.

- **Title Safe:** The image area that might be cropped on a really badly calibrated TV; keep titles inside this area so they will always be readable and not cropped by the edge of the screen.

Premiere Pro can display onscreen overlay guides to indicate the Title Safe and Action Safe areas. You'll want to consider the type of screen you are delivering for carefully before using the guides. Modern screens, for example, have smaller margins than older displays, showing more of the image. See Lesson 4, "Organizing Media," to learn more about configuring onscreen overlays.

Color Management settings

Premiere Pro offers support for High-Dynamic Range (HDR) video, which allows you to capture and produce video content with much more dynamic range between the dark and light areas of the frame and more saturated colors. HDR is beyond the scope of this book but is well worth exploring as it is quickly becoming an industry standard for broadcast and online video delivery.

Producing HDR content requires a camera capable of capturing the content, an editing system that supports it (Premiere Pro), and a screen capable of displaying it.

The Color tab provides advanced options for handling the interpretation and display of color and brightness information in clips and sequences. There are shortcuts for these settings in the Lumetri Color panel, which you will explore in Chapter 13, "Applying Color Correction and Grading."

For now, click the Scratch Disks tab to view the options.

Setting up the scratch disks

Whenever Premiere Pro renders special effects, saves backup copies of the project file, downloads content from Adobe Stock, or imports animated motion graphics templates, or whenever you record a voiceover, it creates new files.

The various *scratch disks* are the storage locations where Premiere Pro stores these files. Although they are described as disks, they are actually folders. Some of the files that are stored will be temporary, and some will be new media created in Premiere Pro or imported.

Scratch disks can be stored on physically separate drives or in any subfolder on your storage. Scratch disks can be located all in the same place or in separate locations, depending on your hardware and workflow requirements. If you're working with really large media files, you may get a performance boost by putting each scratch disk on a physically separate hard drive.

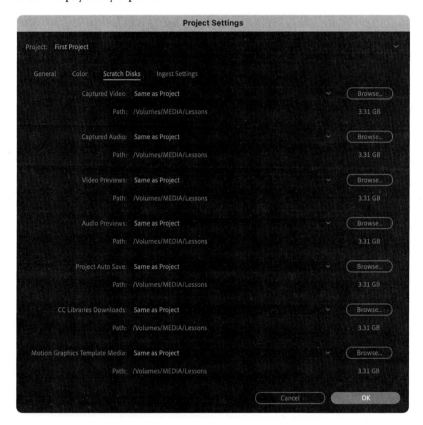

There are generally two approaches to storage for video editing:

- **Project-based setup:** All associated media files are stored with the project file in the same folder. This is the default option in the Scratch Disks menus and the simplest to manage.

- **System-based setup:** Media files associated with multiple projects are saved to one central location (often high-speed network-based storage), and the project file is saved to another location. This might include storing different kinds of media files in different locations.

To change the location of the scratch disk for a particular type of data, choose a location from the menu next to the data type. The choices are:

- **Documents:** Stores the scratch disk in the Documents folder in your system user account, using a subfolder for Premiere Pro.

- **Same As Project:** Stores the scratch disk with the project file. This is the default option.

- **[Custom]:** Enables you to specify any location. This option is automatically chosen if you click Browse and choose a specific location for the scratch disk.

Below each Scratch Disk location menu, a file path shows the current setting and the space available at that location.

Your scratch disks might be stored on local hard drives inside your computer or on a network-based remote storage system; any storage location your computer has access to will work. However, the speed and responsiveness of your scratch disks can have a big impact on both playback and rendering performance—choose fast storage if possible.

Using a project-based setup

By default, Premiere Pro keeps newly created media together with the associated project file (this is the Same As Project option in the Scratch Disk menus). Keeping everything together this way makes finding relevant files simple.

It also makes staying organized easier if you move media files into the same folder before you import them into the project. When you're finished with your project, you can remove everything from your system by deleting the single folder your project file is stored in.

You can use subfolders to keep your project media, notes, scripts, and associated assets organized.

There's a downside: Storing your media files on the same drive as your project file means the drive has to work a little harder while you edit, and this can impact playback performance on slower drives.

Using a system-based setup

Some editors prefer to have all their media stored in a single location, for all projects. Others choose to store their capture folders and preview folders in a different location from their project. This is a common choice in editing facilities where multiple editors share several editing systems, all connected to the same network-based storage. It's also common among editors who have fast hard drives for video media and slower hard drives for everything else.

There's a downside with this setup too: Once you finish editing, it's likely you'll want to gather everything together for archiving. This is slower and more complex when your media files are distributed across multiple storage locations. See the online bonus lesson "Managing Your Projects" for more information.

Typical drive setup and network-based storage

Although all file types can coexist on a single storage drive, a typical editing system will have two storage drives: Drive 1, dedicated to the operating system and programs, and Drive 2 (often a faster drive), dedicated to media, including captured video and audio, video and audio preview files, still images, and exported media. For even better performance, a third storage drive, preferably a solid-state drive (SSD), can be dedicated to temporary Media Cache files.

Modern NVMe SSD drives are so fast that you may never notice any impact on playback performance when storing everything on one drive. Nonetheless, it can make project organization simpler to use a separate drive for media, and you are likely to see an impact when working with particularly large media files, like 8K RAW.

Some storage systems use local computer networks to share storage between multiple systems. If this is the case for you, check with your system administrators to make sure you have the right settings and then check the performance.

Setting up a Project Auto Save location

In addition to choosing where new media files are created, you can set the location to store automatically saved project backup files. These additional copies of your project file are created in the background while you work. Choose a location from the Project Auto Save menu on the Scratch Disks tab.

Storage drives occasionally fail, and you may lose files stored on them without warning. In fact, any computer engineer will tell you that if you have only one copy of a file, you can't count on having the file at all! For this reason, it's a great idea to set the Project Auto Save location to a physically separate storage location.

If you use a synchronized file sharing service like Dropbox, OneDrive, or Google Drive, storing your auto-save files using that service will mean you always have access to all your automatically saved project files.

Creative Cloud Libraries downloads

The Libraries panel provides access to media assets that can be shared between projects and with other users. Assets can be dragged from the Libraries panel into the Project panel or Timeline panel to add them to your current project.

Motion Graphics template media

Premiere Pro can import and display prebuilt animated Motion Graphics templates and titles that have been created with After Effects or Premiere Pro. When you import a Motion Graphics template into the current project, a copy will be stored in the location you choose.

Choosing ingest settings

Professional editors describe adding media to a project as *importing* or *ingesting*. The two words are often used interchangeably but actually have different meanings.

When you *import* a media file into a Premiere Pro project, a clip is created in the project that is linked to the original file. The media file stays in its current location, and you're ready to include the clip in a sequence.

If you select Ingest on the Ingest Settings tab or Copy Media while in Import mode, things are a little bit different. The original media file may also be copied to a different location (which is useful for keeping your media files organized) and/or converted to a new format and codec before it's imported into your Premiere Pro project.

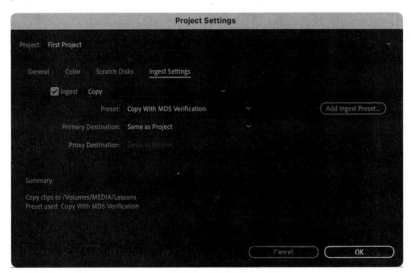

From the Ingest menu you can choose to:

- **Copy** the media files to a new storage location. This option is useful if you want to be sure all your media is in one folder.

- **Transcode** the media files to a new codec and/or format. This option is useful if you choose to standardize your media as part of a larger-scale organization-wide workflow.

- **Create Proxies** of the media file. This option creates lower-resolution copies of media files that are easier for a lower-powered computer to play and that take up less storage space. The original media is always available too, and you can switch between the full-quality and proxy-quality files whenever you like.

- **Copy And Create Proxies** to copy the media files to a new location and create proxies for them in a single step.

  You'll be exploring these settings in Lesson 3, "Importing Media." They can be changed at any time; for now, leave Ingest deselected.

  Now that you have checked that the settings are correct for this project, click OK to apply any changes. Save, and close the project by choosing File > Close Project.

Note: There are several ways to import clips into a project. Once you enable the ingest options, Premiere Pro applies them regardless of the import method you use. Note that existing clips that have already been imported into your project will not have new ingest options applied automatically.

VR video

Premiere Pro offers exceptional support for 360° video and 180° video. Both are often described as *VR video* or *immersive video*, where multiple cameras or an extremely wide lens are used to capture a video image that can be viewed with a VR headset to create an immersive experience.

On the VR Video tab in the New Sequence dialog box, you can specify the angle of view captured so Premiere Pro can accurately display the image.

VR video is beyond the scope of this book, but it is well worth exploring when you have mastered the basics of video editing.

Review questions

1 What is the purpose of the Settings tab in the New Sequence dialog box?

2 How should you choose a sequence preset?

3 What is timecode?

4 How do you create a custom sequence preset?

5 How can you choose where to store temporary files created automatically while editing?

Review answers

1 The Settings tab is used to customize an existing sequence preset or to create a new custom preset.

2 It's generally best to choose a preset that matches your original footage to minimize conversion during playback. Premiere Pro makes this easy by describing the presets in terms of camera systems.

3 Timecode is the universal system for measuring time in hours, minutes, seconds, and frames. The number of frames per second varies depending on the recording format.

4 When you've chosen the settings you want for your custom preset on the Settings tab in the New Sequence dialog box, click the Save Preset button, give the preset a name and a description, and click OK.

5 Use the settings on the Scratch Disks tab of the Project Settings dialog box to specify locations for newly created files.

3 IMPORTING MEDIA

Lesson overview

In this lesson, you'll learn how to do the following:

- Use the Media Browser and Import mode to add video files.

- Use the Import command to load graphic files, including files from Photoshop and Illustrator.

- Work with proxy media.

- Record a voice-over.

- Choose where to store cache files.

 This lesson will take about 75 minutes to complete. To get the lesson files used in this chapter, download them from the web page for this book at *peachpit.com/PremiereProCIB2024.* For more information, see "Accessing the lesson files and Web Edition" in the "Getting Started" section at the beginning of this book. Store the files on your computer in a convenient location.

However you approach editing sequences, importing clips to the Project panel and getting them organized are the first steps. In this lesson, you'll learn multiple methods for browsing and importing media.

Starting the lesson

Note: To ensure that the tools function and the defaults are set exactly as described in this lesson, reset the Premiere Pro preferences by holding the Option/Alt key while launching the application and then clicking Continue.

Before creating a sequence, you'll probably need to import media files into your project. This might include video footage, animation files, narration, music, atmospheric sound, graphics, or photos. In brief, anything that you might incorporate into a sequence will be imported into your project first.

With the exception of the graphics, titles, and captions that you create in Premiere Pro, items in sequences always also appear in the Project panel. For example, if you import a video clip directly to a sequence, it will also automatically appear in the Project panel. If you delete that clip in the Project panel, it will also be removed from sequences that it appears in (you'll be given a warning and the option to cancel before this happens).

In this lesson, you'll learn to import media assets into Adobe Premiere Pro. For most media, you'll import using Import mode or the Media Browser, a robust asset browser that works with many media types you'll import into Premiere Pro. You'll also learn about special cases, such as importing single and multilayer graphics.

For this lesson, you can continue to use the project file you created in Lesson 2, "Setting Up a Project." If you do not have the previous lesson file, you can open the file Lesson 03.prproj from the Lessons folder.

Note: When you open a project created on another computer, you may see a message warning you about a missing renderer. It's fine to click OK in this message. It indicates that the project was last saved with project settings configured for a different (or missing) GPU.

1 Continue to work with your project file from the previous lesson, or open it from your hard drive.

2 Choose File > Save As.

3 Browse to Lessons, and save the project with the name **Lesson 03 Working.prproj**.

4 Click the Workspaces menu ▣, choose Editing; then click the Workspaces menu again and choose Reset To Saved Layout.

Importing media files

When you import items into a Premiere Pro project, you are not actually copying the file into the project. Instead, importing creates a link to the media file with a pointer that lives inside your project.

The pointer is called a *clip*. Think of a clip as a special kind of alias (macOS) or shortcut (Windows).

When you work with a clip in Premiere Pro, you are not making a copy of the original file or modifying it; instead, you're selectively playing a part of, or all of, that file from its current location, nondestructively.

For example, if you choose to include only part of a clip in your sequence, you're not throwing away the unused media. A copy of the clip is added to the sequence with built-in instructions to play only the part you selected. This changes the apparent duration in the sequence, even though the full original duration in the media file is unchanged and still available.

Also, if you add an effect to a clip to brighten the image, the effect is applied to the clip, not the media file it links to. In a sense, the original media file is played "through" the clip, with interpretation settings and effects applied.

You can import media in four principal ways:

- Choose File > Import.
- Drag media files directly from Finder (macOS) or Explorer (Windows) into the Project panel or Timeline panel in Premiere Pro.
- Use Import mode.
- Use the Media Browser.

Tip: Another way to open the Import dialog box is to double-click an empty area of the Project panel.

Let's explore the benefits of each.

When to use Import mode or the Media Browser

If in doubt, use Import mode. It has a robust, user-friendly interface that automatically manages reviewing your media assets and makes it simple to import them into Premiere Pro. If your camera has produced footage made up of multiple fragmented files, they will automatically be presented as whole clips; you'll see each recording as a single item, with the video and audio combined, regardless of the original recording format.

This means you can avoid dealing with complex camera folder structures and instead work with easy-to-browse thumbnails.

For more advanced media browsing tools, use the Media Browser while in Edit mode. This panel offers similar media previewing and navigation options to Import mode, with the additional option to preview clips in the Source Monitor before importing them, and full access to clip metadata. Being able to see this metadata (which contains important information, such as clip duration, recording date, and file type) makes it easier to select the correct clip in a long list. The Media Browser also supports Illustrator files and image sequences, which are not supported by Import mode.

Accessing Import mode is straightforward. Click to select the mode at the top-left corner.

To browse for files in Import mode, select a location from the list on the left and double-click folders displayed in the middle of the window to access their contents. As you navigate into subfolders, you'll see the folder path displayed at the top—click a folder name inside the path to navigate to that folder.

If you have a cloud-based storage location on your computer, you'll find it listed under the Cloud heading at the end of the locations list.

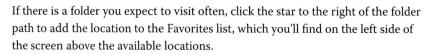

If there is a folder you expect to visit often, click the star to the right of the folder path to add the location to the Favorites list, which you'll find on the left side of the screen above the available locations.

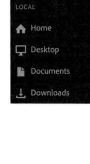

Switching back to Edit mode, in the default layout of the Editing workspace, you'll find the Media Browser in the lower-left corner of your Premiere Pro Editing workspace. It's docked in the same panel group as the Project panel.

▶ **Tip:** You can also quickly access the Media Browser by pressing Shift+8 (be sure to use the 8 key at the top of the keyboard, not the one in the numerical keypad, if you have one).

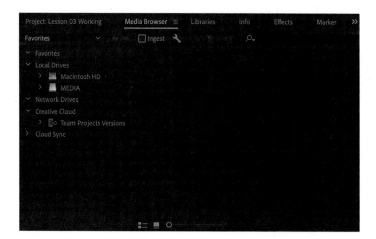

As you can any other panel, you can position the Media Browser in another panel group by dragging its panel tab (identified by the panel name).

You can also undock it to make it a floating panel by clicking the panel menu next to the panel name and choosing Undock Panel.

Browsing for files in the Media Browser is similar to browsing with Finder (macOS) or Explorer (Windows). The contents of your storage are displayed as navigation folders on the left, with buttons to navigate forward and backward at the top.

After you select a folder or media file in the Media Browser, you can use the arrow keys to select items.

You can use Import mode and the Media Browser interchangeably at any time. As your familiarity with Premiere Pro grows, you'll quickly discover the occasions you prefer one option over the other.

Both Import mode and the Media Browser offer several benefits over the regular Import option:

- Filtering the display while browsing a folder. In fact, while Import mode allows you to filter video, audio, or image files, the Media Browser's File Types Displayed menu  enables you to narrow the clips displayed to a specific file type, such as JPEG, PSD, XML, or ARRIRAW files.

- Autosensing camera data—AVCHD, Canon XF, P2, RED, Cinema DNG, Sony HDV, or XDCAM (EX and HD)—to correctly display and import the clips.

- Correctly displaying and importing media files that span multiple camera media cards. Premiere Pro will automatically import the files as a single clip even if a longer video file filled a storage card and continued onto another.

- In the Media Browser, viewing and customizing the kinds of metadata to display.

- In Import mode, automatically creating a bin or sequence when importing new clips.

Opening or browsing projects

Premiere Pro allows you to open multiple project files at the same time. This makes it simple to copy clips from one project to another.

All open projects are editable, which means you'll need to be careful not to make unwanted changes to a project you have opened just to copy a clip from it.

You can switch between projects by choosing Window > Projects, followed by the project you would like to work on.

You can also browse inside another project file using the Media Browser. Use the Media Browser to locate the project file and double-click it to view its contents. You can then select and import clips and sequences to your current Project panel.

Projects you browse inside using the Media Browser are locked, meaning you cannot make unwanted changes.

Remember, when copying clips or sequences from one project to another, you are not copying media files—only clips that link to the media files.

When to use the Import command

Using the Import command is straightforward (and may match your experience in other applications). To import a file, just choose File > Import.

You can also use the keyboard shortcut Command+I (macOS) or Ctrl+I (Windows) to open the Import dialog box.

This method works best for self-contained assets such as graphics and audio files or video files like MOV (QuickTime) or MP4 (H.264), especially if you know exactly where those assets are on your drive and can quickly navigate to them.

This import method is not ideal for RAW media files or when camera media has separate folders for audio, video, and important additional data describing the footage (metadata). For most camera-originated media, you'll want to use Import mode or the Media Browser.

Showing source clip names and labels in the Timeline panel

In the Project panel, it's possible you will change a clip name or label color to help keep everything organized. If you then add it to a sequence, the new name and label color will be displayed in the Timeline panel. However, by default, instances of that clip already in the Timeline panel will still show their original name and label color.

You can choose to display the original clip names and label colors or the updated names and label colors in the Timeline panel. Make sure that a sequence is open in the Timeline panel to enable access to the Timeline Display Settings menu . Click the menu and choose Show Source Clip Name And Label.

Both options can be useful, depending on your chosen workflow for a particular project, and you can switch between them at any time.

Working with ingest options and proxy media

Tip: When project ingest options are enabled, they are applied to all newly imported media, regardless of the way it is imported.

Premiere Pro offers excellent performance when playing back, and applying special effects to, a broad range of media formats and codecs. However, there may be occasions when your system hardware will struggle to play media, especially if it's ultra-high resolution or RAW footage.

You may decide it will be more efficient to work with low-resolution copies of your media while you edit and then switch to the full, original-resolution media to check your effects and output your finished work. This is a *proxy workflow*—creating low-resolution "proxy" files to use temporarily instead of your original content. You can switch between the two types of media whenever you like.

Premiere Pro can automatically create proxy files during import. If you're happy with the performance on your system when working with original footage, you'll probably skip this feature. Still, it offers significant advantages, both for system performance and for collaboration, particularly if you're working with high-resolution media on a less powerful computer.

You define the options for ingesting media and creating proxy files using the Ingest Settings tab of the Project Settings dialog box. Choose File > Project Settings > Ingest Settings and select Ingest to access them.

- **Copy:** When you import media files, Premiere Pro will copy them to a location you choose from the Primary Destination menu below, leaving the original files in place. This is a valuable option if you are importing media files directly from your camera storage, because media files must be available to Premiere Pro when your cards are not connected to the computer.

- **Transcode:** When you import media files, Premiere Pro will convert the files to a new format and codec based on the preset you choose and will place the new files in a destination location you choose. This is useful if you are working in a post-production facility that has adopted a standard format and codec for all projects—sometimes called a *mezzanine media* file.

- **Create Proxies:** When you import media files, Premiere Pro creates additional copies that may have smaller file sizes, are lower resolution, and may be easier for your system to play. They are stored in the location you choose from the Proxy Destination menu. Proxies are useful if you are working on a lower-powered computer or you want to temporarily save on storage space while traveling with a copy of your project. You would not want to use these files for your final delivery because they are usually lower quality, but they facilitate a number of collaborative workflows as well as speed up visual effect setup.

- **Copy and Create Proxies:** When you import media files, Premiere Pro will copy the original files to a location you choose in the Primary Destination menu *and* create proxies that are stored in the Proxy Destination menu.

    Note: Adobe Media Encoder does the work of transcoding files and creating proxies in the background, so you can use your original media right away, and as the new proxy files are created, they'll automatically be used instead of the original media files.

    If proxy media exists for clips in your project, it's easy to switch between displaying your original, full-quality media and your low-resolution proxy versions. Click the Toggle Proxies button 🔳 in the Source Monitor or Program Monitor.

Let's check out the options.

1   Choose File > Project Settings > Ingest Settings.

    Tip: You can also open the Project Settings dialog box to the Ingest Settings tab from the Media Browser by selecting the box for Ingest or by clicking the Open Ingest Settings button.

    By default, all the Ingest options are deselected. It's worth noting that whichever options you choose for ingesting, those actions will be performed regardless of the way you import media files from now on. Importantly, files you have already imported are not affected by these settings.

Tip: When copying media files, Premiere Pro can perform MD5 verification. This checks that the files have copied correctly at the expense of extra time to perform the copy.

2 Enable Ingest by selecting it, and open the adjacent menu to see the options.

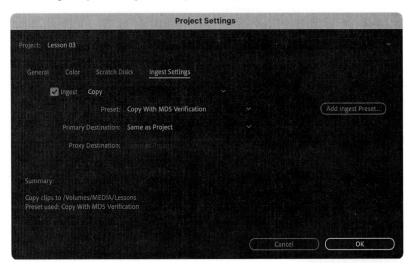

3 Choose Create Proxies, open the Preset menu, and try choosing a few options. Look at the Summary in the lower part of the dialog box for an explanation of each option.

4 When you finish looking at the settings, click Cancel to exit without applying any of the options.

✓ H.264 Low Resolution Proxy
H.264 Medium Resolution Proxy
H.264 High Resolution Proxy
ProRes Low Resolution Proxy
ProRes Medium Resolution Proxy
ProRes High Resolution Proxy
DNxHR VR Monoscopic Proxy
DNxHR VR Stereoscopic Proxy

This was just an introduction to the proxy media work-flow. For more information about managing and viewing proxy files, linking proxy media, and creating new proxy file presets, see the Adobe Premiere Pro Help. For a deep dive into this subject, visit:
blog.frame.io/2023/10/02/guide-to-premiere-pro-proxies-proxy-workflows/.

● **Note:** By default, when you output a sequence that is set to display proxy media, the full-quality original media is automatically used rather than the low-resolution proxy media for the export.

Working with Import mode and the Media Browser

● **Note:** To complete this lesson, you will import files from your computer. Be sure you have copied all the lesson files included with this book to your computer. For more details, see "Getting Started" at the beginning of the book.

You can switch to Import mode at any time to browse your available media files and add clips to your current project. Alternatively, you can open the Media Browser while in Edit mode. This panel can stay open as part of your editing workspace, allowing you to quickly access and compare available media with clips already in your project.

Working with media files

Premiere Pro can use footage from file-based cameras without conversion, including compressed native media from camera systems such as P2, XDCAM, and AVCHD;

RAW media from Canon, Sony, RED, and ARRI; and post-production-friendly codecs such as Avid DNxHD, Apple ProRes, and GoPro Cineform.

For best results, follow these guidelines (no need to follow along for now):

- Create a separate media folder for each project. This will make it easier to differentiate between projects when cleaning up your storage.

- Copy camera media to your editing storage with the existing folder structure intact. For example, transfer the complete data folder directly from the root directory of the memory card. For best results, consider using the transfer application that is often included by the camera manufacturer to move your video files. Check that all media files have been copied and that the original card and the copied folder sizes match.

- Clearly name the copied folder of the media with the camera information, including card number and the date of the shoot.

- Create a second copy of the media on a physically separate drive, in case of hardware failure.

- Really do actually create that second copy of your media on a physically separate drive, and consider making a third copy! Storage fails without warning.

- Ideally, create a long-term archive copy of your media using another backup method, such as Linear Tape-Open (LTO—a popular long-term storage system), an external storage drive, or cloud-based file storage.

Understanding supported video file types

It's not unusual to work on a project with video clips from multiple cameras using different file types, media formats, and codecs. This is no problem for Premiere Pro because you can mix different types of media in the same sequence. Also, Import mode and the Media Browser can display and import almost any media file type.

Premiere Pro supports media from many camera manufacturers, including:

- Most DSLR cameras

- Panasonic

- RED

- ARRI

- Canon

- Sony

- Blackmagic Design

Many standard media types are also supported, including QuickTime, MXF, DPX, and OMF. For a full list of supported camera and delivered media types, see the Adobe Help.

AAF
ARRIRAW Files
AVI Motion JPEG
Adobe After Effects Projects
Adobe After Effects Text Templates
Adobe Audition Tracks
Adobe Illustrator File
Adobe Premiere Pro Projects
Adobe Premiere Pro Text Style
Adobe Rough Cut File
Audio Interchange File Format
Audio Interchange File Format AIFF-C
Biovision Hierarchy
Bitmap
Blackmagic RAW
CMX3600 EDLs
Canon Cinema RAW Light
Canon RAW
Character Animator Project
Cinema DNG Files
Cineon/DPX File
Comma-separated values
Distribution Format Exchange Profile File
EBU N19 Subtitle File
Final Cut Pro XML
GIF File
HEIF files
JPEG File
JSON
MBWF / RF64
MP3 Audio
MPEG Movie
MXF
MacCaption VANC File
Matroska
Motion Graphics JSON
Motion Graphics Template
OpenEXR
PNG File
Phantom Files
Photoshop
QuickTime Movie
RED R3D Raw File
Scenarist Closed Caption File
SonyRAW Format
SubRip Subtitle Format
TIFF image file
Tab-separated values
Text Template
Truevision Targa File
W3C/SMPTE/EBU Timed Text File
WEBP files
Waveform Audio
All Files

Adding clips using Import mode

Import mode offers a simplified, easy-access approach to locating and importing media. Storage locations and favorites are listed on the left, with their contents displayed in the middle and additional import options available on the right.

Note: When importing media, be sure to copy the files to your local storage, or use the project ingest options to create copies before removing your memory cards or external drives.

Add some clips to your project using Import mode, and then try using the Media Browser to compare the experience.

1 Switch to Import mode by clicking Import at the top-left corner.

Notice that now that you are importing to an existing project, rather than creating a new project, the option to create a project is not displayed.

2 By using the locations listed on the left and double-clicking subfolders in the middle, browse to the folder Lessons/Assets/Video And Audio Files/Theft Unexpected.

Selecting versus browsing

Be careful not to single-click a folder while in Import mode, as that will select the entire contents of the folder for import. If you do (but don't want everything in the folder to be imported), single-click the folder again to deselect it; then you can double-click the folder to browse into it.

Alternatively, select the unwanted folder icon at the lower-left corner of the interface (which will display the number of items in the folder), and press Delete (macOS) or Backspace (Windows).

3 If it is not already selected, click the Grid View button ⊞ at the top, and drag the Resize slider next to it to enlarge the thumbnails of the clips. Choose any size you like.

You can hover your pointer over any clip thumbnail to see a preview of the clip contents. Hovering over the left edge shows the start of the clip; hovering over the right edge shows the end of the clip.

4   Select the following clips by single-clicking them:

Excuse Me Tilted – 00036

HS Suit – 00017

Mid John – 00028

5   Check that all of the Import settings (Copy Media, New Bin, and New Sequence) are deselected, and click Import.

You have now imported some clips! The Edit mode is restored, and your newly imported clips have been added to the Project panel.

You can easily switch between the Import and Edit modes at any time while working on a project, so it's quick to add new content to your project as it becomes available. Now let's compare this import method with importing using the Media Browser.

Adding clips using the Media Browser

The Media Browser is even more like the Finder (macOS) or Explorer (Windows). It has Forward and Back buttons to go through your recent navigation. If you select a storage location in the left area, its contents are displayed on the right.

1   Begin by resetting the workspace to the default: From the Workspaces menu, choose Editing. Then, open the menu again and choose Reset To Saved Layout.

2 Click the Media Browser's name to bring the panel to the front of the panel group (it should be docked with the Project panel by default).

▶ **Tip:** Finding the ` (accent grave) key can be difficult in some keyboard layouts. If you can't locate the correct key, you can double-click the name of a panel to enlarge it to fill the screen.

● **Note:** The Media Browser filters out non-media and unsupported files, making it easier to browse for video or audio assets.

3 To make the Media Browser easier to see, position your pointer over the panel, and then press the ` (accent grave) key (it is often in the upper-left corner of a keyboard; non-English keyboards may use a different key) or double-click the panel name.

The Media Browser should now fill the screen.

4 In the navigation area, browse to and select the folder Lessons/Assets/Video And Audio Files/Theft Unexpected.

▶ **Tip:** As you browse a folder system, the navigation area on the left of the Media Browser can fill up with folders. Drag the vertical divider to resize the navigation area or scroll within the navigation area to display the folders you are interested in.

5 If it is not already selected, click the Thumbnail View button ▣ at the lower left of the Media Browser, and drag the Resize slider next to it to enlarge the thumbnails of the clips. Choose any size you like.

Just as in Import mode, you can hover your pointer over any clip thumbnail that is *not* selected, without clicking, to see a preview of the clip contents. Hovering over the left edge shows the start of the clip; hovering over the right edge shows the end of the clip.

6   Click any clip once to select it.

You can now preview the clip using keyboard shortcuts. When a clip is selected while in Thumbnail view, a small preview timeline appears under the clip.

7   Press the L key or the spacebar to play a clip.

8   To stop playback, press the K key or press the spacebar again.

9   To play backward, press the J key.

10 Experiment with playing other clips. You should be able to hear the clip audio during playback.

> **Note:** If you can't hear audio, check the Audio Hardware preferences to make sure the correct output device is selected.

You can press the J or L key multiple times to increase the playback rate for fast previews. Use the K key or the spacebar to pause playback.

11 Now you'll import the two remaining clips into your project. Click once on the clip Cutaways – 00042 to select it. Next, hold Command (macOS) or Ctrl (Windows) and click the clip Reveal - 00038. This selects both clips.

12 Right-click one of the selected clips and choose Import.

> **Tip:** You can also drag selected clips onto the Project panel's tab and then down into the empty area to import the clips.

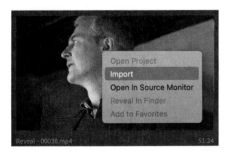

The Project panel opens automatically and displays the clips.

13 Position your pointer over the Project panel and press the ` (accent grave) key or double-click the Project panel name to restore the panel group to its original size.

As in Import mode and the Media Browser, you can view clips in the Project panel as icons or as a list, with information about each clip displayed. There is an additional, more flexible viewing mode for working with icons, called Freeform view. You can switch between these three viewing modes by clicking the List View button ▤, Icon View button ▨, or Freeform View button ▥ at the bottom left of the Project panel.

Making the most of Import mode and the Media Browser

Both Import mode and the Media Browser have a number of features that make it easy to navigate your storage.

- If you expect to import files from a location often, you can add the folder to a list of favorites at the top of the navigation area. To create a favorite in the Media Browser, right-click the folder and choose Add To Favorites. In Import mode, click the Favorite Location button ⭐. Whichever way you add a favorite location, it will appear in both views.

- To ignore regular media file types and just display media from a particular camera system, open the Directory Viewers menu ◉.

- The Media Browser Forward and Back buttons ⬅ ➡ work like those in a web browser, allowing you to navigate to locations you have viewed previously.

- You can limit the types of files displayed to make it easier to browse large folders by opening the File Types Displayed menu ▼.

- In the Media Browser, just above the navigation area on the left, there's a menu with recent storage locations. Choose an option to jump straight to that location.

- You can open multiple Media Browsers and access the contents of several folders at once. To open a new Media Browser, open the panel menu ☰ and choose New Media Browser Panel.

- By default, the Media Browser List view displays limited information about clips (unlike the Project panel, which displays lots of information by default). To display more information while in List view, you can add multiple columns of metadata by clicking the Media Browser panel menu and choosing Edit Columns. In the Edit Columns dialog box, select each type of metadata you would like to display.

Importing still image files

Graphics are an integral part of post-production. People expect graphics to both convey information and add to the visual style of a project. Premiere Pro can import almost any image file type. Support is especially excellent when you use the native file formats created by Adobe's leading graphic tools, Adobe Photoshop and Adobe Illustrator.

Anyone who works with print graphics or performs photo retouching has probably used Adobe Photoshop. Photoshop is a powerful tool with great depth and versatility, and it's an important part of the video production world. Let's explore how to properly import files from Photoshop.

First, you'll import a basic graphic.

Importing single-layer image files

Most graphics and photos you will work with will have a single layer—one flat grid of pixels that you can work with as a simple media file. Let's import one.

1   Choose File > Import, or press Command+I (macOS) or Ctrl+I (Windows).

2   Navigate to Lessons/Assets/Graphics.

3   Select the file Theft_Unexpected.png, and click Import.

    This PNG graphic is a simple logo file, and it appears in the Premiere Pro Project panel. If the Project panel is in Icon view, it will display the contents of the graphic as a thumbnail.

Introducing Dynamic Link

Premiere Pro integrates beautifully with the other tools available as part of Adobe Creative Cloud. In fact, there are several workflows, unique to Creative Cloud, that speed up your post-production workflow.

A good example is Dynamic Link. This technology allows you to import Adobe After Effects compositions (which are a little like Premiere Pro sequences) into a Premiere Pro project while maintaining a live connection between the two applications. Once added in this way, the After Effects compositions will look and behave like any other clip in your Premiere Pro project.

However, when you make changes in After Effects, the imported compositions continuously and automatically update in Premiere Pro—a great time-saver.

Dynamic Link works automatically, creating links between Premiere Pro and After Effects and between Premiere Pro and Adobe Audition, provided the same versions of the applications are installed and used.

Importing layered Adobe Photoshop files

Adobe Photoshop can create graphics with multiple layers, which are saved as files in PSD or TIFF format. Layers are similar to tracks in a Premiere Pro sequence and allow for separation between visual elements. While TIFF files with layers are imported as flattened images, you can import Photoshop document layers into Premiere Pro individually to perform layer-specific adjustments and create animations.

As with any other media you import, changes made to the PSD file in Photoshop will update automatically in Premiere Pro when the file is saved. This means a designer can continue to work on an image you have already incorporated into a sequence.

If you import a layered Photoshop file, the Import Layered File dialog box appears automatically, allowing you to choose options for handling the layers.

- **Merge All Layers:** Merges all layers into one, importing the file into Premiere Pro as a single, flattened clip.

- **Merged Layers:** Merges only the specific layers you select in this dialog box into a single, flattened clip.

- **Individual Layers:** Imports only the specific layers you select in this dialog box, with each layer becoming a separate clip in a bin in the Project panel.

- **Sequence:** Imports only the layers you select in this dialog box, each as a single clip. Premiere Pro then automatically creates a new sequence (with its frame size based on the imported PSD dimensions) containing each clip on a separate track (matching the original stacking order).

If you choose Sequence or Individual Layers, you can choose one of the following from the Footage Dimensions menu:

- **Document Size:** Brings all the selected layers into Premiere Pro at the frame size of the original Photoshop document.

- **Layer Size:** Matches the frame size of the new Premiere Pro clips to the frame size of their individual layers in the original Photoshop file. Layers that do not fill the entire canvas will be cropped tightly, as transparent areas outside of the rectangle containing the layer's pixels are automatically removed. Layers are also then centered in the frame, losing their original relative positioning.

Let's import a layered Photoshop file into our project.

1 Double-click an empty area of the Project panel to open the Import dialog box, or choose File > Import.

2 Navigate to Lessons/Assets/Graphics.

3 Select the file Theft_Unexpected_Layered.psd, and click Import.

The Import Layered File dialog box appears.

> **Tip:** There are good reasons to import individual PSD layers with different layer sizes. For example, some graphic designers create multiple images for editors to incorporate into video edits, with each image occupying a different layer in the PSD. The PSD itself is a kind of one-stop image store when used this way.

> **Note:** There are some deselected layers in this PSD. These are layers with layer visibility turned off in Photoshop but not deleted. Premiere Pro honors this layer selection automatically on import.

4 For this exercise, choose Sequence from the Import As menu, and make sure Document Size is chosen from the Footage Dimensions menu. Click OK.

5 Look in the Project panel for the newly created bin  called Theft_Unexpected_Layered (named after the file). Double-click it to open it.

> ● **Note:** In the Project panel, when you double-clicked the Theft_Unexpected_Layered bin, it opened in a new panel in the same group as the Project panel. Bins have the same options as the Project panel, and opening multiple bins to browse their contents is a common way to navigate the available media in a project.

● **Note:** Bins in the Project panel look and behave a lot like folders in your computer file system, but they exist only inside the project file. They are a great way to stay organized.

6 Inside the bin, double-click the sequence Theft_Unexpected_Layered to open it in the Timeline panel.

Sequences have a particular icon in List view ⊞. A similar icon is displayed as an overlay on their thumbnail in Icon view ⊞.

If you're unsure which item is which, hover your pointer over an item name (not the icon) to display a detailed tool tip, which will tell you if it's a clip or a sequence.

The sequence opens in the Timeline panel and is displayed in the Program Monitor.

Theft_Unexpected_Layered
Sequence, 1280 x 720 (1.0)
00:00:05:00, 25.00p
48000 Hz - Stereo

7 There's a navigator along the bottom of the Timeline panel.

Drag one end of the navigator to shorten it, and zoom in so you can see the clips in the sequence more clearly.

8 Look at the sequence in the Timeline panel. The contents of the sequence are displayed in the Program Monitor. Try clicking the Toggle Track Output button ◉ at the left of the timeline for each track to reveal and hide the content on each layer.

9 Close the Theft_Unexpected_Layered bin by choosing Close Panel from its panel menu ☰.

Working with Adobe Photoshop files

Here are a few tips for working with images from Adobe Photoshop:

- Remember that importing a layered Photoshop document as a sequence with Footage Dimensions set to Document Size produces a clip in Premiere Pro with the same frame size as the pixel dimensions of the Photoshop document.

- Even if you don't plan to zoom in or pan around the image, try to use full-frame image files with a frame size at least as large as the frame size of the project. Otherwise, you'll have to scale up the image, and it may appear to lose some of its sharpness.

- If you do plan to zoom or pan, create images so that the resulting zoomed or panned area of the image has a frame size at least as large as the frame size of the sequence. For example, if you were working in full HD, which is 1920×1080 pixels, and you wanted to perform a 2X zoom, you'd need 3840×2160 pixels in the image to keep it perfectly sharp without scaling up the pixels.

- Importing large image files uses more system memory and can slow down your system. If you are working with original photos (which can be massive), consider processing them to make them smaller before using them.

- If possible, use 16-bit RGB color. The CMYK color mode is for print workflows (and is not supported by Premiere Pro). For video editing, use RGB or YUV color modes.

Importing Adobe Illustrator files

Another important graphics component in Adobe Creative Cloud is Adobe Illustrator. Unlike Photoshop, which is primarily designed to work with pixel-based (or raster) graphics, Adobe Illustrator is a vector-based application. *Vector graphics* are mathematical descriptions of shapes rather than drawn pixels. This means you can scale them to any size in Adobe Illustrator and they always look sharp—useful for titles and graphics.

Vector graphics are typically used for technical illustrations, line art, or complex graphics.

Let's import a vector graphic.

1 Switch back to the Project panel by clicking the panel name.

2 In the Project panel, make sure the Theft_Unexpected_Layered bin is deselected (otherwise the item you are about to import will be imported into that bin).

3 Double-click an empty area of the Project panel to open the Import dialog box, or press Command+I (macOS) or Ctrl+I (Windows).

4 Navigate to Lessons/Assets/Graphics.

5 Select the file Brightlove_film_logo.ai and click Import, or double-click its icon.

6   A clip linked to the Illustrator file you imported appears in the Project panel. Double-click the clip icon to view the logo in the Source Monitor.

There's black text in the logo that disappears into the black background of the Source Monitor. That's because the logo has transparent areas, and the background of the Source Monitor is black.

7   The Source Monitor has a Settings menu 🔧 with options that change the way clips are displayed. Use this menu to choose Transparency Grid.

● **Note:** If you right-click Brightlove_film_logo.ai in the Project panel, you have the option to choose Edit Original. If you have Adobe Illustrator installed on your computer, choosing Edit Original will open the graphic in Illustrator, ready to be edited. This means, even though the layers are merged in Premiere Pro, you can return to Adobe Illustrator, edit the original layered file, and save it; the changes will update automatically in Premiere Pro.

Now you can see the text more clearly because the background of the Source Monitor has been replaced with a grid.

8   Use the Source Monitor Settings menu to select Transparency Grid again to disable it. You'll learn more about working with layers and transparency in Lesson 14, "Exploring Compositing Techniques."

How Premiere Pro deals with Adobe Illustrator files

- Like the Photoshop file you imported earlier, Illustrator files can be layered. However, Premiere Pro doesn't give you the option to import Adobe Illustrator files in separate layers. It always merges them into a single-layer clip.

- Premiere Pro uses a process called *rasterization* to convert the vector-based Adobe Illustrator art into the pixel-based image format used by Premiere Pro. This conversion happens during import automatically, so be sure your graphics are configured in Illustrator to be high enough resolution before importing them into Premiere Pro.

- Premiere Pro automatically anti-aliases (smooths the edges of) Adobe Illustrator art.

- Premiere Pro sets all empty areas of Illustrator files as transparent so that clips on lower tracks in your sequence will show through.

- Illustrator files (which end in .ai) cannot be imported using Import mode. Instead, use the File > Import command, double-click the background of the Project panel to browse to the file, or use the Media Browser.

Importing subfolders

When you bring media into Premiere Pro, you don't have to select individual files. You can select a whole folder. If your files are organized into folders and subfolders on your storage drive, when you import them, Premiere Pro will re-create the folders as bins.

This method is not suitable for importing fragmented camera media, with video and audio files stored in different folders. You'll want to use Import mode or the Media Browser for those file types.

For self-contained media file types like QuickTime movies or MP4 files, regular importing works perfectly.

Try this now.

1　Choose File > Import, or press Command+I (macOS) or Ctrl+I (Windows).

2　Navigate to Lessons/Assets, and select the Stills folder. Don't browse inside the folder; just select it.

3　Click the Import (macOS) or Import Folder (Windows) button. Premiere Pro imports the folder and its contents, including two subfolders containing photos. In the Project panel, you'll find bins were created to match the folders. In List view, you can click the disclosure triangle next to any bin to toggle the display of its contents.

> ● **Note:** You can import folders and subfolders this way using the Media Browser too. Select a folder on the right side of the Media Browser, and import it to achieve the same result. Importing folders this way while in Import mode will always merge the contents of the subfolders into a single collection in the Project panel.

● **Note:** If you import an entire folder, it's possible some of the files will not be media supported by Premiere Pro. If so, a message will inform you that some files could not be imported.

Working with VR (360) video

What is often referred to as *VR video* is really 360° video that is best viewed using a VR headset as it captures an image in all 360 degrees. When wearing a VR headset to view this kind of video, you can turn your head to look in different directions. Premiere Pro has excellent built-in support and dedicated visual effects for 360° video and the 180° video standard, with a dedicated viewing mode, native support for VR headsets, and special effects designed for the particular needs of video footage that surrounds the viewer.

There is no special import process for 360° video. You can use the regular Import option, or you can use the Media Browser and import as you would any other video file.

Premiere Pro supports prestitched equirectangular media, so you will have to use another application to prepare your 360° media in this way prior to import.

360° video workflows are beyond the scope of this book. Check the online help for more information.

Recording a voice-over

You may be working on a video project that includes a narration track. It's likely you will have the narration recorded by professionals (or at least recorded in a location quieter than your desk), but with the right hardware, you can record high-quality audio right into Premiere Pro.

This can be helpful because it will give you a sense of timing for your edits.

Try recording a scratch audio track.

1   If you're not using a built-in microphone, make sure your external microphone or audio mixer is properly connected to your computer. You may need to consult the documentation for your computer or sound card.

2   In the Timeline panel, make sure the Theft_Unexpected_Layered sequence is displayed by clicking its name in the Timeline panel. If you have closed the sequence, re-open it by double-clicking the sequence icon in the Project panel.

3   Every audio track has a set of buttons and options on the far left. This area is called the *track header*. There's a Voice-Over Record button 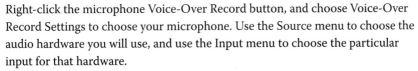 for each audio track.

   Right-click the microphone Voice-Over Record button, and choose Voice-Over Record Settings to choose your microphone. Use the Source menu to choose the audio hardware you will use, and use the Input menu to choose the particular input for that hardware.

▶ **Tip:** The dialog box that appears when recording a voice-over also allows you to name the new audio file.

   Then click the Close button.

4   Turn down your computer speakers, or use headphones to prevent feedback or echo.

5   To see the result more clearly, increase the height of the A1 track.

   To increase the height of an audio track, double-click an empty space on the right side of the track header (next to the Voice-Over Record button), drag down on the horizontal dividing line between two audio track headers (including the Mix track), or hover the pointer over the track header, while holding Option (macOS) or Alt (Windows), and scroll.

6 In the Timeline panel, time moves from left to right, just as it does with any online video. At the top of the Timeline panel, where the time ruler is displayed, a playhead indicates the current frame displayed in the Program Monitor. You can click at any point in the time ruler, and the playhead will move to show that frame. You can also drag on the time ruler itself to view the contents of the current sequence. This is called *scrubbing* (like scrubbing a floor).

Position the Timeline playhead at the beginning of the sequence, as far left as it will go, and click the Voice-Over Record button ⬤ for track A1 to begin recording.

7 After a brief countdown in the Program Monitor, recording will begin. Say a few words, and press the spacebar to stop recording.

Premiere Pro creates a new audio clip and adds it to the Project panel and the current sequence.

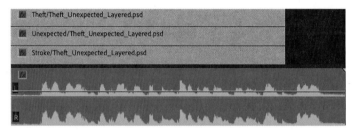

The newly recorded audio file is added to the location specified in the project Scratch Disks settings. By default, this is the same as the location of the project file. In this example, you will have created a new audio file in a subfolder that is automatically created called Adobe Premiere Pro Captured Audio.

8 Choose File > Save to save the project. You can close the project or keep it open, ready for the next lesson.

Customizing the media cache

Note: The word *conform* is used to describe both the way clip playback is adjusted to match sequence settings and the way certain formats are processed when imported to Premiere Pro. That's because the principle is the same: The original material is adapted to improve performance.

When you import files in certain video and audio formats, Premiere Pro may need to process and cache (temporarily store) a version of the file or additional files to make clip playback or waveform display smoother. This is particularly true for highly compressed formats, and the process is called *conforming*.

If necessary, imported audio files are automatically conformed to a new CFA file (conformed audio file). Most MPEG files are *indexed*, resulting in an extra MPGINDEX file that makes it easier to read the file (it's a little like creating a map of the file to make playback easier).

You'll know that the cache is being built if you see a small progress indicator in the lower-right corner of the screen when importing media.

The media cache improves preview playback performance by making it easier for your editing system to decode and play media. You can customize the cache to further improve performance. A media cache database helps Premiere Pro manage these cache files, which are shared between multiple Creative Cloud applications.

Let's take a look at the options. Choose Premiere Pro > Settings > Media Cache (macOS) or Edit > Preferences > Media Cache (Windows).

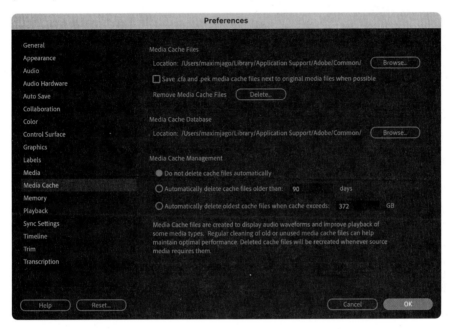

Here are the options:

- To move the media cache files or the media cache database to a new location, click the appropriate Browse button, select the desired location, and click Choose (macOS) or Choose Folder (Windows).

- To keep media cache files stored on the same drive as the media, select Save .cfa And .pek Media Cache Files Next To Original Media Files When Possible. This can be useful if your audio is stored on an external drive that you intend to move between editing systems as it saves you waiting for them to be automatically re-created after changing systems. If you want to keep everything in one central folder, leave this option unselected. Remember, the faster the drive for the media cache, the better the playback performance you're likely to experience in Premiere Pro.

- You should clean the media cache database on a regular basis to remove old conform and index files that are no longer required. To do so, click the Delete button. In the Delete Media Cache Files dialog box, click OK.

It's a good idea to do this after you wrap up projects because it removes unnecessary preview render files too, saving space.

- The Media Cache Management options allow you to configure a degree of automation in the management of cache files. Premiere Pro will automatically re-create these files if they are needed, so it's safe to enable these options to save space.

- To remove *all* media cache files, including those that are in use, restart Premiere Pro while holding Option, Cmd, or Shift (macOS) or Alt, Ctrl, or Shift (Windows) and select Clear Media Cache Files. It's a good idea to do this after updating to a new version of Premiere Pro to maintain a well-organized cache.

For now, click Cancel to close the Preferences dialog box without saving any changes.

Review questions

1   Does Premiere Pro need to convert P2, XDCAM, R3D, ARRIRAW, or AVCHD footage when it is imported?

2   What is an advantage of using Import mode or the Media Browser rather than the File > Import method to import multiple media files that are part of one clip?

3   When you're importing a layered Photoshop file, what are the four ways to import the file?

4   Where can media cache files be stored?

5   How can you enable automatic proxy media file creation when video is imported?

Review answers

1   No. Premiere Pro can edit P2, XDCAM, R3D, ARRIRAW, and AVCHD, as well as many other formats, natively.

2   Import mode and the Media Browser automatically honor the complex folder structures for P2, XDCAM, and many other formats, automatically stitching multiple media files together into a single clip where it's needed.

3   You can merge all the visible layers in the Photoshop file into a single clip by choosing Merge All Layers from the Import As menu in the Import Layered File dialog box; or select the specific layers you want by choosing Merged Layers. If you want layers as separate clips, choose Individual Layers and select the layers to import, or choose Sequence to import the selected layers and create a new sequence from them.

4   You can store media cache files in any specified location or automatically on the same drive as the original files (when possible). The faster the storage for your cache files, the better the playback performance.

5   You can enable proxy media file creation in the Ingest Settings dialog box. You'll find these in the Project Settings dialog box. You can also enable proxy creation by selecting the box at the top of the Media Browser. There's an Ingest Settings shortcut button there too.

4 ORGANIZING MEDIA

Lesson overview

In this lesson, you'll learn how to do the following:

- Navigate the Project panel.

- Organize your project with bins.

- Add clip metadata.

- Use essential playback controls.

- Configure footage interpretation.

- Make changes to your clips.

 This lesson will take about 90 minutes to complete. To get the lesson files used in this chapter, download them from the web page for this book at *peachpit.com/PremiereProCIB2024*. For more information, see "Accessing the lesson files and Web Edition" in the "Getting Started" section at the beginning of this book. Store the files on your computer in a convenient location.

Once you have some video and audio assets in your project, you'll begin looking through your footage and adding clips to a sequence. Before you do, it's well worth spending a little time organizing the assets you have—this can save you from spending hours hunting for things later.

Starting the lesson

When you have lots of clips in your project, especially many imported from several different media types, it can be a challenge to stay on top of everything, let alone finding that magic shot when you need it.

In this lesson, you'll learn how to organize your clips using the Project panel. You'll create special containers, called *bins*, to divide your clips into categories. You'll also learn about adding important metadata and labels to your clips.

● **Note:** To ensure that the tools function and the defaults are set exactly as described in this lesson, reset the Premiere Pro preferences by holding Option (macOS) or Alt (Windows) while launching the application and then clicking Continue in the Reset Options dialog box.

You'll begin by getting to know the all-important Project panel and organizing your clips.

1 For this lesson, open the project file Lesson 04.prproj from the Lessons folder.

2 To begin, reset the workspace to the default. Choose Window > Workspaces Editing. Then choose Window > Workspaces > Reset To Saved Layout.

3 Choose File > Save As.

4 Rename the file to **Lesson 04 Working.prproj**.

5 Browse to the Lessons folder, and click Save to save the project.

   By saving a new version of the project file you can always go back to the previous version—it's an electronic paper trail.

▶ **Tip:** You can choose Save As or Save A Copy from the File menu. Save As saves the current project file with a new name, leaving the previous version untouched. Save A Copy creates a new separate project file while you continue to work on your existing project file.

Using the Project panel

Everything you import into your Adobe Premiere Pro project will appear in the Project panel. The Project panel has folder-like bins that you can use to stay organized and tools for browsing your clips and working with their metadata.

In addition to acting as the repository for all your clips, the Project panel gives access to important options for interpreting media. All your footage will have a frame rate (frames per second, or fps), a pixel aspect ratio (pixel shape), and a color space, usually set by the camera. You may want to change these interpretation settings for creative or technical reasons.

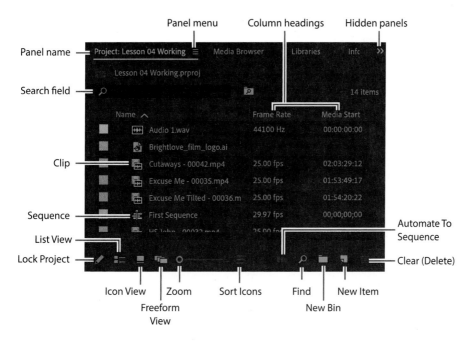

For example, if a video file is tagged with the wrong playback frame rate, you could change the clip interpretation to correct it. You might also receive a video file that has the wrong pixel aspect ratio setting and want to correct it.

Premiere Pro uses metadata associated with footage to know how to play it back and can display and edit additional metadata (such as location log notes) in the Project panel or the dedicated Metadata panel. If you want to change the clip metadata, you can also do so in the Project panel.

Customizing the Project panel

It's likely that you'll want to resize the Project panel from time to time. You'll also alternate between looking at your clips as a list or as thumbnail icons. Sometimes it's quicker to resize the panel than to scroll to see more information.

> **Tip:** You can access a lot of clip information by scrolling the List view or by hovering your pointer over a clip name.

Name ∧	Frame Rate	Media Start	Media End	Media Duration
Audio 1.wav	44100 Hz	00:00:00:00	00:00:04:22	00:00:04:23
Brightlove_film_logo.ai				
Cutaways - 00042.mp4	25.00 fps	02:03:29:12	02:04:34:10	00:01:04:24
Excuse Me - 00035.mp4	25.00 fps	01:53:49:17	01:54:20:20	00:00:31:04
Excuse Me Tilted - 00036.m	25.00 fps	01:54:20:22	01:56:02:18	00:01:41:22
First Sequence	29.97 fps	00;00;00;00	23;00;00;01	00;00;00;00

The default Editing workspace is designed to keep the interface as clean as possible so you can focus on your creative work. Part of the Project panel that's hidden from view by default, called the Preview Area, gives additional information about your clips.

Let's take a look.

1   While still working in the default Editing workspace, open the Project panel menu ☰.

Tip: There's a quick way to toggle between seeing the Project panel in a frame and seeing it full-screen: Hover your pointer over the panel, and press the ` (accent grave) key. You can do this with any panel. If your keyboard does not have a ` (accent grave) key, you can double-click the panel name.

2   Choose Preview Area.

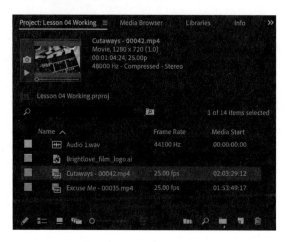

When you select a clip, the Preview Area shows you several kinds of useful information, including the frame size, pixel aspect ratio, and duration.

Tip: Click the Set Poster Frame button to select the clip thumbnail displayed in the Project panel.

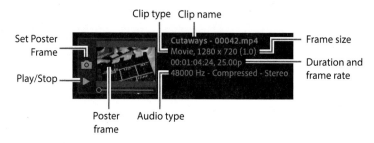

Clip type   Clip name

Set Poster Frame

Frame size

Play/Stop

Cutaways - 00042.mp4
Movie, 1280 x 720 (1.0)
00:01:04:24, 25.00p
48000 Hz - Compressed - Stereo

Duration and frame rate

Poster frame   Audio type

Tip: You can scroll the Project panel view up and down using the scroll wheel on your mouse or a gesture on your touchpad.

3   If it's not already selected, click the List View button ▤ at the bottom left of the Project panel. In this view, you'll find a lot of information about each clip listed in the Project panel organized in columns, but you need to scroll horizontally to see it.

4   Choose Preview Area from the Project panel menu again to hide it.

There is also a Freeform view ▦ in the Project panel, which can be used to organize clips or even begin to build sequences.

Finding assets in the Project panel

Working with clips is a little like working with pieces of paper at your desk. If you have just one or two clips, it's easy. But when you have 100 to 200, you need an organizational system.

One way you can help make things smoother throughout the edit is to invest a little time in organizing your clips right at the beginning. If you rename your clips after importing them, you can more easily locate content later (see "Changing names" in this lesson). It also helps to know how to sort items in the Project panel.

1 Click the Name column heading at the top of the Project panel. Each time you click the Name heading, items in the Project panel are displayed in alphabetical order or reverse alphabetical order. A direction indicator next to the heading shows the current sort order.

Note: You may need to drag a heading divider to expand the width of a column before you can see its sort order indicator or all of the information available in the column.

If you're searching for several clips with particular features—such as a duration or a frame size—it can be helpful to change the order in which the headings are displayed, from left to right.

2 Scroll to the right until you can see the Media Duration heading in the Project panel. This shows the total duration of each clip's media file. You may find it helpful to resize the Project panel to see more columns.

Note: When you scroll to the right in the Project panel, Premiere Pro always maintains the clip names and labels on the left so you know which clips you're seeing information about.

3 Click the Media Duration heading. Premiere Pro now displays the clips in order of media duration. Notice the direction arrow is now on the Media Duration heading.

Each time you click the heading, the direction arrow toggles between showing clips in order of increasing duration and decreasing duration.

Tip: The Project panel display configuration is saved with workspaces, so if you want to always have access to a particular setup, save it as part of a custom workspace.

4 Drag the Media Duration heading to the left until you see a blue divider between the Frame Rate heading and the Name heading. When you release the heading, it will be repositioned right next to the Name heading.

Note: Graphic and photo files such as Adobe Photoshop PSD, JPEG, and Adobe Illustrator AI files import with a default frame rate (timebase) and duration. You can choose a new default frame rate in the Media Preferences, using the Indeterminate Media Timebase menu. You can choose a new default duration in the Timeline Preferences, using the Still Image Default Duration menu.

Filtering bin content

Premiere Pro has search tools to help you find your media. Even if you're using the nondescriptive original clip names assigned in-camera, you can search for clips based on a number of factors, such as frame size or file type.

At the top of the Project panel, you can type in the Search (or Filter Bin Content) field to display only clips with names or metadata matching the text you enter. This is a quick way to locate a clip if you remember its name (or even part of its name). Clips that don't match the text you enter are hidden, and clips that do match are revealed, even if they are inside a closed bin.

Try this now.

● **Note:** The name *bin* comes from film editing. The Project panel is also effectively a bin; it can contain clips and functions like any other bin.

1 Click in the Filter Bin Content box, and type **jo**.

Premiere Pro displays only the clips with the letters *jo* in the name or in the metadata, expanding bins if necessary. Notice that the name of the project is displayed above the text-entry box, along with *(filtered)*. This, along with the letters you typed, is the only indication that some of the clips in the Project panel may be hidden.

▶ **Tip:** Look out for *(filtered)* in the search box. It's easy to press Spacebar while the Filter Bin Content box is active, which adds an otherwise invisible filter—the space you typed!

2 Click the X on the right of the Search field to clear your search.

3 Type **psd** in the box.

Premiere Pro displays only clips that have the letters *psd* in their name or metadata, along with all project bins.

● **Note:** When filtering bin contents, all bins remain visible, even if they don't contain the letters you are filtering with.

Using the Filter Bin Content box in this way, you can search for particular types of files. Notice that the clips are inside a closed bin, which opens automatically to display clips that meet your search criteria.

Some types of metadata can be edited directly in the Project panel. For example, you can add notes to the Description field, and these notes will immediately be searchable.

Be sure to click the X on the right of the Search field to clear your filter when you have found the clips you want. Do this now to reveal all the clips in the project.

● **Note:** In this context, *field* means a box or space into which you can enter text or numerical information. For clips in the Project panel, many fields are already filled, but there are several you can use freely to help organize your project.

Using advanced Find

Premiere Pro also has an advanced Find feature. To learn about it, let's import some more clips.

Using any of the methods described in Lesson 3, "Importing Media," import these items:

- Seattle_Skyline.mov from the Assets/Video and Audio Files/General Views folder
- Under Basket.mov from the Assets/Video and Audio Files/Basketball folder

At the bottom of the Project panel, click the Find button 🔍. Premiere Pro displays the Find dialog box, which has more advanced options for locating your clip.

You can perform two searches at once with the advanced Find dialog box. You can choose to display clips that match *all* search criteria or *any* search criteria. For example, depending on the setting you choose from the Match menu, you could do either of the following:

- Search for a clip with the words *dog* **and** *boat* in its name.

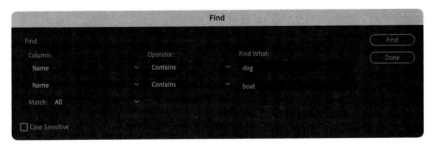

- Search for a clip with the word *dog* **or** *boat* in its name.

You can refine your search by choosing items from the following menus:

- **Column:** This menu lists the columns in the Project panel. When you click Find, Premiere Pro will search only within the column you choose.
- **Operator:** This menu contains a set of standard search options. You can choose to have the search return clips that contain your search term, match it exactly, begin with it, end with it, or lack it entirely.

Tip: You can find clips in sequences too. With a sequence open and the Timeline panel active, choose Edit > Find.

- **Match:** Choose All to find a clip with both your first *and* your second search text. Choose Any to find a clip with *either* your first or your second search term.

- **Case Sensitive:** Select this option to return only results that exactly match the uppercase and lowercase letters you enter.

- **Find What:** Type your search text here.

When you click Find, Premiere Pro highlights a clip that matches your search criteria. Click Find again, and Premiere Pro highlights the next clip that matches your search criteria.

Click Done now to exit the Find dialog box.

Working with bins

Bins allow you to organize clips, sequences, graphics, and so on, by dividing them into named groups.

Just as with folders on your hard drive, you can have multiple bins inside other bins, creating an organizational system as complex as your project requires.

There's an important difference between bins and the folders on your storage drive, however: Bins exist only in your Premiere Pro project file. You won't find individual folders representing project bins on your storage drive.

Creating bins

Let's create a bin.

Tip: If you accidentally create a new bin inside an existing bin, drag the new bin out of the selected bin or choose Edit > Undo to remove the new bin and create it again after deselecting.

1   Click the New Bin button ▪ at the bottom of the Project panel.

Premiere Pro creates a new bin and automatically highlights the name, ready for you to rename it. It's a good habit to name bins as soon as you create them.

Tip: If your keyboard has a Function (fn) key, you may find that you can hold the key to switch the way the Return/Enter key works. Try this now to apply the next new bin name.

2   You have already imported some clips from a short film, so let's give them a bin. Name the new bin **Theft Unexpected,** and press Return (macOS) or Enter (Windows). But wait—what happened?

If your new bin is at the end of the list of items in the Project panel, pressing Return/Enter applies the new name and highlights the first item on the list. However, if the new bin is anywhere else on the list, pressing this key applies the new name and then automatically highlights the next item name on the list, so you can easily rename it too.

This useful shortcut allows you to quickly rename several items in your project. If you want to apply a new name without highlighting the next item, just click elsewhere and continue your work. If you have a numerical keyboard, you can also press that Enter key to apply a new entry without highlighting the next item.

3   You can also create a bin using the File menu. Let's do this now: Make sure the Project panel is active, and deselect the bin you just created. (If a bin is selected when you create a new bin, Premiere Pro places the new bin inside the selected bin.) Choose File > New > Bin.

4   Name the new bin **Graphics**.

5   You can also make a new bin by right-clicking a blank area in the Project panel and choosing New Bin. Try this now.

6   Name the new bin **Illustrator Files**.

7   Drag the clip Seattle_Skyline.mov onto the New Bin button  at the bottom of the Project panel and release it.

> **Note:** It can be difficult to find a blank part of the Project panel to click when it's full of clips. Try clicking just to the left of the icons, inside the panel, or choose Edit > Deselect All.

    The clip is moved into a new bin. This is one of the quickest and easiest ways to create a new bin for selected clips you have already imported into your project.

8   Name the newly created bin **City Views**.

9   Make sure the Project panel is active but no existing bins are selected. Press the keyboard shortcut Command+B (macOS) or Ctrl+B (Windows) to make another bin.

10 Name the bin **Sequences**.

If your Project panel is set to List view, with the Name heading selected for sorting at the top of the panel, bins appear in alphabetical order among the clips. Newly created bins in List view are automatically expanded, with their disclosure triangles set open. You may need to click the Name heading to reset the sorting order after creating the new bins. Click the heading twice to sort in ascending order again.

> **Note:** To rename a bin, you can right-click it and choose Rename. Type the new name, and click away from the text to apply it.

Managing media in bins

Even for this small example project, the Project panel already contains quite a lot of items, including bins. Suppose you were working on a larger project with 200 or even 2,000 clips—it's not hard to imagine how useful bins would be!

Now that you have some bins, let's put them to use. As you move clips into bins, use the disclosure triangles to hide their contents and tidy up the view.

1   Drag the clip Brightlove_film_logo.ai onto the Illustrator Files bin icon. This will move the clip into the bin.

2   Drag Theft_Unexpected.png into the Graphics bin.

Note: When you import a Photoshop file with multiple layers and choose to import it as a sequence, Premiere Pro automatically creates a bin for the layers and their sequence. For more information on this workflow, see "Importing layered Adobe Photoshop files" in Lesson 3.

3 Drag the whole bin called Theft_Unexpected_Layered (created automatically when you imported the layered PSD file as individual layers) into the Graphics bin.

4 Drag the clip Under Basket.mov into the City Views bin. You may need to resize the panel or switch it to full-screen to see both the clip and the bin.

5 Drag the sequence called First Sequence into the Sequences bin.

6 Drag all the remaining clips into the Theft Unexpected bin.

   ▶ **Tip:** You can Shift-click, as well as Command-click (macOS) or Ctrl-click (Windows), to make selections in the Project panel, just like you can with files on your hard drive.

   You should now have a nicely organized Project panel, with each kind of clip in its own bin.

   ▶ **Tip:** To expand or collapse all disclosure triangles, hold Option (macOS) or Alt (Windows) while you click any disclosure triangle.

7 Click the disclosure triangle for the Graphics bin to display the contents.

   You can copy and paste clips to make extra copies if this helps you stay organized. In the Graphics bin, you have a PNG file that might be useful for the Theft Unexpected content. Let's make an extra copy.

8 Right-click the Theft_Unexpected.png clip and choose Copy.

9 Click the disclosure triangle for the Theft Unexpected bin to display the contents.

10 Right-click the Theft Unexpected bin and choose Paste to add a copy of the clip to the Theft Unexpected bin.

   When you make copies of clips, you are not making duplicate copies of the media files they are linked to. You can make as many copies as you like of a clip in your Premiere Pro project. Those copies will all link to the same original media file.

Finding your media files

If you would like to know where a media file is on your hard drive, you can right-click the clip in the Project panel and choose Reveal In Finder (macOS) or Reveal In Explorer (Windows).

The folder in your storage drive that contains the media file will open. This can be useful if you are working with media files stored on multiple hard drives or if you renamed your clips in Premiere Pro.

If you moved all the remaining clips into the Theft Unexpected bin, you should have an Audio 1.wav clip in that bin now, which is the voice-over you recorded in an earlier exercise (in this instance, it's a version provided with the project file). If you tried recording that voice-over multiple times, you may have more than one audio clip, each with a different number. Let's remove the clip but keep the audio:

1   Right-click that voice-over clip and choose Reveal In Finder (macOS) or Explorer (Windows).

2   Switch back to Premiere Pro. Click the icon for the Audio 1.wav clip to select it, and press Delete (macOS) or Backspace (Windows) to remove it.

Premiere Pro displays a warning message to remind you that the clip is currently used in a sequence.

▶ **Tip:** Notice that the No option in this dialog box is highlighted in blue. If you press Return/Enter, this is the option that you are selecting.

Clicking Yes will remove the clip from the Project panel *and* any sequence that contains the clip.

Click Yes to remove the clip.

3   Switch back to the folder containing the file in your storage. The audio file is still there!

Removing a clip in Premiere Pro does not remove the linked media file from your storage. Also, making changes to a clip in Premiere Pro does not make changes to the linked media file.

Changing bin views

Although there is a distinction between the Project panel and the bins inside it, they have the same controls and viewing options. For all intents and purposes, you can treat the Project panel as a bin; many Premiere Pro editors use the terms *bin* and *Project panel* interchangeably.

Bins have three views. You choose between them by clicking the buttons at the lower left of the Project panel.

* **List view** ▣ : By default, this view displays your clips and bins as a list, with a significant amount of metadata displayed. You can scroll through the metadata and use it to sort clips by clicking column headers.

* **Icon view** ▣ : This view displays your clips and bins as thumbnails you can rearrange and use to preview clip contents.

- **Freeform view** : This view displays clips and bins as thumbnails that you can assign different sizes, group together, and place freely in a large area.

Note: You can change the List view font size in the Project panel or a bin by clicking the panel menu and choosing Font Size. This is particularly useful if you are working on a high-resolution screen.

The Project panel has a Zoom control, next to the List View, Icon View, and Freeform View buttons, which changes the size of the clip icons or thumbnails.

1 Double-click the Theft Unexpected bin. The bin opens in a new panel in the same group as the Project panel. You can keep as many bin panels open as you like and place them anywhere in the interface to help you stay organized.

> **Tip:** The option to open bins in a new panel when double-clicking, rather than the same panel, can be changed in the General preferences.

2 Click the Icon View button on the Theft Unexpected bin to display thumbnails for the clips. You may want to resize the Project panel to view more thumbnails.

3 Try adjusting the Zoom control.

Premiere Pro can display large thumbnails to make browsing and selecting your clips easier.

You can also apply various kinds of sorting to clip thumbnails in Icon view by clicking the Sort Icons menu ▤ ⌄.

4 Switch to List view ▤.

When you're in List view, it doesn't help that much to zoom, unless you turn on the display of thumbnails in this view.

5 Open the panel menu ▤ next to the Theft Unexpected bin name at the top of the panel, and choose Thumbnails.

Premiere Pro now displays thumbnails in List view, as well as in Icon view.

6 Drag the Zoom control to the right to increase the size of thumbnails.

Notice the numbers in the clip names. These are the original media filenames that were retained when you added descriptive names. For these lessons, we'll only refer to the descriptive clip names and omit the numbers taken from the original media.

By default, the clip thumbnails show the first frame of the media. In some clips, the first frame will not be particularly useful. Look at the clip Cutaways, for example. The thumbnail shows the clapperboard, but it would be useful to see the content.

7 Switch to Icon view ▤.

In this view, you can hover the pointer over clip thumbnails to preview clips.

⬤ **Note:** While in Icon view or Freeform view, selecting a clip by clicking its thumbnail reveals a small timeline control under it. Drag this timeline to view the contents of the clip.

Tip: You can also change the poster frame by pressing the I key, which is the keyboard shortcut for Mark In, a command that sets the beginning of a selection when choosing part of a clip that you intend to add to a sequence. This shortcut will only update the poster frame if you haven't already set one.

8   Hover your pointer over the Cutaways clip. Without clicking, move the pointer until you find a frame that better represents the shot.

9   While the frame you have chosen is displayed, press Command+P (macOS) or Shift+P (Windows).

This keyboard shortcut sets the poster frame for the clip.

10 Switch back to List view.

Premiere Pro shows your newly selected frame as the thumbnail for this clip.

11 Choose Thumbnails from the panel menu to turn off thumbnails in List view.

12 Drag the Zoom control to the left to restore the default size for the clip icons.

Creating Search Bins

When using the Search field to display specific clips, you have the option to create a special kind of virtual bin, called a Search Bin.

After typing in the Search field, click the Create New Search Bin From Query button .

A new Search Bin appears in the Project panel. Search Bins display the results of a search performed when using the Search field. You can rename Search Bins and place them in other bins.

The contents of Search Bins update dynamically, so if you add new clips to a project that meet the search criteria, they'll appear in matching Search Bins automatically. This can be a fantastic time-saver when working with documentary material that might change over time as you obtain new footage.

Assigning labels

Tip: Once your clips have the right label colors, you can right-click a clip at any time and choose Label > Select Label Group to select and highlight all visible items with the same label.

Every item in the Project panel has a label color. In List view, the Label column shows the label color for every clip. When you add clips to a sequence, they are displayed in the Timeline panel with this label color.

Let's change the label color for a title clip.

1   In the Theft Unexpected bin, right-click Theft_Unexpected.png and choose Label > Forest.

You can change label colors for multiple clips in a single step by selecting them and then right-clicking them to choose another label color.

2   Press Command+Z (macOS) or Ctrl+Z (Windows) to change the
    Theft_Unexpected.png label color back to Lavender.

When you add a clip to a sequence, Premiere Pro creates a new *instance*, or
copy, of that clip—you'll have one copy in the Project panel and one copy in the
sequence. Both link to the same media file.

When you change the label color for a clip in the Project panel or rename a clip,
it may or may not update copies of the clip in sequences.

If a sequence is open in the Timeline panel, you can toggle this setting by opening the Timeline Display Settings menu 🔧 and choosing Show Source Clip
Name And Label.

Changing the available label colors

You can assign up to 16 colors as labels to items in your project. Premiere Pro can
automatically assign label colors to eight types of items (video, audio, still, etc.),
which means you have eight spare label colors.

If you choose Premiere Pro > Settings >
Labels (macOS) or Edit > Preferences > Labels
(Windows), you'll see the list of colors, each
with a color swatch. You can click the color
swatch to change the color, and you can click
the name to rename it.

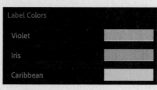

You can use the Label Defaults options to choose different default labels for each
kind of item in your project.

Changing names

Because clips in your project are separate from the media files they link to, you can
rename items in Premiere Pro without affecting the names of your original media
files on the hard drive. This makes it safe to rename clips, which can be helpful when
organizing a complex project.

If you opened the Theft Unexpected bin by double-clicking it, it will have opened
as a new panel in the same group as the Project panel. Let's begin by navigating
between these bins.

At the top left of the Theft Unexpected bin, notice the button to navigate up 🔼.
This button appears whenever you are viewing the contents of a bin by opening it.
Just as Finder (macOS) and Explorer (Windows) have navigation buttons, you can
use this button to browse "up" to the container of the current bin. In this case, it's
the Project panel, but it could just as easily be another bin.

1   Click to navigate up to the Project panel.

The Project panel comes to the front and becomes the active panel, with an underline for the panel name. The Theft Unexpected bin is still open.

Whenever you navigate between bins that are already open, Premiere Pro brings the existing open instance to the front. This way, you won't have multiple instances of the same bin taking up screen space.

2   Open the Graphics bin by double-clicking it.

3   Right-click the clip Theft_Unexpected.png and choose Rename.

4   Change the name to **TU Title BW** (that is, Theft Unexpected Title Black and White). After typing the new name, click the background of the Project panel to apply it.

5   Right-click the newly renamed clip, TU Title BW, and choose Reveal In Finder (macOS) or Reveal In Explorer (Windows).

The original media file is displayed in its current location. Notice that the original filename has not changed.

Earlier you deleted a clip in this project and the original media file remained untouched—in a sense this is similar to renaming a clip in a project. Changing the clip in Premiere Pro does not change the media file.

It's helpful to be clear about the relationship between your original media files and the clips inside the Premiere Pro project because it explains much of the way the application works.

Reviewing footage

The greater part of video editing is spent reviewing clips and making creative choices about them.

In Premiere Pro, you can perform common tasks, such as playing video clips, in multiple ways. You can use the keyboard, click buttons with your pointer, or use an external device such as a jog/shuttle controller.

1   Navigate to the Theft Unexpected bin.

> **Tip:** To rename an item in the Project panel, you can also click the item name, wait a moment, and click again, or you can select the item and press Return (macOS) or Enter (Windows). Be sure to use the Return or Enter key on the right edge of the main alphanumeric keyboard rather than the Enter key on the numeric keyboard, if you have one.

> **Note:** When you change the name of a clip in Premiere Pro, the new name is stored in the project file. Different Premiere Pro project files may use different names for the same clip. In fact, you could have two copies of a clip in the same project with different names.

2 Click the Icon View button  at the lower-left corner of the bin, and use the Zoom control to set the thumbnails to a size you are happy with.

3 Hover your pointer over any of the thumbnails in the bin.

Premiere Pro displays the contents of the clip as you move your pointer, which is called *hover scrubbing.* The left edge of the thumbnail represents the beginning of the clip, and the right edge represents the end. In this way, the width of the thumbnail represents the whole clip. While you're hover scrubbing, a tiny navigator appears at the bottom of the thumbnail.

4 Select a clip by clicking it once (be careful not to double-click, which will open the clip in the Source Monitor).

When you select the clip and hover your pointer over it, the navigator at the bottom of the thumbnail grows larger, and a small gray playhead appears. Try dragging through the clip using this playhead. When you do so, the clip audio will also play.

When a clip is selected, you also can use the J, K, and L keys on your keyboard to perform playback.

- **J:** Play backward
- **K:** Pause
- **L:** Play forward

Customizing bins

When set to List view, the Project panel displays a number of columns of information about each clip. Depending on the clips you have and the types of metadata you are working with, you might want to change the columns that are displayed.

To accomplish this, open the Project panel menu ☰ and choose Metadata Display.

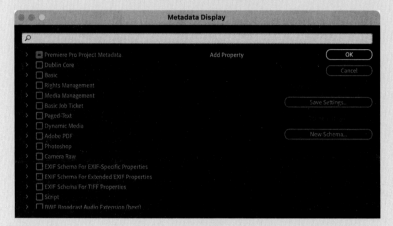

The Metadata Display dialog box allows you to select the kinds of metadata to display in the List view of the Project panel (and any bins). The dialog box lists the types of data in groups; click the disclosure triangle for a group to display the properties in that group.

Select a single property to add it as a column heading in the Project panel or bin. Select a group to add all the properties in that group.

Keep in mind that metadata display settings for individual bins are saved in the project file, while metadata display settings for the Project panel are saved with the workspace.

Any bins that you have not yet opened will inherit the settings from the Project panel, so make changes in that panel if you want them to be applied to every bin.

5 Select a clip, and use the J, K, and L keys to play the video in the thumbnail. You can also use the spacebar to play and stop.

▶ **Tip:** If you press the J or L key multiple times, the video will play at multiple speeds. Pressing Shift+J or Shift+L reduces or increases playback speed in 10% increments.

When you double-click a clip, Premiere Pro displays the clip in the Source Monitor and also adds it to a list of recent clips.

6   Double-click four or five clips from the Theft Unexpected bin to open them in the Source Monitor.

7   Open the Source Monitor panel menu to browse your recent clips.

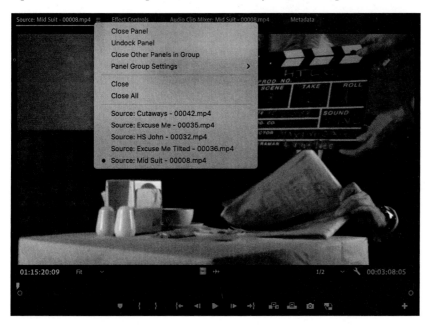

Tip: Notice that you have the option to close a single clip or close all clips, clearing the menu and the monitor. Some editors like to clear the menu and then open several clips that are part of a scene by selecting them in the bin and dragging them into the Source Monitor together. You can then use the Recent Items menu to browse only the clips from that selection. You can also quickly cycle through clips on this recent list by pressing Shift+2 with the Source Monitor active.

8   Open the Zoom Level menu at the bottom left of the Source Monitor.

By default, this is set to Fit, which means Premiere Pro will display the whole frame, regardless of the original size. The resolution of your clips will often be higher than that of your Source Monitor. Change the setting to 100%.

Tip: Premiere Pro has multiple tools for different purposes. You can use the Hand tool (with the keyboard shortcut H) to drag the view around in the Source Monitor and Program Monitor. Be sure to switch back to the Selection tool when you are finished.

It's likely scroll bars have appeared at the bottom and on the right of your Source Monitor so you can view different parts of the image. However, if you are working on a very high-resolution screen, it's possible the image got smaller.

The benefit of viewing with Zoom set to 100% is that you see every pixel of the original video, which is useful for checking the quality.

9 Now choose Fit from the Zoom Level menu.

Using essential playback controls

Let's look at the Source Monitor playback controls.

1 Double-click the shot Excuse Me (not Excuse Me Tilted) in the Theft Unexpected bin to open it in the Source Monitor.

Tip: Hover the pointer over each button to see the name and keyboard shortcut (in parentheses).

2 At the bottom of the Source Monitor, you'll find a blue playhead marker. Drag it along the bottom of the panel to view various parts of the clip. You can also click wherever you want the playhead to go, and it will jump to that spot.

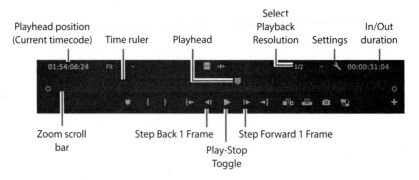

3 Below the time ruler and its playhead, there's a scroll bar that doubles as a Zoom control. Drag one end of this scroll bar toward the other to zoom in on the time ruler. This will make it easier to navigate longer clips precisely.

Drag here   Drag here

4 Click the Play-Stop Toggle button to play the clip. Click it again to stop playback. You can also use the spacebar to start and stop playback.

5 Click the Step Back 1 Frame ◀ and Step Forward 1 Frame ▶ buttons to move through the clip one frame at a time. You can also use the Left Arrow and Right Arrow keys on your keyboard.

6 Try using the J, K, and L keys to play your clip.

7 Try holding K while you press and release the J or L key. The playhead will move one frame and play the associated audio, making it useful when seeking a precise moment in dialogue.

● **Note:** Panel selection is important when using keyboard shortcuts (and menus). If you find the J, K, and L keys don't work, double-check that the Source Monitor is selected (it will be outlined in blue).

Lowering the playback resolution

If you have an older or slower computer processor or are working with large frame sizes, such as Ultra High-Definition (UHD, 4K, 8K, or above), your computer may struggle to play all the frames of your video clips. Clips will play with the correct timing (10 seconds of video will still take 10 seconds), but some frames may not be displayed.

To work with a wide variety of computer hardware configurations, from powerful desktop workstations to lightweight portable laptops, Premiere Pro can lower the playback resolution to help make playback smoother.

There are separate menus in the Source Monitor and Program Monitor to set the playback resolution. The default resolution is 1/2.

You can change the playback resolution using the Select Playback Resolution menu on the Source Monitor and Program Monitor.

Some lower resolutions are available only when working with particular media types. This is because, for other media types, the work of converting the image to a lower resolution might be more than the work saved by not playing full resolution (not all codecs can be played back at a lower resolution efficiently). In that case, some resolutions will automatically be dimmed and unavailable.

▶ **Tip:** If you are working with a particularly powerful computer, you may want to choose High Quality Playback from the monitor Settings menu 🔧. This maximizes preview playback quality, particularly for compressed media like H.264 video, graphics, and stills (potentially at the expense of playback performance).

Getting timecode information

At the bottom left of the Source Monitor, a timecode display in blue shows the current position of the playhead in hours, minutes, seconds, and frames (00:00:00:00), according to the clip's timecode. For example, 01:54:06:24 is 1 hour, 54 minutes, 6 seconds, and 24 frames.

01:54:06:24

Clip timecode may not begin at 00:00:00:00, so you should not count on this number to assess the duration of a clip.

00:00:31:04

At the bottom right of the Source Monitor, a timecode display in light gray shows the duration of your current clip selection.

By default, this shows the whole clip duration, but later you'll add special *In point* and *Out point* marks to make a partial selection. When you do, the duration shown will update.

In and Out points are simple to use: Click the Mark In button ![Mark In] to set the beginning of the part of a clip you want to use, and click the Mark Out button ![Mark Out] to set the end of the part of a clip you want. You'll learn more about this in Lesson 5, "Editing Video—the Essentials."

Displaying safe margins

Television monitors often crop the edges of the picture to achieve a clean edge. Open the Settings menu ![Settings] at the bottom of the Source Monitor, and choose Safe Margins to display useful white outlines over the image.

The outer box is the *action-safe zone*. Aim to keep important action inside this box so that when the picture is displayed, edge cropping does not hide what's going on.

The inner box is the *title-safe zone*. Keep titles and graphics inside this box so that even on a badly adjusted display, your audience will be able to read the words.

Modern televisions crop the frame less, and online videos are not cropped at all. You'll probably want to adjust the size of the safe zones according to your intended delivery medium.

Premiere Pro has advanced overlay options that you can configure to display useful information in the Source Monitor and Program Monitor. To enable or disable overlays, open the monitor's Settings menu and choose Overlays.

You can access the specific settings for overlays and safe margins by clicking the monitor's Settings menu and choosing Overlay Settings > Settings.

You can disable Safe Margins or Overlays by choosing them from the Source Monitor or Program Monitor's Settings menu again. Do so now so you can see the image clearly.

Customizing the monitors

To customize the way a monitor displays video, open each monitor's Settings menu 🔧.

The Source Monitor and Program Monitor have similar options. In the Source Monitor, you can view the waveform of the audio in the clip, which shows amplitude over time (useful if you are searching for a particular sound or the start of a word).

For now, make sure Composite Video is chosen from the Source Monitor Settings menu.

You can quickly switch between viewing the clip audio waveform and the video by clicking Drag Video Only ▣ or Drag Audio Only ᴴ, just under the middle of the video display.

These icons are mainly used to drag only the video or only the audio part of a clip into a sequence, but they also provide this useful shortcut to view the audio waveform.

You can add, move, or remove buttons at the bottom of the Source Monitor and Program Monitor. Note that any customizations you make to the buttons on one of the monitor panels are applied only to that panel.

1 Click the Button Editor ➕ at the lower right of the Source Monitor.

The complete set of available buttons appears on a floating panel.

> **Tip:** If you are working with 360° video, you can switch to a VR video viewing mode using the Source Monitor and Program Monitor Settings menus.

2 Drag the Loop Playback button  from the floating panel to a spot to the right of the Play button on the Source Monitor (the other buttons will automatically make space for it), and click OK to close the Button Editor.

3 Double-click the Excuse Me clip in the Theft Unexpected bin to open it in the Source Monitor, if it isn't open already.

4 Click the Loop Playback button you added to activate it. The button is blue when it's activated.

▶ **Tip:** If you are comfortable using keyboard shortcuts only, you can hide all of the buttons along the lower edge of the Source Monitor or Program Monitor. To do so, choose Show Transport Controls in the Source Monitor or Program Monitor Settings menu. Select this item again to restore the buttons.

5 Click the Play button to play the clip. Play the video using the spacebar or the Play button on the Source Monitor. Stop the playback when you see the video start again.

With Loop turned on, Premiere Pro continuously repeats playback of a clip or sequence. If there are In and Out points set, playback loops between them. This is a great way to review a section of a clip.

Exploring Freeform view

While bins provide a convenient way to organize your clips, as lists of items or as thumbnails, Freeform view, the Project panel's third viewing mode, allows you to group clips *within* a bin. Freeform view looks a lot like Icon view except that now you can position clips anywhere, including beyond the edges of the panel. You also can set different thumbnail sizes for different clips and organize clips as stacks or groups. You can snap the edges of thumbnails together. By placing clips next to each other in a line, you can use hover scrubbing to quickly review multiple clips.

Freeform view is an open canvas for you to arrange clips into groups and experiment with possible combinations before adding them to a sequence.

Modifying clips

Premiere Pro uses metadata associated with media files to know how to play linked clips. For example, information about the playback frame rate is stored in the media file as metadata. This metadata is normally added when the media is created (by the camera, for example), but occasionally it might be missing or set wrong. Sometimes, you'll need to tell Premiere Pro how to interpret clips.

You can change the interpretation for one clip or multiple clips in a single step. All instances of selected clips (including copies already edited into a sequence) are affected by changes you make to interpretation.

Choosing audio channels

Premiere Pro has advanced audio management features. You can create complex sound mixes and selectively target output audio channels with original clip audio. You can work with mono, stereo, 5.1, Ambisonics, and even 32-channel sequences and clips with precise control over the routing of audio channels.

If you're just starting out, you'll probably want to produce sequences mastered in stereo using mono or stereo source clips. In this case, the default settings are most likely all you will need.

When recording audio with a professional camera, it's common to have one microphone record onto one audio channel and a second microphone record onto another audio channel. These are the same audio channels that would be used for regular stereo audio, but they now contain completely separate sound.

> **Tip:** If you are not familiar with terms like *metadata*, check out the glossary provided for download with the rest of the book's online content at peachpit.com (see "Getting Started" earlier in the book). It offers explanations for many of the specialized terms used when describing post-production.

> **Note:** Changes made to clip interpretation are applied to the clip, not the media file it is linked to. This means you could have two copies of a clip, both linked to the same media file but with different interpretation settings. The media file is not changed.

What is an audio channel?

When an audio recording is created, it's always captured and stored as one or more audio channels. Think of a channel as a single signal—something you could hear with one ear.

Because we have two ears, we are able to hear in stereo—sensing where a sound comes from by comparing differences in the way the sound arrives at each ear. The process happens automatically and precognitively (your conscious mind doesn't do any analysis to sense where a sound comes from).

To capture stereo (the sound two ears can detect), you need two signals, so two channels are recorded using microphones.

One signal (let's say the sound a microphone captures) is captured as one channel in an audio recording. For output, one channel will play through one speaker or headphone ear. The more channels you have for recording, the more sources you can capture independently (think of capturing an entire orchestra with many channels to be able to adjust the volume of each instrument separately in post-production).

To play audio with different volume levels on multiple speakers (for surround sound, for example), you need multiple playback channels. You'll learn more about working with audio in Lesson 10, "Editing and Mixing Audio."

Your camera adds metadata to the audio to tell Premiere Pro whether the sound is meant to be mono (separate audio channels) or stereo (channel 1 audio and channel 2 audio combined to produce the complete stereo mix).

You can tell Premiere Pro how to interpret audio channels when new media files are imported by choosing Premiere Pro > Settings > Timeline > Default Audio Tracks (macOS) or Edit > Preferences > Timeline > Default Audio Tracks (Windows).

The Use File option means Premiere Pro will use the audio channel settings applied to the clip when it was created. You can override that option for each media type using the appropriate menu.

If the setting was wrong when you imported your clips, it's easy to set a different way to interpret the audio channels in the Project panel.

1 Click the name of the Theft Unexpected bin to bring it to the front. If the bin is not open, double-click it to open it in the Project panel.

2 Right-click the Reveal clip in the Theft Unexpected bin and choose Modify > Audio Channels.

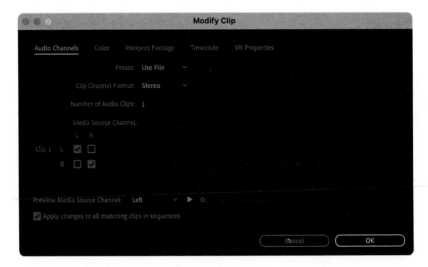

When the Preset menu is set to Use File, as it is here, Premiere Pro will use the file's metadata to set the channel format for the audio.

In this case, Clip Channel Format is set to stereo, and Number Of Audio Clips is set to 1—that's the number of audio clips that will be added to a sequence if you edit this clip into it.

Now look at the channel matrix below those options. The Left and Right audio channels of the source clip (described as Media Source Channel) are both assigned to a single clip (described as Clip 1).

When you add this clip to a sequence, it will appear as one video clip and one audio clip, with both audio channels in the same audio clip.

3   Open the Preset menu, and choose Mono. Be sure to use the Preset menu and not the Clip Channel Format menu.

Premiere Pro switches the Clip Channel Format menu to Mono, so the Left and Right source channels are now linked to two separate clips.

This means that when you add the clip to a sequence, each audio channel will go on a separate track, as separate clips, allowing you to work on them independently.

4   Click OK.

A few tips on audio clip channel interpretation

Here are some things to keep in mind when working with audio clip channel interpretation:

- In the Modify Clip dialog box, every available audio channel will be listed. If your source audio has channels you don't need, you can deselect them, and those empty channels won't take up space in your sequence as clips.

- If you override the original file audio channel interpretation (mono, stereo, etc.), you may need a different type of audio track when the clip is added to a sequence.

- The list of clips on the left (which may be as short as one clip) shows how many audio clips will be added to a sequence when edited in.

- Use the checkboxes to choose which source audio channels are included when the clip is edited into a sequence. This means you can combine multiple source audio channels into a single sequence clip or separate them into different clips in any way that works for your project.

- Changes made to audio clip channel interpretation will not update clip instances that are already edited into a sequence. The next time you edit a modified clip into a sequence, the new interpretation will apply. This means you could have two instances of the same clip in a sequence with different audio channels.

Merging clips

It's common for professional video to be recorded on a camera with relatively low-quality audio, while high-quality sound is recorded on a separate device. When working this way, you'll want to combine the high-quality audio with the video by merging them in the Project panel.

The most important factor when merging video and audio files in this way is synchronization for the audio. You will either manually define a sync point—like a clapperboard mark—or allow Premiere Pro to sync your clips automatically based on their original timecode information or by matching up their audio.

If you choose to sync clips using audio, Premiere Pro will analyze both the in-camera audio and the separately captured sound and match them up. The option to sync automatically using the audio in both clips makes it worthwhile attaching a microphone to your camera, even if you know you won't use the audio in post-production. The following steps are described for your information only—no need to follow along.

1 If you don't have matching audio in the clips you are merging, you can manually add a marker to each clip you want to merge on a clear sync point like a clapper-board or a visible and audible hand clap. The keyboard shortcut to add a marker is M.

2 Select the camera clip and the separate audio clip, right-click either item, and choose Merge Clips.

   There's an option to use audio time-code (sometimes useful for older, archived tape-based media).

   There's also an option to automatically remove the unwanted audio included with the audio-video clip. You may want to keep that audio, though, just in case there's a momentary issue with the external microphone audio, like something bumping the microphone.

3 Under Synchronize Point, select your sync method, and click OK to create a new clip that combines the video and the "good" audio in a single item.

   ▶ **Tip:** You can also use the more advanced Multicamera Source Sequence workflow to synchronize multiple clips in a single step. For more information on this workflow, check out the Best Practices and Workflow Guide for Long Form and Episodic Post Production, available at *helpx.adobe.com*.

Interpreting video footage

For Premiere Pro to play a clip correctly, it needs to know the frame rate for the video, the pixel aspect ratio (the shape of the pixels), the color space, and, if your clip is interlaced, the order in which to display the fields. Premiere Pro can usually find out this information from the file's metadata, but you can override the interpretation easily. Let's try this now:

1   Use the Media Browser panel to import RED Video.R3D from the Assets/Video and Audio Files/RED folder. Then double-click the clip to open it in the Source Monitor. It's full anamorphic widescreen, which is wider than regular 16×9 footage. This wider aspect ratio is achieved by using pixels that are wider.

2   Right-click the clip in the Project panel and choose Modify > Interpret Footage.

    The option to modify audio channels is unavailable because this clip has no audio.

    Right now, the clip is set to use the pixel aspect ratio setting from the file: Anamorphic 2:1. This means the pixels are twice as wide as they are tall.

3   In the Pixel Aspect Ratio section, select Conform To, choose Square Pixels (1.0), and click OK.

    Take a look at the clip in the Source Monitor. The clip looks almost square!

4   Try another aspect ratio. Right-click the clip in the Project panel and choose Modify > Interpret Footage. Choose DVCPRO HD (1.5) from the adjacent menu. Click OK, and take a look at the clip again in the Source Monitor.

From now on, Premiere Pro will interpret the clip as having pixels that are 1.5 times wider than they are tall. This reshapes the picture to make it standard 16:9 widescreen.

Changing the pixel aspect ratio is rarely a good solution when making creative decisions because it widens or compresses horizontal space in the picture—all circles will become ovals, for example. However, if all circles already appear to be ovals and all squares appear to be rectangles, it may be that you need to correct the pixel aspect ratio interpretation for technical reasons.

Review questions

1 How do you change the List view column headings displayed in the Project panel?

2 How can you quickly filter the display of clips in the Project panel to make finding a clip easier?

3 How do you create a new bin?

4 If you change the name of a clip in the Project panel, does it change the name of the media file it links to on your hard drive?

5 What keyboard shortcuts can you use to play video and sound clips?

6 How can you change the way clip audio channels are interpreted?

Review answers

1 Open the Project panel menu, and choose Metadata Display. Select the checkbox for any column heading you want to appear. You can also right-click a heading and choose Metadata Display to access these settings.

2 Click the Search field, and start typing the name of the clip you are looking for. Premiere Pro hides clips that don't match what you typed and reveals those that do, even if they are in a closed bin. Any clips with the characters you type in their metadata will be displayed.

3 There are several ways to create a new bin: by clicking the New Bin button at the bottom of the Project panel, by choosing File > New > Bin, by right-clicking a blank area in the Project panel and choosing New Bin, or by pressing Command+B (macOS) or Ctrl+B (Windows). You can also drag clips onto the New Bin button on the Project panel. Premiere Pro can even automatically create a new bin when importing media.

4 No. You can duplicate, rename, or delete clips in your Project panel, and nothing will happen to your original media files.

5 The spacebar starts and stops playback. You can use J, K, and L like a shuttle controller to play backward and forward, and the arrow keys can be used to move one frame backward or one frame forward. If you are using a trackpad, you may be able to position your pointer over the video in a monitor or over the Timeline panel and use gestures to scrub through the content.

6 In the Project panel, right-click the clip you want to change and choose Modify > Audio Channels or press the keyboard shortcut, Shift+G. Choose the correct option (usually by selecting a preset), and click OK.

5 EDITING VIDEO— THE ESSENTIALS

Lesson overview

In this lesson, you'll learn how to do the following:

- Work with clips in the Source Monitor.
- Create sequences.
- Use essential editing commands.
- View timecode.
- Understand tracks.

This lesson will take about 75 minutes to complete. To get the lesson files used in this chapter, download them from the web page for this book at *peachpit.com/PremiereProCIB2024*. For more information, see "Accessing the lesson files and Web Edition" in the "Getting Started" section at the beginning of this book. Store the files on your computer in a convenient location.

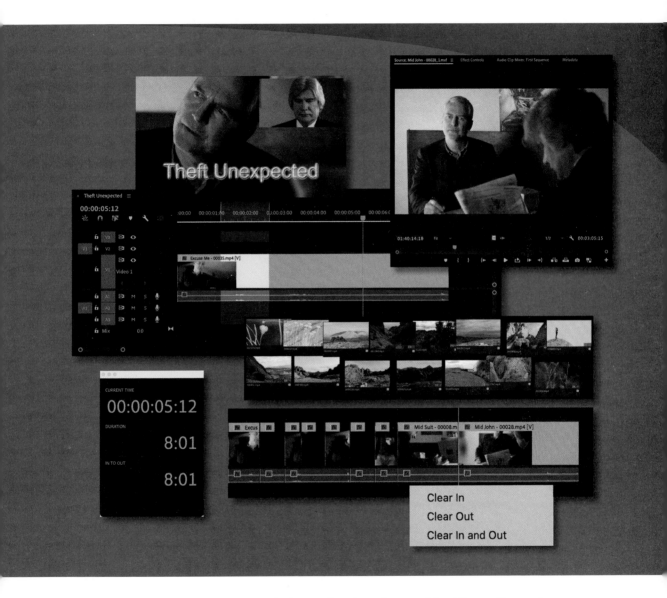

This lesson will teach you the core editing skills you will use again and again in Adobe Premiere Pro. Editing is much more than choosing shots. You'll choose your edits precisely, place clips in sequences at exactly the right point in time and on the tracks you want (to create layered visual effects), add new clips to existing sequences, and remove unwanted content (that you can restore later if you want—this is *nonlinear* editing, after all).

Starting the lesson

Note: To ensure that the tools function and the defaults are set exactly as described in this lesson, reset the Premiere Pro preferences by holding Option (macOS) or Alt (Windows) while launching the application and then clicking Continue in the Reset Options dialog box.

There is much more to video editing than cutting and pasting footage into sequences—it's the art and craft of visual storytelling. Many of the exercises in this book will walk you through the steps of crafting a short video narrative, making creative decisions for you, so you can focus on learning the tools and techniques.

For the following examples, you'll use footage of a chance encounter between two strangers in a London café. The footage was shot from a variety of angles to allow the editor to choose the way the story will be told, from the points of view of either a participant or of a nonparticipating, hypothetical observer.

Editing helps to propel the story and maintain the viewer's interest by switching between the viewpoints of the participants and by revealing events to the audience that neither participant is conscious of.

The start of the process is to review all the available footage and to choose the best shots. To save time, the sifting has already been done for you, and you will be guided to the shots to use and given the precise timing for the edits.

Working with clip names

Clip names are important. Having well-organized and clearly named clips can save hours of post-production time.

The clip names in this project are unusual because they incorporate new regular names to help identify the contents and the original media file numbers to help track the footage.

There are no fixed rules about naming and organizing clips, and throughout these lessons you will encounter various naming conventions. In the later sidebar "Shot types and clip names," you'll learn about common abbreviations.

Throughout these exercises, the additional numbers in the clip names will be ignored for brevity.

No matter how you approach video editing, you'll use a few simple techniques time and again. Most of the practice of video editing is carefully reviewing and making partial selections of your clips and placing them in your sequence. There are several ways of doing this in Premiere Pro.

Before you begin, you'll make sure you're using the Editing workspace.

1   Open the Lesson 05.prproj project file from the Lessons folder.

2   Choose File > Save As.

3   Rename the file **Lesson 05 Working.prproj**.

4 Choose a preferred location on your hard drive, and click Save to save the
   project.

5 Open the Workspaces menu in the upper-right corner of the Premiere Pro interface and make sure Editing is selected. Then use the same menu to choose Reset
   To Saved Layout.

You'll begin by learning more about the Source Monitor and how to add In and Out
points to your clips to select the parts that will be added to a sequence. Then you'll
learn about the Timeline panel, where you'll work on your sequences.

Using the Source Monitor

The Source Monitor is the main place you'll go when you want to review your assets
before including them in a sequence.

▶ **Tip:** Change clip
interpretation by
right-clicking the clip
in the Project panel
and choosing Modify >
Interpret Footage.

When you view a video clip in the Source Monitor, you watch it in its original format. That is, it will play back with its frame rate, frame size, field order, audio sample
rate, and audio bit depth exactly as when recorded, unless you changed the way the
clip is interpreted. For more on how to do this, see Lesson 4, "Organizing Media."

However, when you add a clip to a sequence, Premiere Pro conforms it to the
sequence settings. For example, if the clip and the sequence don't match, the clip
frame rate and audio sample rate will be adjusted so that all the clips in the sequence
play back the same way.

As well as being a viewer for multiple types of media, the Source Monitor provides
important additional functions. You can add comments to a clip in the form of
markers that you can refer to later or use to remind yourself about important facts
relating to a clip. For example, you might include a note about part of a shot you
don't have permission to use. You can also use two special kinds of markers, called
the *In point* and *Out point*, to select part of a clip for inclusion in a sequence.

Opening a clip in the Source Monitor

Opening clips in the Source Monitor is a little like opening files in the Finder (macOS) or Explorer (Windows). First, you'll try navigating the Project panel:

1   In the Project panel, presuming your preferences have default settings, double-click the Theft Unexpected bin while holding Command (macOS) or Ctrl (Windows). This opens the bin in the existing panel.

In the same way that you would double-click a folder in the Finder (macOS) or Explorer (Windows), you have navigated into the bin.

> ▶ **Tip:** Notice that the currently active panel has a blue outline. It's important to know which panel is active because menus and keyboard shortcuts sometimes give different results depending on your current selection.

When you finish working in a bin that you opened in the current panel, you can navigate back to the Project panel contents by clicking the Navigate Up button ![icon] at the top left of the bin panel. Navigate up now.

2   Double-click the RED Video.R3D video clip, or drag it into the Source Monitor. You may need to scroll down in the Project panel to find the clip.

Premiere Pro displays the clip in the Source Monitor, ready for you to review and add In and Out points.

3   Position your pointer so that it is over the Source Monitor, and press the ` (accent grave) key. The panel fills the Premiere Pro application frame, giving you a larger view of your video clip. Press the key again to restore the Source Monitor to its original size. If your keyboard does not have a ` (accent grave) key, you can double-click the panel name to toggle the full-screen view.

Viewing video on a second monitor

If you have a second monitor connected to your computer, Premiere Pro can use it to display full-screen video.

Choose Premiere Pro > Settings > Playback (macOS) or Edit > Preferences > Playback (Windows), make sure Mercury Transmit is enabled, and select the checkbox for the monitor you want to use for full-screen playback.

You also have the option of playing video via third-party hardware, if it is installed. It's common to use third-party hardware to make different physical connections available for monitoring purposes. Check your third-party hardware user guide for installation and setup.

Using Source Monitor controls

As well as playback controls, there are some important additional buttons in the Source Monitor.

- **Add Marker:** Adds a marker to the clip at the location of the playhead. Markers can provide a simple visual reference, can be various colors, and can store comments.

- **Mark In:** Sets the In point at the current playhead location. The In point is the beginning of the part of the clip you intend to use in a sequence. You can have only one In point per clip or sequence, so a new In point will automatically replace an existing one.

- **Mark Out:** Sets the Out point at the current playhead location. The Out point is the end of the part of the clip you intend to use in a sequence. You can have only one Out point, so the new Out point will automatically replace an existing one.

- **Go To In:** Moves the playhead to the clip In point.

- **Go To Out:** Moves the playhead to the clip Out point.

- **Insert:** Adds the clip to the active sequence displayed in the Timeline panel using the *insert edit* method (see "Using essential editing commands" later in this lesson).

- **Overwrite:** Adds the clip to the active sequence displayed in the Timeline panel using the *overwrite* edit method (see "Using essential editing commands" later in this lesson).

- **Export Frame:** Allows you to create a still image file from whatever is displayed in the monitor. See Lesson 16, "Exporting Frames, Clips, and Sequences," for more on this.

- **Toggle Proxies:** If your media has proxies attached, click to toggle between viewing the proxy media and original media.

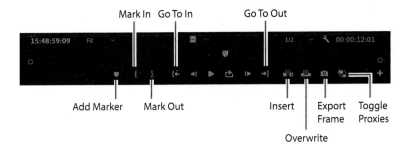

Selecting a range in a clip

You will often want to include only a specific part of a clip in a sequence. Much of an editor's time is spent watching video clips and choosing not only which ones to use but also which *parts* to use, including only the best performances and excluding technical mistakes or fluffed lines. Let's make some partial selections:

1 In the Theft Unexpected bin, double-click the clip Excuse Me (not Excuse Me Tilted) to open it in the Source Monitor. It's a shot of John nervously asking whether he can sit down.

2 Play the clip to get an idea of the action.

   John walks on-screen about halfway through the shot but takes a moment to speak.

Tip: Most cameras will record timecode in such a way that repetition is avoided, which can result in large numbers. If you want the timecode for all clips to be displayed as starting at 00:00:00:00, you can choose this option in the Media preferences, using the Timecode menu.

3 Position the playhead around 01:54:06:00, just as John pauses briefly and speaks. Note that the timecode for this clip does not start at 00:00:00:00.

4 Click the Mark In button ▌. You can also press the I key on your keyboard.

   Premiere Pro highlights the section of the clip that you selected. You have excluded the first part of the clip, but you can easily reclaim this part later if you need to do so—that's the freedom of nonlinear editing!

5 Position the playhead just as John begins to sit down. Around 01:54:14:00 is perfect.

Using a numeric keypad

If your keyboard has a separate numeric keypad, you can use it to enter timecode numbers directly. For example, if you type 700 and press the Enter key when the Source Monitor is active, Premiere Pro will position the playhead at 00:00:07:00. There's no need to enter the leading zeros or number separators. Be sure to use the numeric keypad, on the right on your keyboard, and not the numbers along the top of your keyboard (these have a different use). This works in the Program Monitor and Timeline panel too.

Note: In and Out points added to clips are persistent. That is, they will still be present if you close and reopen the clip—or even the project.

6 Click the Mark Out button ▌ or press the O key on your keyboard to add an Out point.

Tip: If you hover your pointer over a button, a tool tip appears displaying the name of the button followed by its keyboard shortcut in parentheses (if it has one).

Some editors prefer to go through all the available clips, adding In and Out points as required, before building a sequence. Some editors prefer to add In and Out points only as they use each clip. Your preference may depend on the kind of project you are working on.

Now you'll add In and Out points for two more clips. Double-click the icon for each clip in the Project panel to open it in the Source Monitor.

Our goal is to produce an edited sequence with natural-looking movement from one shot to the next and nuanced timing for dialogue.

As an editor, you would normally carefully review content to find the ideal moments to cut between shots. To save time, the precise timing has already been worked out and included in these steps.

First, we'll get a couple of seconds of the man in the suit giving John permission to share his table; then, we'll get another clip from the opposite angle showing John taking his seat.

▶ **Tip:** If you have added the Loop Playback button to the Source Monitor (see Lesson 4) and the option is activated (the button is blue), clips will loop between In and Out points when you play them.

▶ **Tip:** To help you find your way around your footage, Premiere Pro can display timecode on the Source Monitor and Program Monitor time rulers. Toggle this option on and off by clicking either monitor's Settings menu and choosing Time Ruler Numbers.

Editing from the Project panel

In points and Out points remain active in your project until you change them, so you can add clips to a sequence directly from the Project panel, as well as from the Source Monitor. If you have already looked at all your clips and selected the parts you want, this can be a quick way to create a rough version of a sequence. You can add In and Out points directly in the Project panel too.

Premiere Pro applies the same editing controls when you're working from the Project panel as it does when you're using the Source Monitor, so the experience is similar—and a few clicks quicker.

Of course, although it's faster to work this way, there's also value in having one last look at your clips in the Source Monitor before you add them to a sequence.

7 For the HS Suit clip, add an In point just after John's line of dialogue, about a quarter of the way into the shot at 01:27:00:16.

8 Add an Out point when John passes in front of the camera, blocking our view at 01:27:02:14.

▶ **Tip:** If the Source Monitor is active, you can press Tab to make the Playhead Position timecode active and selected, ready to type in new timecode. You can copy and paste new timecode in or type new numbers.

9 For the Mid John clip, add an In point just as John begins to sit down at 01:39:52:00.

10 Add an Out point after he has a sip of tea at 01:40:04:00.

Shot types and clip names

Filmmakers use common names for types of shot framing, and these are often abbreviated when naming clips to make identifying footage quicker and easier.

For example, the HS Suit clip is a *head and shoulder shot* of the Suit character, while the Mid John clip is a *mid shot* of the John character.

Here are some common shot types and their abbreviations. These descriptions vary, and there are subtle differences from one cinematographer to another, but this brief list shows the broad differences in coverage between the types:

- **Extreme Close-Up (ECU):** A very close shot of a character's face—close enough to crop out their hair and/or chin.
- **Close-Up (CU):** A close shot of a character's face that usually incorporates just the character's head.
- **Head and Shoulder (HS):** A close shot that incorporates the character's head and shoulders.
- **Mid/Medium (Mid or MS):** A shot that includes the character's head to their waist.
- **Mid-Wide or Medium Wide (MWS):** A shot that includes the character's head to their knees.
- **Wide (WS or Wide):** A shot that includes the whole body of the character from their head to their toes.
- **Extreme Wide (EWS):** A shot that includes the whole body of the character and a substantial amount of space around them.
- **Two Shot (2S):** A shot that includes two characters.
- **Group Shot (GS):** A shot that includes several characters.
- **General Views (GV):** Views of the environment or exteriors, often used for story exposition to introduce the location.
- **Cutaways/B-Roll (Alt or B-Roll):** Shots that the editor can cut to during a scene, allowing cuts between takes to be disguised. Cutaways also add to the scene by offering additional visual cues to inform the audience. For example, as a character describes an object they are looking at, we might cut away to a shot of that object.

Creating subclips

If you are working with a long clip, you might want to use more than one part in your sequence. It can be useful to separate the sections so they can be organized in the Project panel prior to building your sequence.

This is exactly what subclips let you do. *Subclips* are partial copies of clips. They are commonly used when working with long clips, such as interview footage, where there are several parts of the same original clip that might be used in a sequence.

Subclips have a few notable characteristics.

- They can be organized in bins and renamed, just like regular clips, although they have a different icon 🖼️ in the Project panel.

- They have a limited duration based on the In and Out points used to create them, which makes viewing their contents easier when compared with viewing potentially much longer original clips.

- They share the same media as the original clip they are based on, so if an original media file is deleted or moved to a different folder, both the original clip and any subclips will go "offline"—with no media displayed.

- They can be edited to change their contents and even converted into a copy of the original full-length clip.

The short film *Theft Unexpected* depicts a comic moment between two characters at a railway café. Our protagonist, John, believes a stranger at his table is shamelessly stealing his cookies. At the last moment, it's revealed that John's cookies were safe under his newspaper the whole time; John has been stealing the other man's cookies accidentally.

Let's make a subclip to make it easier to find a critical moment with the packet of cookies.

1 In the Theft Unexpected bin, double-click the Cutaways clip to view it in the Source Monitor.

2 While viewing the contents of the Theft Unexpected bin, click the New Bin button at the bottom of the panel to create a new bin. The new bin will appear inside the existing Theft Unexpected bin.

3 Name the bin **Subclips**, and hold Command (macOS) or Ctrl (Windows) while double-clicking the new Subclips bin to open it in the same frame, rather than in a new panel.

4 Choose a section of the clip to turn into a subclip by marking the clip with an In point and an Out point. Around 02:04:05:00, before the second time the packet is removed, would make a good In point. Around 02:04:15:00, after the packet is placed back on the table, would make a good Out point.

As with many workflows in Premiere Pro, there are several ways to create subclips, and the outcome is always the same.

5 Try one of the following:

- Right-click in the picture display of the Source Monitor and choose Make Subclip.

- With the Source Monitor active, choose Clip > Make Subclip.

- With the Source Monitor active, press Command+U (macOS) or Ctrl+U (Windows).

- While holding Command (macOS) or Ctrl (Windows), drag the picture from the middle of the Source Monitor into the Project panel bin.

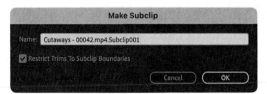

6 Name the new subclip **Packet Moved**, and click OK.

● **Note:** If Restrict Trims To Subclip Boundaries is selected, you won't be able to access the parts of your clip that are outside your selection when viewing the subclip. This might be exactly what you want to help you stay organized (and you can change this setting by right-clicking the subclip in the bin and choosing Edit Subclip).

Premiere Pro adds the new subclip to the Subclips bin, with the duration you specified with your In and Out points.

Scene Edit Detection

If your original footage contains multiple different shots as part of a continuous clip, you may find it helpful to separate the parts. This is common when working with archive footage, for example. Each time a new shot begins, it's considered to be a scene change.

In the Timeline panel, Premiere Pro can detect scene changes in a clip and separate the clip into multiple clips automatically.

To do so, select a clip in a sequence and choose Clip > Scene Edit Detection.

Choose the result you would like (adding cuts, subclips, or markers), and click Analyze.

Editing in the Timeline panel

The Timeline panel is your creative canvas. In this panel, you'll add clips to your sequences, make editorial changes to them, add visual and audio special effects, mix soundtracks, and add titles and graphics.

Here are a few facts about the Timeline panel. Refer to this list as you make progress through these lessons to make sure you are comfortable with all the features of the Timeline panel.

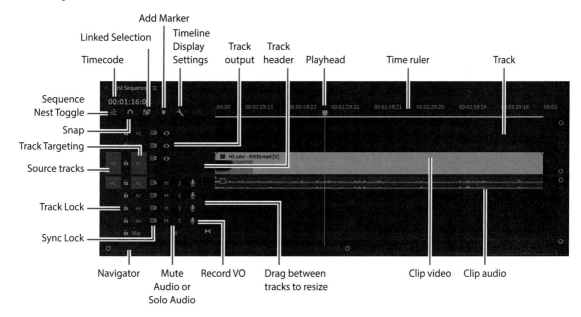

- You view and edit clips in sequences in the Timeline panel.

- The Program Monitor shows the contents of the currently displayed sequence, at the position of the playhead.

- You can open multiple sequences at the same time, with each displayed in its own Timeline panel.

- The terms *sequence* and *timeline* are often used interchangeably by editors, as in "the clip is in the sequence" or "the clip is on the timeline." Sometimes *timeline* (lowercase) is used when speaking of a sequence of clips in the abstract, without reference to a specific panel.

- If you add clips to a completely empty Timeline panel, a new sequence is created automatically with settings that match the clip you selected first.

- You can add any number of video tracks. Preview playback is limited only by your system's hardware resources.

- Upper video tracks appear "in front" of lower ones, so foreground graphic clips should be placed on tracks above background video clips.

- You can add any number of audio tracks, and they all play at the same time to create an audio mix. Audio tracks can support mono clips (1 channel), stereo clips (2 channels), 5.1 clips (6 channels), or adaptive audio—with up to 32 channels.

- You can change the height of tracks in the Timeline panel to gain access to additional controls and thumbnails on your video clips.

- Each track has a set of controls, shown on a track header on the far left, to change the way it functions.

- Time moves from left to right in the Timeline panel, so when you play a sequence, the playhead will move in that direction.

- You can zoom in and out of the sequence using the = (equals) and – (minus) keys (at the top of your keyboard). Use the \ (backslash) key, if your keyboard has one, to toggle the zoom level between your current setting and to show your whole sequence. You can also double-click the navigator at the bottom of the Timeline panel to view the whole sequence.

  If your keyboard doesn't have dedicated = (equals) and – (minus) keys, it's straightforward to assign alternative keyboard shortcuts. See Lesson 1, "Touring Adobe Premiere Pro," for more information about setting keyboard shortcuts.

Note: The modes, markers, and settings buttons at the top left of the Timeline panel are available only when a sequence is open.

- The series of buttons at the top left of the Timeline panel gives you access to alternative modes, markers, and settings. You will learn about most of these buttons later. For now, unless described otherwise, if the Timeline panel seems to be acting strangely, check to make sure these modes are set as shown here.

Selecting a tool

Premiere Pro makes use of tools that change the way the pointer works. In this way, it's similar to Adobe Photoshop.

For most operations in the Timeline panel and some operations in the Program Monitor, you will use the standard Selection tool , which you will find at the top of the Tools panel. Make a tool active by clicking its icon in the Tools panel; an active tool has a blue icon .

There are several other tools that serve different purposes, and each tool has a keyboard shortcut. If in doubt, press the V key—the keyboard shortcut for the Selection tool.

What is a sequence?

A *sequence* is a series of clips that play one after another—sometimes with multiple blended layers and often with special effects, titles, and audio—making a complete film.

You can have as many sequences as you like in a project. Sequences are stored in the Project panel, just like clips, and have their own icon.

Let's make a new sequence for the Theft Unexpected project.

1   In the Project panel, if you are still browsing inside the Subclips bin you created, click the Navigate Up button in the upper-left corner to view the contents of the Theft Unexpected bin.

2   In the Theft Unexpected bin, drag the clip Excuse Me (not Excuse Me Tilted) onto the New Item menu at the bottom of the panel. You may need to resize the Project panel to see the button.

This is a shortcut to make a sequence with playback settings that perfectly match your media.

The newly created sequence has the same name as the clip you used to create it. If you already have a sequence open when you create a new sequence, the new sequence opens in a new panel in the same Timeline panel group.

3   The sequence is highlighted in the bin, and it would be a good idea to rename it right away. Right-click the sequence in the bin and choose Rename. Name the sequence **Theft Unexpected**. Notice that the icon used for sequences in List view (shown here) and in Icon view is different from that used for clips.

The sequence is automatically opened in the Timeline panel, and it contains the clip you used to create it. This works for our purposes, but if you had used a random clip to perform this shortcut (just to make sure you had the right sequence settings), you could select that clip in the sequence now and delete it by pressing Delete (macOS) or Backspace (Windows).

> **Tip:** As with clips, you can edit sequences into other sequences, in a process called *nesting*. This creates a dynamically connected set of sequences for advanced editing workflows.

▶ Tip: You can use the Timeline Display Settings menu 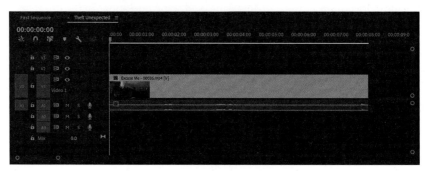 to choose Minimize All Tracks or Expand All Tracks to change the height of all tracks in a single step.

You can zoom into the sequence, with its single clip, using the navigator at the bottom of the Timeline panel. To see a thumbnail on the clip, increase the height of the V1 track by dragging the dividing line between the V1 and V2 tracks in the track header area (where the track controls are located).

Opening a sequence in the Timeline panel

To open an existing sequence in the Timeline panel, do one of the following:

- Double-click the icon for the sequence in a bin.

- Right-click the sequence in a bin and choose Open In Timeline.

You can also drag a sequence into the Source Monitor to use it as if it were a clip. Be careful not to drag a sequence into the Timeline panel to open it because this will add it to your current sequence or create a new sequence from it instead.

Conforming

Sequences have a frame rate, a frame size, and an audio mastering format (mono or stereo, for example). They *conform*, or adjust, any clips you add to match these settings.

You can choose whether clips should be scaled to match your sequence frame size. For example, for a sequence with a frame size of 1920x1080 (high-definition HD) and a video clip that is 3840x2160 (ultra-high-definition UHD), you might decide to automatically scale the high-resolution clip down to match your sequence resolution or leave it as it is, viewing only part of the picture through the reduced "window" of the sequence.

When clips are scaled, the vertical and horizontal sizes are scaled equally to keep the original aspect ratio. If a clip has a different aspect ratio from your sequence, it may not completely fill the frame of your sequence when it is scaled. For example, if your clip has a 4:3 aspect ratio and you add it, scaled, to a 16:9 sequence, you'll see gaps at the sides.

Using the Motion controls in the Effect Controls panel (see Lesson 9, "Putting Clips in Motion"), you can adjust which part of the picture you see or even create a dynamic pan-and-scan effect inside the picture.

Understanding tracks

Much as railway tracks keep trains in line, sequences have video and audio tracks that constrain the positions of the clips you add to them. The simplest form of sequence would have just one video track and perhaps one audio track. You add clips to tracks, one after another, from left to right, and they play in the order you place them.

Sequences can have multiple video and audio tracks. They become layers of video and additional audio channels in the complete sound mix. Higher video tracks appear in front of lower ones, so you can place clips on different tracks to produce layered compositions.

For example, you might use an upper video track to add titles to a sequence or to blend multiple layers of video using visual effects to create a complex composition.

— Title

— Picture-in-picture overlay

— Video

You might use multiple audio tracks to create a complete audio composition for your sequence, with original source dialogue, music, spot audio effects such as gunshots or fireworks, atmospheric sound, and voice-over.

You can scroll through clips and sequences in multiple ways, depending on the location of your pointer.

- If you hover your pointer over the Source Monitor or Program Monitor, you can navigate earlier or later using the scroll wheel; trackpad gestures work too.

- You can navigate sequences in the Timeline panel this way if you choose Horizontal Timeline Mouse Scrolling in the Timeline preferences.

- If you hold Option (macOS) or Alt (Windows) while scrolling with your pointer, the Timeline view will zoom in or out horizontally.

- If you hover your pointer over a track header and scroll while holding Option (macOS) or Alt (Windows), you'll increase or decrease the height of the track.

- If you double-click a blank space in a track header, you'll toggle the header between being tall or flattened.

- If you hover your pointer over a video or audio track header and scroll while holding the Shift key, you'll increase or decrease the height of all tracks of that type (video or audio tracks).

▶ **Tip:** If you're scrolling to change track height while holding Option/Alt or while holding Shift, you can also hold Command or Ctrl for finer control.

Targeting tracks

The portion of each Timeline track header to the right of its Track Lock button is for selecting, or *targeting*, tracks in a sequence.

Source tracks

Timeline tracks

At the far-left end of the track headers are the source track indicators. These represent the tracks available in the clip currently displayed in the Source Monitor or selected in the Project panel. They are numbered just like the Timeline tracks. This helps keep things clear when performing more advanced edits.

When you use a keyboard shortcut or the buttons on the Source Monitor to add a clip to a sequence, source track indicators are important. The position of a source track indicator relative to a Timeline track header sets the track to which the new clip will be added. A source track indicator also needs to be selected, in blue, for the contents of that track to be added to the sequence.

In the example shown, the position of the source track indicators means a clip with one video track and one audio track would be added to the Video 1 (V1) and Audio 1 (A1) tracks in the Timeline panel when using buttons or a keyboard shortcut to add a clip to the current sequence.

● **Note:** Remember, enabling or disabling Timeline track targeting buttons will not impact the video or audio added to a sequence when you apply an edit; only the source track indicators do.

In the example at left, the source track indicators have been moved to new positions relative to the Timeline panel track headers. In this example, the clip would be added to the Video 2 (V2) and Audio 2 (A2) tracks on the Timeline when using buttons or a keyboard shortcut to add a clip to the current sequence.

Click a source track indicator to enable it or disable it. A blue highlight indicates a track is enabled.

When performing edits in this way, enabling or disabling timeline tracks won't affect results. The source track indicator and sequence track selection controls look very similar, but they have different functions.

If you drag a clip into a sequence, Premiere Pro adds content from enabled (highlighted in blue) source tracks but ignores the position of the source track indicators, adding the content to the tracks you drag them to.

● **Note:** If you accidentally click a source track indicator while holding Alt (Windows) or Option (macOS), it will have a black border. This indicates that blank space will be added to the sequence when you perform the edit—an option that is sometimes used to maintain sync or leave space for alternative content. To remove the black border, click the source track indicator while holding Alt/Option again.

Using In and Out points in the Timeline panel

The In and Out points set in the Source Monitor define the part of a clip you will add to a sequence.

The In and Out points you use in the Timeline panel have two primary purposes.

- To tell Premiere Pro where, in time, a new clip should be positioned when it is added to a sequence.
- To select parts of a sequence you want to remove. You can make precise selections to remove whole clips, or parts of clips, from specific tracks by using In and Out points in combination with the track selection buttons.

Selected parts of a sequence, defined by In and Out points, are highlighted in the Timeline panel. The highlighting (and selection) doesn't extend to tracks that are not targeted.

In the following example, all the timeline tracks are targeted except V2, so there's a gap in the highlight where In and Out points define a selection. Notice the Source track V1 is enabled, but this does not impact sequence track selection.

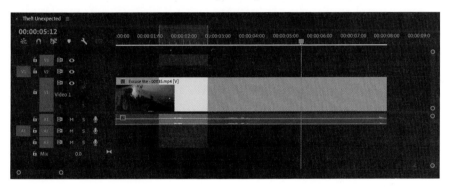

Setting In and Out points

Adding In and Out points in the Timeline panel or in the Program Monitor is almost the same as adding them in the Source Monitor.

One key difference is that unlike the controls in the Source Monitor, the Mark In and Mark Out buttons on the Program Monitor also apply changes to the currently displayed sequence.

To add an In point to a sequence at the current position of the playhead, make sure either the Timeline panel or the Program Monitor is active and then press the I key or click the Mark In button █ on the Program Monitor.

To add an Out point to a sequence at the current position of the playhead, make sure either the Timeline panel or the Program Monitor is active and then press the O key or click the Mark Out button █ on the Program Monitor.

Clearing In and Out points

If you open a clip that already has In and Out points, you can change them by adding new ones; your new In and Out points will replace the existing ones.

You can also simply remove existing In and Out points from a clip or from a sequence. It's the same technique to remove In and Out points on the Timeline, in the Program Monitor, and in the Source Monitor.

1 In the Timeline panel, position the playhead over the Excuse Me clip.

2 Press the X key. This adds an In point to the Timeline at the start of the clip (on the left) and an Out point at the end of the clip (on the right). Both appear on the time ruler at the top of the Timeline panel.

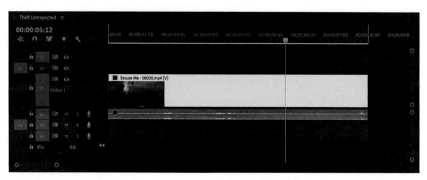

3 Right-click the time ruler at the top of the Timeline panel, and take a look at the menu commands.

Choose the command you need from this menu, or use one of the following keyboard shortcuts:

Clear In
Clear Out
Clear In and Out

- **Clear In:** Removes the In point (Option+I, macOS; Ctrl+Shift+I, Windows)

- **Clear Out:** Removes the Out point (Option+O, macOS; Ctrl+Shift+O, Windows)

- **Clear In And Out:** Removes both the In point and Out point (Option+X, macOS; Ctrl+Shift+X, Windows)

4 That last option is particularly useful. It's easy to remember and quickly removes both In and Out points. Try it now to remove the In point and Out point you just added.

Using time rulers

The time rulers at the bottom of the Source Monitor and Program Monitor, as well as at the top of the Timeline panel, all serve the same purpose: They help you navigate through your clips or sequences in time.

Time goes from left to right in Premiere Pro, and the location of the playhead gives you a visual reference in relation to your clips.

- Drag left and right in the Timeline panel time ruler now. The playhead moves to follow your pointer. As you drag across the Excuse Me clip, you see the contents of the clip in the Program Monitor. Dragging through your content in this way is called *scrubbing*.

  Notice that the Source Monitor, Program Monitor, and Timeline panel all have navigation bars at the bottom.

- You can zoom the time ruler by hovering over the navigation bar and using your mouse wheel to scroll (trackpad gestures work too).

- Once you have zoomed in, move through the time ruler by dragging the navigator.

- Adjust the zoom level of the time ruler by dragging the ends of the navigator.

Using the Timecode panel

There is a dedicated Timecode panel that, like other panels, can float in its own window or be added to a panel group. To open it, choose Window > Timecode.

The Timecode panel offers multiple lines of timecode information. Each line can be configured to show a particular type of time information. Because the panel can be set to a large size, it's particularly useful when you want to sit back and review your footage—and read the numbers from a distance.

The default configuration shows the current time, the total duration, and the duration set by In and Out points for the active panel—Source Monitor, Program Monitor, or Timeline panel.

The current time matches the timecode displayed at the bottom left of the Source Monitor or the Program Monitor and the top left of the Timeline panel.

You can add or remove lines of timecode information to make it easier to monitor your clips and sequences by right-clicking the Timecode panel and choosing Add Line or Remove Line.

To configure the type of information displayed in a line, right-click the line and choose the option you would like.

Right-click any line and choose Save Preset to store a configuration you would like to use again. The preset you create will appear in the menu when you right-click the Timecode panel.

You can also right-click and choose Manage Presets to assign a keyboard shortcut to presets or delete presets.

There's a compact mode for the Timecode panel that shows the same information in a smaller panel. To switch modes, right-click the panel to choose between Compact and Full Size.

The Timecode panel has no active controls—that is, you won't use it to add In or Out points or make edits—but it provides useful additional information to guide your decisions. Seeing the difference between total duration and selected duration, for example, can help you gauge your total available media for multiple edits.

▶ Tip: If a panel is active/selected, you can press Command+W (macOS) or Ctrl+W (Windows) to close it.

Close the Timecode panel now.

Customizing track headers

Just as you can customize the Source Monitor and Program Monitor controls, you can change several options on the Timeline track headers.

1   To access the options, right-click a video or audio track header and choose Customize, or click the Timeline Display Settings menu 🔧 and choose Customize Video Header or Customize Audio Header from the menu.

There are no additional video track header buttons, but opening the editor allows you to move, remove, and restore buttons by clicking Reset Layout. Additional audio track header buttons allow you to extend the functionality of the track headers.

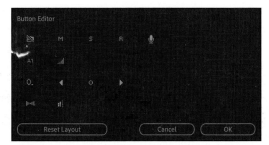

2   Hover your pointer over buttons in the Button Editor to see the tool tip. Some of these will be familiar to you already; others will be explained in later lessons.

3   Add a button to a track header by dragging it from the Button Editor onto a track header. You can remove a button from a track header by dragging it away while the Button Editor is open.

Note that all audio or video track headers update to match the one you adjust.

4   Experiment with this feature a little more. You can always click the Reset Layout button on the Button Editor to return the track header to the default options.

5   When you have finished, click Cancel to leave the Button Editor.

Using essential editing commands

No matter how you add a clip to a sequence—by dragging, clicking a button on the Source Monitor, or using a keyboard shortcut—you'll choose one of two kinds of edits: an insert edit or an overwrite edit.

When a sequence has existing clips at the location where you want to add a new clip, these two choices—insert and overwrite—will produce markedly different results.

Performing one or other of these two types of edit is at the absolute heart of nonlinear editing. Of all the skills you will learn in this book, this is the one you will perform most often. Fundamentally, this *is* nonlinear editing, so take a little extra time to be sure you are comfortable with this workflow before you continue.

Performing an overwrite edit

Continue working on the Theft Unexpected sequence. So far, you have just one clip, in which John asks if a seat is free.

First, let's use an overwrite edit to add a reaction shot to John's request for a chair.

Tip: Professional editors use the terms *shot* and *clip* interchangeably.

1   Open the shot HS Suit in the Source Monitor. We've already added In and Out points to this clip.

   ▶ **Tip:** You can copy and paste timecode into the current time indicator at the bottom left of the Source Monitor or Program Monitor. Click to select the timecode, paste the new timecode, and press Return or Enter to move the playhead to that time. This is a useful feature when working with camera logs that allow you to quickly locate a particular part of a clip.

   You'll next need to set up the Timeline panel carefully. This may seem like a slow process at first, but after practice, you'll find editing is fast and easy. Also, it's common to perform several edits with the same settings before you need to change them.

2   Position the Timeline playhead (rather than the Source Monitor playhead) just after John makes his request. Around 00:00:04:00 is perfect.

   Unless an In point or Out point has been added to the Timeline, the playhead is used to position new clips when editing with the keyboard or on-screen buttons (it becomes the In point). When you drag a clip into a sequence, the location of the playhead and existing In or Out points are ignored.

3   Though the new clip has an audio track, you don't need it. You'll keep the audio that is already in the timeline. Click the source track selection indicator A1 to turn it off. The button should be gray rather than blue.

4 Check that your track headers look like the example shown, with only the Source Track Indicator for V1 enabled, and positioned next to the sequence track V1.

● **Note:** When editing clips into a sequence, the track targeting buttons have no effect.

5 Click the Overwrite button 🖳 in the Source Monitor.

Premiere Pro adds the clip to the sequence on the Video 1 track, replacing part of the existing clip. When you perform an overwrite edit, existing sequence clips do not move to make room for the incoming clip.

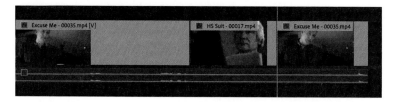

● **Note:** Editors often use the words *sequence* and *edit* interchangeably. In this case, the word *edit* means any change made to one or more clips in a sequence.

Congratulations! You have completed an overwrite edit.

By default, when you drag a clip into a sequence, rather than using an on-screen button or keyboard shortcut, you'll perform an overwrite edit. You can perform an insert edit instead by holding down Command (macOS) or Ctrl (Windows) while you drag.

6 Now position the playhead at the beginning (far-left end) of either the Timeline panel or the Program Monitor, and click the Play button ▶ on the Program Monitor (or press the spacebar) to play the result of your edit.

The timing might not be perfect, but you're now editing dialogue!

Performing an insert edit

Now try an insert edit.

1 In the Timeline panel, position the playhead over the Excuse Me clip, just after John says, "Excuse me," at around 00:00:02:16. Make sure there is no In point or Out point in the sequence.

2 From the Theft Unexpected bin, open the clip Mid Suit in the Source Monitor, add an In point at 01:15:46:00, and add an Out point at 01:15:48:00. This is actually from a different part of the action, but the audience won't know, and it works well enough as a reaction shot—we'll adjust the timing later.

3 In the Timeline panel, adjust the Source Track Indicators as necessary to match the example at left.

4 Click the Insert button 🖫 in the Source Monitor.

▶ **Tip:** As your sequence gets longer, you may find yourself often zooming in and out to get a better view of your clips. It can speed things up to use the keyboard shortcuts. At the top of the keyboard (not on the numeric keypad), the = key zooms in, while the – key zooms out.

The clip Excuse Me, already in the sequence, splits, with the part after the playhead moved later to make space for the new clip. This is the major difference between insert edits and overwrite edits: When you apply an insert edit, it makes your sequence longer. The clips already on the selected tracks, located to the right of the new clip, will move later (to the right) in the sequence to make room for the new clip.

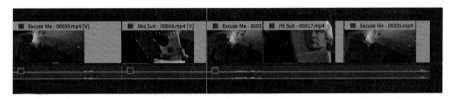

5 Position the playhead at the beginning of the sequence and play through your edit again. If your keyboard has a Home key, you can use it to jump to the beginning, you can drag the playhead with your pointer to move forward or back, or you can press the Up Arrow key to jump the playhead to earlier edits (the Down Arrow key jumps to later edits).

▶ **Tip:** If your Mac keyboard has no Home key, press Fn+Left Arrow.

There is more work to be done, and there's a continuity issue near the start as John moves his jacket from one arm to the other, but this is beginning to look like a story unfolding.

6 Now open the Mid John (not the Mid Suit) clip in the Source Monitor. We've already added In and Out points to this clip.

7 Position the Timeline playhead at the end of the sequence—on the frame after the Excuse Me clip. When dragging the playhead, you can hold the Shift key to have the playhead snap to the ends of clips.

8 Click either the Insert or Overwrite button in the Source Monitor. Because the Timeline playhead is at the end of the sequence, there are no clips in the way, and it makes no difference which kind of edit you perform.

Now you'll insert one more clip.

9 Position the Timeline playhead just before John takes a sip of tea, around 00:00:14:00 in the sequence.

10 Open the clip Mid Suit in the Source Monitor, and use In and Out points to choose a part you think would go well between John sitting down and his first sip of tea. An In point around 01:15:55:00 and an Out point around 01:16:00:00 might work well.

Notice that the existing In and Out points are replaced when you add new ones.

Note: You can also edit clips into a sequence by dragging them from the Project panel or Source Monitor into the Program Monitor.

11 Edit the clip into the sequence using an insert edit.

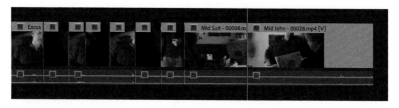

The timing of the edit may not be perfect, but that's okay; you can change your mind about the timing later—that's the beauty of nonlinear editing. The important thing, to begin with, is to get the order of the clips right.

Performing a three-point edit

When adding clips to a sequence by dragging, the duration of the part of the clip that will be added is set by In and Out points on the clip. The timing in the sequence is set by the location you drop the clip in the sequence.

When adding a clip to a sequence using a keyboard shortcut or button, Premiere Pro needs to know where and when and it should be placed.

This means there should be two In points and two Out points:

- An In point for the clip

- An Out point for the clip

- An In point for the sequence setting the beginning of the clip once it has been added

- An Out point for the sequence setting the end of the clip once it has been added

In fact, you need to specify only three of these points; Premiere Pro calculates the fourth automatically based on the selected duration.

Here's an example: If you choose four seconds of a clip in the Source Monitor, Premiere Pro automatically knows it will take four seconds of time in your sequence. Once you have set the location for the clip to be placed, you're ready to perform the edit.

Using just three points to perform edits in this way is called *three-point editing*.

When you performed your last edit, Premiere Pro aligned the In point from the clip (the start of the clip) with the In point in the sequence (the playhead is used as the In point if no In point has been added).

Even though you didn't manually add an In point to the sequence, you're still performing a three-point edit, with the duration calculated from the selection you made in the Source Monitor.

You can achieve a similar result by adding an Out point to the sequence instead of an In point. In this case, Premiere Pro will align the Out point of the clip in the Source Monitor with the Out point in the sequence when you perform the edit.

You might choose to do this, for example, if you have a piece of timed action, like a door closing at the end of a clip in the sequence, and your new clip needs to line up in time with it.

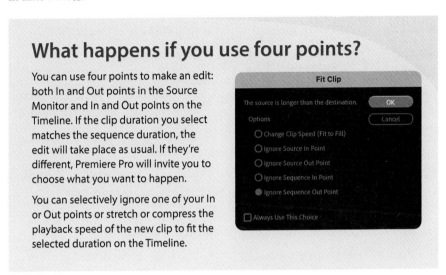

What happens if you use four points?

You can use four points to make an edit: both In and Out points in the Source Monitor and In and Out points on the Timeline. If the clip duration you select matches the sequence duration, the edit will take place as usual. If they're different, Premiere Pro will invite you to choose what you want to happen.

You can selectively ignore one of your In or Out points or stretch or compress the playback speed of the new clip to fit the selected duration on the Timeline.

Fit Clip

The source is longer than the destination.   OK

Options   Cancel

○ Change Clip Speed (Fit to Fill)
○ Ignore Source In Point
○ Ignore Source Out Point
○ Ignore Sequence In Point
● Ignore Sequence Out Point

☐ Always Use This Choice

Performing storyboard-style editing

The term *storyboard* usually describes a series of drawings that show the intended camera angles and action for a film. Storyboards are often quite similar to comic strips, although they usually include additional technical information, such as intended camera moves, lines of dialogue, and sound effects.

You can use clip thumbnails in Icon view and Freeform view in a bin as storyboard images.

Drag the thumbnails to arrange them in the order you want the clips to appear in your sequence, from left to right and from top to bottom; select them; and then drag them all into your sequence. The order the clips are selected is the order they will be added to the sequence.

Using a storyboard to build an assembly edit

An assembly edit is a sequence in which the order of the clips is correct but the timing of the edits has yet to be worked out. It's common to build sequences as an assembly edit first, just to make sure the structure works, and then adjust the timing later.

You can use storyboard editing to quickly get your clips in the right order.

1 Save your current project. This is good practice when you reach any major milestone in the development of your project.

2 Open Lesson 05 Desert Sequence.prproj in the Lessons folder.

3 Make sure the Project panel is the active panel, and choose File > Save As. Save the project as **Lesson 05 Desert Sequence Working.prproj**.

4 Double-click the Desert Montage sequence to open it in the Timeline panel.

This sequence has music but no visuals. You'll add some shots using a storyboard edit.

The audio track A1 has been locked (click the track padlock 🔒 to lock and unlock a track). This means you can make adjustments to the sequence without risking making changes to the music track.

● **Note:** You now have two project files open at the same time. You can switch between them by choosing one of them from Window > Projects, and you can close all projects by choosing File > Close All Projects.

▶ **Tip:** Project filenames can become quite long. It's fine to include useful information to help you identify a project, but avoid making the name so long it's hard to manage the file.

▶ **Tip:** You can use the Zoom control at the bottom of the bin window to resize the clip thumbnails.

Arranging your storyboard

It's not necessary to pre-arrange clips in the Project panel prior to adding them to a sequence. However, it's a helpful step to quickly give you a sense of the sequence structure.

1 Double-click the Desert Footage bin to open it in a new panel.

2 Click the Freeform View button 🖼 at the lower-left corner of the bin to see thumbnails for the clips.

You can set the Project panel to Icon view to arrange clips as a storyboard, but Freeform view gives you more…freedom! It's a more flexible way to display clip thumbnails.

3 Double-click the Desert Footage bin name to toggle it to full screen. Then, right-click the background of the bin and choose Reset To Grid > Name.

This neatly arranges the clips, sorted by name.

4   Drag the thumbnails in the bin to position them in the order in which you want them to appear in the sequence, from left to right and from top to bottom—just like a comic strip or storyboard. This will make it easier to select them in the correct order in the next step. In Freeform view, thumbnails can overlap and be arranged loosely. The order in which clips will be selected in the next step is the order that Premiere Pro will add them to a sequence.

5   Drag around the clips to select them in the order you'd like them to appear in the sequence, or select them in the correct order while holding Command (macOS) or Ctrl (Windows).

6   Double-click the Desert Footage bin name to toggle it back to its original position. Drag the clips into the sequence, positioning them on the Video 1 track right at the beginning of the timeline, above the music clip.

The clips are added to the sequence in the order you selected them in the Project panel.

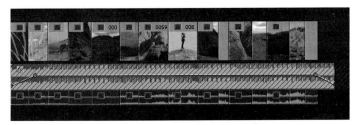

Freeform view gives great flexibility when reviewing and arranging clips, ready to add them to a sequence, but Icon view offers an even faster workflow:

1   Press Command+Z (macOS) or Ctrl+Z (Windows) to undo the last step.

2   Double-click the Desert Footage bin name to toggle it to full screen, and click the Icon View button ▣ to switch to that view.

3   Drag the clip thumbnails into the order you'd like them to appear in the sequence. In this view, the thumbnails always stay in an ordered grid.

4   Double-click the Desert Footage bin name to toggle it back to its original position.

Tip: You may need to scroll to see the clips after toggling the bin panel back to its original size.

5   Make sure the Desert Footage bin is selected (with a blue outline), but click the background of the bin to deselect any clips. Now press Command+A (macOS) or Ctrl+A (Windows) to select all the clips based on their position in the bin.

6   Drag the clips into the sequence, positioning them on the Video 1 track right at the beginning of the Timeline, above the music clip.

Premiere Pro adds the clips to the sequence in the order you originally selected them in the Project panel. Because you selected the clips in one step by selecting them all, the selection order is based on the thumbnail placement in the bin.

7   Position the Timeline panel playhead at the beginning of the sequence. Play your sequence to see the result.

Although you chose an order for the clips to play in the bin, remember that you are always free to change the order, or the timing, of the clips in the sequence.

Now that you have two projects open at the same time, it may not be clear which project you are working on. If in doubt, look at the project file location, displayed at the top of the Premiere Pro interface. The word *Edited* after a project name indicates changes have been made to that project since it was last saved.

> Lesson 05 Desert Sequence Working - Edited

8   Close each project by choosing File > Close Project twice or by choosing File > Close All Projects. If you are asked if you would like to save, do so.

Setting the duration for still images

These video clips already had In and Out points, which were used automatically when you added them to the sequence.

Graphics and photos can have any duration in a sequence. However, they have default In and Out points that are applied as you import them.

To change the default duration, choose Premiere Pro > Settings > Timeline (macOS) or Edit > Preferences > Timeline (Windows) and enter a new number in the Still Image Default Duration field. This setting applies to clips when you import them, so it won't affect clips that have already been imported.

Still images and still image sequences (a series of images intended to play one after another, as animation) have no timebase—that is, the number of frames that should play per second (fps or frame rate). You can set the default timebase for still images by choosing Media in the Preferences dialog box and setting an option for Indeterminate Media Timebase.

Review questions

1 What do In and Out points do?

2 Is the Video 2 track in front of the Video 1 track or behind it?

3 How do subclips help you stay organized?

4 How would you select a time range in a sequence to work with in the Timeline panel?

5 What is the difference between an overwrite edit and an insert edit?

6 How much of your source clip will be added to a sequence if the source clip has no In or Out points and there are no In or Out points in the sequence?

Review answers

1 In the Source Monitor and in the Project panel, In and Out points define the part of a clip you would like to use in a sequence. On the Timeline, In and Out points are used to define parts of your sequence you want to remove, edit, render effects, or export as a file.

2 Upper video tracks are always in front of lower ones, so the Video 2 track is in front of the Video 1 track.

3 Although subclips make no difference to the way Premiere Pro plays back video and sound, they make it easier for you to divide your footage into different bins. For larger projects with lots of longer clips, it can make a big difference to be able to organize content this way.

4 You'll use In and Out points to define parts of your sequence you want to work with. For example, you might render when working with effects or export parts of your sequence as a file.

5 Clips added to a sequence using an overwrite edit replace any content already in the sequence where they are placed. Clips added to a sequence using an insert edit displace existing clips, pushing them later (to the right) and making the sequence longer.

6 If you don't add In or Out points to your source clip, the entire clip will be added to the sequence. Setting an In point, an Out point, or both will limit the portion of the source clip used in the edit.

6 WORKING WITH CLIPS AND MARKERS

Lesson overview

In this lesson, you'll learn how to do the following:

- Understand the differences between the Program Monitor and the Source Monitor.

- Use markers.

- Apply sync locks and track locks.

- Select items in a sequence.

- Move clips in a sequence.

- Remove clips from a sequence.

 This lesson will take about 90 minutes to complete. To get the lesson files used in this chapter, download them from the web page for this book at *peachpit.com/PremiereProCIB2024*. For more information, see "Accessing the lesson files and Web Edition" in the "Getting Started" section at the beginning of this book. Store the files on your computer in a convenient location.

Adobe Premiere Pro makes it easy to fine-tune your edits with markers and advanced tools for syncing and locking tracks when you're editing clips in your video sequence.

Starting the lesson

The art and craft of video editing is perhaps best demonstrated during the fine-tuning phase after the first version of your sequence is completed. Once you've chosen your shots and put them in approximately the right order, the process of carefully adjusting the timing of your edits begins.

You'll move clips around in your sequence and remove the parts you don't want. You can also add markers with comments to store information about clips and sequences, which can be useful during your edit or when you send your sequence to other Adobe Creative Cloud applications.

In this lesson, you'll learn about additional controls in the Program Monitor and discover how markers help you stay organized.

You'll also learn about making changes to clips that are already on the timeline—the "nonlinear" part of nonlinear editing with Adobe Premiere Pro.

Before you begin, make sure you are using the Editing workspace.

Note: To ensure that the tools function and the defaults are set exactly as described in this lesson, reset the Premiere Pro preferences by holding Option (macOS) or Alt (Windows) while launching the application and then clicking Continue in the Reset Options dialog box.

1 Open the file Lesson 06.prproj from the Lessons folder.

2 Choose File > Save As.

3 Rename the file **Lesson 06 Working.prproj**.

4 Choose a location on your hard drive, and click Save to save the project.

5 Open the Workspaces menu and choose Editing. Then open the menu again to choose Reset To Saved Layout.

Using the Program Monitor controls

The Program Monitor is almost identical to the Source Monitor, but there are a small number of important differences.

What is the Program Monitor?

The Program Monitor displays the frame your sequence playhead is sitting on or playing. In the Timeline panel, the sequence is presented as clip segments and tracks, while the Program Monitor shows the resulting video output. The Program Monitor time ruler is a smaller version of the one in the Timeline panel, and the two are linked.

In the early stages of editing, you're likely to spend a lot of time working with the Source Monitor, reviewing and marking your clips. Once your sequence is roughly edited together, you will spend most of your time using the Program Monitor and the Timeline panel.

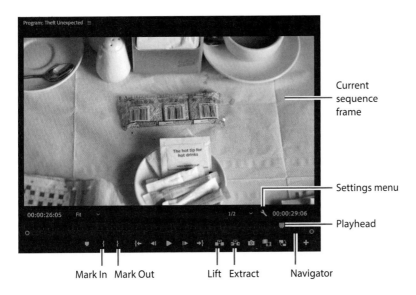

Current sequence frame

Settings menu

Playhead

Mark In Mark Out   Lift Extract   Navigator

Comparing the Program Monitor and the Source Monitor

Key differences between the Program Monitor and the Source Monitor include the following:

- The Source Monitor is usually used to show the contents of a clip; the Program Monitor shows the contents of whichever sequence is currently displayed in the Timeline panel. In particular, it shows whatever is under the playhead in the Timeline panel.

- The Source Monitor has Insert and Overwrite buttons for adding clips (or parts of clips) to sequences. By contrast, the Program Monitor has Extract and Lift buttons for removing clips (or parts of clips) from sequences (more on extract and lift edits is coming up).

- Both monitors have a time ruler. The playhead on the Program Monitor matches the playhead in the sequence you're currently viewing in the Timeline panel (the name of the current sequence is displayed at the top left of the Program Monitor). As one playhead moves, the other moves as well, so you can use either panel to change the currently displayed frame.

- When you work with special effects in Premiere Pro, you'll see the results in the Program Monitor. There's one exception to this rule: Source clip effects are viewed in both the Source Monitor and the Program Monitor (for more information about effects, see Lesson 12, "Adding Video Effects").

- The Mark In and Mark Out buttons in the Program Monitor work in the same way as the ones in the Source Monitor. In and Out points are added to the currently displayed sequence when you add them in the Program Monitor, and they are persistent in sequences in the same way that they are persistent in clips.

Adding clips to a sequence with the Program Monitor

You've already learned how to make a partial clip selection with the Source Monitor and then add the clip to a sequence by pressing a key, clicking a button, or dragging.

You can also drag a clip from the Source Monitor or Project panel into the Program Monitor to add it to a sequence.

When you do so, several overlay images appear in the Program Monitor, each highlighting a drop zone that gives different options for the edit you're about to perform.

Take a look at the options now (you'll put them to work in this section's second exercise):

1 If it's not open already, in the Sequences bin, open the Theft Unexpected sequence (not Theft Unexpected 02).

2 From the Theft Unexpected bin, drag the clip HS Suit over the viewing area of the Program Monitor, but don't release it yet (remember to always drag the icon rather than the clip name). Take note of the drop zones that appear in the Program Monitor.

3 Move the pointer over each drop zone. As you do, Premiere Pro highlights the drop zone to indicate the type of edit you will apply if you release the clip (don't, though).

4 Continue to drag the clip into the Source Monitor and release it. Most of the time you will double-click to open clips in the Source Monitor, but intuitive steps like dragging work too.

You can drag clips into the Program Monitor from the Project panel or Source Monitor. Here's the list of overlay options:

- **Insert:** This performs an insert edit, using the source track selection indicators to choose the track (or tracks) the clip will be added to.

- **Overwrite:** This performs an overwrite edit, using the source track selection indicators to select the track (or tracks) the clip will be added to.

- **Overlay:** If there is already a clip under the Timeline panel's playhead in the current sequence, this adds the new clip to the next available track above it. If there's already a clip on the next track, the one above that is used, and so on.

- **Replace:** This replaces the clip currently under the timeline playhead with the new clip (more on replace edits in Lesson 8, "Editing Video—Advanced Techniques"). Replace edits cannot be used to replace graphics and titles created in the Timeline panel but will work when replacing imported photos and graphics.

- **Insert After:** This inserts the new clip immediately after the clip currently under the timeline playhead.

- **Insert Before:** This inserts the new clip immediately before the clip currently under the timeline playhead.

● **Note:** The Overlay, Insert Before, and Insert After edits are available only when dragging a clip onto the appropriate drop zone in the Program Monitor. There are no buttons or single-key shortcuts that achieve the same results.

The Program Monitor overlays give maximum flexibility when editing by touch, with a computer screen that allows touch interaction. You can use the mouse or trackpad to drag clips in, as well as drag clips by touch.

Now that you are familiar with the options, let's add that HS Suit clip to the sequence. Continue working on the Theft Unexpected sequence.

1 Position the Timeline panel's playhead anywhere over the last clip in the sequence, Mid John. Somewhere around 00:00:20:00 would work.

2 If it's not already open, open the clip HS Suit from the Theft Unexpected bin in the Source Monitor. This is a clip that has already been used in the sequence, but you'll choose a different part.

   ▶ **Tip:** When the Project panel is set to List view, you can use the Left Arrow and Right Arrow keys to expand and collapse bins that are selected in the Project panel or to navigate up and down a list of items.

3 Set an In point for the clip around 01:26:49:00. There's not much going on in the shot, so it works well as a cutaway. Add an Out point around 01:26:52:00 so you have a little time with the man in the suit.

4 Click in the middle of the picture in the Source Monitor and drag the clip into the Program Monitor, but don't release it yet.

● **Note:** Even if you drag a clip directly into a sequence, Premiere Pro still uses the Timeline panel's source track indicators to control which components of the clip (video and audio channels) are used.

▶ **Tip:** You can press the End key to move the playhead to the end of the sequence, and pressing the Home key moves the playhead to the start of the sequence. If your macOS keyboard lacks these keys, you can use Fn+Right Arrow in place of the End key and Fn+Left Arrow in place of Home.

For this edit, release the clip in the Insert After drop zone. Though the Timeline panel playhead was in the middle of the Mid John clip, the new clip is edited into the sequence immediately after it.

The Insert After and Insert Before drop zones can make it easier to place new clips precisely in sequences without replacing or splitting existing clips.

Typing timecode

You can click a timecode display, type the timecode you want the playhead to move to *without punctuation*, and then press Return (macOS) or Enter (Windows).

For example, if you want the playhead to move to 00:00:27:15, you can type **2715**. There's no need to enter leading zeros.

When typing timecode, you can use a period (full stop) as a replacement for two zeros or to skip to the next number type.

For example, if you want the playhead to move to 01:29:00:15, you can type **1.29..15**.

You can also type incremental amounts. For example, typing **+200** will move the playhead 2 seconds later (because the punctuation will be added automatically, making this 00:00:02:00).

Insert editing with the Program Monitor

Let's try an insert edit into the middle of the current sequence using the same technique.

1 Position the Timeline panel playhead around 00:00:13:00, at the beginning of the Mid Suit shot. Play through the next edit, between this shot and the following shot, Mid John.

   The continuity of movement isn't perfect on this cut, so let's add another part of that HS Suit clip.

2 Once again, position the timeline playhead anywhere over the Mid John shot toward the end of the sequence. Somewhere around 00:00:20:00 would work, just to try out this technique.

3 Add a new In point and Out point to the HS Suit clip in the Source Monitor. Choose any part you like, selecting about two seconds in total. You can see the selected duration at the lower-right corner of the Source Monitor.

4 Drag the clip from the Source Monitor onto the Insert Before drop zone in the Program Monitor viewing area. When you release it, the clip is inserted into your sequence before the Mid John clip.

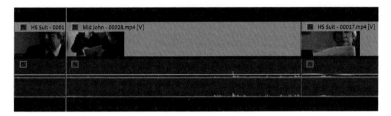

Drag only video or audio into a sequence

If you prefer to drag clips into the Timeline panel, there's a way to bring in just the video or audio part of a clip.

Now try an Overlay edit.

1 Position the Timeline panel playhead at 00:00:25:20, just before John takes out his pen.

2 Open the Mid Suit clip in the Source Monitor. At about 01:15:54:00, John is wielding his pen. Add an In point there.

3 Add an Out point at about 01:15:56:00. You just need a quick alternative angle for now, to give the audience a better perspective on the action.

4 At the bottom of the Source Monitor, you'll see the Drag Video Only and Drag Audio Only icons ▣ ⁺⁺⁺.

These icons serve three purposes:

- They tell you whether your clip has video, audio, or both. If there is no video, for example, the filmstrip icon is dimmed. If there is no audio, the waveform is dimmed ▣ ⁺⁺⁺.

- You can click one or the other icon to switch between viewing the clip audio waveform or video.

- You can drag them to selectively edit video or audio into your sequence.

Note: Remember, only the source track selection indicators matter when editing clips into a sequence, not the track targeting controls next to them in the Timeline panel.

Drag the filmstrip icon from the bottom of the Source Monitor into the Program Monitor, and release it on the Overlay drop zone. When you release, just the video part of the clip is added to the Video 2 track in the sequence (the next available empty track).

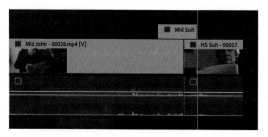

This works even if both the Source Video and Source Audio selection buttons in the Timeline panel are enabled, so it's a quick, intuitive way to select the part of a clip you want. You could achieve the same effect by selectively disabling source track selection buttons in the Timeline panel, but it would require more clicks.

5 Play your sequence from the beginning.

The timing may not be perfect, but this edit is off to a good start. The clip you just added plays in front of the end of the Mid John clip and the start of the HS Suit clip, changing the timing. Because Premiere Pro is a nonlinear editing system, you can adjust the timing later. You'll learn how to do this in Lesson 8.

Why are there so many ways to edit clips into a sequence?

As you continue to develop your editing skills and build experience, you'll find that some ways of adding clips to sequences work better than others depending on the particular situation. Perhaps you need to be absolutely sure you've got the timing right, so you carefully select options in the Source Monitor and Timeline panel. Perhaps you are in a hurry to throw something together, so you drag clips from the Project panel into the Timeline panel and worry about timing later.

In addition, you'll find you naturally tend toward one editing style or another. To ensure editors can work flexibly according to their own styles, Premiere Pro includes multiple workflows for the same outcome.

Setting the playback resolution

The Mercury Playback Engine enables Premiere Pro to play multiple media types, special effects, and more in real time—without pre-rendering. Mercury uses the power of your computer hardware to boost performance. This means the speed (and number of cores and type) of your CPU, the amount of RAM (memory) you have, the power of your GPU (video card), and the speed of your storage drives are all factors that impact playback performance.

If your system has difficulty playing back every frame of video in your sequence (in the Program Monitor) or in your clips (in the Source Monitor), you can lower the playback resolution to make playback smoother. If you see your video playback stuttering, stopping, and starting, it usually indicates that your system is unable to play the file because of a hardware limitation.

It's worth remembering that playing high-resolution video files is *hard!* A single frame of uncompressed full HD video is roughly equivalent to more than 8 million letters of text. And, of course, there are usually at least 24 frames per second, adding up to 192 million letters of text a second for HD video playback. UHD video (often described as 4K video) is four times that!

Reducing the playback resolution means you won't see every pixel in your pictures, but for some media formats it can dramatically improve performance, making creative work much easier. It's common for video to have a higher resolution than can be displayed, because your Source Monitor and Program Monitor are often smaller than the original media size. For this reason, you may not always see a difference in the display in any case.

Choosing playback resolution

Let's try adjusting playback resolution.

1   Open the clip Snow_3 from the Boston Snow bin in the Source Monitor. At the bottom right of the Source Monitor and Program Monitor, you'll see the Select Playback Resolution menu.

    1/2

    By default, playback is set to half-resolution. If it isn't, choose that option now. In fact, it's half-horizontal resolution and half-vertical resolution, so it's really quarter-resolution.

2   Play the clip to get a sense of the quality when it's set to half-resolution.

3   Change the resolution to Full and play it again to compare. It probably looks similar. With some media formats, changing the playback resolution can make a big difference to the visual quality.

© Maxim Jago 2016

4 Try reducing the resolution to 1/8 and play the clip—a dramatic difference! Notice that the picture is sharp when you pause playback. This is because the pause resolution is an independent setting from the playback resolution (see the next section).

© Maxim Jago 2016

You'll notice the biggest differences in images with lots of detail, like text. Compare the detail in the tree branches, for example.

5 Try dropping the playback resolution to 1/16. Premiere Pro makes an assessment of each kind of media you work with, and if the benefits of reducing resolution are less than the effort it takes to drop the resolution, the option is unavailable. In this case, the media is full 4K (4096×2160 pixels), and the 1/16 option is available.

You certainly wouldn't want to work at 1/16 resolution all of the time, but it can make an enormous difference when working with very high-resolution media on a low-powered computer.

6   Return the setting to 1/2, ready for the other clips in this project.

⬤ **Note:** The choices on the Playback Resolution menu are the same on the Source Monitor and the Program Monitor, but the option you choose on one of the menus is independent of the other.

If you're working on a powerful computer, you may want to maximize the playback quality when previewing at full resolution. There's an extra option to do this. You can choose High Quality Playback from the Settings menu 🔧 for the Source Monitor or Program Monitor.

With High Quality Playback selected, playback is performed at the same quality as file export. Without this option enabled, a small amount of quality loss is allowed in exchange for better playback performance.

Choosing resolution when playback is paused

The playback resolution control is also available in the Settings menu on the Source and Program Monitors.

If you look in the Settings menu on either monitor, you'll find a second set of options related to display resolution: Paused Resolution.

This menu works in the same way as the menu for playback resolution, but as you might have guessed, it changes the resolution only when the video is paused.

Most editors choose to leave Paused Resolution set to Full. That way, during playback you may see lower-resolution video to get the timing right, but when you pause playback, Premiere Pro reverts to showing you a full-resolution image. When adjusting effects, you'll see the video at the playback resolution. As soon as you stop adjusting settings, the pause resolution is applied.

Some third-party special effects may not make use of your system hardware as efficiently as Premiere Pro does. As a consequence, it might take a long time to update the picture when you adjust the effect settings. You can speed things up by lowering the paused resolution.

The playback resolution and paused resolution settings have no impact on output quality when exporting to a file.

Playing back VR video

Virtual reality headsets are now commonplace. Premiere Pro has built-in support for 360° video and 180° video for VR headset display, with clip interpretation options, dedicated immersive video visual effects, desktop playback controls, and Ambisonics Audio support.

For more information about VR Video support in Premiere Pro, check out the Adobe Help at *helpx.adobe.com* and search for "VR Video."

What's the difference between 360° video and virtual reality?

360° video is captured a little like a panoramic photo. Video is recorded in multiple directions, and the different camera angles are merged (a process called *stitching*) into a complete sphere that surrounds the viewer. The sphere is flattened into 2D video footage that's described as *equirectangular*. This is the same term used to describe a globe of the Earth that has been flattened into an atlas you can view in a book.

Equirectangular video looks distorted, which makes it hard to view. However, although the appearance is strange for human eyes, it's still a regular video file like any other, and Premiere Pro can work with it.

To view 360° video properly, it's usually necessary to wear a virtual reality headset. In the headset you can turn your head to see different parts of the image. Because a VR headset is required to see 360° video properly, it's often referred to as *VR video*.

True VR isn't actually video. It's a complete 3D environment you can move around in, viewing things from different directions, like 360° video, but also viewing things from different locations in the virtual reality space. In a sense, VR is a little like a 3D gaming experience.

The key difference is this: In 360° video, you can view in different angles, but in true VR you can view from different locations within the scenario.

Using markers

Sometimes it can be difficult to remember where you saw that useful part of a shot or what you intended to do with it. Wouldn't it be useful if you could mark clips with comments and flag areas of interest for later?

What you need are markers.

What are markers?

Markers allow you to identify specific times in both clips and sequences and add comments to them. These temporal (time-based) markers are a fantastic aid to help you stay organized and communicate with co-editors.

You can use markers for personal reference or for collaboration. You can add markers to clips or sequences.

Exploring the types of markers

More than one type of marker is available, and, like clips, markers can be assigned a color. You can change a marker type and color by double-clicking it.

- **Comment Marker:** This is a general marker; you can assign it a name, duration, and comments.

- **Chapter Marker:** This is a marker that DVD and Blu-ray Disc design applications can convert into a regular chapter marker.

- **Segmentation Marker:** This marker makes it possible for video distribution servers to divide content into parts.

- **Web Link:** Certain video formats can use this marker to automatically open a web page while the video plays. When you export your sequence to create a supported format, web link markers are included in the file.

- **Flash Cue Point:** This is a marker used by other Adobe animation tools. By adding these cue points to the timeline in Premiere Pro, you can begin to prepare your Animate project while still editing your sequence.

Note: If a single clip is selected in a sequence in the Timeline panel when you add a marker, the marker will be added to the selected clip rather than the sequence. See "Selecting clips" later in this lesson for more information about selecting clips in sequences.

Sequence markers

Let's add some markers to a sequence.

1 Open the City Views sequence from the Sequences bin.

   This is a simple assembly edit with a few shots from a travelogue program.

2 Set the Timeline panel playhead to around 00:01:12:00, and make sure no clips are selected (you can click the background of the timeline or press the Escape key to deselect clips).

3 Add a marker in one of the following ways:

- Click the Add Marker button  at the top left of the Timeline panel or the left end of the Program Monitor transport controls.

- Right-click the Timeline panel's time ruler and choose Add Marker.

- Press M.

Premiere Pro adds a green marker to the timeline, just above the playhead.

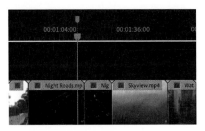

The same marker appears at the bottom of the Program Monitor.

You can use this as a visual reminder of an important moment in time or change it into a different kind of marker. You'll do that in a moment, but first let's look at this marker in the Markers panel.

● **Note:** The Markers panel will display markers associated with the currently active sequence or a clip you open in the Source Monitor. If the panel is blank, try clicking in the Timeline panel or Source Monitor to make it active.

4 Open the Markers panel. By default, the Markers panel is grouped with the Project panel. If you don't see it there, choose Window > Markers.

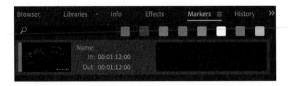

The Markers panel shows you a list of markers, displayed in time order. The same panel shows you markers for a sequence or for a clip, depending on whether the Timeline panel, a sequence clip, or the Source Monitor is active (selected).

▶ **Tip:** The Markers panel has a Search box at the top that works the same way as the Search box in the Project panel. Next to the Search box are marker color filters. Click one (or several) of these to see only markers with matching colors in the Markers panel.

5 Double-click the thumbnail for the marker in the Markers panel. This displays the Marker dialog box.

▶ **Tip:** You can open the Marker dialog box by double-clicking a marker in the Markers panel or by double-clicking the marker icon in the Timeline panel or a monitor.

▶ **Tip:** You can quickly add a marker and immediately display the Marker dialog by pressing M twice.

▶ **Tip:** Each type of marker, including different colors, can have a keyboard shortcut assigned. Working with markers using the keyboard is generally faster than using the mouse or trackpad.

6 Notice the insertion point is already flashing in the Name box. Type a production note, such as **Replace this shot**.

7 Click the Duration field (the blue numbers), and type **400**. Avoid the temptation to press Enter or Return, as this will close the panel. Premiere Pro automatically adds punctuation, turning this into 00:00:04:00 (four seconds) as soon as you click away or press the Tab key to move to the next field.

Press the Tab key now so you can review the new setting.

8 Click OK, or press Return/Enter.

The marker now has a visible duration in the Timeline panel and Program Monitor. Zoom in to the timeline a little, and you'll see the text you typed into the Name field.

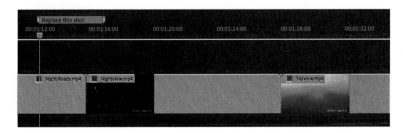

The name of the marker is also displayed in the Markers panel.

9 Take a moment to open the Markers menu, at the top of the screen on the main menu bar, to see the available commands.

At the bottom of the Markers menu is the Ripple Sequence Markers command. With this enabled, sequence markers will move in sync with clips when you insert and extract clips—these are editing operations that change the sequence duration and timing. With this option disabled, markers stay where they are when your clips move.

At the very bottom of the same menu, you'll find a command with the "snappy" name Copy Paste Includes Sequence Markers.

With this option enabled, when you copy a section of a sequence that you've selected using In and Out points and then paste that content somewhere else, any sequence markers in the selection are included.

Clip markers

Let's add markers to a clip.

1 Open the clip Seattle_Skyline.mov from the Further Media bin in the Source Monitor.

2 Play the clip, and while it plays, press the M key several times to add markers.

▶ **Tip:** You can add markers using a button or a keyboard shortcut. If you use the keyboard shortcut, M, it's easy to add markers that match the beat of your music because you can add them during playback.

3 Look in the Markers panel. If the Source Monitor is active, every marker you added will be listed. You may need to scroll down to see all the markers.

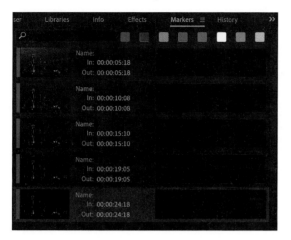

When clips with markers are added to a sequence, they retain their markers.

4 Make sure the Source Monitor is active by clicking it. Choose Markers > Clear Markers to remove all the markers from the clip.

Exporting markers

You can export markers associated with a clip or sequence as a text file, as an HTML page with thumbnails, or as a CSV (comma-separated value) file readable by spreadsheet-editing applications. This is great for collaboration and as a reference.

To export markers, select a sequence or clip with markers and choose File > Export > Markers.

Finding clips in the Timeline panel

As well as searching for clips in the Project panel, you can search for them in a sequence. Depending on whether you have the Project panel active or the Timeline panel active, choosing Edit > Find or pressing Command+F (macOS) or Ctrl+F (Windows) will display search options for that panel.

▶ **Tip:** The Markers panel groups with the Project panel by default. If you can't locate a panel, you'll discover it in the Window menu.

▶ **Tip:** You can use markers to quickly navigate your clips and sequences. If you single-click a marker icon or select a marker in the Markers panel, the playhead will move to the location of the marker—a fast way to find your way around. If you double-click a marker, Premiere Pro will display the Marker dialog box.

▶ **Tip:** To clear markers—or the current marker—right-click in the Source Monitor, in the Program Monitor, or on the Timeline panel time ruler and choose Clear Markers or Clear Selected Marker.

When clips in a sequence are found that match your search criteria, Premiere Pro highlights them. If you choose Find All, Premiere Pro will highlight all clips that meet the search criteria.

Using Sync Locks and Track Locks

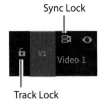

Sync Lock

Track Lock

There are two distinct ways to lock clips on tracks in the Timeline panel.

- Sync locks keep clips in sync, so when you apply an insert edit or extract edit, clips on other tracks stay synchronized.
- Track locks enable you to lock a track so that absolutely no changes can be made to it.

Using sync locks

If an actor's lips move out of time with the audio of the person's voice, it's considered bad lip-sync. It's obvious when this kind of synchronization (sync) goes wrong, but other types of sync issues may be harder to detect.

It's helpful to think of syncing as coordinating any two things that are meant to happen at the same time. It might be a musical event that happens at the same time as a climactic visual or something as simple as a lower-third title that identifies a speaker. If it happens at the same time, it's synchronized.

1 Open the Theft Unexpected 02 sequence from the Sequences bin.

This sequence contains two takes of John arriving and saying, "Excuse me." We'll fix that later.

When John arrives, at the beginning of the sequence, the audience won't know what he's looking at. Let's add a new opening shot of the other actor to set the scene.

2 Open the Mid Suit clip, from the Theft Unexpected bin, in the Source Monitor. Add an In point around 01:15:35:18, and add an Out point around 01:15:39:00.

3 Position the Timeline panel playhead at the beginning of the sequence, and make sure there are no In or Out points on the timeline.

4 Click the Sync Lock for the Video 2 track to turn it off.

5 Check that your Timeline panel is configured as in the example at right, with the Source V1 track patched to the timeline V1 track (drag it into position or click to select a new position if necessary). The timeline track targeting indicators are not important for the edit you are about to perform, but having the right source track selection buttons enabled is.

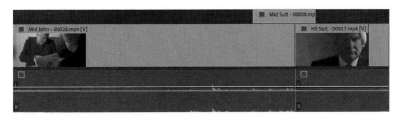

Take a quick look at the position of the Mid Suit cutaway clip on the Video 2 track, toward the end of the sequence.

It's just over the cut (the edit) between the clips Mid John and HS Suit on Video 1, covering that edit for the viewer.

● **Note:** You may need to zoom out to see the other clips in the sequence.

6 Insert edit the Mid Suit source clip into the beginning of the sequence (you can click the Source Monitor Insert Edit button 🔳).

Take another look at the location of the Mid Suit cutaway clip.

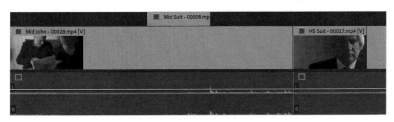

The Mid Suit cutaway clip on the Video 2 track did *not* move when you inserted the new clip because the sync lock was turned off for that track. The other clips, on the Video 1 track, have moved to the right to accommodate the new clip.

This is a problem! The cutaway is now out of position with the clips to which it relates—it no longer covers up the cut!

● **Note:** Overwrite edits do not change the duration of your sequence, so they are not affected by sync locks.

7 Undo by pressing Command+Z (macOS) or Ctrl+Z (Windows).

8 Turn on the Sync Lock 🔳 for the Video 2 track, and perform the insert edit again.

This time, the cutaway clip moves with the other clips on the timeline, even though nothing is being edited onto the Video 2 track. This is the power of sync locks: They keep things in sync!

Sometimes you will choose to turn off sync locks, as, for example, when you have music clips that you don't want to move while you add visuals.

Using track locks

Track locks (which are separate from sync locks) prevent any changes being made to a track. They are an excellent way to avoid making accidental changes to your sequence and to fix clips on specific tracks in place while you work.

For example, you could lock your music track while you insert different video clips. By locking the music track, you can simply forget about it while editing because no changes can be made to it.

The content of a locked track is still included in the sequence; you just can't make changes to that content.

Lock and unlock a track by clicking the Track Lock button ![lock icon]. Clips on a locked track are highlighted with diagonal lines.

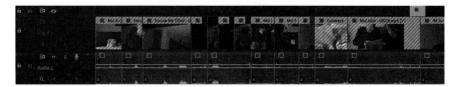

Track locks override sync locks, so even though the sync locks are enabled in this example, you'd break sync with the video clips if you were to change the position of the audio clips.

Working with gaps in the sequence

Until now, you've been exclusively *adding* clips to a sequence (not removing them). Part of the power of nonlinear editing is in having the freedom to move clips around in a sequence and remove the parts you don't want.

When removing clips or parts of clips, you'll either leave a gap by performing a *lift edit* or not leave a gap by performing an *extract edit*. You will learn more about these two types of edit later in this lesson.

An extract edit is a little like an insert edit but in reverse. Rather than other clips in a sequence moving out of the way to make space for a new clip, the other clips move in to fill the gap left behind by a clip you are removing.

When you zoom out of a long complex sequence, it can be difficult to see smaller gaps between clips. To automatically locate the next gap, choose Sequence > Go To Gap > Next In Sequence.

Once you've found a gap between clips, you can remove it by selecting it (click the gap) and pressing Delete (macOS) or Backspace (Windows). Clips after the gap will move to close the gap.

If you have set In and Out points in the sequence and used the track targeting buttons to select tracks, you can remove multiple gaps by choosing Sequence > Close Gap. Only gaps between the marks will be removed.

Let's explore working with clips in a sequence a little more. Continue working with the Theft Unexpected 02 sequence in the next section.

Selecting clips

Selection is an important part of working with Premiere Pro. For example, depending on the panel you have selected to be active (with a blue outline), different menu options will be available. Select clips in your sequences carefully before applying adjustments.

When working with clips in sequences that have both video and audio, you'll have two or more segments for each clip: one video segment and one or more audio segments.

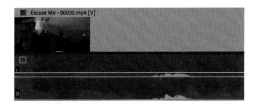

When the video and audio clip segments come from the same original media file, they are automatically linked together when added to a sequence. If you select one, the other is automatically selected too.

By default, the Linked Selection button is on ![icon]. To ignore links between clips, toggle Linked Selection off ![icon], at the top left of the Timeline panel. All clip linking will be ignored. For example, if there are linked video and audio segments, you'll select just the one you click.

There's a quick way to ignore linked selections without clicking the Linked Selection button: Hold Option (macOS) or Alt (Windows) while selecting clip segments in a sequence.

Leave the Linked Selection option on for now.

> **Tip:** Because video and audio track locks are separate, you can easily move video and audio clips apart that are linked without unlinking them first by locking one or other track first. Be warned, though, that this can lead to unwanted sync issues!

Selecting a clip or range of clips

When selecting clips in a sequence, there are two approaches.

- Make time selections by using In and Out points.

- Make clip segment selections.

The simplest way to select a clip in a sequence is to click it. Be careful not to double-click, which will open the sequence clip instance in the Source Monitor, ready for you to adjust the In or Out points (these will update, live, in the sequence).

When making selections, you'll generally use the Selection tool ![selection tool icon], which is selected in the Tools panel by default. This tool has the keyboard shortcut V.

If you hold the Shift key while selecting sequence clip segments, you'll add or remove clips from the selection. Selected clips do not have to be contiguous.

You can also drag the Selection tool over multiple clips to select them. Begin by placing the pointer over an empty part of the Timeline panel and then dragging to create a selection box. Any clip you drag over (even partially) with the selection box will be selected.

Note: If no tracks are enabled, pressing D will select all clips under the Timeline panel's playhead.

There is also an option to automatically select whichever clip the Timeline panel's playhead passes over, on the highest targeted track. This is particularly useful for keyboard-based editing workflows and effects setup. You can enable the option by choosing Sequence > Selection Follows Playhead.

If you enable this option, note that clips will not be selected automatically during playback.

You can also press the keyboard shortcut D to select the clips under the timeline playhead. Clips on targeted tracks (highlighted in blue) will be selected.

Selecting all the clips on a track

If you want to select every clip on every track, make sure the Timeline panel is active and press Command+A (macOS) or Ctrl+A (Windows).

There are also two handy tools to select all clips in a particular direction in a sequence: the Track Select Forward tool , which has the keyboard shortcut A, and the Track Select Backward tool , which has the keyboard shortcut Shift+A. You can click and hold the Track Select Forward tool to access the Track Select Backward tool.

Try this now. Select the Track Select Forward tool and click any clip on the Video 1 track.

Every clip on every track, from the one you select until the end of the sequence, is selected. This is useful if you want to add a gap to your sequence to make space for more clips; you can drag all the selected clips to the right.

When you click a clip with the Track Select Backward tool, every clip up to and including the one you clicked is selected.

If you hold the Shift key while using either of the tools, you'll select clips on only one track.

When you have finished, switch to the Selection tool by clicking it in the Tools panel or by pressing the V key.

Tip: The V key is a useful shortcut. If the Timeline panel seems to be acting strangely, try pressing V to return to the Selection tool.

Splitting a clip

It's also common to add a clip to a sequence and then realize you need it in two parts. Perhaps you want to take just a section of a clip and use it as a cutaway, or maybe you want to separate the beginning and the end to make space for new clips.

You can split clips in several ways.

- Use the Razor tool . If you hold the Shift key while clicking with the Razor tool, you'll split the clips on every track.

Tip: The keyboard shortcut for the Razor tool is C.

- Make sure the Timeline panel is selected, and choose Sequence > Add Edit. Premiere Pro adds an edit at the location of your playhead to clips on any tracks that are targeted (with the track targeting indicators on). If you have selected one or more clips in the sequence, Premiere Pro adds the edit only to the selected clips, ignoring track selections.

- Choose Sequence > Add Edit To All Tracks to add an edit to clips on all tracks, regardless of whether they are targeted.

- Use the Add Edit keyboard shortcuts. Press Command+K (macOS) or Ctrl+K (Windows) to add an edit to targeted tracks or selected clips, or press Shift+Command+K (macOS) or Shift+Ctrl+K (Windows) to add an edit to all tracks.

Clips that were originally continuous will still play back seamlessly unless you move them apart or make separate adjustments to different segments.

If you click the Timeline Display Settings  menu, you can choose Show Through Edits to see a special icon on edits of this kind, between two clips that were originally continuous.

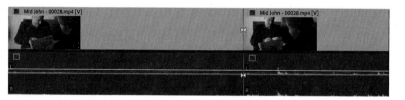

Using the Selection tool, click a Through edit icon, and press Delete/Backspace to rejoin the two parts of the clip. You don't need the Through Edits icons to be displayed for this to work, but they are a handy visual indicator.

Try splitting some clips in your current sequence using these techniques. Then try rejoining them. When you're done, be sure to use the Undo command repeatedly until you've removed all of the new cuts you added.

Grouping clips

If there are several clips in a sequence that you would like to select, move, and apply effects to in a single step, you can group them.

Select the clips, right-click the selection, and choose Group. From now on, selecting any of the clips in the group selects them all.

To separate the clips from the group, right-click any of the clips and choose Ungroup.

Linking and unlinking clips

The link between specific connected video and audio segments can be switched off and on easily. Just select the clip or clips you want to change, right-click the selected clips, and choose Unlink.

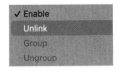

You'll find the command in the Clip menu too. You can link the clip segments again by selecting both segments, right-clicking one of them, and choosing Link. There's no harm in linking or unlinking clips—it won't change the way Premiere Pro plays your sequence. It just gives you flexibility when selecting clips.

Even if video and audio clip segments are linked, you'll need to make sure the Timeline Linked Selection option is enabled ▣ to select linked clips together.

Moving clips

Insert edits and overwrite edits add new clips to sequences in dramatically different ways. Insert edits push existing clips out of the way, whereas overwrite edits simply replace them. This theme of having two ways of working with clips extends to the techniques you'll employ to move clips around a sequence and to remove clips.

When moving clips using Insert mode, you may want to ensure the sync locks are switched on for all tracks to avoid losing sync.

Let's try a few examples.

Dragging clips

At the top left of the Timeline panel, you'll find the Snap button ▣, which is on by default. When snapping is enabled, clip segments snap automatically to each other's edges. This simple but useful feature will help you position clip segments frame-accurately.

The keyboard shortcut to toggle snapping on or off is S. Even if you have already begun dragging an item to perform an edit, you can still press S to enable or disable snapping—while dragging. It's common to forget if snapping is off or on, so this can be a useful shortcut to learn.

1   Select the last clip on the timeline, HS Suit, and drag it a little to the right.

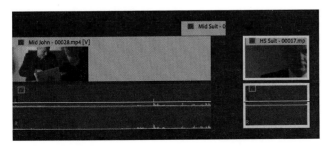

Because there are no clips after this one in the sequence, you simply introduce a gap before the clip. No other clips are affected.

2 Make sure the Snap option is enabled (in blue), and drag the clip back to its original position. If you move slowly, you'll notice that the clip segment jumps into position at the last moment. When this happens, you can be confident it's perfectly positioned. Notice that the clip also snaps to the end of the cutaway shot on the Video 2 track, and the playhead.

3 Drag the clip left until the right edge of the clip snaps to the right edge of the previous clip so they are overlapping. When you release it, the new clip replaces the end of the previous clip.

When you drag clips, the default editing mode is Overwrite.

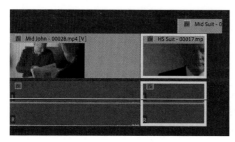

4 Undo enough times to return the clip to its original position.

Nudging clips

Many editors prefer to use the keyboard as much as possible, minimizing the use of the mouse or trackpad because working with the keyboard is usually faster.

You can reposition clip segments in a sequence using the arrow keys in combination with a modifier key, nudging the selected items left and right (earlier or later in time) or up and down between tracks.

Because of the separator between the video and audio tracks in the Timeline panel, when you nudge linked video and audio clips up or down, one of the clips may be left in its original position. This introduces a vertical gap between the linked clips. This won't impact playback but can make it a little harder to see which clips are linked together.

● **Note:** When you nudge clips, an overwrite edit is performed, removing clips or parts of clips overlapped by the clip you are moving. If you nudge a clip back into its original position, you will leave a gap.

Rearranging clips in a sequence

If you hold the Command (macOS) or Ctrl (Windows) key while you drag clip segments in the Timeline panel, Premiere Pro uses Insert mode (rather than Overwrite mode) to place the clip when you release it.

To try this out, click the name of the Theft Unexpected sequence to bring it into view (or open it from the Sequences bin).

> **Tip:** You may need to zoom in to the timeline to see the clips clearly and move them easily.

The HS Suit shot that begins around 00:00:16:00 might work better if it appeared before the previous shot—and it might help to hide the poor continuity between the two shots of John.

1   Make sure Snapping is enabled, with a blue icon at the top left of the Timeline panel.

2   Start dragging the HS Suit clip to the left of the clip before it. After you have begun dragging, but before you release the clip, hold the Command (macOS) or Ctrl (Windows) key.

> **Tip:** Be careful when dropping the clip into position. The ends of clips snap into position just like the beginnings do.

3   Drag until the left edge of the HS Suit clip snaps to the left edge of the Mid Suit clip. Release the drag to drop the clip, and then release the modifier key.

4 Play the result. This creates the edit you want, but it introduces a gap where the clip HS Suit was originally placed.

Let's try that again with an additional modifier key.

5 Undo to restore the clips to their original positions.

6 Holding Command+Option (macOS) or Ctrl+Alt (Windows), drag the HS Suit clip to the beginning of the previous clip again.

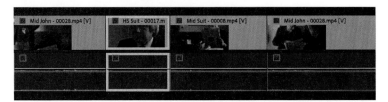

This time, no gap is left in the sequence after you drop it—you have performed an extract edit followed by an insert edit in a single step.

Play through the edit to see the result.

Using the clipboard

You can copy and paste clip segments on the Timeline panel just as you might copy and paste text in a word processor.

1 In a sequence, select any clip segment (or segments) you want to copy, and then press Command+C (macOS) or Ctrl+C (Windows) to add them to the clipboard.

2 Position your playhead where you would like to paste the clips you copied, and press Command+V (macOS) or Ctrl+V (Windows).

Premiere Pro adds copies of the clips to your sequence based on their original track location. For example, if a clip that you copied was originally on the V1 track, when you paste it will be added to the V1 track at the location of the sequence playhead.

Pressing Command+V (macOS) or Ctrl+V (Windows) adds the copied clips using an overwrite edit. To insert the copied clips instead, use Shift+Command+V (macOS) or Shift+Ctrl+V (Windows).

You can use In points and Out points combined with track selection buttons to select the parts of clips that you'll copy.

Extracting and deleting segments

Now that you know how to add clips to a sequence and how to move them around, all that remains is to learn how to remove them. Once again, you'll be operating in either a kind of Insert or Overwrite mode.

Premiere Pro offers two ways to select the parts of a sequence you want to remove. You can use In and Out points combined with track selections, or you can select clip segments.

Performing a lift edit

A lift edit will remove the selected part of a sequence, leaving blank space. It's similar to an overwrite edit but in reverse.

1 For this exercise, if you have turned on the Selection Follows Playhead option, turn it off now by choosing Sequence > Selection Follows Playhead.

2 Click the name of the Theft Unexpected 02 sequence in the Timeline panel to bring it into view. This sequence has two unwanted clips.

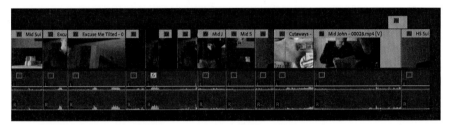

Next, you'll set In and Out points on the timeline to select the part that will be removed. You could do this by positioning the playhead and pressing I or O, but the next step will show you a handy shortcut.

3 Position the playhead so that it's somewhere over the first unwanted clip, Excuse Me Tilted.

4 Make sure the Video 1 and Audio 1 tracks are targeted, and then press X. There's no need to select the clip first.

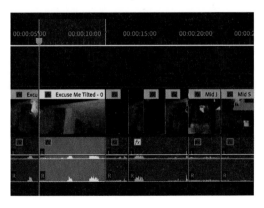

Tip: When you perform a lift or extract edit, the content you remove is added to the clipboard just as if you had copied it, allowing you to paste the content somewhere else in your sequence.

This adds an In point and an Out point that match the beginning and end of the clip. You'll see a highlight that shows the selected part of the sequence.

5   Click the Lift button 🖳 at the bottom of the Program Monitor. If your keyboard has a ; (semicolon) key, you can press it instead.

Premiere Pro removes the part of the sequence you selected, leaving a gap. This might be fine on another occasion, but on this occasion, we don't want the gap. You could remove the gap now, but for the next exercise you'll try performing an extract edit so no gap is left.

Different shortcuts for In and Out points

You can set In and Out points at the beginning and end of a selected clip (or multiple selected clips) by pressing the / (forward slash) key. This is the keyboard shortcut for the Mark Selection command. This shortcut is a little different from using the X key after positioning the playhead over the clip (without selecting it) with the correct tracks selected.

The difference is subtle, but X is perhaps even faster than using the selection-based / key, provided your track selections are already set up and you only want to select one clip.

Performing an extract edit

An extract edit removes the selected part of your sequence and does not leave a gap. It's similar to an insert edit but in reverse.

1   Undo the last edit.

> ● **Note:** Non-English keyboards may not include an ' (apostrophe) key. If your keyboard lacks that key, set up a new keyboard shortcut in the Keyboard Shortcuts preferences.

2   Click the Extract button 🖳 at the bottom of the Program Monitor. If your keyboard has an ' (apostrophe) key, you can press it.

This time, Premiere Pro removes the selected part of the sequence, and the other clips in the sequence move to close the gap.

Performing a delete and ripple delete edit

Just as there are two ways to remove part of a sequence based on In and Out points, there are also two similar ways to remove clips by selecting clip segments: Delete and Ripple Delete.

Click once to select the Cutaways clip in the sequence, and try these two options:

- Pressing the Delete/Backspace key removes the selected clip (or clips), leaving a gap behind. This is similar to a lift edit but the contents are not copied to the Clipboard.

- Pressing Shift+Forward Delete (macOS) or Shift+Delete (Windows) removes the selected clip (or clips) without leaving a gap behind. This is similar to an extract edit.

  If you're using a Mac keyboard without a dedicated Forward Delete key, you can achieve the same result by pressing Option+Delete.

The result is similar to that achieved when performing a lift or extract edit. You can even use Delete or Ripple Delete selectively on parts of clips by combining In and Out points with track targeting selections.

However, when you perform an extract or a lift edit to remove content, the content is added to the clipboard and can be pasted somewhere else in your sequence. When you delete content, it is simply removed.

Disabling a clip

You can turn a whole track's output off or on, or you can turn the output of individual clips off or on. Clips that you disable are still in your sequence, but they cannot be seen or heard.

This is a useful feature for selectively hiding parts of a complex, multilayered sequence when you want to see background layers or compare different versions or different performance takes that you have placed on different tracks.

Try this on the cutaway shot on the Video 2 track, toward the end of the sequence.

1 Right-click the Mid Suit clip on the Video 2 track and choose Enable to deselect the option.

   ● **Note:** When right-clicking clips in a sequence, be careful not to right-click the small clip FX badge ▨ as this will give you options relating to effects instead of the general clip options.

   Play through that part of the sequence, and you'll notice that the clip is present, but you can no longer see it.

2 Right-click the clip again and choose Enable to make the clip visible once more.

3 Choose File > Close to close the current project. Click Yes to save the file if you are prompted.

Review questions

1 When dragging clips directly into the Timeline panel, what modifier key (Command/Ctrl, Shift, or Option/Alt) should you use to make an insert edit rather than an over-write edit?

2 How do you drag just the video or audio part of a clip from the Source Monitor into a sequence?

3 How do you reduce the playback resolution in the Source Monitor or Program Monitor?

4 How do you add a marker to a clip or sequence?

5 What is the difference between an extract edit and a lift edit?

6 What is the difference between Delete and Ripple Delete?

Review answers

1 Hold the Command (macOS) or Ctrl (Windows) key when dragging a clip into the Timeline panel to make an insert edit rather than an overwrite edit.

2 Rather than dragging the picture from the Source Monitor, which will bring both the video and the audio if they are available, drag the filmstrip icon or the audio waveform icon at the bottom of the monitor to take only the video or audio part of the clip, respectively. You can also use the source patching buttons in the Timeline panel to deselect the parts you want to exclude when dragging the picture from the Source Monitor or dragging a clip from the Project panel or a bin.

3 Use the Select Playback Resolution menu at the bottom of the monitor to change the playback resolution.

4 There are several ways add a marker:

• Click the Add Marker button at the bottom of a monitor or on the Timeline panel.

• Press the M key.

• Use the Markers menu.

5 When you extract a section of your sequence using In and Out points, no gap is left behind. When you lift, a gap remains.

6 When you delete one or more clip segments in a sequence, a gap is left behind. When you ripple delete, no gap is left.

7 ADDING TRANSITIONS

Lesson overview

In this lesson, you'll learn how to do the following:

- Understand edit points and handles.

- Understand transitions.

- Add video transitions.

- Modify transitions.

- Fine-tune transitions.

- Apply transitions to multiple clips.

- Work with audio transitions.

 This lesson will take about 75 minutes to complete. To get the lesson files used in this chapter, download them from the web page for this book at *peachpit.com/PremiereProCIB2024*. For more information, see "Accessing the lesson files and Web Edition" in the "Getting Started" section at the beginning of this book. Store the files on your computer in a convenient location.

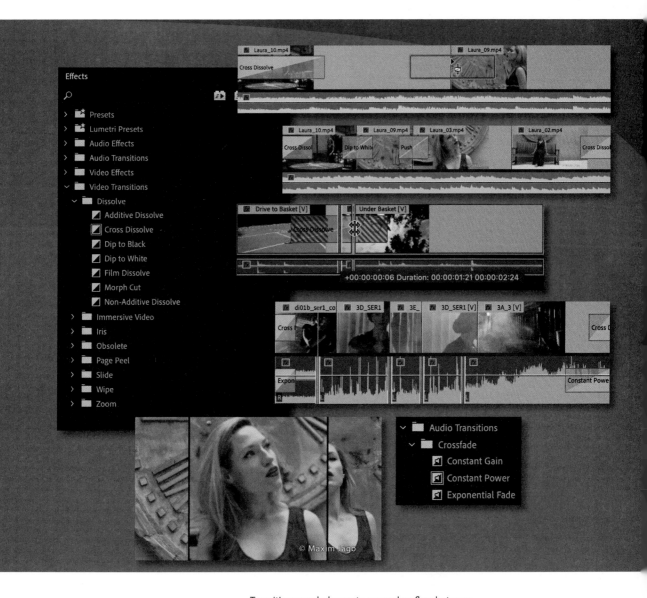

Effects

- > Presets
- > Lumetri Presets
- > Audio Effects
- > Audio Transitions
- > Video Effects
- ∨ Video Transitions
  - ∨ Dissolve
    - Additive Dissolve
    - Cross Dissolve
    - Dip to Black
    - Dip to White
    - Film Dissolve
    - Morph Cut
    - Non-Additive Dissolve
  - > Immersive Video
  - > Iris
  - > Obsolete
  - > Page Peel
  - > Slide
  - > Wipe
  - > Zoom

© Maxim Jago

∨ Audio Transitions
  ∨ Crossfade
    Constant Gain
    Constant Power
    Exponential Fade

Transitions can help create a seamless flow between
two video or audio clips or inform the viewer that
a change of scene has begun. Video transitions are
often used to signify a change in time or location.
Audio transitions provide a useful way to avoid abrupt
edits that jar the listener or to blend the significance
of two scenes.

Starting the lesson

Although the most common transition is a *cut*—where one clip abruptly ends and another begins—there are great opportunities for creativity using transition effects you can animate.

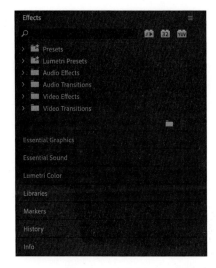

In this lesson, you'll learn to use transitions between video and audio clips to help your edits flow more smoothly. You'll also learn best practices for choosing the most appropriate transitions.

For this lesson, you'll use a new project file.

1   Start Adobe Premiere Pro, and open the project Lesson 07.prproj from the Lessons folder.

2   Save the project as **Lesson 07 Working.prproj** in the same folder.

3   Use the Workspaces menu to choose Effects. Reset the workspace to the saved layout.

This changes the workspace to a preset optimized for working with transitions and effects.

The workspace uses stacked panels to maximize the number of panels that can be onscreen at a time.

You can enable stacked panels for any panel group by opening the panel menu ▤ and choosing Panel Group Settings > Stacked Panel Group. The same option will toggle off stacked panels.

Keep stacked panels enabled for now.

You can click the name of any stacked panel to view it. In the Effects panel, you can click effect category disclosure triangles to display their contents. The stacked panel automatically changes height to accommodate the listed items.

What are transition effects?

Adobe Premiere Pro offers several special effects and preset animations to help you bridge neighboring clips in a sequence. These transitions—such as dissolves, wipes, dips to color, and so on—provide a way to ease viewers from one scene to the next. As well as smoothing the join between two clips, transitions can be used to focus attention on a major jump in the story.

Choosing and configuring transitions is an art. Applying them is simple enough: Drag the transition you want from the Effects panel onto the edit between two clips in a sequence.

The skill comes in their placement, length, and settings, such as direction, motion, and start/end positions.

You can adjust some transition settings in the Timeline panel, but it's usually easier to make precise adjustments in the Effect Controls panel. To view the settings for a transition effect in the Effect Controls panel, select it in a sequence.

In addition to the unique options for each transition, the Effect Controls panel features a helpful *A/B timeline display* (more on this later).

This display makes it easy to change the timing of transitions relative to an edit point, change the transition duration, and apply transitions to clips that don't have enough head or tail frames—that is, additional content to provide an overlap at the beginning (head) or end (tail) of a clip.

Knowing when to use transitions

Transitions are a standard storytelling tool in video editing, and the rules for their use are similar to the rules of screenwriting. They're effective when they help the viewer understand the story.

For example, you may switch from indoors to outdoors in a video, or you may jump forward in time. An animated transition, a fade to black, or a dissolve can help the viewer understand that the location has changed, that time has passed, or that a character's perspective has changed.

A fade to black at the end of a scene is a clear indication that the scene has finished. The trick with transitions is to be intentional—and this often means using restraint—unless, of course, a total lack of restraint is the creative result you want!

As long as it looks like you intended to include a particular effect, your audience will tend to trust your decision (whether or not they agree with your creative choice). It takes practice and experience to develop sensitivity for the right time, and the wrong time, to use effects such as transitions. If in doubt, less is usually best.

There is an established visual language that modern audiences recognize and respond to. For example, if a character falls asleep and the picture goes soft-focus, with everything in the frame glowing and bright, your audience will immediately know that we are witnessing that character's dream. Studying this kind of visual language can help you make creative choices.

Following best practices with transitions

You may be tempted to use a transition effect on every cut. Don't! Or at least, get them out of your system with your first project.

Most TV shows and feature films use cuts-only edits. You'll rarely see any transition visual effects. Why is this? An effect should be used only if it gives an additional benefit; transition effects can sometimes be a distraction from the video, reminding viewers they are watching a story and preventing them from connecting with it emotionally.

If a news editor uses a transition effect, it's for a purpose. The most frequent use in newsroom editing is to transform what would have been a jarring or abrupt edit into a more comfortable experience.

A jump cut is a good example of a scenario where a transition effect can help. A *jump cut* is a cut between two similar shots. Rather than looking like a continuation of the story, they look a little like a piece of the video is unintentionally missing. By adding a transition effect between the two shots, you can make a jump cut look intentional and less distracting.

Dramatic transition effects do have their place in storytelling. Consider the *Star Wars* movies with their highly stylized transition effects, such as obvious, slow wipes. Each of those transitions has a purpose. In this case, it's to create a look reminiscent of old serialized movies and TV shows. The transition effects send a clear message: "Pay attention now. We're transitioning across space and time."

Understanding the importance of clip handles

To understand transition effects, you'll need to understand edit points and handles. An edit point is the point in your sequence where one clip ends and the next begins. This is often called a *cut* and sometimes simply called an *edit*. These are easy to see because Premiere Pro displays vertical lines to show where one clip ends and another begins (much like two bricks next to each other).

When you first edit a clip into a sequence, you set an In point and an Out point to select the part you want. When you edit that selected part of the clip into a sequence, the unused sections at the beginning and end are still available but hidden in the Timeline panel. Those unused sections are referred to as *clip handles* or simply *handles*.

There's a handle between a clip's original beginning and the In point you set. There's also a handle between a clip's original end and the Out point you set. The time ruler in the Source Monitor shows you how much footage is available in your handles.

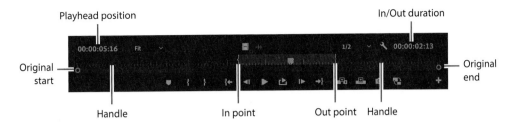

Of course, you may not have used In or Out points, or you may have set just an In point or an Out point at the very beginning or end of the clip. In this case, you would have either no unused media or unused media at only one end of the clip.

In the Timeline panel, if you see a tiny triangle in the upper-right or upper-left corner of a clip, it means you've reached the end of the original clip and there are no additional frames available.

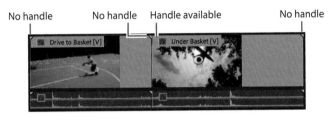

For transition effects to work, you need handles because the effect creates an overlap between the outgoing clip and the incoming clip.

For example, if you want to add a two-second Cross Dissolve transition centered between two video clips, you need at least a one-second handle available on both clips (one additional second each that would not normally be visible in the sequence). In the Timeline panel, the transition effect icon gives a visual indication of the duration of the effect and, therefore, the clip overlap.

Adding video transition effects

Premiere Pro gives you multiple video transition effects to choose from. Most options are available in the Video Transitions group in the Effects panel.

Video transitions are organized into eight subcategories. You'll find some additional transitions in the Video Effects > Transition group in the Effects panel. However, these effects are meant to be applied to an entire clip and are used to reveal the visual contents of the clip over time between its start and end frames (not using clip handles overlapping another clip). This second category works well for superimposing text or graphics.

Applying a single-sided transition

The easiest transition to understand is one that applies to just one end of a single clip. This could be a fade from black on the first clip in a sequence or a dissolve into an animated graphic. Let's give it a try.

Note: To ensure that the tools function and the defaults are set exactly as described in this lesson, reset the Premiere Pro preferences by holding the Option (macOS) or Alt (Windows) while launching the application and then clicking Continue in the Reset Options dialog box.

1 If it's not already open, open the sequence called Transitions.

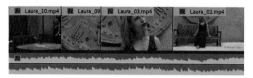

This sequence has four video clips and background music. The clips have handles, so transition effects can be applied between them (no tiny triangles are visible at the ends of the clips, which would indicate the last frame is already visible).

Note: You can use the Search field, at the top of the Effects panel, to locate an effect by name or keyword, or you can browse the folders of effects.

2 In the Effects panel, open the Video Transitions > Dissolve group. Find the Cross Dissolve effect.

3 Drag the effect onto the start of the first video clip. A highlight shows you where the transition effect will be added. When the transition is in the right position, release it.

4 Drag another Cross Dissolve effect onto the end of the last video clip.

The Cross Dissolve icon shows the timing of the effect. For example, the effect you just applied to the last clip in the sequence will start before the end of the clip and complete by the time it reaches the clip's end.

Transitions of this kind don't extend the clip (using a handle) because the transition doesn't reach past the end of the clip.

Because you're applying the Cross Dissolve transition effect at the end of the last clip, where there is no connected clip, the picture dissolves into the background of the Timeline, which is black. The result is that this looks like a Dip To Black effect.

In reality you are causing the clip to become gradually transparent in front of a black background. The difference is clearer when you work with multiple layers of clips, with different-colored background layers.

5 Play the sequence to see the result.

You should see a fade from black at the start of the sequence and a fade to black at the end.

Applying a transition between two clips

Let's apply transitions between a few clips. For the purposes of exploration, you'll break the less-is-best rule and try several options in one sequence. As you go through these steps, play the sequence regularly to view the results.

1 Continue working with the previous sequence, called Transitions.

2 Move the Timeline playhead to the edit point between clip 1 and clip 2 on the Timeline and then press the equal sign (=) key two or three times to zoom in fairly close. If your keyboard does not have the = key, use the navigator at the bottom of the Timeline panel to zoom. You can also create a custom keyboard shortcut for this purpose (see Lesson 1, "Touring Adobe Premiere Pro").

▶ **Tip:** On an English-language keyboard, it's easy to remember that pressing the = key (if your keyboard has one) zooms in because there is usually a + symbol on the same key.

3 Drag the Dip To White transition effect from the Dissolve group in the Effects panel onto the edit point between the first clip and the second clip. The effect will snap to one of three positions, and the pointer will change to indicate which position the transition will occupy.

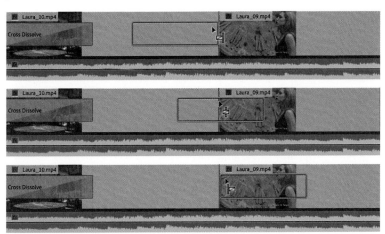

Be sure to line up the effect with the middle of the edit, not the end of the first clip or beginning of the second clip.

The Dip To White transition effect gradually builds to a completely white screen, which obscures the cut between the first clip and the next.

4. In the Effects panel, click the disclosure triangle for the Slide group of video transitions to display its contents. Drag the Push transition onto the edit point between the second clip and the third clip in the sequence, centered on the cut.

5. Play through the transition to see the result, and then position the playhead on the edit between clip 2 and clip 3 by pressing the Up Arrow key. The Up and Down Arrow keys are shortcuts to move the Timeline playhead to the previous or next edit on targeted tracks.

6. Click the Push transition effect icon in the Timeline panel once to select it, and open the Effect Controls panel (remember, if you can't see a panel, it will always be listed in the Window menu).

7. Change the direction of the clip from West To East to East To West by clicking the small direction control triangle to the right of the A/B thumbnail at the top left of the Effect Controls panel.

Select direction

▶ **Tip:** If the Effect Controls panel is empty when you open it, click once on the Push transition effect again to re-select it.

Each small white triangle changes the direction for the Push transition effect. Hover the pointer over a triangle to see a tool tip describing the option.

In the Timeline panel, play through the transition to see the result.

8. In the Effects panel, expand the Page Peel group in the Video Transitions category. Drag the Page Turn transition effect onto the edit point between the third clip and the fourth clip, centered on the cut.

9. Review the sequence by playing it from beginning to end.

Having watched this sequence, you can probably see why it's a good idea to use transitions with restraint!

Let's try replacing an existing transition effect.

10 Drag the Barn Doors transition from the Wipe group onto the existing Push transition effect icon, between the second clip and the third clip. The new transition effect replaces the old one, taking the duration and timing of the existing effect.

> **Note:** When you drag a new video or audio transition effect from the Effects panel on top of an existing transition, it replaces the existing effect. It also preserves the alignment and duration of the transition it replaces. This is a quick way to experiment with alternative transition effects.

11 Select the Barn Doors transition effect icon on the timeline so its settings are displayed in the Effect Controls panel. Using the controls in that panel, set Border Width to 7 and Anti-aliasing Quality to Medium to create a thin black border at the edge between the two clips.

> **Note:** You may need to scroll down in the Effect Controls panel to access further controls.

12 Play through the transition to view the result. The best way to do this is probably to click a little earlier in the sequence to watch the video leading up to the transition.

© Maxim Jago

If the video does not play smoothly during transition effects, press the Return (macOS) or Enter (Windows) key to render, wait for the rendering to complete, and try again. See the sidebar "Red, yellow, and green render bars" later in this lesson for more information about rendering.

Video transitions have a default duration, which can be set in seconds or frames (it's frames by default). If the default duration is set in frames, the effective playback duration of a transition effect will change depending on the sequence frame rate. The default transition duration can be changed in the Timeline section of the Preferences panel.

13 Choose Premiere Pro > Settings > Timeline (macOS) or Edit > Preferences > Timeline (Windows). Depending on your geographic region, you may see a default Video Transition Duration setting of 30 Frames or 25 Frames.

14 This is a 24-frames-per-second sequence, but this doesn't matter if you change the Video Transition Default Duration option to 1 second. Do so now, and click OK.

Existing transition effects keep their existing settings when you change the preference, but any future transitions you add will have the new default duration.

The duration of an effect can dramatically change its impact, and later in this lesson, you'll learn about adjusting the timing of transitions.

Apply the default transition effect to multiple clips

So far, you've been applying transitions to video clips. You can also apply transitions to still images, graphics, color mattes, and even audio, as you'll see shortly.

It's common for editors to create a photomontage, which might look good with transitions between the multiple photos. Applying transitions between two or three photos is quick and easy, but if you have 100 images, it will take a long time!

Premiere Pro makes it straightforward to automate this process by allowing you to set a default transition effect.

1 In the Project panel, find and open the sequence Slideshow.

This sequence consists of several images placed in a particular order. Notice that a Constant Power audio crossfade has already been applied to the beginning and end of the music clip to create a fade in and out.

2 Play the sequence by making sure the Timeline panel is active and pressing the spacebar.

There's a cut between each clip.

3 Press the backslash (\) key to zoom out the Timeline panel so the whole sequence is visible. If your keyboard does not have a \ key, drag the right end of the Timeline panel navigator to adjust the zoom.

▶ **Tip:** If you discover a useful keyboard shortcut that uses a key not included on your keyboard, you can use the Keyboard Shortcuts dialog box to assign a different key.

4   If necessary, increase the height of the V1 track to see thumbnails on the clips (you can drag the dividing line between V1 and V2 in the track header).

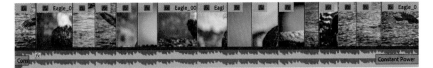

5   Using the Selection tool, draw a marquee around all the video clips to select them. Begin dragging in an empty area, away from the clips, or you'll move the first clip you click instead.

6   Choose Sequence > Apply Default Transitions To Selection.

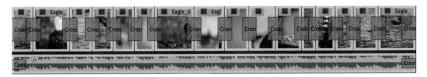

▶ **Tip:** You'll find the option to apply audio-only or video-only transition effects in the Sequence menu too.

This applies the default transition between all the currently selected clips. Notice that the Constant Power audio crossfade at the beginning and end of the music clip is now shorter because the default audio transition duration has been applied.

The default video transition effect is a 30-frame or 25-frame Cross Dissolve (though you changed this earlier to 1 second), and the default audio transition effect is a 1-second Constant Power crossfade. The shortcut you used replaced the existing audio crossfades with new, shorter ones.

You can set the default transition by right-clicking any transition effect in the Effects panel and choosing Set Selected As Default Transition. The icon for the selected default transition effect has a blue outline.

● **Note:** If you're working with clips that have linked video and audio and Linked Selection is enabled in the Timeline panel, you can select just the video or audio portions by Option-dragging (macOS) or Alt-dragging (Windows) with the Selection tool. Then choose Sequence > Apply Default Transitions To Selection.

7   Play the sequence to see the difference the new Cross Dissolves make to the montage.

Copy a transition effect to multiple edits

You can copy an existing transition effect to multiple edits using the keyboard.

Let's try it.

1   Press Command+Z (macOS) or Ctrl+Z (Windows) to undo the last step, and press Esc to deselect the clips.

2   Select any transition effect in the Effects panel, and drag it onto the cut between the first two video clips in the Slideshow sequence.

3   Select the transition you just applied by clicking its effect icon once in the sequence.

4 Press Command+C (macOS) or Ctrl+C (Windows) to copy the effect. Then hold Command (macOS) or Ctrl (Windows) while you use the Selection tool to drag a marquee around multiple other edits to select them, rather than clips.

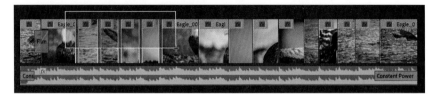

5 With the edits selected, press Command+V (macOS) or Ctrl+V (Windows) to paste the transition effect onto all the selected edits.

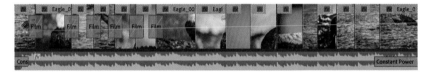

This is a great way to add transition effects with matching settings to multiple edits, especially if you have taken the time to customize the effect.

Red, yellow, and green render bars

When you add a transition to a sequence, a red or yellow horizontal line (or *render bar*) may appear above it in the Timeline panel. A yellow bar indicates that Premiere Pro expects to be able to play the effect smoothly. A red bar means that this section of the sequence may need to be rendered before you can play a preview without dropped frames.

You can choose to render at any time to make these sections preview more smoothly on a less powerful computer.

The easiest way to render is to press the Return/Enter key. If you add In and Out points to select a part of your sequence and then render, only the selected section of the sequence will render. This is useful if you have many effects that need to render but you're concerned with only one part for now.

Red or yellow bars will turn to green when those sections of a sequence are rendered. Premiere Pro creates a video file for each section where the bar has turned green. The new video files are stored in the Preview Files folder (as set in the project's Scratch Disk settings). As long as the render bar is green, playback should be smooth.

Using A/B mode to fine-tune a transition

When you review transition effect settings in the Effect Controls panel, you have access to an *A/B editing mode* that splits a single video track into two. What would normally be displayed as two consecutive and contiguous clips on a single timeline track are now displayed as individual clips on separate tracks, with a transition between them. Separating the elements of the transition in this way allows you to manipulate the head and tail frames (or handles) and to change other transition options.

Changing parameters in the Effect Controls panel

You can customize all transitions in Premiere Pro. A major benefit of the Effect Controls panel is that, in addition to it giving you access to the settings for transition effects, you can see the outgoing and incoming clip handles (unused media in the original clip). This makes it easier to adjust the timing of an effect.

Let's modify a transition.

1 In the Timeline panel, switch back to the Transitions sequence.

2 Position the Timeline playhead over the Barn Doors transition you added between clips 2 and 3, and click the transition to select it.

3 In the Effect Controls panel, select the box for Show Actual Sources to view frames from the actual clips.

This makes it easier to assess the changes you'll make.

4 In the Effect Controls panel, open the Alignment menu, and choose Start At Cut.

The transition in the Effect Controls panel timeline, and in the sequence, switches to show the new position.

5   Click the small Play The Transition button 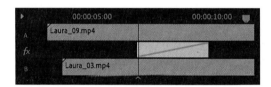 at the upper-left corner of the Effect Controls panel to preview the transition beneath the button.

6   Now change the transition duration. In the Effect Controls panel, click the blue numbers for the Duration, type **300**, and click away from the numbers or press the Tab key to apply the new setting. Premiere Pro will add the correct punctuation automatically, changing 300 into 00:00:03:00—that is, 3 seconds.

The Alignment menu changes to Custom Start because the effect now reaches beyond the beginning of the next transition effect. To make the new transition duration fit, Premiere Pro automatically sets its start two frames earlier.

● **Note:** If the Effect Controls panel timeline is not visible, click Show/Hide Timeline View ▶ at the upper-right corner of the panel. You may need to resize the panel to make the button visible.

Examine the A/B timeline display in the Effect Controls panel timeline, at the right side of the panel. There is a zoom navigator at the bottom of the Effect Controls panel timeline that works just like the one in the Monitors and Timeline panel. Zoom out by dragging one of the circles on the navigator to make it longer, so you can see the ends of the clips.

In this example, the Effect Controls panel playhead is centered on the cut, and you can see the way the effect timing has been adjusted automatically.

● **Note:** It's possible to shorten a transition to a duration of one frame. This can make it hard to grab and position the transition effect icon, so try using the Duration and Alignment controls. If you want to remove a transition, select it in the sequence in the Timeline panel and press Delete (macOS) or Backspace (Windows).

7   In the Timeline panel, play through the transition to see the change.

These automated adjustments can be subtle, so always double-check the results of new settings by playing through the effect. This way you can be sure you're happy with the newly revealed media taken from the clip handles—the media that was hidden from view until you added the transition effect. Although it's useful that Premiere Pro automatically modifies the timing of effects when necessary, it makes it even more important to check the transition before you move on.

Now let's customize the transition.

▶ **Tip:** You can position the start time of a dissolve asymmetrically by dragging it to a new position. This means you don't have to settle for the Centered, Start At Cut, and End At Cut options. You can drag the position of a transition effect directly on the Timeline too.

8   In the Effect Controls panel timeline, hover the pointer over the middle part of the vertical black line that crosses all three layers (the two video clips and the transition effect between them). The line is the edit point between the two clips. If your pointer is correctly positioned, it will change to the red Rolling Edit tool.

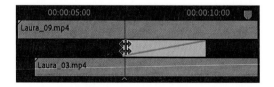

This edit line is close to the left edge of the effect, so you might want to zoom in to the Effect Controls panel timeline to conveniently make adjustments.

In the Effect Controls panel, the Rolling Edit tool lets you reposition the timing of an edit between two clips by dragging the edit line.

Tip: You may need to move the playhead out of the way—earlier or later—to see the edit point between two clips in the Effect Controls panel timeline.

9 Still in the Effect Controls panel, drag left and right with the Rolling Edit tool. As you do, you're changing the timing of the cut. The Out point of the clip on the left of the edit and the In point of the clip on the right of the edit update in the Timeline panel when you release the drag. This is a form of *trimming*.

You'll explore trimming in more detail in Lesson 8, "Editing Video—Advanced Techniques."

10 Move the pointer over the transition to the left or right of the edit line in the Effect Controls panel, and the pointer changes to the Slide tool. If there is a blue line, it's the time ruler playhead.

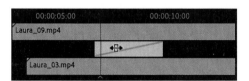

Using the Slide tool changes the start and end points of the transition without changing its overall duration. Unlike using the Rolling Edit tool, moving the transition rectangle by using the Slide tool does not change the edit point between the two sequence clips. Instead, it changes the timing of the transition effect.

11 Use the Slide tool to drag the transition rectangle left and right and compare the results.

Using a Morph Cut effect

Morph Cut is a special transition effect that aims to be invisible. It's designed to help with "talking head" video interviews, where a single speaker looks in the direction of the camera. If your subject pauses a lot or there is inappropriate content in the footage, you may want to remove a section of the interview.

This would normally produce a jump cut (when the image seems to jump suddenly from one piece of content to another), but with media that changes very little over time, and a little experimentation, the Morph Cut effect might yield an invisible transition that seamlessly hides what you have removed. Let's try it.

1 Open the sequence Morph Cut. Play the beginning of the sequence.

This sequence has one clip, with a jump cut near the start. It's a small jump cut but enough to jar the audience.

2   In the Effects panel, look in the Video Transitions > Dissolve group for the Morph Cut effect. Drag this effect to the join between the two clips.

The Morph Cut transition effect begins by analyzing the two clips. If the playhead is over the transition effect, you'll see a banner across the screen while the analysis takes place, but you can continue to work on your sequence without waiting.

Depending on your media, you may achieve improved results with the Morph Cut transition effect by experimenting with different durations.

3   Double-click the Morph Cut transition effect to display the Set Transition Duration dialog box. Change the duration to **16** frames (you can double-click any transition effect to access this setting).

4   When the analysis is complete, press Return/Enter to render the effect (if your system requires it) and play a preview.

The result is not perfect, but it's close, and it's unlikely an audience will notice the join.

Dealing with inadequate (or nonexistent) head or tail handles

If you try to extend a transition for a clip that doesn't have enough frames in the handle for the new duration of the effect, the transition still appears but has diagonal warning bars through it. This means Premiere Pro is using a freeze frame to extend the duration of the clip. The last available frame is held onscreen to complete the transition effect.

You can adjust the duration and position of the transition to resolve the issue.

1 Open the sequence called Handles.

2 Locate the edit between the two clips.

These two sequence clips have no heads or tails. You can tell this immediately because of the little triangles in the corners of the clips; a triangle indicates the first or last frame of the original clip.

3 Select the Ripple Edit tool  in the Tools panel, and use it to drag the right edge of the first clip to the left (begin dragging just to the left of the cut between the two clips). Drag to shorten the duration of the first clip to about 1:10, and then release. A tool tip appears while you trim to show the new clip duration.

The clip to the right of the edit point ripples (moves) left to close the gap. Notice that the little triangles at the end (the right edge) of the clip you just trimmed are no longer present.

4 Drag the Cross Dissolve transition effect from the Effects panel onto the edit point between the two clips.

You'll discover that you can drag the transition onto the right side of the edit but not the left. That's because there's no handle available at the beginning of the second clip to create a dissolve that overlaps the end of the first clip without using freeze frames.

5 Press the V key to select the Selection tool, or click to select the tool ◤ in the Tools panel. In the Timeline panel, click the Cross Dissolve transition once to select it. You may need to zoom in to make it easier to select the transition.

6 In the Effect Controls panel, set the duration of the effect to **1:12**.

The clip handle is not long enough to create this effect; the diagonal lines on the transition, both in the Effect Controls panel and in the Timeline panel, indicate Premiere Pro automatically added a freeze frame to fill the duration you set.

7 Play the transition to see the result.

8 In the Effect Controls panel, change the alignment of the transition to Center At Cut.

9 Drag the Timeline panel playhead slowly through the transition and watch the result.

- For the first half of the transition (up to the edit point), the B clip is a freeze frame, while the A clip continues to play.

- At the edit point, the A clip and the B clip start to play.

- After the edit, a short freeze frame is used.

There are several ways to fix this kind of issue.

- You can change the duration or timing of the transition effect.

● **Note:** The Rolling Edit tool lets you move the transition earlier or later but does not change the overall length of the sequence because it extends one clip while shortening another.

- You can drag the edit in the Timeline panel using the Rolling Edit tool ![rolling edit icon] (click and hold the Ripple Edit tool in the Tools panel to access it) to change the timing of the transition in the Timeline panel. Be sure to drag the edit between the clips and not the transition effect. This won't necessarily remove all the freeze frames, but it may improve the overall result.

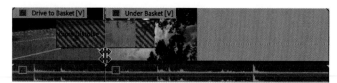

- You can drag one side of the edit in the Timeline panel using the Ripple Edit tool ![ripple edit icon] to shorten a clip, increasing the length of the handle. Again, be sure to click the edit between the clips and not the effect icon.

You'll learn more about the Rolling Edit and Ripple Edit tools in Lesson 8. For now, make sure you have the Selection tool selected.

Adding audio transition effects

Audio transitions can dramatically improve a sequence's soundtrack by removing unwanted audio pops or abrupt edits. Audiences are usually much more aware of inconsistency in the soundtrack than they are of the overall quality of the soundtrack, and crossfade transitions can have a big impact in smoothing variation between clips.

Creating a crossfade

There are three styles of crossfade.

- **Constant Gain:** The Constant Gain crossfade (as its name implies) transitions audio by using a constant audio gain (volume) adjustment between the clips. Although this transition can lead to a slight perceived dip in the audio level for the listener, some editors find it useful. It's most useful in situations where you do not want much blending between two clips but rather more of a dip out and in between the clips.

- **Constant Power:** This is the default audio transition. It creates a smooth, gradual transition between two audio clips. The Constant Power crossfade works in a similar way to a video dissolve. The outgoing clip fades out slowly at first and then faster toward the end of the clip. For the incoming clip, the opposite occurs—the audio level increases quickly at the start of the incoming clip and more slowly toward the end of the transition. This crossfade is useful in situations where you want to blend the audio between two clips, without a noticeable drop in level in the middle.

- **Exponential Fade:** The Exponential Fade transition creates a fade between clips. It uses a logarithmic curve to fade out and fade up audio. Some editors prefer the Exponential Fade transition when performing a single-sided transition (such as fading in a clip from silence at the start or end of a program).

Applying audio transitions

There are several ways to apply an audio crossfade to a sequence. You can, of course, drag an audio transition effect just as you would a video transition effect, but there are also useful shortcuts to speed up the process.

Audio transitions have a default duration, measured in seconds or frames. You can change the default duration by choosing Premiere Pro > Settings > Timeline (macOS) or Edit > Preferences > Timeline (Windows).

Let's take a look at the three methods for applying audio transitions.

1 Open the sequence called Audio and switch to the Selection tool.

The sequence has several clips with audio.

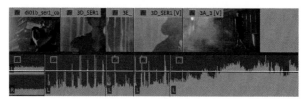

2 Play the sequence to review the contents.

3 Open the Audio Transitions > Crossfade group in the Effects panel.

4 Drag the Exponential Fade transition to the start of the first audio clip.

5 Right-click the right edge of the last clip in the sequence and choose Apply Default Transitions.

Note: To add only an audio transition, hold Option (macOS) or Alt (Windows) when right-clicking to select only the audio clip.

A default video transition and default audio transition are added to the end of the clip.

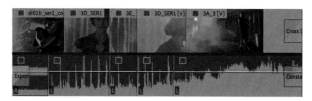

6 You can change the length of any transition by dragging its edge in the Timeline. Drag to extend the audio transition you just created, and then listen to the result.

To polish the project, next you'll add an opening Cross Dissolve transition effect to the video clip at the beginning of the sequence. Press Esc to deselect the transition effect you just adjusted.

▶ **Tip:** When using keyboard shortcuts to apply transition effects, Premiere Pro uses track targeting or clip selection to work out where exactly the effects should be applied.

7 Move the playhead near the beginning of the sequence, and press Command+D (macOS) or Ctrl+D (Windows) to add the default video transition.

You now have a fade from black at the beginning and a fade to black at the end. Now let's add a series of short audio dissolves to smooth out the sound mix.

8 Ordinarily, making a marquee selection in the Timeline panel would select clips, but you can override this by holding a modifier key and select edits instead.

Note: The selection of clips does not have to be contiguous in the Timeline panel. You can Shift-click clips to select individual clips in a sequence.

Using the Selection tool, while holding Command+Option (macOS) or Ctrl+Alt (Windows), drag a marquee selection over all of the audio edits between the clips on track Audio 1, being careful not to select any video clips—drag from below the audio clips to avoid accidentally selecting items on the video track.

Holding Command/Ctrl allows you to select edits rather than clips. Holding Option/Alt temporarily unlinks the audio clips from the video clips to isolate those edits while making a selection.

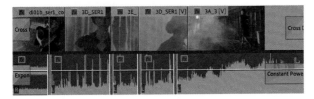

9 Press Shift+D to apply the default transition effect to all selected clips. You exclusively selected audio clips, so Premiere Pro knows to add only audio transition effects.

You could have pressed Shift+Command+D (macOS) or Shift+Ctrl+D (Windows), which is the shortcut to add an audio-only transition. This is useful if you have selected both video and audio clips and want to apply audio transition effects only.

Command+D (macOS) or Ctrl+D (Windows) applies the default video-only transition.

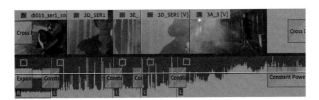

▶ **Tip:** You could choose Apply Audio Transition from the Sequence menu to add transitions exclusively to audio clips, but if you have already chosen audio-only clips, there's no need, as the default transition option will have the same effect.

10 Deselect the transitions by clicking an empty area of the Timeline panel or by pressing Escape. Play the sequence to see and hear the changes you have made.

11 Choose File > Close to close the current project. Click Yes to save the file if you are prompted.

It's common for audio editors to add one-frame or two-frame audio transitions to every cut in a sequence to avoid jarring pops when an audio clip begins or ends. If you set the default duration for audio transitions to two frames, you can select multiple clips and then choose Sequence > Apply Audio Transition to quickly smooth your audio mix.

● **Note:** If you'd like more transition effects, check the Adobe website. Visit *helpx.adobe.com/ premiere-pro/plug-ins.html*. There, you'll find several third-party effects to explore.

Review questions

1 How can you apply the default transition to multiple clips in a sequence?

2 In the Effects panel, how can you locate a transition effect by name?

3 How do you replace one transition with another?

4 What are three ways to change the duration of a transition?

5 What is an easy way to gradually increase the audio level at the beginning of a clip?

Review answers

1   Select the clips, and choose Sequence > Apply Default Transitions To Selection.

2   Start typing the transition name in the search box in the Effects panel. As you type, Premiere Pro displays all effects and transitions (audio and video) that have that letter combination anywhere in their names. Type more letters to narrow your search.

3   Drag the replacement transition on top of the transition you're rejecting. The new transition inherits the timing of the effect it replaces (but not other settings, like border colors).

4   Use the Selection tool to drag the edge of the transition icon in the Timeline, do the same thing in the A/B timeline display in the Effect Controls panel, or change the Duration value in the Effect Controls panel. You can also double-click the transition icon in the Timeline panel and change the Duration value in the dialog box that appears.

5   Apply an audio crossfade transition to the beginning of the clip.

8 EDITING VIDEO—ADVANCED TECHNIQUES

Lesson overview

In this lesson, you'll learn how to do the following:

- Perform a four-point edit.

- Change the speed or duration of clips in your sequence.

- Replace a clip in a sequence.

- Replace footage in a project.

- Use Text-Based Editing.

- Perform basic trimming on media to refine edits.

- Apply slip and slide edits to refine your edit.

- Trim clips dynamically.

This lesson will take about 120 minutes to complete. To get the lesson files used in this chapter, download them from the web page for this book at *peachpit.com/PremiereProCIB2024*. For more information, see "Accessing the lesson files and Web Edition" in the "Getting Started" section at the beginning of this book. Store the files on your computer in a convenient location.

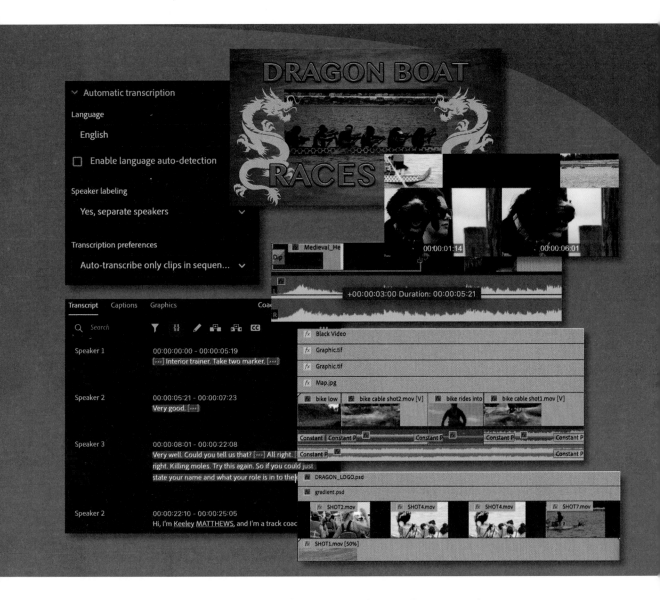

In Adobe Premiere Pro, the main editing commands are straightforward to learn. More advanced techniques take a little time to learn, but they're worth it! They'll accelerate your editing and provide the understanding you'll need to produce the highest-level professional results.

Starting the lesson

● **Note:** To ensure that the tools function and the defaults are set exactly as described in this lesson, reset the Premiere Pro preferences by holding Option (macOS) or Alt (Windows) while launching the application and then clicking Continue in the Reset Options dialog box.

In this lesson, you'll use several short sequences as you explore advanced editing concepts in Adobe Premiere Pro. The goal is to get hands-on with the techniques you'll need for advanced editing.

1   Open the project Lesson 08.prproj in the Lessons folder.

2   Save the project as **Lesson 08 Working.prproj** in the Lessons folder.

3   Click Editing in the Workspaces menu, or choose Window > Workspaces > Editing.

4   Reset the workspace to the saved version by clicking the Workspaces menu and choosing Reset To Saved Layout, or by choosing Window > Workspaces > Reset To Saved Layout.

Performing a four-point edit

In previous lessons, you used the standard technique of three-point editing. You used a combination of three In and Out points (split between the Source Monitor as well as the Program Monitor or Timeline panel) to set the source, duration, and location of an edit.

But what happens if you set four points?

The short answer is that you have to make a choice. It's likely that the duration you've marked in the Source Monitor differs from the duration you've marked in the Program Monitor or in the Timeline panel.

In this case, when you attempt to perform the edit using a keyboard shortcut or onscreen button, a dialog box warns you the durations don't match and asks you to make a decision about what to change. Most often, you'll discard one of the points.

Setting editing options for four-point edits

If you perform a four-point edit with mismatched selected durations in the clip and the sequence, the Fit Clip dialog box appears with options to resolve the issue. You can ignore one of the four points or automatically change the speed of the clip to fit the new duration in the sequence.

• **Change Clip Speed (Fit To Fill):** The first choice assumes that you set four points with different durations deliberately. Premiere Pro preserves the source clip's In and Out points but adjusts its playback speed to match the duration you set in the Timeline panel or in the Program Monitor. This is a good choice if you want to precisely adjust clip playback speed to fill a gap.

- **Ignore Source In Point:** The source clip's In point is ignored, converting your edit back to a three-point edit. When you have an Out point and no In point in the Source Monitor, Premiere Pro works out the In point automatically based on the duration set in the Timeline panel or Program Monitor (or the end of the clip). This option is available only if the source clip is longer than the duration set in the sequence.

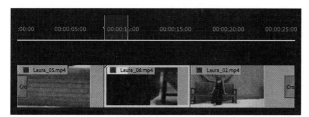

- **Ignore Source Out Point:** The source clip's Out point is ignored, converting your edit back to a three-point edit. When you have an In point and no Out point in the Source Monitor, Premiere Pro determines the Out point based on the duration set in the Timeline panel or Program Monitor (or the end of the clip). This option is available only if the source clip is longer than the targeted duration.

- **Ignore Sequence In Point:** The sequence In point is ignored, making this a three-point edit. The duration is taken from the clip In and Out points.

- **Ignore Sequence Out Point:** The sequence Out point is ignored, making this a three-point edit. The duration is taken from the clip In and Out points.

You can set a default option to apply automatically when performing a four-point edit by selecting an option and selecting Always Use This Choice in the Fit Clip dialog box. If you change your mind, open the Premiere Pro Preferences, select Timeline, and select Reset Fit Clip Dialog. The Fit Clip dialog box will then open when an edit duration mismatch occurs.

Making a four-point edit

Let's perform a four-point edit. You'll change the playback speed of a clip to fit a duration set in the sequence.

1 If it's not already open in the Timeline panel, open the sequence 01 Four Point. Play through the sequence to review the content.

2 Locate the section with In and Out points already set. You should see a high-lighted range in the Timeline panel.

3 Browse inside the bin called Clips To Load, and open the clip called Laura_04 in the Source Monitor.

In and Out points are already set on this clip.

4   Take a look at the selected duration at the lower-right corner of the Source Monitor—8 seconds and 4 frames of this clip have been selected. Next, take a look at the selected duration at the lower-right corner of the Program Monitor—only 2 seconds and 5 frames of this sequence have been selected.

This duration difference is important when performing a four-point edit because the way you decide to resolve the difference can have a huge impact on the result.

5   In the Timeline panel, check that the source track indicators are patched correctly, with Source V1 positioned next to Timeline Video 1. There's no audio in this source clip, so you just need to check the Source V1 (also, note the track targeting buttons have no effect on editing clips into a sequence).

6   In the Source Monitor, click the Overwrite button to perform the edit.

7   In the Fit Clip dialog box, select the Change Clip Speed (Fit To Fill) option, and click OK.

● **Note:** Changing the playback speed of a clip counts as a visual effect. Notice the small FX badge on the clip changes color to indicate an effect has been applied.

Premiere Pro applies the edit, replacing the selected part of the clip in the sequence with the selected part of the source clip and adjusting the clip playback speed to fit the new duration.

8   Zoom in to the Timeline panel using the Navigator controls at the bottom of the panel until you can see the name and speed information on the Laura_04 clip you just edited into the sequence.

The percentage between square brackets shows the new playback speed. The speed has been adjusted perfectly to fit the new duration.

9   Play the sequence to see the result of your edit and the speed change. The playback may not be super smooth, but you'll learn ways to improve the results when applying speed adjustments next.

Changing clip playback speed

Slow motion is one of the most commonly used effects in video post-production. It can be an effective way to add drama or to give the audience more time to experience a moment. You might change the speed of a clip for technical reasons or for artistic impact.

The fit-to-fill edit you just learned about is one way to change clip playback speed, and its results can vary. If the media originally had clear, smooth motion, you'll probably get better results. Also, fit-to-fill edits can result in partial frame rates, and this can produce inconsistent motion.

When changing the speed of a clip, you will usually achieve smoother playback if the new speed is an even multiple or a fraction of the original clip playback speed. For example, changing a 24-fps clip to play back at 25% speed will result in 6 fps, and this will usually look smoother than if the clip is set to an unequally divided playback speed, like 27.45%. Sometimes you'll get the best results by changing clip speed to an even-numbered frame rate and then trimming to get a precise duration.

You can achieve high-quality slow motion by recording at a higher frame rate than your sequence playback frame rate. If you play the video at a slower frame rate than it was recorded at, you'll see slow motion—provided the new frame rate is still at least as high as your sequence frame rate.

For example, imagine a 10-second video clip was recorded at 48 frames per second but your sequence is set to 24 frames per second. You can set your footage to play at 24 frames per second, matching the sequence. Playback will be smooth, with no frame rate conversion when the clip is added to the sequence. However, the clip will be playing at half its recording frame rate, resulting in 50% slow motion. It will take twice as long to play back, so the clip will now have a 20-second duration.

Overcranking

Recording video footage at a higher frame rate than you intend to play it back at is a technique called *overcranking* because early film cameras were driven by turning a crank handle.

The faster the handle was turned, the more frames per second were captured. Slower turning would capture fewer frames per second. When the film was played back at a regular speed, filmmakers would achieve slow motion or fast motion.

Modern cameras often allow recording at faster frame rates to provide excellent-quality slow motion in post-production. The camera assigns a playback frame rate to the clip metadata that might differ from the recorded rate (the camera's system frame rate is used for playback).

This means clips may play in slow motion automatically when you import them into Premiere Pro. Use the Interpret Footage dialog box to tell Premiere Pro how to play clips.

Let's try this.

1 Open the sequence 02 Laura In The Snow. Play the sequence.

   The clip plays in slow motion for two reasons:

   • The clip was recorded at 96 frames per second but…

   • The clip is set to 24-fps playback (this was set by the camera and stored in the metadata for the media file).

   The sequence is configured for 24-fps playback, so it matches the clip playback setting and no conforming is necessary.

2 In the Timeline panel, right-click the clip and choose Reveal In Project to high-light the clip in the Project panel.

3 Right-click the clip in the Project panel and choose Modify > Interpret Foot-age. You'll use the Interpret Footage tab in the Modify Clip dialog box to tell Premiere Pro how to play back this clip.

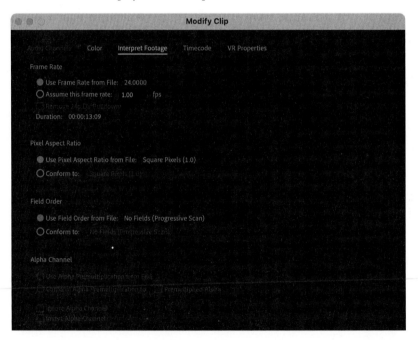

4 In the Frame Rate area, select Assume This Frame Rate and enter **96** in the fps box. This tells Premiere Pro to play the clip at 96 frames per second (the original recording speed). Click OK.

   Look back at the Timeline panel. The sequence clip has changed appearance.

You have given the clip a faster frame rate, and with the new playback speed it has a shorter duration. Rather than change the sequence clip segment duration, which might impact the timing of your edit, Premiere Pro displays diagonal lines to indicate the portion of the clip that now has no media (because the faster playback means the clip has finished playing earlier).

5   Play the sequence again.

The clip plays at regular speed because it was originally recorded at 96 fps. It's much less smooth—not because there's anything wrong with the clip but because the original camera recording was bumpy!

6   Drag a new instance of the Laura_01.mp4 clip from the Clips To Load bin to the beginning of the sequence, on the V2 track above the existing instance, so you can see both versions to compare them.

● **Note:** If you're using a system with slow storage, you may need to lower the playback resolution in the Program Monitor to play clips with fast frame rates without dropping frames.

The new clip instance is shorter, matching the playback time at the new frame rate. The faster frame rate clip was conformed to match the sequence frame rate, so only one frame in four is playing.

If you were to slow the sequence clip playback speed to 25% of its current playback speed, the missing frames would be restored, producing slow motion.

The duration of the clip that was already in the sequence hasn't changed (to ensure the overall timing of the sequence isn't impacted). However, the content of that original clip uses the new faster-playback interpretation setting, leaving an empty section of the clip segment.

Be sure to re-check your sequences after modifying clip interpretation settings.

Changing clip speed or duration in a sequence

Although it's more common to slow clips down, speeding up clips is a useful effect as well. The Speed/Duration command in the Timeline panel can change the playback speed for a clip in two ways. You can set a specific duration for a clip, or you can set clip playback speed as a percentage.

For example, if you set a clip to play at 50% speed, it will play at half speed; 25% would be one-quarter speed. Premiere Pro allows you to set playback speeds up to two decimal places, so you could have 27.13% if you wanted (though only whole frames will be displayed during playback).

Let's explore this technique.

1 Open the sequence 03 Speed/Duration. Play the sequence to get a sense of the normal playback speed. It's a 20-second drone shot of the Nevada desert.

2 Right-click the clip in the sequence and choose Speed/Duration. You can also select the clip in the sequence and choose Clip > Speed/Duration.

The Clip Speed/Duration dialog box gives you several options for controlling the clip playback speed.

- If you click the small chain icon , you can toggle on and off linking the sequence clip duration and clip contents playback speed. If the chain is broken , you can change the speed or duration settings without them updating each other. When settings are linked or unlinked in this way, they are described as *ganged* or *unganged*. The result is that more or less of the clip contents will be displayed during playback within the duration of the sequence clip segment.

- By default, if there are other clips in the sequence after this one, shortening the clip will leave a gap. If you make the clip longer than the space available before the next clip, the clip will be trimmed to keep the same duration at the new playback speed. That's because the clip can't move the next clip to make room for the new duration when you change these settings. However, if you select Ripple Edit, Shifting Trailing Clips, the clip will make space for itself, pushing other clips later in the sequence.

- To play a clip backward, select Reverse Speed.

- If a clip has audio, consider selecting Maintain Audio Pitch. This will keep the clip's original pitch at the new speed. With this option disabled, the pitch will naturally go up or down as the speed changes.

3 Make sure Speed and Duration are linked with the chain icon on. Change the speed to 200%, and click OK.

Note: If you set a duration that is longer than the available media, based on the playback speed percentage you set, you won't be able to click OK. The button will be dimmed.

Play the clip in the Timeline panel. Notice that the clip is now 10 seconds long. That's because it's playing at 200% speed: Double the playback speed means playing for half the original time.

4 Choose Edit > Undo, or press Command+Z (macOS) or Ctrl+Z (Windows).

5 Select the clip on the Timeline, and press Command+R (macOS) or Ctrl+R (Windows) to open the Clip Speed/Duration dialog box.

6 Click the chain icon to make sure the Speed and Duration settings are unlinked . Then, change Speed to 50%.

7 Click OK; then play the clip. The clip plays back at 50% speed, so it should play for twice as long. But because you turned off the link between playback speed and duration, the second half has been trimmed to maintain the 20-second duration in the sequence.

Notice the new playback speed is displayed on the sequence clip as a percentage.

Unganging the Speed and Duration options is useful when you want the visual effect of slow motion without changing the timing of your edits. For example, if you want to add a dreamlike quality to footage of waves crashing against a beach, you can reduce the speed just enough for the waves to seem dreamily slow without altering the timing of the next clip.

This kind of aesthetic change often demands trial and error to achieve the result you want—a great reason to learn keyboard shortcuts for quick access to the controls you need.

Now try reversing playback.

8 Select the clip, and open the Clip Speed/Duration dialog box again.

9 Leave Speed at 50%, but this time select Reverse Speed; then click OK.

10 Play the clip. Now it plays in reverse at 50% slow motion. You'll see a negative sign next to the new speed displayed in the sequence.

Changing sequence clip speed with the Rate Stretch tool

Sometimes you'll have the perfect clip for your sequence—but it's just a little too short or a little too long. This is where the Rate Stretch tool helps.

1 Open the sequence 04 Rate Stretch.

This sequence is synchronized to music. The clips contain the desired content, but the first video clip is too short. You'll need to fix the gap before the second clip begins.

You can make a guess and try to make an exact Speed/Duration adjustment, but it's easier and faster to use the Rate Stretch tool to drag the end of the clip to fill the available gap.

2 In the Tools panel, click and hold the Ripple Edit tool ◄|► to select the Rate Stretch tool ◄▪.

▶ **Tip:** If you change your mind about a change made with the Rate Stretch tool, you can always use it to stretch a clip back or use Undo. Alternatively, you can use the Clip Speed/Duration dialog box to enter a Speed value of 100% and restore the clip to its original speed.

3 With this tool, drag the right edge of the first video clip until it reaches the left edge of the second video clip.

The speed of the clip changes to fill the gap. The contents haven't changed (you haven't trimmed the clip); the clip is playing more slowly.

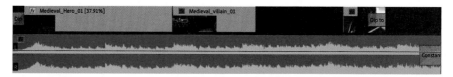

4 Using the same tool, drag the right edge of the second video clip to meet the left edge of the third clip.

5 Check that snapping 🔲 is enabled. Drag the right edge of the third clip until it snaps to the end of the audio.

The duration of the video now matches the music. You may need to zoom in to the Timeline panel to see the new playback speeds of the clips.

6 Play the sequence to view the result. Some of the faster action is noticeably jumpy. Let's fix that.

7 Press the shortcut key V, or click the Selection tool in the Tools panel to select it.

8 With the Timeline panel active, press Command+A (macOS) or Ctrl+A (Windows) to select all the clips.

9 Right-click any clip and choose Time Interpolation > Optical Flow. This smooths playback when changing clip speed. It's a more advanced method for producing playback speed changes, and the effect needs to be rendered before you preview the result.

10 Render by pressing Return (macOS) or Enter (Windows), and play the sequence to see the result.

A great improvement!

Optical Flow is usually worth choosing when adjusting clip playback speed. You can adjust and preview the timing of playback speed changes using the default Frame Sampling renderer. Then, when the timing is right, switch to Optical Flow and preview again.

Optical Flow is also available when choosing a new playback speed using the Clip Speed/Duration dialog box.

● **Note:** Using Optical Flow to render a new playback speed can produce visual artifacts, particularly with footage that has motion blur as a result of a slow camera shutter speed. For example, take a look just after 00:00:11:00 in the current sequence (you may want to scrub through the frames or use the arrow keys to move the playhead frame by frame to see the issues). Always check your results!

Edit timing and playback speed

If you change the speed of a clip that has other clips placed after it in a sequence, those other clips will be affected too. You might see:

- Gaps caused if clips grow shorter because they are playing faster.
- Sequence duration changes because of the Ripple Edit option in the Clip Speed/Duration dialog box.
- Potential audio issues created by changes in speed—including changing pitch.

When making speed or duration changes, check the overall impact on the sequence.

Replacing clips and media

It's common to swap one sequence clip for another as you try different versions of an edit.

This might mean making a global replacement, such as replacing one version of an animated logo with a newer file. You might also want to swap out one clip in a sequence, such as an actor's performance, for another that you have available in a bin. Depending on the task at hand, you'll use different approaches.

Dragging in a replacement clip

You can drag a new shot onto a sequence clip you'd like to replace. This is called a *replace edit*. Let's try it.

1   Open the 05 Replace Clip sequence.

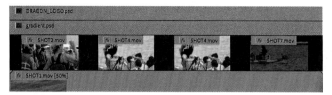

2   Play the sequence.

On the Video 2 track, the second and third clips are actually the same SHOT4 clip repeated. The clip has motion keyframes applied to make it spin onto the screen and spin off again. You'll learn how to create these kinds of animation effects in Lesson 9, "Putting Clips in Motion."

Let's replace the first instance of the clip SHOT4. This clip has the Black & White and Crop effects applied and has keyframes animating the Scale and Rotation settings for the Motion effect. You may not want to re-create these effects, as they are already set perfectly. This is an ideal scenario for replacing a sequence clip.

3   From the Clips To Load bin, drag the Boat Replacement clip straight from the Project panel over the first instance of the SHOT4 clip in the sequence, but don't release it yet. You don't need to position the pointer precisely; just make sure it's over the clip you want to replace.

Even though the new clip already has In and Out points, it's much longer than the existing clip that you intend to replace.

4   Press and hold the Option (macOS) or Alt (Windows) key. While you're holding this modifier key, the replacement clip snaps to fit the length of the clip it's replacing.

Release the clip while still holding the modifier key to replace the existing clip.

Premiere Pro synchronizes the first frame (or In point) of the replacement clip with the first visible frame of the existing clip in the sequence. Just enough of the new clip is used to replace the existing clip in the sequence.

5   Play the sequence. All the picture-in-picture clips have the same effect applied. The new clip inherits the settings and effects from the clip it replaced. This is a quick and easy way to try different shots in a sequence.

Performing a synchronized replace edit

What if you need to synchronize a particular moment in the middle of a clip, such as a hand clap or a door closing?

For this, you can use a more advanced type of replace edit to synchronize a particular frame of the replacement clip with a particular frame of the clip it's replacing.

1   Open the sequence 06 Replace Edit.

This is the same sequence you previously fixed, but this time you'll position the replacement clip precisely.

2   Position the playhead in the sequence at approximately 00:00:06:00. The playhead will be the sync point for the edit you are about to perform.

3   Click the first instance of the SHOT4 clip in the sequence to select it.

4   From the Sources bin, open the clip SHOT5.mov in the Source Monitor.

5   In the Source Monitor, position the playhead about halfway through the clip. There's a marker on the clip for guidance. You can click the marker to line up the playhead with it.

> **Tip:** Because clip markers are displayed in the Timeline panel, they are a useful way to check you have lined up frames as you intended.

6   Make sure the Timeline panel is active, with the first instance of SHOT4.mov selected, and choose Clip > Replace With Clip > From Source Monitor, Match Frame. SHOT5 replaces the SHOT4 clip!

7   Play the newly edited sequence to check the edit.

The playhead position in the Source Monitor and Program Monitor was synchronized. The sequence clip duration, effects, and settings are all applied to the replacement clip. This technique can be a huge time-saver when you need to match the precise timing of action and effects that are applied to the existing sequence clip.

Using the Replace Footage feature

While a replace edit replaces the contents of a clip segment in a sequence, the Replace Footage command replaces footage in the Project panel so that the clip links to a different media file. This can be of great benefit when you need to replace a clip that occurs several times in a sequence or in multiple sequences. You might use this to update an animated logo or a piece of music, for example.

When you replace footage in the Project panel, all instances of the clip you replace are changed anywhere the clip is used.

1   Load the sequence 07 Replace Footage.

Let's replace the graphic on the Video 4 track with something more interesting.

2   In the Clips To Load bin, right-click DRAGON_LOGO.psd and choose Replace Footage.

3   Navigate to the Lessons/Assets/Graphics folder, and open the DRAGON_LOGO_FIX.psd file.

4 Play the sequence.

● **Note:** The Replace Footage command cannot be undone. To switch back to the original clip, choose Clip > Replace Footage again to navigate to and relink the original file, or choose File > Revert to restore the current project to the last saved version (you'll lose changes made since you last saved).

The clip name has been updated to match the new file, both in the bin and in the sequence.

Using Text-Based Editing

Premiere Pro can transcribe spoken word content to make it easier to navigate your footage and to produce captions and titles. You can even edit video using text-based tools.

So far, you have added clips to sequences using insert and overwrite edits. You've also moved clips within sequences and removed clips. Text-Based Editing allows you to perform these standard editing tasks for your sequences based on text alone. This process can be extraordinarily fast compared to watching content like interviews in real time to make selections and edits.

You can choose to have clips transcribed automatically when they are imported or manually using the Text panel. Let's try both.

Removing content using Text-Based Editing

Removing content with Text-Based Editing is as straightforward as editing a document in a word processing application.

1 Switch to Import mode.

2 Navigate to Lessons/Assets/Video and Audio Files/Interview and select only one clip, Coach_Interview_DCAM.

3 Under the Import settings turn on the option to create a new bin, and name the bin **Interview**.

4 Turn on Automatic Transcription. Leave the Language menu set to English; set Speaker Labeling to Yes, Separate Speakers; and set Transcription Preferences to Auto-Transcribe Only Clips In Sequence.

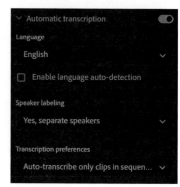

Click Import. Premiere Pro switches back to Edit mode, and in the upper-right corner, a progress indicator ⊙ shows that the transcription analysis is taking place.

If you click the progress indicator, Premiere Pro will display a list of recent processing tasks as well as the status of the current analysis.

You can access this list at any time by clicking the Open Progress Dashboard button ▤.

5 Open the new Interview bin, right-click the Coach_Interview_DCAM.mp4 clip, and choose New Sequence From Clip. This creates a new sequence with settings that match the format of the clip.

6 From the Workspaces menu, choose Text-Based Editing. Then from the same menu again, choose Reset To Saved Layout.

The Text-Based Editing workspace includes the Text panel, moves the Project panel to the upper-right corner, and combines the Source Monitor and Program Monitor in one frame.

The Text panel should already be displaying the transcription for the interview clip. If not, click to make the Timeline panel or Program Monitor active and make sure the Transcript tab is selected in the Text panel.

The Text panel allows you to click a word to move the playhead to that part of your content, to search for words (and replace words), and to perform edits.

As you are currently viewing the contents of a sequence, the editing buttons at the top of the Text panel are for lift and extract edits. If you were viewing the contents of a clip, the buttons would be for insert and overwrite edits. These buttons are similar to those found on the Source Monitor and Program Monitor.

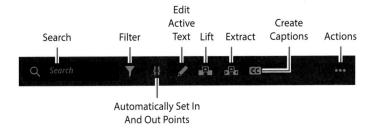

Removing content from a sequence using Text-Based Editing is straightforward.
Select the text you want to remove and press Delete (macOS) or Backspace
(Windows).

7 Make sure the option to Automatically Set In/Out Points ⬚ is turned on at the
top of the Text panel. With this option on, every time you select text, In and Out
points are added to the sequence, making it easy to see the part of the sequence
you have selected.

Select all of the text from the beginning up to and including the phrase *what
your role is in to the camera* (the first three pieces of text). Press Delete/
Backspace.

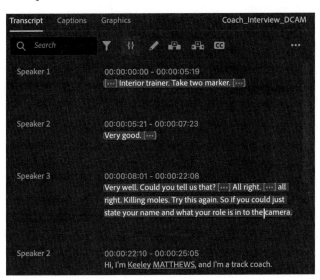

Premiere Pro removes the first part of the interview clip from the sequence.

8 The transcription shows our subject as Speaker 2, while the interviewer is shown
as Speaker 3. In the Text panel, drag or shift-click to select and delete all of the
Speaker 3, Unknown, and Speaker 5 text items (all items that aren't Speaker 2) to
remove them from the sequence.

In just a few moments, you will have removed all the content that is not the subject speaking.

9 There are quite a few pauses in this interview, and you can remove them all in a single step. In the Text panel, click the three dots in the upper-right corner and choose Transcript View Options. To remove all but the shortest pauses, drag the slider to set the Minimum Pause Length to 0.5 seconds, and click Save.

10 Click the Filter button  and choose Pauses. All the pauses that are over 0.5 seconds are highlighted, and a Delete button appears. Click Delete.

11 Additional options appear. You have the option to perform an extract or lift, and you can choose to delete all the pauses in one step or delete them one by one.

Keep Extract, the default option, selected. Click Delete All.

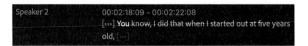

12 You can also remove individual words or sentences. Type the word **football** in the search box to highlight that word in the transcript. Within that section of text, select and delete the words *I played football as well. But track was my mainstay.*

You have now removed all other speakers from this interview, removed all pauses, and removed selected sentences—all by selecting and deleting text. Now let's add some content using Text-Based Editing.

Adding content using Text-Based Editing

To add content to this sequence, you'll import a new clip and open it in the Source Monitor.

1 In the Text panel, click the word *You* that is just after the section you removed. This will move the sequence playhead to the beginning of the word.

Speaker 2
00:02:18:09 – 00:02:22:08
[···] You know, I did that when I started out at five years old, [···]

2   In the Project panel, click the Interview bin to select it. When you import a new clip, it will automatically be added to the selected bin.

3   Switch to Import mode, and select the clip Coach_Interview_ECAM. This is an alternative angle for the same interview.

4   Turn off all the Import settings, including Automatic Transcription, and then click Import.

    Premiere Pro imports the new clip and adds it to the Interview bin.

5   Double-click the clip Coach_Interview_ECAM in the Interview bin to open it in the Source Monitor. In the Text panel, click the blue Transcribe button. In the Create Transcription For Source Media dialog, make sure the Language is set to English and Speaker Labeling is set to Yes, Separate Speakers. Click Transcribe.

6   In the Text panel, select the text *I played football as well. But track was my mainstay.*

    Click the Insert button at the top of the panel, or press the , (comma) key.

    The clip is added to the sequence at the location of the playhead.

7   Play the sequence to review the edits you made. There are lots of jump cuts, where the content switches from one moment to the next without changing camera angle. The timing of the edits is pretty good, though, and with some more visuals and graphics, this might work well as a social media post.

You can switch between Text-Based Editing and the other editing tools at any time. This powerful and extremely fast editing workflow is ideal for interviews, podcasts, presentations to camera—any kind of content that has a lot of speech.

Transcripts can be exported and imported, speakers can be named, and captions can be generated automatically. For more information about Text-Based Editing, see the Adobe Premiere Pro help.

Experiment with adding and removing content using Text-Based Editing. When you have finished practicing, use the Workspaces menu to return to the Editing workspace.

Performing regular trimming

You can adjust the part of a clip that is used in a sequence in several ways. This process is generally called *trimming*. When you trim, you can make the selected part of the original clip shorter or longer in the sequence by restoring or removing content.

Some trimming methods affect just one clip, while others can adjust the relationship between two adjacent clips, or even multiple clips.

Trimming in the Source Monitor

A clip edited into a sequence is a separate instance from the original clip in the Project panel. You can view a sequence clip in the Source Monitor by double-clicking it in the Timeline panel. Once the clip is open in the Source Monitor, you can adjust its In and Out points. The clip will update in the sequence.

By default, when you open a sequence clip segment in the Source Monitor, the Source Monitor navigator will automatically zoom in to the existing selection.

You can use the navigator to explore all of the available content in the clip.

There are two basic ways to change existing In and Out points in the Source Monitor.

- **Add new In and Out points:** In the Source Monitor, set new In or Out points, replacing the current selection. If the clip has another clip adjacent to it in the sequence, before or after the current clip, you cannot extend the In or Out point in that direction.

- **Drag In and Out points:** Position your pointer over an In or Out point in the mini timeline at the bottom of the Source Monitor. The pointer changes into a red-and-black pointer with two-way arrows, indicating that a trim can be performed. Now you can drag left or right to change the In or Out point.

  Once again, if the clip has another clip adjacent to it in the sequence, you cannot extend the current clip in that direction.

Trimming in a sequence

Another, faster way to trim clips is directly in the Timeline panel. Making a single clip shorter or longer is called a *regular* trim, and it's fairly straightforward.

1   Open the sequence 10 Regular Trim.

2   Play the sequence to review the contents.

    Too little of the last shot was added to the sequence, and it needs to be extended
    to match the end of the music.

3   Make sure you have the Selection tool ▶ selected.

4   Position the pointer over the right edge of the last video clip in the sequence.

    The pointer changes into the red Trim Out pointer with a directional arrow.

▶ **Tip:** The keyboard
shortcut for the Selec-
tion tool is V.

Precisely hovering the pointer over the end of a clip, you can change between
trimming the Out point (end of a clip, to the left) and trimming the In point of
the next clip (beginning of a clip, to the right). In this case, there's no next clip,
of course.

This clip has a transition effect applied to the end. You may need to zoom in to
make it easier to trim the clip and not adjust the transition effect.

5   Drag the edge to the right until it meets the end of the audio file. A tool tip
    shows you how much you've trimmed.

Note: Making a clip
shorter will leave a gap
between it and any
adjacent clips. Later in
this lesson you'll learn
to use the Ripple Edit
tool to automatically
remove gaps or push
clips later in a sequence
when you trim a clip
(just like insert and
extract edits).

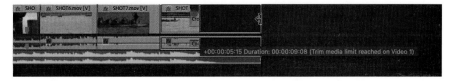

In this instance, the tool tip also shows that the trim has reached the end of the
original media.

6   Release the drag to apply the trim.

Performing advanced trimming

The trimming methods you've learned so far have their limitations. They leave gaps
in the sequence caused by shortening a clip or prevent you from lengthening a shot
if there's an adjacent clip.

Fortunately, Premiere Pro offers several more ways to trim. Let's check out ripple
edits.

Performing ripple edits

▶ **Tip:** The keyboard shortcut for the Ripple Edit tool is B.

● **Note:** When performing a ripple edit, you might shift items on other tracks out of sync. By default, sync locks keep items on all tracks in sync.

You can avoid introducing gaps when trimming by using the Ripple Edit tool 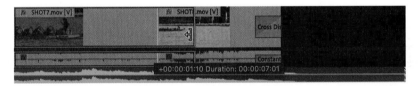 rather than the Selection tool.

You can use the Ripple Edit tool to trim a clip in the same way that you use the Selection tool. When you use the Ripple Edit tool to change the duration of a clip, the adjustment ripples through the sequence. That is, clips after the clip you have trimmed slide to the left to fill the gap, or they slide to the right to make room if the clip gets longer.

Let's try it.

1   Open the sequence 11 Ripple Edit.

2   The Ripple Edit tool is usually available in the Tools panel. Because you recently used the Rate Stretch tool , the Ripple Edit tool will be hidden. Click and hold the Rate Stretch tool to reveal and select the Ripple Edit tool.

3   Hover the Ripple Edit tool over the inside-right edge of the seventh clip (SHOT7) until it turns into a yellow, left-facing bracket and arrow.

The shot is too short, so let's add some more footage from the clip handle.

4   Drag to the right until the timecode in the tool tip reads +00:00:01:10.

▶ **Tip:** To use the Selection tool as a temporary Ripple Edit tool, hold Command (macOS) or Ctrl (Windows). Be sure to click to one side of the edit to avoid performing a rolling edit (described next).

Notice that while you're using the Ripple Edit tool, the Program Monitor displays the last frame of the clip on the left side of the edit and the first frame of the clip on the right side. The image updates dynamically while you trim.

5   Release the drag to complete the edit.

The clip you have trimmed now has a longer duration, so the clip to its right slides right (later in the sequence) to make space for it. Play that part of the sequence to see whether the timing of the edit works.

6 Make another trimming adjustment—add another +2:00 seconds to the end of the SHOT7 clip. Play through the newly trimmed edit between SHOT7 and SHOT8.

This time, trimming has exposed a slight on-camera shake that you'll work on next.

Making ripple edits with keyboard shortcuts

Though the Ripple Edit tool gives fine control when trimming, there are two useful keyboard shortcuts that apply the same type of trim adjustment, based on the location of the Timeline panel playhead.

For these shortcuts to work, the correct timeline tracks must be targeted. Whichever tracks are targeted will be trimmed.

Position the Timeline panel playhead over a clip (or multiple layers of clips), and press one of the following shortcuts:

- **Q:** Ripple trims clips from their current start to the playhead position.
- **W:** Ripple trims clips from their current end to the playhead position.

This can be a fast way to trim clips, particularly in the early stages of editing, when you may simply want to "top and tail" (remove unwanted content at the start or end) your clips.

Performing rolling edits

Trimming with the Ripple Edit tool changes the overall length of the sequence. This is because one clip gets shorter or longer, and the rest of the sequence moves to close the gap (or moves out of the way).

There's another way to change the timing of an edit: a rolling edit, sometimes referred to as a *double-roller* or *dual-roller* trim.

When you perform a rolling edit, the overall length of the sequence does not change. Instead, a rolling edit shortens one clip and lengthens another at the same time, adjusting the clips by the same number of frames.

For example, if you use the Rolling Edit tool to extend a clip by two seconds, you will also shorten the adjacent clip by two seconds.

1 Continue working with the sequence 11 Ripple Edit.

2 In the Tools panel, press and hold the Ripple Edit tool ◄▮► to select the Rolling Edit tool ✛.

> **Tip:** The keyboard shortcut for the Rolling Edit tool is N.

> **Tip:** You can use the Selection tool while holding the Command (macOS) or Ctrl (Windows) key as a shortcut for either the Ripple Edit tool or the Rolling Edit tool. Position the pointer just before or just after the edit to perform a ripple trim. If you place the pointer exactly on the edit, you perform a rolling trim.

> **Note:** When trimming, it's possible to trim a clip to a 0 (zero) duration (removing it from the timeline altogether).

3 Use the Rolling Edit tool to drag the edit point between SHOT7 and SHOT8 (the last two clips on the timeline). Use the Program Monitor split-screen display to find a better-matching edit between the two shots, dragging the edit left to remove the camera shake.

You may need to zoom in to the Timeline panel to make more accurate adjustments.

Try rolling the edit to the left 1 second and 19 frames (−1:19). You can use the Program Monitor timecode as a reference or the tool tip that appears in the Timeline panel. If you pre-position the playhead, the edit will snap to it as you drag (if snapping is enabled).

Performing slip edits

A *slip trim* changes both the In point and Out point of a single sequence clip segment at the same time, by the same amount, "rolling" the visible contents in position.

Because a slip trim changes the beginning and end by equal amounts, it doesn't change the duration of your sequence. In this way, it's similar to a rolling trim.

▶ Tip: The keyboard shortcut for the Slip tool is Y.

Slip trims change only the clip you select; adjacent clips before or after the clip you adjust are not affected. Using the Slip tool to adjust a clip is a little like moving a conveyor belt: The visible part of the original clip changes inside the timeline clip segment without changing the length of the clip or the sequence.

1 Continue working with the sequence 11 Ripple Edit.

2 Select the Slip tool [↔].

3 Drag SHOT5 left and right to adjust both the In point and Out point for the clip.

4 Take a look at the Program Monitor while you perform the slip edit.

SHOT4 Out point (unchanged)   SHOT6 In point (unchanged)

SHOT5 In point (changed)   SHOT5 Out point (changed)

The two top images in the Program Monitor are the Out point of SHOT4 and the In point of SHOT6, before and after the clip you are adjusting. They don't change. The two larger images are the In point and Out point of SHOT5, the clip you are adjusting. These edit points *do* change.

The Slip tool is well worth taking time to get to grips with. It's usually the case that the timing for action at the beginning or the end of a clip is critical but not both, and so this is sometimes the fastest tool for adjusting timing when cutting action.

Making slide edits

The Slide tool works by leaving the duration of the clip you're sliding unchanged. Instead, the Out point of the previous clip and the In point of the following clip are changed by equal amounts, in opposite directions. It's another form of dual-roller trim. In a sense, it's the opposite of a slip trim.

Because you're changing the previous and next clip durations by an equal number of frames, the length of the sequence doesn't change.

▶ **Tip:** The keyboard shortcut for the Slide tool is U.

1   Continue working with the sequence 11 Ripple Edit.

2   Click and hold the Slip tool [⊩⊣] in the Tools panel to select the Slide tool [⊕].

3   Position the Slide tool over the middle of the second clip in the sequence, SHOT2.

4   Drag the clip left or right.

5   Take a look at the Program Monitor as you perform the slide edit.

SHOT2 In point (unchanged) — SHOT2 Out point (unchanged)

SHOT1 Out point (changed) — SHOT3 In point (changed)

00:00:07:06   00:00:09:00

The two top images are the In point and Out point of SHOT2, the clip you are dragging. They do not change because you are not changing the selected part of SHOT2.

The two larger images are the Out point and In point of the previous and next clips. These edit points change as you slide the selected clip over those adjacent clips.

Trimming in the Program Monitor

If you'd like to trim with even more control, you can use the Program Monitor Trim mode. In this mode, Premiere Pro displays both the outgoing and incoming frames of the trim you're working on and offers dedicated buttons for making precise adjustments.

When the Program Monitor is set to Trim mode, pressing the spacebar to play the sequence loops playback around the edit you have selected. This means you can continually adjust the timing of an edit and view the result immediately.

You can perform three types of trims using the Program Monitor Trim mode controls. You learned about each of these earlier in this lesson.

- **Regular trim:** This trim moves one edit point of the selected clip. This method trims only one side of the edit point. It moves the selected edit point either earlier or later in the sequence, but it doesn't shift any of the other clips.

- **Ripple trim:** Like the Regular trim, this trim moves one edit point of the selected clip either earlier or later. This method trims only one side of the edit point. Clips after the edit shift to close a gap or make room if trimming extends the clip.

- **Roll trim:** The roll trim moves the tail of one clip (the end) and the head of the adjacent clip (the beginning) in one step. It lets you adjust the timing of an edit point (provided there are handles). No gap is created, and the sequence duration doesn't change.

Accessing Trim mode in the Program Monitor

When the Program Monitor is in Trim mode, the controls change to make it easier to focus on trimming. To use Trim mode, you need to activate it by selecting an edit point between two clips. There are three ways to do this.

- Double-click an edit point (the left or right end of a clip) on the timeline with a selection tool or a trimming tool.

- With the correct Timeline panel track targeted (with a blue highlight), press Shift+T. The playhead will move to the nearest edit point.

- Drag around one or more edits using the Ripple Edit tool or Rolling Edit tool to select them.

   ▶ **Tip:** You also can select edits and enter Trim mode by dragging a rectangle around them using the Selection tool if you hold Command (macOS) or Ctrl (Windows).

When invoked, the Program Monitor Trim mode shows two video clips. The box on the left shows the outgoing clip (also called *A side*). The box on the right shows the incoming clip (also called *B side*). Below the frames are five additional buttons and two indicators.

A **Out Shift Counter:** This shows how many frames the Out point for the A side has changed.

B **Trim Backward Many:** This performs the selected type of trim, adjusting the A side earlier by five frames.

C **Trim Backward:** This performs the selected type trim, adjusting by one frame earlier.

D **Apply Default Transitions To Selection:** This applies the default transition effect to the selected edit point.

E **Trim Forward:** This performs the selected type of trim, adjusting the edit one frame later.

F **Trim Forward Many:** This is like the Trim Backward Many button except it adjusts the edit five frames later.

G **In Shift Counter:** This shows how many frames the In point for the B side has changed.

> **Tip:** By default, the Trim Backward Many and Trim Forward Many buttons will trim five frames. You can change this setting in Premiere Pro preferences > Trim > Large Trim Offset.

Choosing a trimming method in the Program Monitor

You've already learned about the three types of trims you can perform (regular, roll, and ripple). Using Trim mode in the Program Monitor makes the process easier because it provides rich visual feedback. It also provides subtle control when dragging, regardless of the Timeline panel view scale: Even if the Timeline panel is zoomed a long way out, you'll be able to make frame-accurate trim adjustments by dragging inside the Program Monitor while in Trim mode. Let's try this:

1 Open the sequence 12 Trim View. Play the sequence to familiarize yourself with the timing of the edits.

2 With the Selection tool (keyboard shortcut V), hold down Option (macOS) or Alt (Windows) and double-click the video edit between the first video clip and the second video clip in the sequence. Holding this modifier key overrides Linked Selection, selects just the video edit, and leaves the audio tracks untouched.

3 In the Program Monitor, hover the pointer over the A and B (left and right) clip images (but don't click).

As you move the pointer from left to right, you'll see the tool change from Trim Out (left side) to Roll (center) to Trim In (right).

4 Now drag in between both clips in the Program Monitor to perform a rolling edit trim.

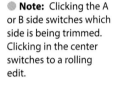 **Note:** Clicking the A or B side switches which side is being trimmed. Clicking in the center switches to a rolling edit.

Adjust the timing until the A-side source clip timecode overlay on the lower-left side of the Program Monitor frame reads 01:54:08:13 and the overlay on the B-side clip image reads 01:26:59:01.

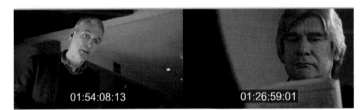

5 Press the Down Arrow key three times to jump between edits until you have selected the edit between the third and fourth clips (the cut in the audio track counts as one jump because that track also has targeting turned on).

The shot before the edit plays too long and shows the actor beginning to sit down, which is repeated in the next shot.

When you drag in the Program Monitor to trim, the color of the tool indicates the type of trim you'll perform. Red indicates a regular trim, and yellow indicates a ripple trim.

You can quickly change the trim type by holding Command (macOS) or Ctrl (Windows) and clicking one of the images in the Program Monitor. After clicking, you may need to move the pointer in order for the color of the tool to update.

6 Command-click (macOS) or Ctrl-click (Windows) one of the images in the Program Monitor until the Trim tool pointer turns yellow. This indicates that you've selected the Ripple Trim tool.

7 Drag to the left on the outgoing clip (on the left side of the Program Monitor) to make the clip shorter.

Make sure the time display on the left reads 01:54:12:18, and stay in Trim Mode, in the Program Monitor.

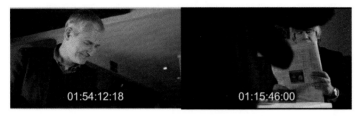

8 Play the edit by pressing the spacebar. While the Program Monitor is in Trim mode, playback loops over the edit to allow you to review it.

Modifier keys

You can use modifier keys to make precise selections before trimming.

- Hold Option (macOS) or Alt (Windows) when selecting clips to temporarily ignore Linked Selection between audio and video clip segments in a sequence. (You can also disable Linked Selection by clicking the button in the Timeline panel 🔳.)

- Hold Shift to select multiple edit points. You can trim multiple tracks or even multiple clips at the same time. Wherever you see a trim "handle," adjustments will be made when you apply a trim.

- You can combine these two modifier keys to make advanced clip selections for trimming.

Performing dynamic trimming

Much of the trimming work you perform will be to adjust the pace and rhythm of an edit. In many ways, perfecting the timing of a cut is the point at which the craft of editing becomes the art.

Because playback using the spacebar will loop in Trim mode, it's easier to get a feel for the timing of an edit. You can also trim using keyboard shortcuts or buttons while the sequence plays back in real time.

1 Continue working with the sequence 12 Trim View.

2 Press the Down Arrow key to move to the next video edit point, between the fourth and fifth video clips. Set the trim type to a rolling trim by clicking in the middle of the Program Monitor between the two frames.

The trim handles in the Timeline panel change to indicate a rolling edit.

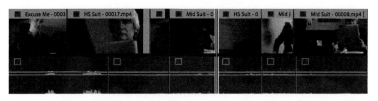

3 Press the spacebar to loop playback.

Note: To adjust the pre-roll and post-roll durations, open the Premiere Pro Preferences and select the Playback category. You can set the duration in seconds.

You'll see a playback loop lasting a few seconds, showing the shot before the cut (*pre-roll*) and after the cut (*post-roll*). This should help you get a feel for the timing of the edit.

4 Try adjusting the trim using the methods you've learned while the playback continues to loop.

The Trim Forward and Trim Backward buttons at the bottom of Trim mode view work well and can adjust the edit while the clip plays back.

5 Click Stop or press the spacebar to stop the playback loop. Now let's try using the keyboard for more dynamic control. The same J, K, and L keys you use to control playback can also be used to control trimming, as long as the Program Monitor is in Trim mode.

6 Press the L key to shuttle the trim to the right.

Pressing once trims in real time. You can tap the L key multiple times to trim faster.

If you are in Regular Trim mode and trimming a clip extends to the next clip, the trim will be blocked. If you are in Ripple Trim mode, clips will move to accommodate the new clip duration.

These clips are quite short, so you'll reach the end quickly. Let's refine and trim with a little more precision.

Note: Timeline panel clip segments update after you press K to stop dynamic trimming.

7 Press the K key to stop trimming.

8 Hold down the K key and press the J key to shuttle left in slow motion.

9 Release both keys to stop the trim.

10 Exit Trim mode by clicking an empty track in the Timeline panel.

Trimming with the keyboard

Here are some of the most useful keyboard shortcuts to use when trimming. If you have a color-coded keyboard, it's easier to remember which key is which.

MACOS	WINDOWS
Trim Backward: Option+Left Arrow	**Trim Backward:** Ctrl+Left Arrow
Trim Backward Many: Option+Shift+Left Arrow	**Trim Backward Many:** Ctrl+Shift+Left Arrow
Trim Forward: Option+Right Arrow	**Trim Forward:** Ctrl+Right Arrow
Trim Forward Many: Option+Shift+Right Arrow	**Trim Forward Many:** Ctrl+Shift+Right Arrow
Slide Clip Selection Left Five Frames: Option+Shift+, (comma)	**Slide Clip Selection Left Five Frames:** Alt+Shift+, (comma)
Slide Clip Selection Left One Frame: Option+, (comma)	**Slide Clip Selection Left One Frame:** Alt+, (comma)
Slide Clip Selection Right Five Frames: Option+Shift+. (period)	**Slide Clip Selection Right Five Frames:** Alt+Shift+. (period)
Slide Clip Selection Right One Frame: Option+. (period)	**Slide Clip Selection Right One Frame:** Alt+. (period)
Slip Clip Selection Left Five Frames: Command+Option+Shift+Left Arrow	**Slip Clip Selection Left Five Frames:** Ctrl+Alt+Shift+Left Arrow
Slip Clip Selection Left One Frame: Command+Option+Left Arrow	**Slip Clip Selection Left One Frame:** Ctrl+Alt+Left Arrow
Slip Clip Selection Right Five Frames: Command+Option+Shift+Right Arrow	**Slip Clip Selection Right Five Frames:** Ctrl+Alt+Shift+Right Arrow
Slip Clip Selection Right One Frame: Command+Option+Right Arrow	**Slip Clip Selection Right One Frame:** Ctrl+Alt+Right Arrow

Review questions

1 If you change the playback speed of a clip to 50% using the Clip Speed/Duration dialog box, what effect will this have on the clip duration?

2 Which tool allows you to stretch a sequence clip to change its playback speed?

3 What's the difference between a slide edit and a slip edit?

4 What is the difference between replacing a sequence clip and replacing footage?

Review answers

1 The clip will be twice as long. Reducing a clip's speed results in the clip playing for longer, unless the Speed and Duration parameters are unlinked in the Clip Speed/Duration dialog box or the clip is blocked by another clip.

2 The Rate Stretch tool allows you to adjust playback speed as if you were trimming. This is useful when you need to fill a small extra amount of time in a sequence or shorten a clip just a little.

3 You slide a clip over adjacent clips, retaining the selected clip's original In and Out points. You slip a clip under adjacent clips (or roll the contents like a conveyor belt), changing the selected clip's In and Out points.

4 Replacing a sequence clip replaces that single instance of the clip in the sequence with a new clip from the Project panel. Replacing footage replaces a clip in the Project panel with a new source clip. Any instance of the clip in any sequence in the project is replaced. In both cases, effects that were applied to the clip that is replaced are maintained.

9 PUTTING CLIPS IN MOTION

Lesson overview

In this lesson, you'll learn how to do the following:

- Adjust the Motion effect for clips.

- Change clip size and add rotation.

- Adjust the anchor point to refine rotation.

- Work with keyframe interpolation.

- Automatically reframe content for square video.

 This lesson will take about 75 minutes to complete. To get the lesson files used in this chapter, download them from the web page for this book at *peachpit.com/PremiereProCIB2024*. For more information, see "Accessing the lesson files and Web Edition" in the "Getting Started" section at the beginning of this book. Store the files on your computer in a convenient location.

The Motion effect controls can add movement to a clip. You can animate a graphic or resize and reposition a video clip within the frame. You can animate an object's position using keyframes and enhance that animation by controlling the way those keyframes are interpreted.

Starting the lesson

Note: To ensure that the tools function and the defaults are set exactly as described in this lesson, reset the Premiere Pro preferences by holding Option (macOS) or Alt (Windows) while launching the application and then clicking Continue in the Reset Options dialog box.

Video projects are often motion graphics-oriented, and it's common to see multiple shots combined as complex multi-layered compositions. These layers are often put into motion. Perhaps you'll see multiple video clips streaming past in floating boxes, or you'll see a video clip shrunk down and placed next to an on-camera host. You can create those effects (and many more) using the Motion effect in the Effect Controls panel or using a number of other clip-based effects that offer Motion settings.

The Motion effect allows you to position, rotate, or change the size of a clip within the frame. Some adjustments can be made directly in the Program Monitor. The Effect Controls panel displays controls for only one selected clip at a time. That clip could be a segment in a sequence, or a clip opened in the Source Monitor.

You can animate effect settings over time using *keyframes*. A *keyframe* is a special kind of marker that stores settings at a particular point in time. If you use two (or more) keyframes with different settings, the settings automatically animate over time. For example, you could animate the Position setting to have a graphic move across the screen. You can apply subtle adjustments to the timing of animation using different types of keyframes.

Most settings for most visual effects can be *keyframed*, that is, animated using keyframes.

Adjusting the Motion effect

Every visual clip segment in a Premiere Pro sequence has certain effects applied automatically. These are referred to as *fixed effects* (also sometimes called *intrinsic effects*), and the Motion effect is one of them.

Tip: If you expand or collapse the settings for the fixed effects, the settings will remain expanded or collapsed for all clips.

To adjust a clip's Motion effect, select the clip in a sequence and look in the Effect Controls panel. Expand the Motion effect to adjust the settings.

The Motion effect allows you to adjust the position, scale, or rotation of a clip. Let's look at the way this effect has been used to reposition a clip in a sequence.

Tip: Because you have been saving projects with new names while working on them, you can go back to earlier lessons and experiment again with a fresh copy of the original project file.

1   Open Lesson 09.prproj in the Lessons folder.

2   Save the project as **Lesson 09 Working.prproj**.

3   Choose Window > Workspaces > Effects. Reset the workspace.

4   If it's not already open, open the sequence 01 Floating. This simple sequence has just one clip in it (Gull.mp4).

> **Tip:** Click the Name heading in the Project panel to sort items in alphanumeric order.

5 Make sure Fit is chosen from the Select Zoom Level menu in the Program Monitor.

It's important to see the whole composition when setting up visual effects. This menu does not change the contents of the sequence, only the way the contents are viewed. It can be helpful to zoom in or out to see fine details in an image or set up effects, but generally you will want to keep this menu set to Fit.

6 Play the sequence.

This clip's Position, Scale, and Rotation settings have been animated using keyframes added to the Motion effect. The keyframes have different settings at various points in time, so the clip animates into the frame.

Understanding Motion settings

Though these controls are called Motion, there's no movement until you configure them. By default, clips are positioned in the center of the Program Monitor, at their original scale. Select the clip in the sequence now, and click the name of the Effect Controls panel to bring it into view. If necessary, click the disclosure triangle 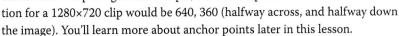 next to Motion in the Video Effects section of the Effect Controls panel to display the available settings.

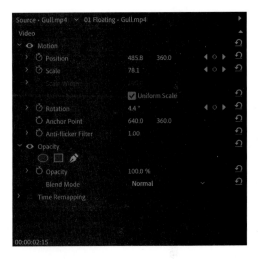

Here are the options:

- **Position:** This places the clip along the x-axis (horizontal) and y-axis (vertical). The position is calculated based on the location of an anchor point, which is at the center of the image by default, measured from the upper-left corner of the clip image. For example, the default position for a 1280×720 clip would be 640, 360 (halfway across, and halfway down the image). You'll learn more about anchor points later in this lesson.

- **Scale (including Scale Height, when Uniform Scale is deselected):** Clips are set to their full original size by default (100%). To shrink a clip, reduce this number. You can scale up to 10,000%—though be warned, scaling up will make images pixelated and soft.

- **Scale Width:** Deselect Uniform Scale to make Scale Width available. This lets you change the clip width and height independently.

- **Rotation:** You can rotate an image in a flat spin (as if viewing a spinning turntable or carousel from above). You can enter degrees or a number of rotations. For example, 450° is the same as 1x90 (one full 360° turn plus an additional 90°). Positive numbers result in clockwise rotation, and negative numbers result in counterclockwise rotation.

Tip: The anchor point position can be animated using keyframes, just like every other Motion control.

Note: If the Effect Controls panel is too narrow, some of the controls will overlap or be hidden. Resize the panel as necessary before working on effect settings.

- **Anchor Point:** Rotation, Position, and Scale adjustments are all based on the anchor point, which is at the center of a clip image by default. This can be changed to any point, including one of the clip's corners or even a point outside the clip image.

  For example, if you set the anchor point to the corner of the clip, when you adjust the Rotation setting, the clip will rotate around that corner rather than around the center of the image. If you change the anchor point in relation to the image, you may have to reposition the clip in the frame to compensate for the adjustment.

- **Anti-flicker Filter:** This feature is useful for interlaced video clips and for images that contain high detail, such as fine lines, hard edges, or parallel lines (which can cause moiré effects). Such high-detail images sometimes flicker during motion. To add some blurring and reduce flicker, set this to 1.00.

Let's look closer at the animated clip. Continue working with the sequence 01 Floating.

1 Click the clip in the Timeline panel once to make sure it is selected.

2 Make sure the Effect Controls panel is visible. It should be in the same panel group as the Source Monitor, but if you can't find it, look for it in the Window menu.

3 Still in the Effect Controls panel, if the integrated timeline is not visible, click the small triangle ⚏ at the top-right corner of the panel to toggle it open.

   The timeline in the Effect Controls panel displays keyframes.

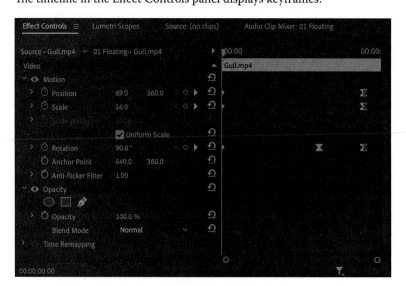

4 Each setting control has its own keyframes. Click the Go To Previous Keyframe or Go To Next Keyframe arrows to jump between existing keyframes for a particular control.

Every effect and each individual control also has its own Reset button . If you reset the whole effect, every control returns to its default state at the time where your playhead is positioned. If animation is enabled for the control, this adds a keyframe with the default setting at the current time (existing keyframes are not removed).

5 Drag the playhead back and forth in the Effect Controls panel timeline to see the way the position of the keyframe markers relates to the animation.

Now that you know how to view the settings for an existing animation, let's begin by resetting the clip.

6 The Toggle Animation stopwatch button for each setting turns animation on or off. When the stopwatch is blue, animation is enabled for a setting. Click the stopwatch for the Position property to turn off its keyframes.

7 Because the setting already has some keyframes, a warning message lets you know they will be deleted if you continue. Click OK to continue.

8 Turn off keyframes for the Scale and Rotation properties in the same way.

9 Click the curved-arrow Reset Effect button to the right of the Motion effect heading in the Effect Controls panel.

Now the Motion settings are all set to their default values, and the clip no longer animates onscreen.

Exploring Motion settings

The Position, Scale, and Rotation properties are spatial. The changes you make to these settings are easy to see because the object will change in size and position. You can adjust these settings by entering numerical values, by using the scrubbable numbers (drag on the blue numbers), or by dragging the Transform controls.

1 Open the sequence 02 Motion.

2 In the Program Monitor, make sure the zoom level is set to 25% or 50% (or a zoom amount that allows you to see space around the active frame).

Note: It can be difficult to line up the playhead with an existing keyframe. Using the Previous/Next Keyframe buttons can help you avoid adding extra unwanted keyframes.

Note: When the Toggle Animation button is on, clicking the Reset button will not change any existing keyframes. Instead, a new keyframe will be added with a default setting. It's important to turn off animation before resetting the effect to avoid this.

Setting the zoom small like this makes it easier to position items outside the sequence's frame.

Tip: You may find it easier to work with the Motion effect in the Program Monitor if you toggle the panel full screen (double-click the Program Monitor panel name).

3 Scrub the Timeline panel playhead over the video clip so you can see the contents in the Program Monitor.

4 Click the clip in the sequence once to select it and to display its settings in the Effect Controls panel.

5 In the Effect Controls panel, click the Motion effect name to select it. This highlights the effect heading in gray.

When you select the Motion effect name, a bounding box with a crosshair and handles appears around the clip in the Program Monitor.

6 Click inside the clip bounding box in the Program Monitor, avoiding the circular crosshair ⊞ in the center (that's the anchor point).

This makes the Program Monitor the active panel, which enables menu items associated with it.

7 Open the View menu and make sure that Snap In Program Monitor option is checked. If not, choose the option now.

8 Drag the clip down and to the right so that it's partially out of the frame, with the anchor point aligned with the lower-right corner of the frame.

While dragging, the clip edges and anchor point will snap to the edges of the frame and guides will appear.

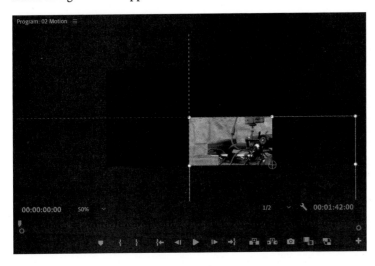

In the Effect Controls panel, the Position control values update as you move the clip.

9   Now position the clip so that it's *almost* centered in the upper-left corner of the screen but not quite—keep the clip slightly away from the center of the frame.

This is difficult to do! With snapping turned on in the Program Monitor, any items moved close to an edge will snap to that edge.

The anchor point is used for the Position, Rotation, and Scale settings. Be careful not to click the anchor point control when repositioning a clip in the frame or you'll move it in relation to the image.

Note: When positioning items, the upper-left corner of the frame is 0 x-axis and 0 y-axis. All x and y values to the left of the left edge of the frame or above the top of the frame are negative values. All other values are positive.

Note: Several effects, like the Motion effect, allow you to use direct manipulation in the Program Monitor when you select the effect heading. Try this with Corner Pin, Crop, Mirror, Transform, and Twirl.

Tip: You can temporarily enable or disable snapping in the Program Monitor by holding Command (macOS) or Ctrl (Windows).

The Position settings in the Effect Controls panel should now be close to 0, 0. You can click the numbers and type **0** into each Position field to exactly position the clip onscreen.

This is a 1280×720 sequence, so the position at the lower-right corner of the screen is 1280, 720. The middle of the screen is 640, 360.

10 In the Effect Controls panel, click the Reset button for the Motion effect to restore the clip to its default position.

11 Scrub the blue number for the Rotation value in the Effect Controls panel. As you scrub left or right, the control updates and the clip rotates.

12 Click the Reset button for the Motion effect to restore the clip to its default position.

▶ Tip: Hold Shift while scrubbing numbers, and they'll change 10 times faster. Hold Command (macOS) or Ctrl (Windows), and they'll change 10 times slower, allowing more precise adjustment.

Changing clip position, size, and rotation

The Motion effect can combine multiple independent settings changes. In the next example, you'll build an intro segment for a behind-the-scenes featurette adjusting Motion settings for multiple clips in a sequence.

Changing position

Let's begin by using keyframes to animate the position of a layer. For this exercise, the first thing you'll do is change the clip position. The picture will begin offscreen and then move fully across the screen from right to left.

1 Open the sequence 03 Montage. Scrub through the sequence to get familiar with the content.

The sequence has several tracks, some of which have their output switched off 🚫. You'll use those tracks later.

2 Position the Timeline panel playhead at the start of the sequence.

3 Set the Program Monitor zoom level to Fit.

4 Click once to select the first video clip on track V3. You might want to make the track taller to see the thumbnails more clearly.

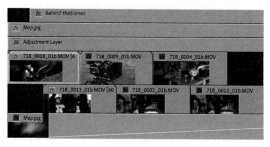

Once the clip is selected, its effect controls appear in the Effect Controls panel.

5 In the Effect Controls panel, click the Toggle Animation stopwatch button  for Position (the icon should turn blue). This turns on keyframing for that setting and automatically adds a keyframe at the current playhead position, visible in the Effect Controls panel. The keyframe icon is partially obscured because it's applied to the very first frame of the clip.

Now that animation is enabled for Position, whenever you change the setting Premiere Pro will automatically add a keyframe at the playhead's current position.

6 The Position control has two numbers. They are the values for the x-axis and the y-axis, respectively. Click the blue number and enter a Position setting of **–640** for the x-axis value (the first number) as a starting position.

The clip moves offscreen to the left, revealing the contents of the V1 and V2 tracks below. Track V2 is empty at the current playhead position, so the clip Map.jpg on V1 fills the frame.

7 Drag the playhead to the last frame of the selected clip (00:00:4:23). You can do this in the Timeline panel or in the Effect Controls panel.

8 Enter **1920** for the x-axis position. The clip is now positioned off the right edge of the screen, and a second keyframe has been added to the Position setting.

Tip: If you drag all the way to the right edge of the Effect Controls panel timeline, the playhead will be on the first frame of the next clip. Be sure to move the playhead back one frame to line up with the last frame of the current clip.

9 Play the first part of the sequence to see the clip animated from off-screen left to off-screen right. As it moves, the clip on the V2 track is revealed, but then the second clip on V3 appears suddenly. You'll animate this clip and others next.

Reusing Motion settings

Now that you've applied keyframes with new settings to a clip, you can save time by reusing those settings on other clips. Applying effects from a clip to one or more other clips is as easy as copying and pasting. In the following example, you'll apply the left-to-right floating animation you configured to other clips in the sequence.

There are several methods for reusing effects. Let's try one now.

1   In the Timeline panel, make sure the clip you just animated is still selected. It's the first clip on V3.

2   Choose Edit > Copy, or press Command+C (macOS) or Ctrl+C (Windows).

The clip, with its effects and settings, is now temporarily stored on your computer's clipboard.

3   With the Selection tool (keyboard shortcut V), beginning on the background of the Timeline panel, drag from the right across the five other clips on the V2 and V3 tracks (you may need to zoom out a little to see all the clips). This selects the clips, but the selection should not include the first video clip.

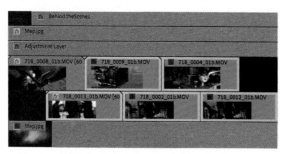

4   Choose Edit > Paste Attributes.

The Paste Attributes dialog box opens, letting you selectively apply effects and keyframes copied from another clip.

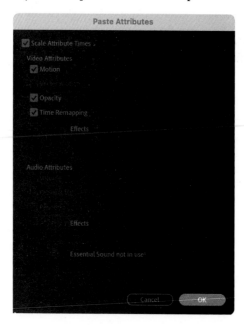

5 For the purposes of this exercise, leave the checkboxes with their default values, and click OK.

You can have only one set of fixed effects, so pasting settings from another clip will replace any existing adjustments that you may have made. You should ordinarily review the available options in the Paste Attributes dialog box carefully before clicking OK.

6 Play the sequence to see the result.

Adding rotation and changing the anchor point

Moving clips around the screen can be effective, but you can really bring things to life by combining multiple animated properties. Let's start with Rotation.

The Rotation property revolves a clip around its anchor point. By default, the anchor point is in the center of the clip image. However, you can change the relationship between the anchor point and the image for more interesting animation.

Let's add some rotation to a clip.

1 In the Timeline panel, click the Toggle Track Output button  for V6 to enable it . The one clip on the track is a title graphic that reads *Behind the Scenes*.

This clip is a title graphic created in Premiere Pro, using vector-based design tools. This means it can be scaled to any size and will always look sharp, with smooth curves and no pixelation. Vector graphics work the same way as non-vector graphics; you can use the same controls, effects, and adjustments.

2 Move the playhead to the first frame of the graphic clip (00:00:01:13). Try holding the Shift key while you scrub on the Timeline panel time ruler to do this—the playhead will snap to the ends of clips.

3 Select the graphic clip in the sequence. The clip's effect controls appear in the Effect Controls panel.

Because this is a vector graphic, there are two types of Motion effects available:

- **Graphics—Vector Motion:** Treats the contents of the graphic as vectors, allowing you to scale up the image and retain clean lines without pixelation.

- **Video—Motion:** Treats the contents of the graphic as pixels. When you scale up, the pixels will increase in size, producing jagged edges and softening the image. Believe it or not, there may be a time that you want to achieve exactly this effect!

Every graphic and text layer created in Premiere Pro appears (with full properties) in the Effect Controls panel. This graphic has just one layer, and you can see it under the Vector Motion effect.

Note: As an alternative to copying a whole clip in the Timeline panel, you can always select one or more specific effect headings in the Effect Controls panel. Command-click (macOS) or Ctrl-click (Windows) to select multiple effects and choose Edit > Copy. You can then select another clip (or clips) and choose Edit > Paste to paste the selected effects, with their current settings, onto other clips.

4 In the Effect Controls panel, select the Vector Motion effect heading (not the regular Motion effect) to display the anchor point and bounding-box controls in the Program Monitor. Notice the position of the anchor point , a small circle with a cross, in the center of the title.

Let's adjust the Rotation property in the Effect Controls panel and see the effect it has.

5 Click the disclosure triangle ❯ to reveal the Vector Motion effect controls, and enter a value of **90.0** in the Rotation field.

The title rotates in the center of the screen.

6 Choose Edit > Undo.

7 Make sure the Vector Motion settings heading is still selected in the Effect Controls panel.

8 In the Program Monitor, drag the anchor point until the crosshair sits in the upper-left corner of the letter *B* in the first word.

The Position property and Anchor Point property control similar but separate settings:

- The Anchor Point settings control the position of the anchor point in relation to the original clip image.

- The Position settings in the Effect Controls panel control the location of the anchor point in relation to the sequence frame.

⬤ **Note:** The position settings update automatically when you reposition the anchor point in the Program Monitor. If you change the Anchor Point property in the Effect Controls panel, you will need to adjust the Position property separately.

The clip image position within the frame follows the anchor point, so when you reposition the anchor point, the clip position will update.

Now that you have moved the anchor point in the image, both the Anchor Point and Position properties have been updated in the Effect Controls panel.

9 In the Vector Motion effect settings, click the Animation stopwatch button for Rotation to toggle on animation. This adds a keyframe for the Rotation setting automatically.

10 Set the rotation to **90.0**. This updates the keyframe you just added.

11 Move the playhead forward to 00:00:06:00, and click the reset button for the Rotation property (returning it to the default setting of 0.0). This adds another keyframe automatically.

12 Play the sequence to see your animation.

With careful positioning (or even animation) of anchor points, you can achieve advanced animation effects using the Motion or Vector Motion effects.

Changing clip size

There are a few approaches to changing the size of items in a sequence. By default, items added to a sequence are displayed at 100% of their original size. If a clip image size does not match the sequence frame size, it may be cropped by the edge of the sequence frame, or there may be black space around it.

There are several ways to adjust clip image size in a sequence:

- In the Effect Controls panel, adjust the Scale property of the Video > Motion effect or Graphics > Vector Motion effect.

- Right-click the clip in the sequence and choose Set To Frame Size. This automatically adjusts the Scale property of the Video > Motion effect to fit the clip in the frame. The Scale property remains fully adjustable.

- Right-click the clip in the sequence and choose Scale To Frame Size. This has a similar result to the Set To Frame Size option, but Premiere Pro resamples the image at the new (often lower) resolution. If you scale back up now using the Motion > Scale setting, the image might look soft, even if the original clip was very high resolution.

- You can also select Scale To Frame Size or Set To Frame Size automatically by choosing Premiere Pro > Settings > Media > Default Media Scaling (macOS) or Edit > Preferences > Media > Default Media Scaling (Windows). The setting is applied to assets as you import them (but won't change assets you have already imported).

For maximum flexibility, use the first or second method so you can scale as required without sacrificing quality. Let's try this.

1 Open the sequence 04 Scale.

2 Scrub through the sequence to view the clips.

The second and third clips on the V1 track are much larger than the first clip—and the sequence frame size. They are dramatically cropped by the edge of the frame.

Tip: To see the full contents of a clip, set the Source Monitor Zoom level to fit.

3 To view the original full image frame at 100% resolution, move the Timeline playhead over the last clip in the sequence on the V1 track. Click to select the clip, and press the F key or choose Sequence > Match Frame to open the clip in the Source Monitor at its original resolution.

© Maxim Jago 2016

The Match Frame command is a useful shortcut to locate a precise frame in a source clip that you are viewing in a sequence.

4 In the Timeline panel, right-click the clip and choose Scale To Frame Size.

Scale to Frame Size
Set to Frame Size
Adjustment Layer

This conveniently scales and resamples the image to fit the sequence resolution. However, there's an issue: The clip is full DCI standard 4K, with a resolution of

4096×2160, and that is not a perfect 16:9 image. What is often referred to as 4K is actually ultra-high definition (UHD), a slightly different frame size standard with the dimensions 3840×2160 and a 16:9 aspect ratio.

This clip doesn't fit the aspect ratio of the sequence, and thin black bars are introduced at the top and bottom of the image. These bars are often called *letterboxing*.

This is a common outcome when working with content that has a different aspect ratio than your sequence, and there is no easy way around it. It's time to make a manual adjustment.

5   Right-click the clip and choose Set To Frame Size. This seems to achieve the same result, but now the change has been achieved by modifying the Scale setting—and you can modify it further in the Effect Controls panel.

Choosing Set To Frame Size automatically deselects Scale To Frame Size.

⬤ **Note:** The settings in the Effect Controls panel don't indicate if they are pixels, percentages, or degrees. This can take a little getting used to, but you'll find the controls for each setting do make sense with experience.

6   With the clip selected, open the Effect Controls panel. The Scale setting has been automatically changed to 31.3% to fit the image in the sequence frame.

Use the Scale setting to adjust the clip's image size until it fits the sequence frame without showing letterboxing; a setting of 34% should work. You can adjust the Position settings to reframe the shot if necessary.

When clip and sequence aspect ratios don't match, you'll have to choose how to resolve the mismatch: letterboxing, *pillarboxing* (black bars at the sides), cropping, or changing the aspect ratio of the image by deselecting the Uniform Scale option in the Effect Controls panel.

Animating clip size changes

In the previous example, the clip image had a different aspect ratio compared to the sequence.

Now try another example; this time you'll animate the adjustment.

1   Position the Timeline playhead over the first frame of the second clip in the 04 Scale sequence, at 00:00:05:00.

This clip is 3840×2160-pixel UHD, which is the same image aspect ratio (shape) as the sequence, which is 1280×720 (16:9). It's also the same aspect ratio as full HD, at 1920×1080. This makes shooting UHD content convenient if you intend to mix media sources.

2   Select the clip and look in the Effect Controls panel. The scale setting is 100%.

3   Right-click the clip in the Timeline panel and choose Set To Frame Size.

In the Effect Controls panel, the Scale setting changes to 33.3% to fit the image in the sequence frame. You now know you can scale this clip between 33.3% and 100% and maintain quality (without magnifying pixels), while still filling the frame.

4   In the Effect Controls panel, turn on keyframing for the Scale control by clicking the Toggle Animation stopwatch button .

5   Position the playhead over the last frame of the clip.

6   Click the Reset button ↩ for the Scale setting in the Effect Controls panel.

7   Scrub through the clip to see the result.

This creates an animated zoom effect for the clip. Because the clip never scales to more than 100%, it maintains full quality.

This clip includes motion, and it already looks like the ground is coming up to meet the camera.

8   Try reversing the timing of the keyframes, so the first keyframe sets Scale to 100% and the second keyframe sets Scale to 33.3%. To switch the settings, drag the keyframes to each other's positions in the Effect Controls panel timeline or change the settings for each keyframe in their current positions.

The result is reminiscent of the famous Dolly Zoom effect.

9   Use the Undo command to restore the timing, with the clip starting at 33.3% and animating to 100%. It's safe to experiment with effect configuration, because you can always undo to restore a recent setup.

10   Turn on the Track Output option for the V2 track.

This track has an adjustment layer clip on it. Adjustment layers apply effects to all footage on lower video tracks.

11   Select the Adjustment Layer clip in the Timeline panel to display its settings in the Effect Controls panel.

A Brightness & Contrast effect has been added. You'll learn more about adjustment layers in Lesson 12, "Adding Video Effects."

12   Play the sequence.

You may need to render the sequence to see smooth playback because some of the clips are high resolution and will take a lot of computer processing power to play. To render the sequence, make sure the Timeline panel is active and choose Sequence > Render Effects In To Out or press Return (macOS) or Enter (Windows).

Filtering Effect Controls panel properties

If you have applied lots of effects to a clip and made several adjustments to specific controls, you might have a long list of headings and controls to navigate in the Effect Controls panel.

At the lower-right corner of the Effect Controls panel you can use the Filter Properties menu ![icon] to reduce the number of items displayed, making it easier to navigate the controls you are using.

There are three options that you can choose from:

- **Show All Properties:** This is the default option—all effects and controls are displayed.
- **Show Only Keyframed Properties:** Only properties that you have added keyframes to are displayed.
- **Show Only Edited Properties:** Only properties that you have modified from their default values are displayed.

Working with keyframe interpolation

Throughout this lesson you've been using keyframes to define your animation. The term *keyframe* originates from traditional animation, where the lead artist would draw the major poses, which were the most important (or *key*) frames, and then assistant animators would draw the individual frames illustrating each step of the animation from one key frame to the next. When animating in Premiere Pro, you're the lead animator, and the computer does the rest of the work as it interpolates values in between the keyframes you set.

Choosing a keyframe interpolation method

One of the most useful yet least used features of keyframes is their interpolation method. This is a fancy way of describing the particular way to get from point A to point B.

Premiere Pro has five interpolation methods. Changing the method can create a very different animation. You can access all the available interpolation methods by right-clicking a keyframe icon to see the options (some effects have both spatial and temporal options).

✓ Linear
  Bezier
  Auto Bezier
  Continuous Bezier
  Hold

- ◆ **Linear:** This is the default method of keyframe interpolation. It gives a uniform rate of change between keyframes. Changes begin instantly at the first keyframe and continue to the next keyframe at a constant speed. At the second keyframe, the rate of change switches instantly to the rate between it and the third keyframe, and so on. This can be effective, and even "snappy," but it can also look a little mechanical.

- **Bezier:** This gives the most control over keyframe interpolation. *Bezier* keyframes (named after the French engineer Pierre Bézier) provide manual handles you can adjust to change the shape of the value graph or motion path on either side of the keyframe. By dragging the Bezier handles that appear when the keyframe is selected, you can create smooth curved adjustments or sharp angles. For example, you could have an object move smoothly to a position on-screen and then sharply take off in another direction.

  ▶ **Tip:** If you are familiar with Adobe Illustrator or Adobe Photoshop, you will recognize Bezier handles; they work the same way in Premiere Pro.

- **Auto Bezier:** Auto Bezier keyframes create a smooth rate of change through the keyframe. They automatically update as you change settings. This is a dependable, quick-fix version of Bezier keyframes.

- **Continuous Bezier:** This option is similar to the Auto Bezier option, but it provides some manual control. The motion or value path will always have smooth transitions, but you can adjust the shape of the Bezier curve on both sides of the keyframe with a control handle.

- **Hold:** This is available only for temporal (time-based) properties. Hold-style keyframes hold their value across time, without a gradual transition. This is useful if you want to create staccato-type movements or make an object suddenly disappear. When the Hold style is used, the value of the first keyframe will hold until the next hold keyframe is encountered, and then the value will change instantly.

Temporal vs. spatial interpolation

Some properties and effects offer a choice of temporal and spatial interpolation methods for transitioning between keyframes. You'll find that all properties have temporal controls (which relate to time). Some properties also offer spatial interpolation (which refers to space or movement).

Here's what you need to know about each method:

- **Temporal interpolation:** Temporal interpolation deals with changes in time. It controls the speed at which an object moves. For example, you can add acceleration and deceleration using Bezier keyframes.

- **Spatial interpolation:** The spatial method deals with changes in an object's position. It controls the shape of the path an object takes across the screen. That path is called a *motion path*, and there are ways to display it in the Program Monitor. By making spatial interpolation adjustments, you can make an object appear to bounce around the frame with hard angular ricochets as it moves from one keyframe to the next or give it a more sloping movement with round corners.

Adding Ease to Motion

You can use a keyframe preset to quickly add a feeling of inertia to clip motion. For example, you can create a ramp-up effect for speed by right-clicking a keyframe and choosing Ease In or Ease Out. Ease In is used for approaching a keyframe, and Ease Out is used when leaving a keyframe.

When you choose Ease In or Ease Out, a Bezier interpolation is applied to the keyframe. You'll learn more about applying interpolation methods to keyframes in Lesson 12.

Continue working with the 04 Scale sequence.

1   Select the second video clip in the sequence.

2   In the Effect Controls panel, locate the Rotation and Scale properties.

3   Click the disclosure button ❯ next to the Scale property, and then select the Scale property heading to select the Scale keyframes and reveal the control handles and velocity graphs in the Effect Controls panel timeline.

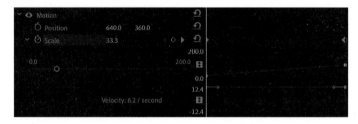

You might want to increase the height of the Effect Controls panel to make room for the extra controls.

Don't be overwhelmed by the new numbers and graphs. Once you understand one of these controls, you'll understand them all because they use a common design.

The graph makes it easier to view the results of keyframe interpolation adjustments. For example, a straight line means a steady speed without acceleration; in other words, you're using linear keyframes.

You can make the graph taller to see it more clearly by dragging the horizontal line below the keyframes down. The line is very faint, so you'll have to look carefully to find it.

4   Click the background of the Effect Controls panel timeline to deselect the keyframes; they will change from blue (selected) to gray (unselected). Right-click the first Scale keyframe (level with the Scale heading) and choose Ease Out. The keyframe is partially obscured by the left edge of the timeline.

5 Right-click the second Scale keyframe and choose Ease In.

The graph now shows a curved line, which translates as a gradual acceleration and deceleration of the animation.

6 Play the sequence to see your animation.

7 Experiment by dragging the blue Bezier handles in the Effect Controls panel to see their effects on speed and ramping.

The steeper the curve you create, the more sharply the animation's movement or speed increases. After experimenting, you can choose Edit > Undo repeatedly if you don't like the changes.

Applying the Auto Reframe effect

Once upon a time…all screens were 4×3. Then they were all manner of aspect ratios until they settled eventually on 16×9 as the standard delivery aspect ratio for television shows and online video distribution platforms today. This standard is sometimes written as 1.78:1—that is, 1.78 times wider than the height.

Theatrical cinema releases tend to be wider, with the two standard aspect ratios being 1.85:1 and 2.39:1.

It's common for major film studios to produce multiple versions of a film with different aspect ratios and color standards, intended for several traditional video distribution standards. Still, these are usually close to 16×9 or 4×3.

With the development of popular social media platforms, in particular on smartphones, demand for dramatically different aspect ratios has returned.

To help you repurpose sequences, Premiere Pro has an Auto Reframe workflow. You can largely automate the process of converting a finished sequence from one aspect ratio to another. The stand-out feature of this workflow is that Premiere Pro analyzes the visuals in your clips and then applies and configures the Auto Reframe effect for each clip, which automatically keeps points of interest—such as faces—onscreen.

You will want to check and adjust results, but this can be a huge time-saver if you intend to deliver your content on multiple platforms. Try it now:

1 Open the sequence 05 Auto Reframe.

2 Play the sequence to familiarize yourself with the content.

The character moves around the screen quite a lot. Sequences crop the edges of clips that don't fit in the frame. If you were to nest this sequence in another sequence and manually add keyframes to reframe the content, it would take quite some time.

3 With the Timeline panel active or the sequence selected in the Project panel, choose Sequence > Auto Reframe Sequence to open the dialog box of the same name.

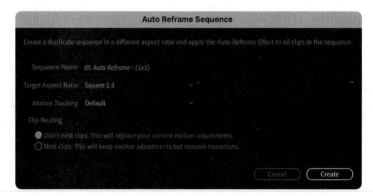

When you click Create in this dialog box, Premiere Pro creates a new separate sequence based on the settings you choose. The original sequence will not be affected. Here are the settings:

- **Sequence Name:** Give the new sequence a name. By default, the new aspect ratio is added to the original name.

- **Target Aspect Ratio:** Specify a new aspect ratio. You can repeat this process and produce multiple sequences with different aspect ratios.

- **Motion Tracking:** Set the number of keyframes that will be used to follow the motion in the sequence. For slower, smoother movements choose Slower Motion, and for faster action choose Faster Motion.

- **Clip Nesting:** Choose whether or not to nest clips. There can be only one Motion effect on each clip, and if you have motion keyframes on your clips already, they will be replaced in the new sequence unless you choose to nest the clips. If you do nest your clips, however, you'll lose transition effects between them.

4 Leave the settings at their defaults for now, with Square 1:1 chosen from the Target Aspect Ratio menu, and click Create. Premiere Pro performs visual analysis of the sequence.

The new sequence appears in the Project panel, inside a new bin called Auto Reframed Sequences, and it opens in the Timeline panel.

5 Play the new sequence to review the results of the reframing.

6 Select the clip in the Timeline panel, and look in the Effect Controls panel. The Motion effect is disabled ![icon], and an Auto Reframe effect is applied.

> ![Note icon] **Note:** Some of the results produced by Auto-Reframe are achieved by scaling clips—particularly graphics—in ways that reduce their resolution. This can result in softer looking images when displayed at full size. To achieve the sharpest possible results, you can manually create a new sequence, copy the original sequence clips into it, and then apply the Auto Reframe effect to the individual clips (available in the Effects panel).

You can use the Auto Reframe controls to make overall adjustments to the results of the effect or select Overwrite Generated Path, and many individual Position keyframes will appear in the Effect Controls panel timeline that you can adjust one by one or delete.

Combining a drop shadow with motion effects

Premiere Pro offers a number of effects to control motion. Although the Motion effect is the most immediately accessible, you may find yourself wanting more.

The Transform and Basic 3D effects are also useful and give more control over an object (including 3D rotation).

These effects are particularly helpful because the order in which visual effects are listed in the Effect Controls panel is the order in which they are applied, with one exception; the fixed effects (including Motion, Opacity, and Time Remapping) are always applied last.

This can lead to complications when effects that impact lighting or effects that change the shape or position of a clip are applied. In this exercise, you'll learn how to combine effects to achieve natural-looking results.

Adding a drop shadow

A drop shadow creates perspective by adding a small shadow behind an object. This is often used to help create a sense of separation between foreground and background elements.

Try adding a drop shadow.

1 Open the sequence 06 Enhance.

2 Make sure the Program Monitor zoom level is set to Fit.

3 In the Effects panel, browse into Video Effects > Perspective.

4 Drag the Drop Shadow effect onto the Journey to New York Title clip on the V3 track.

5 Experiment with the Drop Shadow settings in the Effect Controls panel. You may need to scroll down to see them. When you have finished experimenting, choose the following settings:

- Darken the shadow by changing Opacity to **85%**.

- Drag the Direction value to about 320° to see the shadow's angle change.

- Set Distance to **15** so the shadow is further offset from the clip.

- Set Softness to **25** to soften the edges of the shadow. Generally, the greater the Distance setting, the more softness you should apply.

6 Play the sequence to view the result.

Adding motion with the Transform effect

An alternative to the Motion effect settings is the Transform effect, available in the Effects panel Video Effects > Distort category. These two effects offer similar controls, but the Transform effect offers three key differences.

- Changes to a clip's Anchor Point, Position, Scale, and Opacity settings are processed in the stack with other effects, unlike the Motion settings. This means effects such as drop shadows and bevels can behave differently (usually more correctly).

- There are additional Skew, Skew Axis, and Shutter Angle settings to allow a visual angular transformation to clips.

- The Transform effect can automatically simulate motion blur for more natural-looking movement.

Let's compare the two effects.

1   Open the sequence 07 Motion and Transform.

2   Scrub through the sequence to familiarize yourself with it.

    There are two sections in the sequence. Each has a picture-in-picture (PIP), rotating twice over a background clip while moving from left to right. Look carefully at the position of the shadow on each pair of clips.

    - In the first example, the shadow follows the bottom edge of the PIP and appears on all four sides of the clip as it rotates, which obviously isn't realistic because the light source producing the shadow wouldn't be moving.

    - In the second example, the shadow stays on the lower right of the PIP, which is more realistic.

3   Click the first clip on the V2 track, and view the effects applied in the Effect Controls panel: the Motion effect and the Drop Shadow effect.

4   Now click the second clip on the V2 track. The Transform effect is producing the motion this time, with the Drop Shadow effect again producing the shadow.

▶ **Tip:** Anywhere you see a blue number in Premiere Pro, you can usually drag across it rather than click it to change the value incrementally—this includes the timecode displays for the current playhead position.

5 Experiment with the Transform effect settings. You can click numbers to type in new values or drag across the numbers to make incremental adjustments.

The effect has many of the same options as the Motion effect, with the addition of Skew, Skew Axis, and Shutter Angle. As you can see, the Drop Shadow effect works more realistically when combined with the Transform effect than when it's used with the Motion effect alone because of the order in which the effects are applied; the Motion effect is always applied after other effects.

Manipulating clips in 3D space with Basic 3D

Another option for creating movement is the Basic 3D effect, which can manipulate a clip in 3D space. It allows you to rotate the image around horizontal and vertical axes as well as move it toward or away from you. You'll also find an option to enable a specular highlight, which creates the appearance of light reflecting off the rotating surface.

Let's explore the effect:

1 Open the sequence 08 Basic 3D.

2 Drag the playhead over the sequence in the Timeline panel (scrub) to view the contents.

The light that follows the motion comes from above, from behind, and from the left of the viewer. Because the light comes from above, you won't see the effect until the image is tilted backward to catch the reflection. Specular highlights of this kind can be used to enhance the realism of a 3D effect.

These are the four major properties of the Basic 3D effect:

- **Swivel:** This controls the rotation around the vertical y-axis. If you rotate past 90°, you'll see the back of the image, which is a mirror of the front.

- **Tilt:** This controls the rotation around a horizontal x-axis. If you rotate beyond 90°, again, you'll see the back of the image.

- **Distance To Image:** This moves the image along the z-axis to simulate depth. As the distance value gets larger, the image moves farther away.

- **Specular Highlight:** This adds a glint of light that reflects off the surface of the rotated image, as though an overhead light were shining on the surface. This option is either on or off.

3 Experiment with the Basic 3D options. Note that the Draw Preview Wireframe option applies only when working in Software Only mode (without GPU acceleration enabled in your Project settings).

With this option enabled, Premiere Pro displays only an outline of the clip frame. This is a quick way to set up the effect without your computer rendering the image. If you're working with GPU acceleration enabled, the full image will always be shown.

Review questions

1 Which fixed effect will move a clip in the frame?

2 You want a clip to appear full screen for a few seconds and then spin away. How do you make the Motion effect's Rotation feature start partway through a clip rather than at the beginning?

3 How can you start an object rotating gradually and have it stop rotating slowly?

4 If you want to add a drop shadow to a clip, why might you choose to use a different motion-related effect rather than the Motion effect?

Review answers

1 The Motion effect lets you set a new position for a clip. If keyframes are used, the effect can be animated.

2 Position the playhead where you want the rotation to begin, and click the Add/Remove Keyframe button or the stopwatch icon. Then move to where you want the spinning to end and change the Rotation parameter; another keyframe will appear.

3 Use the Ease Out and Ease In options to change the keyframe interpolation to be gradual rather than sudden.

4 The Motion effect is the last effect applied to a clip. Motion takes whatever effects you apply before it (including Drop Shadow) and spins the entire assemblage as a single unit. To create a realistic drop shadow on a spinning object, use Transform or Basic 3D and then place a Drop Shadow effect below that in the Effect Controls panel.

10 EDITING AND MIXING AUDIO

Lesson overview

In this lesson, you'll learn how to do the following:

- Work in the Audio workspace.

- Understand audio characteristics.

- Adjust clip audio volume.

- Adjust audio levels in a sequence.

- Lower music levels automatically.

- Use the Audio Clip Mixer.

 This lesson will take about 100 minutes to complete. To get the lesson files used in this chapter, download them from the web page for this book at *peachpit.com/PremiereProCIB2024*. For more information, see "Accessing the lesson files and Web Edition" in the "Getting Started" section at the beginning of this book. Store the files on your computer in a convenient location.

Until now, our focus has been primarily on working with visuals. No doubt about it, the pictures count, but professional editors tend to agree that sound is at least as important as the images on the screen— sometimes more important! In this lesson, you'll learn some audio-mixing fundamentals using the powerful tools provided by Adobe Premiere Pro.

Starting the lesson

Consider the difference it makes if you turn the sound off while watching a horror movie. Without an ominous soundtrack, scenes that were scary a moment ago can seem like comedy.

Music works around many of our critical faculties and directly influences our feelings. Your body will react to sound whether you want it to or not. For example, it's normal for your heart rate to be influenced by the beat of the music you're listening to. Fast music tends to raise your heart rate, and slow music tends to lower your heart rate. Powerful stuff!

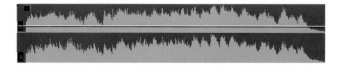

It's rare to record perfect on-camera audio that's ready for output without any adjustments, but Premiere Pro enables you to do many things to improve your audio mix. For instance, you can:

- Interpret recorded audio channels differently from the way they were recorded in-camera. For example, audio recorded as stereo can be interpreted as separate mono tracks.

- Clean up background sound. Whether it's system hum from your recording equipment or the sound of an air-conditioning unit, Premiere Pro has tools for cleaning up your audio.

- Adjust the volume of specific frequencies in your clips (different tones).

- Adjust the volume level on clips in the Project panel and on clip segments in sequences. The adjustments made to clips in sequences can vary over time to create a dynamic sound mix.

- Add music, and then mix levels between music clips and dialogue clips. This can be performed automatically or manually.

- Produce a mono, stereo, or even 5.1 surround sound mix.

- Add audio spot effects, such as explosions, door slams, or atmospheric environmental sounds.

- Change the duration of a music clip to suit your sequence.

In this lesson, you'll begin by learning how to use the audio tools in Premiere Pro, and then you'll make adjustments to clips and a sequence. You'll also use the Audio Clip Mixer to make changes to your volume "on the fly" while your sequence plays.

Setting up the interface to work with audio

Let's begin by switching to the Audio workspace.

1 Open Lesson 10.prproj in the Lessons folder.

    ● **Note:** To ensure that the tools function and the defaults are set exactly as described in this lesson, reset the Premiere Pro preferences by holding Option (macOS) or Alt (Windows) while launching the application and then clicking Continue in the Reset Options dialog box.

2 Save the project as **Lesson 10 Working.prproj**.

3 From the Workspaces menu, choose Audio. Then return to the Workspaces menu and choose Reset To Saved Layout.

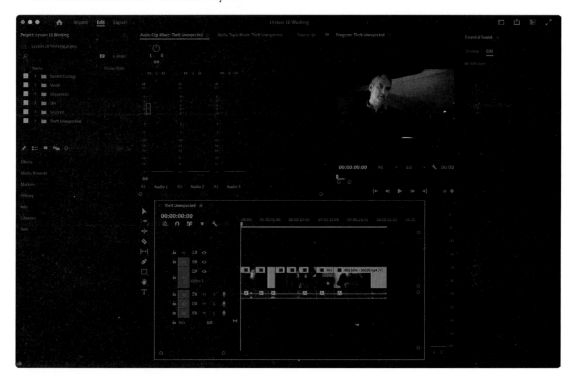

Working in the Audio workspace

You'll recognize most of the components of the Audio workspace from the Editing workspace you've used. One obvious difference is that the Audio Clip Mixer is displayed in place of the Source Monitor. The Source Monitor is still there; it's just hidden right now, grouped with the Audio Clip Mixer.

Clip-based and track-based audio level adjustments are combined for final output. So, if you reduce a clip's audio level by −3 dB *and* reduce the track audio level by −3 dB, you'll have a total drop of −6 dB.

You can apply clip-based audio effects and modify their settings in the Effect Controls panel. In fact, adjustments made using the Audio Clip Mixer appear in the Effect Controls panel, along with any other adjustments.

Track-based audio adjustments can be modified in the Audio Track Mixer only or directly in the Timeline panel.

Premiere Pro applies clip-based audio adjustments and effects before track-based adjustments and effects. It's important to keep this in mind, because the order in which adjustments are applied can have a big impact on results.

You can modify the Timeline panel track headers and add an audio meter for each track, along with track-based level and pan controls. This is useful when mixing audio as it helps you locate the sources of audio levels you might want to adjust.

Let's try this.

Note: You will have noticed that this project has a different bin structure and is organized in a different way. There is no one correct way to organize your project. Try a few options to find a system that works best for your editing style.

1 If it's not open already, open the Theft Unexpected sequence in the Sequences bin.

2 Open the Timeline Display Settings menu ![wrench icon], and choose Customize Audio Header. The Audio Header Button Editor appears, and the Audio 1 track expands to display the full track header.

3 Drag the Track Meter icon ![meter icon] onto the Audio 1 track header, and click OK.

Notice that when you clicked OK, the Audio 1 track header returned to its previous size. Resize the Audio 1 track header vertically to see the new meter.

Changes made to any track header update all track headers. Now every audio track will have a small built-in audio meter—useful for working out which track is contributing most to the overall audio mix.

You can remove items from track headers by dragging them away from the header while the editor is open. You can also click the Reset Layout button in the Audio Header Button Editor to restore the default track header configuration.

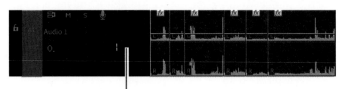

Track Audio Meter

There are two audio mixer panels in Premiere Pro. Let's look at the differences between the two:

- **Audio Clip Mixer:** This provides controls to adjust the audio level and *pan* or *balance* (to distribute audio between the left or right side of the sequence audio mix) of clips in sequences. As you play your sequence, you can make adjustments, and Premiere Pro will add keyframes to clips as the playhead moves over them.

- **Audio Track Mixer:** This adjusts audio level and pan on tracks rather than clips. The controls are similar, but the Audio Track Mixer offers more advanced mixing options. If the Effects And Sends section at the top of the panel has been expanded, you may need to scroll down to view the controls. See Chapter 11, "Improving Audio," for more information about audio mixing.

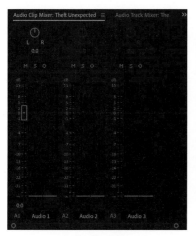
Audio Clip Mixer

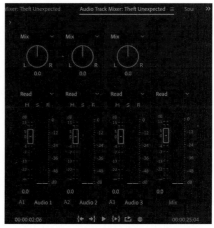
Audio Track Mixer

Configuring the audio mix

Sequences have settings that are similar to media files. For example, sequences have a frame rate, frame size, and pixel aspect ratio.

The Audio Mix setting defines the number of audio channels the sequence will output. This is a little like configuring the audio channels for a media file. In fact, if you export the sequence using the option to automatically match sequence settings, the sequence audio mix setting will be the audio format for the new file.

When you create a new sequence, the Audio Mix setting is in the Tracks tab of the New Sequence dialog box, under Audio.

- **Stereo** has two audio channels: Left and Right. This is the most common option for delivered content.

- **5.1** has six audio channels: Middle, Front-Left, Front-Right, Rear-Left, Rear-Right, and Low Frequency Effects (LFE)—that's the sound that gets played through the subwoofer. At very low frequencies, our ears can't detect the direction sound comes from, so there's no need for two subwoofers.

- **Multichannel** has between 1 and 32 audio channels you can choose. This option is most commonly used for advanced multichannel broadcast television, documentary and feature film workflows, particularly where multilingual delivery is required.

- **Mono** has one audio channel.

You can change most sequence settings at any time, but not the Audio Mix setting. With the exception of multichannel sequences, you cannot change the number of channels that your sequence will output.

You can add or remove audio tracks at any time. If you decide to change your audio mix setting, you can copy and paste clips from a sequence with one audio mix setting to a sequence with a different setting.

What is an audio channel?

It's common to think that Left and Right audio channels are in some way intrinsically different. In fact, they are both actually mono audio channels designated as Left or Right. When recording sound, it's the standard configuration to have Audio Channel 1 as Left and Audio Channel 2 as Right.

What makes Audio Channel 1 Left is only the following:

- It's recorded from a microphone pointing left.
- It's interpreted as Left in Premiere Pro.
- It outputs to a speaker positioned on the left.

Otherwise, it's a single, mono audio channel.

If you also perform the same recording from a microphone pointing right (but with Audio Channel 2), then you have stereo audio. They are, in fact, two separate mono audio channels.

Using the audio meters

When previewing a clip in the Source Monitor or Project panel, the audio meters display the level for each audio channel in the clip separately.

When previewing a sequence, the audio meters display the audio level for each mix channel. Regardless of the number of audio tracks in the sequence, the audio meters will give you the overall mix output volume for your sequence.

If the audio meters are not already displayed, you will find them in the Window menu.

If the audio meters are too narrow, you can resize the panel. If you make the meters wide enough, the audio level will be displayed horizontally.

There is a Solo button for each audio meter. This allows you to exclusively hear the selected channel (or multiple channels). If the Solo buttons are displayed as small circles, drag the edge of the panel a little to make the meters wider and display larger Solo buttons.

● **Note:** The Solo buttons do not display when you use the mono audio mix option.

If you right-click the audio meters, you can choose a different display scale. The default is a range from 0 dB to −60 dB, which clearly shows the main information about the audio level you'll want to see.

You can also choose between static and dynamic peaks. When you get a loud "spike" in audio levels that makes you glance at the meters, the sound is usually gone by the time you look. With static peaks, the highest peak is marked and maintained in the meters so you can identify the loudest level played.

You can click the audio meters to reset the peak. With dynamic peaks, the peak level will continually update, briefly holding before disappearing; keep watching to check the levels.

About audio level

The scale displayed on the audio meters is decibels, denoted by dB. The scale shown is a little unusual in that the highest volume is designated as 0 dB. Lower volumes become larger and larger negative numbers until they reach negative infinity.

If a recorded sound is too quiet, it might get lost in the background noise. Background noise might be environmental, such as an air-conditioning system making a hum. It also might be system noise, such as the quiet hiss you might hear from speakers when no sound is playing.

When you increase the overall volume of your audio, background noise gets louder too. When you decrease the overall volume, background noise gets quieter. This means it's often better to record audio at a higher level than you need (while avoiding such high levels that the audio distorts) and then reduce the volume later to remove (or at least reduce) the background noise.

Depending on your audio hardware, you may have a bigger or smaller signal-to-noise ratio; that's the difference between the sound you want to hear (the signal) and the sound you don't want to hear (the background noise). Signal-to-noise ratio is often described as SNR and is also measured in dB.

Viewing samples

The *audio sample rate* is the number of times per second the recorded sound source is sampled. It's common for professional camera audio to take a sample 48,000 times per second.

Let's look at an individual audio sample.

1   In the Project panel, open the Music bin, and double-click the clip Graceful Tenure - Patrick Cannell.mp3 to open it in the Source Monitor.

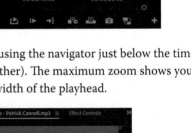

Because this clip has no video, Premiere Pro automatically displays the waveforms for the two audio channels.

At the bottom of the Source Monitor, the width of the time ruler represents the total duration of the clip.

● **Note:** You may have noticed that sometimes timecode indicators separate the numbers with colons, and at other times semicolons are used. Semicolons indicate NTSC video, while colons indicate PAL video.

2   Open the Source Monitor Settings menu 🔧, and choose Time Ruler Numbers. The time ruler now shows timecode indicators.

Try zooming in to the time ruler using the navigator just below the time ruler (drag the handles all the way together). The maximum zoom shows you an individual frame—illustrated by the width of the playhead.

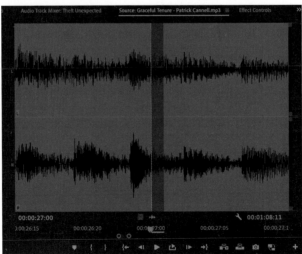

3 Open the Source Monitor Settings menu again, and choose Show Audio Time Units.

This time, you'll see individual audio samples counted on the time ruler. You can zoom in to an individual audio sample—in this case, one 48,000th of a second, the sample rate of this audio!

The Timeline panel has the same option to view audio samples in the panel menu (rather than the Timeline Settings menu).

4 For now, use the Source Monitor Settings menu to disable both the Time Ruler Numbers and Show Audio Time Units options.

Showing audio waveforms

When you view a waveform in the Source Monitor, you'll see an extra navigator zoom control for each channel to the right of the waveform. These controls work in a way that's similar to the navigator zoom control at the bottom of the panel. You can resize the vertical navigator to view the waveforms larger or smaller, which is particularly useful when navigating quiet audio.

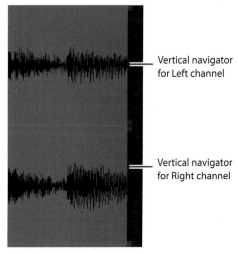

Vertical navigator for Left channel

Vertical navigator for Right channel

You can choose to display audio waveforms for any clip that has audio by choosing Audio Waveform from the Source Monitor Settings menu.

If a clip has video as well as audio, the video will be displayed in the Source Monitor by default. You can quickly switch to viewing the audio waveform by clicking the Drag Audio Only button ⁙.

Let's look at some waveforms.

1 In the Theft Unexpected bin, double-click the clip HS John to open it in the Source Monitor.

2 Open the Source Monitor Settings menu, and choose Audio Waveform.

Note: Viewing an audio waveform is helpful if you are trying to locate specific dialogue and you are not as concerned about the video portion of the footage.

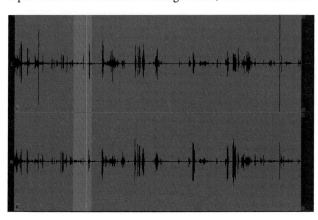

You can easily see where the dialogue begins and ends. Notice the clip's In and Out points are shown as a highlighted region on the waveform.

Notice also, you can click the waveform to move the Source Monitor playhead.

3   Switch back to viewing the composite video using the Source Monitor Settings menu.

You can also turn off and on the display of waveforms for clip segments on the Timeline.

4   The sequence Theft Unexpected should already be open in the Timeline panel. If not, open it from the Sequences bin.

5   Open the Timeline Display Settings menu, and make sure the Show Audio Waveform option is enabled.

6   If necessary, resize the Audio 1 track to make sure the waveform is fully visible. Notice that two audio channels are displayed in each audio clip in this sequence: The clips have stereo audio.

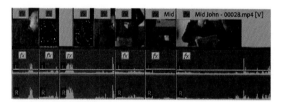

The audio waveforms on these clips look very different from the waveforms in the Source Monitor. That's because, by default, the Timeline panel displays *rectified* audio waveforms that look a little like a highly detailed bar graph. This style of waveform makes it easier to see lower-volume audio, like the dialogue in this scene.

7   Open the Timeline panel menu ▤ (not the Settings menu) and choose Rectified Audio Waveforms to deselect it.

This switches the Timeline panel waveforms to the same type as the Source Monitor.

The regular waveform display works well for louder audio, but notice the quieter parts of the speech; it's harder to follow the level changes.

8   Open the Timeline panel menu, and restore the Rectified Audio Waveforms option.

Working with standard audio tracks

In a sequence, the standard audio track type can accommodate both mono audio clips and stereo audio clips. The controls in the Effect Controls panel, the Audio Clip Mixer, and the Audio Track Mixer work with both kinds of media.

If you're working with a combination of mono and stereo clips, you'll find it more convenient to use the standard track type than separate mono tracks.

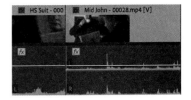

Standard tracks support both mono and stereo audio, automatically displaying one or two waveforms depending on the clip audio channels.

Monitoring audio

You can choose which sequence audio channels you hear when monitoring.

Let's try this with a sequence.

1 Open the Desert Montage sequence from the Sequences bin.

2 Play the sequence, and while you do, try clicking each of the Solo buttons at the bottom of the audio meters on the right side of the Timeline panel.

When you select a Solo button, you'll hear only the channel you select. You can solo multiple channels to hear a specific combination—although in this example it wouldn't help much, as you have only two channels to choose between.

Soloing is useful if you're working with audio where the sound from different microphones is recorded onto different audio channels. This is common with professionally recorded location sound.

● **Note:** The audio meters indicate levels for audio channels when playing clips in the Source Monitor or mix channels when playing sequences in the Timeline panel. To view levels for individual sequence tracks, use the Audio Clip Mixer or Audio Track Mixer.

The number of channels and associated Solo buttons you'll see when previewing a sequence depends on your current sequence Audio Mix setting.

You can also use the small track header Mute button ![M] or Solo button ![S] for specific audio tracks in the Timeline panel.

Examining audio characteristics

When you open a clip in the Source Monitor and view the waveform, you're seeing each channel displayed. The taller the waveform is, the louder the audio for that channel will be. In a sense, you're seeing a plot graph showing the strength of the air pressure wave over time.

Three factors affect the way audio sounds to your ears. Consider them in terms of a television speaker.

- **Frequency:** This refers to how fast the surface of the speaker moves in and out to create high and low air pressure waves. The number of times the surface of the speaker beats the air per second is described as the frequency, measured as Hertz (Hz). Human hearing ranges from approximately 20 Hz to 20,000 Hz (20 KHz). Many factors, including age, affect the frequency range you can hear. The higher the frequency, the higher the perceived pitch of the tone.

- **Amplitude:** This is how far the speaker surface moves. The bigger the movement, the louder the sound will be because it produces a higher air pressure wave, carrying more energy to your ears.

- **Phase:** This is the precise timing with which the surface of the speaker moves out and in. If two speakers push out air and pull in air in sync, they are considered "in phase." If they move out of sync, they become "out of phase," and this can produce problems with sound reproduction. One speaker can reduce the air pressure at exactly the moment the other speaker is attempting to increase it. The result is that you may not hear parts of the sound.

What are audio characteristics?

When the surface of a speaker moves, it creates a high- and low-pressure wave that moves through the air until it arrives at your ears in much the way that surface ripples move across a pond.

As the pressure wave hits your ears, it makes tiny parts of your ear drums move, and that movement is converted into energy that is passed to your brain and interpreted as sound. This happens with extraordinary precision, and because you have two ears, your brain does an impressive job of balancing the two sets of sound information to produce an overall sense of what you can hear.

Much of the way you hear is active, not passive. That is, your brain is constantly filtering out sounds it decides are irrelevant and identifying patterns so you can focus your attention on things that matter—such as speech. For example, you have probably had the experience of being at a party where the general hubbub of conversation sounds like a wall of noise until someone across the room mentions your name. You perhaps didn't realize your brain was listening to the conversation the whole time because you were concentrating on listening to the person standing next to you.

There's a body of research on this subject that broadly falls under the title *psychoacoustics*. For these exercises, we'll be focusing on the mechanics of sound more than on the psychology, though it's a fascinating subject worthy of further study.

Recording equipment makes no such subtle discrimination, which is part of the reason why it's so important to listen to sound with headphones when you're recording on location and to take care to capture the best possible signal. It's usual practice to try to record location sound with no background sound at all. The background sound is added separately in post-production at precisely the right level to add atmosphere to the scene without drowning out the dialogue.

The movement of the surface of a speaker as it emits sound provides a simple example of the way sound is generated, but, of course, the same rules apply to all sound sources, including human voices.

Adding Adobe Stock Audio

As well as importing music files to include in your sequences, you can browse and import music from Adobe Stock Audio using the Essential Sound panel.

The Browse tab of the Essential Sound panel displays Adobe Stock Audio clips ready to search, browse, and preview.

The Search box at the top allows you to seek out clips based on their names or metadata tags. To limit search results, you can expand and select options under the Moods, Genres, and Filters headings.

The Filters heading even allows you to specify a range of tempos or durations. There are additional partner stock audio catalogs available too.

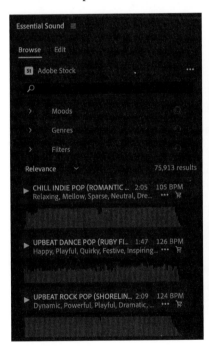

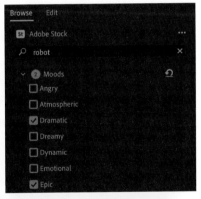

Let's add a preview of a stock audio clip to a sequence.

1 Open the Drone Flight sequence in the Sequences bin. This is a simple sequence with visuals only. Position the playhead at the beginning of the sequence.

2 If the Essential Sound panel is displaying the Edit settings instead, click Browse at the top of the panel.

3 At the bottom of the Essential Sound panel, make sure the Timeline Sync option is selected.

With Timeline Sync enabled, your sequence will play automatically when you play a stock audio clip in the Essential Sound panel. The music will be combined with your existing soundtrack and visuals, so you can preview multiple music options before adding one to your sequence.

▶ **Tip:** You can click anywhere within a stock audio clip waveform preview to jump to another part of the audio. With Timeline Sync enabled, your playhead will also jump by just the right amount.

4 In the Essential Sound panel, click the Play button on a stock audio clip to preview it for your sequence. Then, try clicking Play for several other stock audio options.

If you add an In point to your sequence before playing a stock audio preview, playback will begin at that point. Each time you preview an alternative stock audio clip, playback will begin at the In point.

This makes it easier to compare the timing for different stock clips.

5 Drag one of the stock audio clips from the Essential Sound panel into the sequence. Place the clip at the beginning of the Audio 1 track. Be careful to drag using the name or the description of the audio clip.

The clip also automatically appears in a new Stock Audio Media bin in the Project panel.

6 Preview your sequence.

The audio clips you add to sequences from the Essential Sound panel are preview quality by default. You can license full-quality versions by clicking the License button ⛏ in the Essential Sound panel or next to the clip in the Project panel.

Adobe Stock Audio offers an extensive catalog of royalty-free music. For more information about Adobe Stock Audio, visit *stock.adobe.com/audio*.

Adjusting audio volume

There are several ways to adjust the volume of clips, and they are all nondestructive. Changes you make don't affect your original media files, so you can experiment freely and always restore the original version.

Adjusting audio in the Effect Controls panel

Earlier, you used the Effect Controls panel to make adjustments to the scale and position of clips in a sequence. You can also use the Effect Controls panel to adjust volume.

1   Open the Excuse Me sequence from the Sequences bin.

   This is a simple sequence with two clips in it (if the second clip isn't visible, scroll to the right in the Timeline panel or zoom out). In fact, it's the same clip added to the sequence twice. One version has been interpreted as stereo, and the other has been interpreted as having separate mono channels. For more on clip interpretation, see Lesson 4, "Organizing Media."

2   Click the first clip to select it, and open the Effect Controls panel.

3   In the Effect Controls panel, expand the Volume, Channel Volume, and Panner controls.

   Each control gives appropriate options for the type of audio you have selected.

   - **Volume** adjusts the combined volume of all the audio channels in the selected clip.

   - **Channel Volume** allows you to adjust the audio level for individual channels in the selected clip.

   - **Panner** gives you overall stereo left/right output balance control for the selected clip.

   The keyframe toggle stopwatch icon is automatically enabled (in blue) for all the audio controls, so every change you make adds a keyframe.

   However, if you add just one keyframe to a setting and use it to apply an adjustment, the adjustment will apply to the whole clip.

4   Position the Timeline playhead somewhere over the first clip where you would like to add a keyframe (it doesn't make too much difference where you choose if you intend to make only one adjustment).

5   Click the Timeline Display Settings menu ▧, and make sure Show Audio Keyframes is selected.

6 Increase the height of the Audio 1 track, and the Timeline panel zoom, so you can see the clip audio waveform and the special thin white line for adding keyframes, often referred to as a *rubber band*.

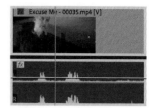

7 In the Effect Controls panel, scrub left across the blue Level number that sets the volume.

Set it to around −25 dB.

Premiere Pro adds a keyframe that's visible in the Effect Controls panel timeline and on the rubber band on the clip in the Timeline panel.

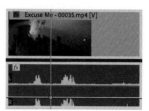

The rubber band on the clip in the Timeline panel moves down, indicating the reduced volume. The difference is subtle, but as you become more familiar with the Premiere Pro interface, it'll stand out more clearly.

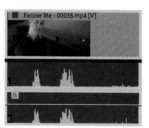

8 Now select the second version of the Excuse Me clip in the sequence.

You'll notice there are similar controls available in the Effect Controls panel, but now there is no Channel Volume option. This is because each audio channel is its own clip segment, so the Volume control for each channel is already an individual one.

The Balance control has now become a Pan control. This has a similar purpose but is suited to mono audio channels, which do not need to balance with other audio channels in the same clip.

9 Experiment with adjusting the volume for these two independent clips, and listen to the results.

Adjusting audio gain

Most music is usually created with the loudest possible usable signal to maximize the difference between the signal and the background noise. This is generally much too loud to use in video sequences. One way to address this issue is to adjust the clip's audio gain.

The following method works in a similar way to the adjustment you made in the previous exercise but is applied to the clip in the Project panel, so any parts of the clip you use in any sequence will already include the adjustment.

You can apply audio gain adjustments to multiple clips in a single step, both in the Project panel and in the Timeline panel.

1 From the Music bin, double-click the clip Graceful Tenure - Patrick Cannell.mp3 to open it in the Source Monitor. You may need to adjust the zoom level on the Source Monitor to see the waveform.

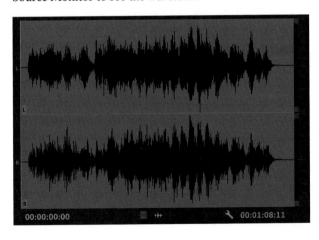

2 Right-click the clip in the Project panel and choose Audio Gain, or select the clip and press G. The Audio Gain dialog box appears with two important options.

- **Set Gain To:** Use this option to specify a particular adjustment for your clip.

- **Adjust Gain By:** Use this option to specify an incremental adjustment for your clip.

For example, if you set Adjust Gain By to –3 dB, this will adjust the Set Gain To setting to –3 dB when you click OK. If you open this dialog box a second time and apply another –3 dB adjustment, the Set Gain To setting will change to –6 dB, and so on.

3 Select the Set Gain To option, set the gain to **–12 dB**, and click OK. Right away, the waveform updates in the Source Monitor.

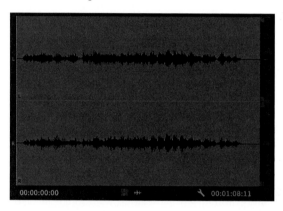

Changes like this, when you are adjusting the audio gain for clips in the bin, will not update clips already edited into a sequence, only new instances of the adjusted clips if you add them to a sequence in the future. However, you can right-click one or more clips in a sequence and choose Audio Gain, or select clips and press G, and make the same kind of adjustment there. Doing so will adjust only the clip instance in the sequence, not the source clip in the bin.

Normalizing audio

Normalizing audio is similar to adjusting gain. In fact, the outcome of normalization is an adjustment to the clip gain. The difference is that normalization is an automatic adjustment, rather than a manual one.

When you normalize a clip, Premiere Pro analyzes the audio to identify the single highest peak—in other words, the loudest moment in the audio. The gain for the clip is then adjusted automatically so that the highest peak matches a level you specify.

You can adjust the volume for multiple clips this way so that they match any peak volume you like.

Imagine working with multiple clips of a voice-over, recorded over several days. Perhaps because of different recording setups, different microphones, or different voices, several clips might have different volumes.

You can select all the clips and, in a single step, have Premiere Pro automatically set their volumes to match. This saves significant time you might have spent manually going through each clip, one by one, to make adjustments.

Let's normalize some clips.

1   Open the Journey to New York sequence from the Sequences bin.

2   Play the sequence, listen, and watch the level on the audio meters.

The voice level varies quite a lot, with the first clip noticeably quieter than the third and fourth clips.

3   Select all the voice-over clips in the sequence on Track A1. To do so, you can lasso them or make an item-by-item selection.

4   Right-click any of the selected clips and choose Audio Gain, or press the G key.

5   You'll normally choose a peak level for audio based on your overall intended mix. For these clips, select Normalize All Peaks To, enter −8 dB, and click OK.

−8 dB is close to 0 dB (full volume) but allows a little headroom. Delivery standards for audio level vary, so always check before deciding on the levels you will set in your mix.

6   Listen again. The music adds to the overall level displayed in the audio meters, making it difficult to assess the voice-over level.

7   To check the level for the voice-over clips only, click the Solo option ⑤ for the Audio 1 track to enable it.

8   Listen again. Every selected clip is adjusted so that the loudest peaks are at −8 dB.

Note: You may need to adjust the track size to see the audio waveforms. Do this by dragging the divider between two track headers.

Notice that the peaks of the clip waveforms now reach approximately the same level.

In the Audio Gain dialog box, if you choose the Normalize Max Peak To option, rather than the Normalize All Peaks To option, gain adjustments are made based on the loudest moment of all the clips combined, as if they were all one clip. The same amount of adjustment will be applied to every clip, maintaining the relative levels of all the clips.

9 Click the Solo option for the Audio 1 track to disable it.

Sending audio to Adobe Audition

While Premiere Pro has advanced tools to help you achieve most audio-editing tasks, it can't compete with Adobe Audition, which is a dedicated audio post-production application.

A component of Adobe Creative Cloud, Audition integrates neatly into your workflow when editing with Premiere Pro. You can send a complete sequence to Adobe Audition, bringing all your clips and a video file based on your sequence, to produce an audio mix that follows along with the video. Audition can even open a Premiere Pro PRPROJ project file natively and convert sequences into multitrack sessions for advanced audio finishing.

If you have Audition installed, you can send a sequence to it by following these steps:

1 Open the sequence you want to send to Adobe Audition.

2 Choose Edit > Edit In Adobe Audition > Sequence.

3 Premiere Pro will create new copies of the associated media files for you to edit in Adobe Audition, keeping your original media safe. Choose a name for the copies, and browse for a location to store them. Choose the remaining options as you prefer, and finally click OK.

4 In the Video menu, you can choose Send Through Dynamic Link to view the video part of your Premiere Pro sequence live in Audition, directly from the Premiere Pro Timeline.

Adobe Audition has fantastic tools for working with sound. It has a special spectral display that helps you identify and remove unwanted noises, a high-performance multitrack editor, and advanced audio effects and controls.

To send your completed mix from Audition to Premiere Pro, choose Multitrack > Export To Adobe Premiere Pro. Choose one of the mixdown options (usually Stereo), specify a location and name for the new media file, and click Export.

You can also send an individual clip to Audition for editing, effects, and adjustment features. To send an audio clip to Audition, right-click the clip in your Premiere Pro sequence and choose Edit Clip In Adobe Audition.

Premiere Pro duplicates the audio clip, replaces the current clip in the sequence with the duplicate, and opens the duplicate in Audition, ready to work on it.

From now on, every time you save changes you have made to the clip in Audition, they'll automatically update in Premiere Pro.

For more information about Adobe Audition, visit *peachpit.com/store/adobe-audition-cc-classroom-in-a-book-9780135228326* and check out *Adobe Audition CC Classroom in a Book*.

Auto-ducking the music level

One of the most common tasks when working on an audio mix is reducing the music level during sections of speech. If there's a voice-over track, for example, you may want the music to get quieter when information is being shared and then quickly become the dominant element in the mix again. This is the way radio DJs speak over music, with the music automatically getting quieter when the DJ speaks. The technique is called *ducking*.

You can manually add audio keyframes to achieve ducking (and you'll explore this technique later), but there's an automated way to do it too, with the Essential Sound panel.

You'll learn about the Essential Sound panel in more detail in Lesson 11, "Improving Audio." Still, this is a quick and easy workflow that saves time when creating your mix, and it's worth learning right away.

1 Continue working in the Journey to New York sequence. Make sure all the voice-over clips on the Audio 1 track are selected.

2 In the Essential Sound panel (which should already be onscreen because you selected the Audio workspace earlier), click the Edit tab to view options that relate to the clips you have selected.

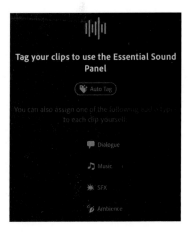

3 By assigning an audio type, you'll get access to tools and controls that are relevant to that type of audio.

Premiere Pro can automatically detect the audio type for clips and assign the correct tags, if you enable the Auto Tag option.

However, it may not be possible to accurately identify the audio type for short clips like these.

Click the Dialogue button to assign the dialogue audio type to the selected clips.

Assigning the Dialog tag means Premiere Pro now knows the audio is dialogue for the purposes of performing automatic ducking.

4 Resize the Audio 2 track so you can see the music clip's audio waveform clearly. Select the clip, and in the Essential Sound panel select the Music audio type.

5 In the Essential Sound panel, select the box to turn on Ducking, and take a look at the options.

If the settings are not showing any values, double-click each slider to restore the defaults.

- **Duck Against:** There are multiple types of audio. You can select whether one, several, or all types of audio will trigger automatic ducking. We're ducking against dialogue, and this option is selected by default.

- **Sensitivity:** The higher the sensitivity, the lower the audio level necessary to trigger ducking.

- **Duck Amount:** This is the amount the music level will be reduced by, measured in dB.

- **Fade Duration:** The slower the fade setting, the longer it will take for the music to get quieter and then louder again.

- **Fade Position:** Adjusts the timing for the fades that are added, producing earlier or later keyframes, which may work better for different sequences.

- **Generate Keyframes:** Click this button to apply the settings and add keyframes to the music clip.

6 Choosing the right settings for audio ducking is a science and an art, and the type of audio you are working with will influence the choices you make. Experimentation is the key.

For this audio, try these settings:

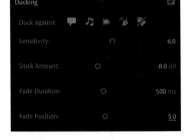

- **Duck Against:** Dialogue Clips should already be selected (it's the default).

- **Sensitivity:** 6.0

- **Duck Amount:** –8.0 dB

- **Fades:** 500 ms

- **Fade Position:** 5.0

7 Click Generate Keyframes.

Keyframes are added to an Amplify effect that the ducking feature automatically applies to the music clip. The effect and keyframes appear in the Effect Controls panel and the Timeline panel.

8 Play the sequence to listen to the result. It's not perfect, but it's closer to a finished mix.

You can adjust the automatic ducking settings and click the Generate Keyframes button repeatedly to remove and replace existing keyframes, making it safe and easy to experiment.

You can also manually adjust the keyframes that have been added. You can remove, move, and add keyframes at any time.

Retiming music with Remix

Music can have an enormous impact on visual storytelling. Just as an action movie might feel tame without a stirring soundtrack, the most nuanced dialogue can be brought to life with exactly the right musical backdrop. In many ways, the music tells the audience how to feel, so naturally getting it right is crucial.

You may discover exactly the piece of music you want, and even have the rights to use it in your project, only to discover it is too long or too short for your visuals. What to do?

For many years, the solution was to spend arduous hours carefully splitting and rejoining pieces of a music track in the hope of seamlessly extending or shortening it—often unsuccessfully, because it can be extremely difficult to avoid jarring joins.

Thankfully, Premiere Pro has an extraordinary solution: Remix. This automated, intelligent technology analyzes the music and applies exactly the right edits to achieve the duration you want—in seconds.

The best way to learn about Remix is to try it.

1 In the Timeline panel, click the name of the Drone Flight sequence to select it.

2 Select the Adobe Stock music clip you added earlier and delete it.

3 From the Music bin, drag the clip Ambient Heavens - Patrick Cannell onto the beginning of the Audio 1 track.

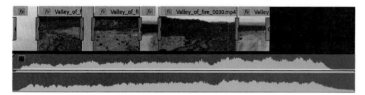

This music track is too long for the sequence. You'll use Remix to adjust it.

4 Click and hold the Ripple Edit tool ![Ripple Edit tool icon] to expand the additional tool options, and select the Remix tool ![Remix tool icon].

5 Check that Snapping ![Snapping icon] is enabled in the Timeline panel, and then use the Remix tool to trim the end of the music clip shorter until it snaps to the end of the video clips.

A progress bar shows the progress of the clip analysis, and clip duration is updated.

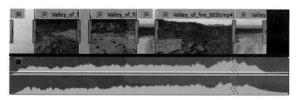

The white jagged lines indicate moments when the music clip was edited. Try playing across the edits—it's difficult to detect them. That's the magic of Remix!

Notice that the music clip does not have exactly the duration you chose. Remix makes an intelligent assessment of the clip and sets a new duration that will best allow for seamless joins.

6   Remix works for making clips longer too. Delete the Ambient Heavens - Patrick Cannell clip.

7   From the Music bin, drag the Ghost Reverie music clip onto the beginning of the Audio 1 track.

8   Use the Remix tool to trim the clip longer to match the duration of the video clips. Review the result.

If you find Remix produces a poor result, you can experiment with the detailed settings in the Duration section of the Essential Sound panel.

For now, select the Selection tool, ready for the next exercise.

Creating a split edit

A *split edit* is a simple, classic editing technique that offsets the cut point for audio and video. The audio from one clip is played with the visuals from another, carrying the feeling of one scene into another.

Adding a J-cut

The *J-cut* gets its name from the shape of the edit. Picture the letter *J* over an edit. The lower part (the audio cut) is to the left of the upper part (the video cut).

1   Open the Theft Unexpected sequence in the Sequences bin.

2 Play the last cut in the sequence. The join in the audio between the last two clips is rather abrupt. You may need to turn up your speaker volume to hear the join. You'll improve things by adjusting the timing of the audio cut.

▶ **Tip:** With the default Premiere Pro preferences, you can use the Selection tool to apply a rolling edit if you hold Command (macOS) or Ctrl (Windows).

3 Select the Rolling Edit tool ⊞ , accessible by clicking and holding the Remix tool icon 🎵 (by default, you'd click and hold the Ripple Edit tool icon ◀▶).

4 Press and hold Option (macOS) or Alt (Windows)—this temporarily overrides linked selections—and drag the audio segment edit between the last two clips (not the video) a little to the left, in a single motion. Congratulations! You've created a J-cut!

▶ **Tip:** For more information on keyboard shortcuts, see "Using and setting keyboard shortcuts" in Lesson 1.

5 Play through the edit.

You might want to experiment with the timing to make the cut seem more natural, but for practical purposes the J-cut works. You could also smooth it over and improve it further with an audio crossfade later.

6 Switch back to the Selection tool (V).

Adding an L-cut

An *L-cut* works in the same way as a J-cut but in reverse. Repeat the steps, but drag the audio segment edit a little to the right while holding Option (macOS) or Alt (Windows). Play through the edit to see (and hear) what you think.

▶ **Tip:** When you have finished working with trimming tools it's a good idea to click the Selection tool. This prevents you from applying adjustments accidentally when you attempt to select clips in a sequence.

Adjusting audio levels for a clip

As well as adjusting clip gain, you can use the rubber band to change the volume of clips in a sequence. You can also change the volume for whole tracks. These three volume adjustments combine to produce an overall output level.

If anything, using rubber bands to adjust volume is more convenient than adjusting gain because you can make incremental adjustments at any time, with immediate visual feedback.

The result of adjusting the rubber bands on a clip is similar to adjusting the volume using the Effect Controls panel. In fact, one control automatically updates the other.

Adjusting overall clip levels

Let's try adjusting clip levels.

1 If it's not already open, open the Desert Montage sequence in the Sequences bin.

   The music already fades up and down at the beginning and end. Let's adjust the volume between those fades.

2 Use the Selection tool to drag the bottom of the A1 track header down, or hold Option (macOS) or Alt (Windows) and hover the pointer over the track header while you scroll to make the track taller. This will make it easier to apply fine adjustments to the volume.

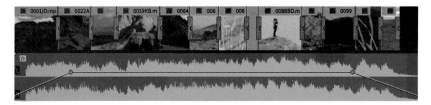

3 The middle part of the music is a little too loud. Drag the middle part of the rubber band on the clip down a little.

   As you drag, a tool tip appears, displaying the amount of adjustment you are making.

4 Each time you make an adjustment of this kind, the only way to review the result is to play the audio. Try this now, and if you are not happy with the result, you can adjust the level and review the result again.

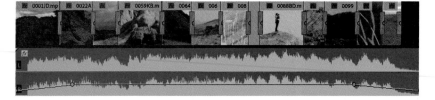

Because you're dragging the rubber band rather than an individual keyframe, you're actually adjusting the two nearest keyframes on either side of the cursor.

If the clip did not have existing keyframes, you'd be adjusting the overall level for the entire length of the clip.

▶ **Tip:** There are additional keyboard shortcuts available to add and adjust keyframe settings. Assign keys to them in the Keyboard Shortcuts dialog box.

Changing clip volume with keyboard shortcuts

If the Timeline panel playhead is over a clip, you can also raise and lower its volume using keyboard shortcuts. The result is the same, although you won't see the tool tip informing you about the amount of adjustment. These are particularly convenient shortcuts for quick, precise audio level adjustments:

- Use the [key to decrease clip volume by 1 dB.
- Use the] key to increase clip volume by 1 dB.
- Use Shift+[to decrease clip volume by 6 dB.
- Use Shift+] to increase clip volume by 6 dB.

If your keyboard does not have square bracket keys, choose Premiere Pro > Keyboard Shortcuts (macOS) or Edit > Keyboard Shortcuts (Windows) to set alternative keys.

Keyframing volume changes

You can use the Selection tool to adjust existing audio keyframes added to sequence clips in the same way that you might adjust visual keyframes. If you drag a keyframe up, the audio will get louder; drag a keyframe down to make the audio quieter.

The Pen tool ✎ adds keyframes to rubber bands. You can also use it to adjust existing keyframes or to lasso multiple keyframes to adjust them as a group.

You don't need to use the Pen tool, though. If you want to add a keyframe using the Selection tool, hold Command (macOS) or Ctrl (Windows) when you click the rubber band.

The result of adding and adjusting the position of keyframes up or down on audio clip segments is that the rubber band is reshaped. Just as before, the higher the rubber band, the louder the sound.

Add a few keyframes to the music now, with dramatic level adjustments, and listen to the results. Go crazy with the keyframes so the adjustments are obvious, and then play the sequence to hear the results and watch the effect on the audio meters.

▶ **Tip:** If you adjust the clip audio gain, Premiere Pro combines that adjustment with any keyframe-based adjustments dynamically. You can change either at any time.

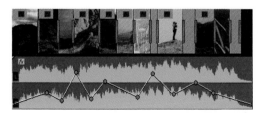

Smoothing volume between keyframes

The adjustments you just made are probably pretty overwhelming. You might want to smooth these or other adjustments.

To do so, right-click any of the keyframes. You'll see a range of standard options, including Ease In, Ease Out, Bezier, and Delete. If you use the Pen tool, you can lasso multiple keyframes and then right-click any one of them to apply a change to them all.

The best way to learn about the different kinds of keyframes is to select each kind, make some adjustments, and see or listen to the results.

Using clip vs. track keyframes

Until now, you've made all your keyframe adjustments to sequence clip segments. When working with the Audio Clip Mixer, as you will in a moment, all adjustments are made directly to clips in the current sequence.

There are similar controls for the audio tracks those clips are placed on. Track-based keyframes work in the same way as the clip-based ones. The difference is that they don't move with the clips.

This means you can set up keyframes for your audio level using track controls and then try different music clips. Each time you put new music into your sequence, you'll hear it via the adjustments you have made to your track.

As you develop your editing skills with Premiere Pro and create more complex audio mixes, explore the flexibility offered by combining clip and track keyframe adjustments.

Working with the Audio Clip Mixer

The Audio Clip Mixer provides intuitive controls to add and adjust clip volume and pan keyframes over time.

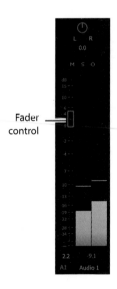

Fader control

Each sequence audio track is represented by a set of controls. Though the controls are organized by track names, the adjustments you make will be applied to clips (not tracks).

You can mute or solo a track in the Audio Clip Mixer, and you can enable an option to write keyframes to clips during playback when dragging a fader or adjusting a pan control.

What's a fader? Faders are industry-standard controls based on real-world audio-mixing decks. You move the fader up to increase the volume and move it down to decrease the volume.

Let's try this.

1   Continue working with the Desert Montage sequence. Use the Timeline Display Settings menu to make sure the Timeline panel is set to show audio keyframes, and increase the height of the Audio 1 track to be able to see the keyframes for clips on that track.

2   Open the Audio Clip Mixer (not the Audio Track Mixer), and play the sequence from the beginning.

    Because you already added keyframes to this clip, the Audio Clip Mixer fader moves up and down during playback, following the currently set level.

3   Position the Timeline panel playhead at the beginning of the sequence again. In the Audio Clip Mixer, enable the Write Keyframes button  near the top of the Audio 1 controls, next to the Mute and Solo buttons.

4   Play the sequence, and while it plays, make some really dramatic adjustments to the Audio 1 fader. Keyframes appear after you stop playback.

5   If you repeat the process, you'll notice that, once again, the fader follows existing keyframes until you make a manual adjustment.

    When you use the fader control to add keyframes, a *lot* of keyframes are added (also, existing keyframes are replaced). By default, Premiere Pro adds a keyframe with every adjustment. However, you can set a minimum time gap for keyframes to make them more manageable.

▶ **Tip:** You can adjust audio pan in the same way as you would adjust volume using the Audio Clip Mixer: Enable keyframing, play your sequence, and make adjustments using the Audio Clip Mixer Pan control.

6   Choose Premiere Pro > Settings > Audio (macOS) or Edit > Preferences > Audio (Windows). Select Minimum Time Interval Thinning and set a minimum time of **500 milliseconds** (half a second is relatively slow, but it provides a balance between precise adjustment and keyframe overload). Click OK.

7   Set the playhead to the beginning of the sequence, and, once again, use the Audio Clip Mixer to add level keyframes using the fader control.

The result is a much more orderly adjustment. Even with dramatic adjustments, the smaller number of keyframes is much more manageable.

You can adjust keyframes you created this way just as you would adjust keyframes that you created using the Selection tool or the Pen tool.

The fundamental building block of animation, whether for visual effects or audio, is the keyframe. You have now explored several ways to add and adjust keyframes in Premiere Pro. There's no right or wrong way to work with keyframes; it's entirely a matter of personal preference or the needs of a particular project.

Experiment and practice to make sure you feel truly comfortable with the concept and application of keyframes, and it will help with your developing understanding of post-production effects.

Review questions

1 How can you isolate an individual sequence audio channel to hear only that channel?

2 What is the difference between mono and stereo audio?

3 How can you view the waveforms for a clip that has audio in the Source Monitor?

4 What is the difference between normalization and gain?

5 What is the difference between a J-cut and an L-cut?

6 Which option in the Audio Clip Mixer must be enabled before you can use the fader controls to add keyframes to sequence clips during playback?

Review answers

1 Use the Solo buttons at the bottom of the audio meters or in the track headers to selectively hear an audio channel.

2 Stereo audio has two audio channels, and mono audio has one. It's the universal standard to record audio from a Left microphone as Channel 1 and audio from a Right microphone as Channel 2 when recording stereo sound.

3 Use the Settings menu on the Source Monitor to choose Audio Waveform. You can also click the Drag Audio Only button at the bottom of the Source Monitor. Clips in a sequence can display waveforms in the Timeline panel.

4 Normalization automatically adjusts the Gain setting for a clip based on the original peak amplitude. You use the Gain setting to make manual adjustments.

5 A J-cut means the sound for the next clip begins before the visuals (this is sometimes described as "audio leads video"). With L-cuts, the sound from the previous clip remains until after the visuals begin (sometimes described as "video leads audio").

6 Enable the Write Keyframes option for each track you would like to add keyframes to.

11 IMPROVING AUDIO

Lesson overview

In this lesson, you'll learn how to do the following:

- Work with the Essential Sound panel.

- Improve the sound of speech.

- Clean up noisy audio.

 This lesson will take about 75 minutes to complete. To get the lesson files used in this chapter, download them from the web page for this book at *peachpit.com/PremiereProCIB2024*. For more information, see "Accessing the lesson files and Web Edition" in the "Getting Started" section at the beginning of this book. Store the files on your computer in a convenient location.

Audio effects in Premiere Pro can dramatically change the feel of your project—and clean up audio. To take your sound mix to the next level, leverage the power of integration with Adobe Audition. In this lesson, you'll learn some quick, easy ways to improve the quality of your sound mix.

Starting the lesson

Note: To ensure that the tools function and the defaults are set exactly as described in this lesson, reset the Premiere Pro preferences by holding Option (macOS) or Alt (Windows) while launching the application and then clicking Continue in the Reset Options dialog box.

You'll find many audio effects in Adobe Premiere Pro. These effects can be used to change pitch, create an echo, add reverb, and remove tape hiss. You can set keyframes for effects and adjust their settings over time.

1 Open the project Lesson 11.prproj.

2 Save the project as **Lesson 11 Working.prproj**.

3 In the Workspaces menu, click Audio. Then open the Workspaces menu again and choose Reset To Saved Layout.

Improving audio with the Essential Sound panel

Video production rarely produces perfect audio. You'll probably need to use audio effects in post-production to fix a few problems and improve the quality of the sound, particularly for vocals, because audiences are acutely sensitive to issues with the sound of a human voice.

Not all audio hardware plays all audio frequencies evenly. For example, listening to deep bass notes on a laptop is never the same as listening on larger speakers.

It's important to listen to your audio using high-quality headphones or studio monitor speakers to avoid compensating for a flaw in your playback hardware as you adjust the sound. Professional audio-monitoring hardware is carefully calibrated to ensure that all frequencies play evenly—a so-called "flat" response, giving you confidence that you'll produce a consistent sound for your listeners.

It can be helpful to listen to your audio on low-quality speakers too. This allows you to confirm that enough of the audio is clear and that low-frequency sound doesn't cause distortion.

Premiere Pro offers a variety of helpful audio effects, including the following, all of which are available in the Effects panel:

- **Parametric Equalizer:** This allows you to make subtle and precise adjustments to the audio level at particular frequencies.

- **Studio Reverb:** This can increase the "presence" in the recording using reverb. For example, it can simulate the atmosphere of a larger room.

- **Dynamics Processing:** This effect allows you to make precise dynamic adjustments to audio to compress, expand, or limit levels.

- **Bass:** This effect can adjust the low-end frequencies of a clip. It works well on narration clips, particularly for male voices.

- **Treble:** This effect adjusts the higher-range frequencies in an audio clip.

Depending upon your operating system and the third party plugins you have installed (if any), you may also see AU, VST, VST3, or custom-named effect folders.

Apply effects by dragging them from the Effects panel onto clips, just as you dragged transition effects onto edits earlier. Select a clip to find its effect controls in the Effect Controls panel. There are many presets to help you get a feel for the ways you can use effects.

You can remove an effect in the Effect Controls panel by selecting it and pressing Delete.

You can use the 01 Effects sequence in this project to experiment with audio effects. The clips in this sequence have a range of audio to make it easy to hear the results of your adjustments.

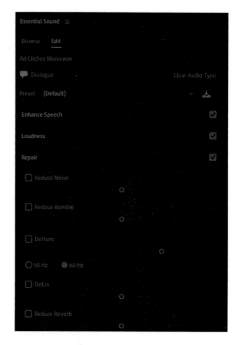

This lesson focuses on the Essential Sound panel, which offers a range of easy-to-apply professional adjustments and effects that are based on common workflows for standard media types like dialogue and music.

The Essential Sound panel should be your go-to set of options for audio cleanup and improvement.

Adjusting dialogue audio

The Essential Sound panel has a comprehensive list of features to help you work with dialogue audio.

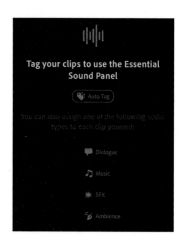

To use the Essential Sound panel, select one or more clips in a sequence, and select a tag that corresponds to the type of audio in the clip.

Selecting each tag displays different tools that are suitable for that type of media. There are more options for dialogue audio than any other—and for good reason! Your dialogue sound is probably the most important, and music, prepared special effects (SFX), and ambient sound files are often already mixed and ready to use.

If the wrong type of audio tag is selected, you can click Clear Audio Type at the top of the Essential Sound panel to remove it.

Every adjustment you apply with the Essential Sound panel actually adds one or more audio effects to your selected clips and modifies the settings for those effects. In a sense, the Essential Sound panel offers an excellent shortcut to achieving great results with simplified controls. After applying adjustments in the Essential Sound panel, you can select a clip and adjust the detailed effect settings in the Effect Controls panel.

In the following exercises, you'll try several of the adjustments available in the Essential Sound panel. All of the options you set can be stored as a preset, accessible at the top of the Essential Sound panel. Several presets are already available.

Setting loudness

The Essential Sound panel makes it easy to set the audio level for multiple clips to an appropriate volume for broadcast television.

Let's try this.

1 Open the sequence 02 Loudness.

   This is the sequence you worked with previously when learning about normalization.

2 Increase the height of the Audio 1 track, and zoom in a little so you can see the voice-over clips clearly.

3 Play the sequence to hear the different levels for the voice-over clips.

4 Select all the voice-over clips. The easiest way is to lasso across them, being careful not to select any of the other clips in the sequence.

5 In the Essential Sound panel, click the Dialogue button. This assigns the Dialogue audio type to these clips.

6 If necessary, click the title of the Loudness category to display the Loudness options. Clicking a category in this way is a little like clicking a disclosure triangle in the Effect Controls panel—options display or hide when you click.

7 Click Auto-Match.

Premiere Pro analyzes each clip and automatically adjusts Audio Gain to achieve the −23 LUFS standard level for broadcast television dialogue. LUFS stands for Loudness Units relative to full scale.

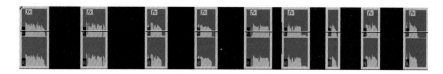

As with normalization, which also adjusts clip gain, this adjustment updates the waveforms for the clips.

If you are producing content for distribution via the internet, there's a good chance you will choose another audio level.

You can adjust the level for multiple selected clips, after using Auto-Match, using the Volume control at the bottom of the Essential Sound panel.

8 Play the sequence to hear the adjustment.

About the Loudness scale

Historically, audio level was described exclusively in *decibels* (dB). You'll find the decibel scale a useful reference all throughout production and post-production as it is still commonly used.

Peak level (the loudest moment of a clip's audio level) is often used to set limits for audio level. Although it's a useful reference, it doesn't account for the overall power or energy in a soundtrack, and it's common to produce a mix that sets every part of the soundtrack louder than is natural, for dramatic effect. A whisper, for example, can sound as loud as a shout. As long as the peak level of the audio is within prescribed limits, it might be allowed for broadcast television.

This is why, in some parts of the world, so many television commercials sound as loud as they do—even the quiet sections of the soundtrack are loud.

Intended to resolve this issue, the widely adopted *Loudness scale* measures the total energy over time. When a Loudness limit is used, it's okay for content to have loud sections, but the total amount of energy in the soundtrack per minute can't rise above the level set.

If you are producing content for broadcast television, you will almost certainly use the Loudness scale when assessing your audio mix, and this is the scale the Essential Sound panel uses.

Repairing audio

However hard you try to capture clean audio on location, it's likely some of your footage will have unwanted background noise.

The Essential Sound panel has a number of ways to clean up dialogue clips. Take a look at the Repair category to reveal the options for repairing dialogue.

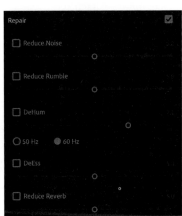

- **Reduce Noise:** Reduce the level of unwanted noises in the background, like the sound of an air-conditioning unit, rustling clothes, or background hiss.

- **Reduce Rumble:** Reduce low-frequency sounds, such as engine noise or some types of wind noise.

- **DeHum:** Reduce electrical interference hum. In North and South America, this is in the 60 Hz range, while in Europe, Asia, and Africa, it's in the 50 Hz range. If your microphone cable was lying next to a power cable, you may have this intrusive but easy-to-remove unwanted sound.

- **DeEss:** Reduce harsh, high-frequency "ess"-like sounds common in the sibilance part of voice recordings.

- **Reduce Reverb:** Reduce the effect of reflected sounds to make vocals clearer. When recording in an environment with a lot of reflective surfaces, some of the sound may be reflected back to the microphone as reverb.

Different clips are likely to benefit from one or more of these cleanup features, and often you will use a combination.

The default settings have high enough intensity to make it clear when a repair is enabled or disabled. In most cases, you will obtain the best results by starting with a setting of 0, playing the audio, and increasing the effect intensity during playback until you are happy with the result, minimizing potential distortion.

Let's try cleaning up some power hum.

▶ **Tip:** You can turn the display of audio and video clip names on and off by choosing the appropriate options from the Timeline Display Settings menu.

1   Open the sequence 03 Noise Reduction.

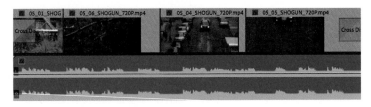

2   Play the sequence to listen to the voice-over.

This is a simple sequence, with a voice-over accompanying some visuals. There's a loud electrical interference power hum in the audio. If you can't hear the hum, your speakers may not be able to reproduce audio at sufficiently low frequencies—try listening with headphones.

3   Select the voice-over clip in the sequence.

The clip has already been designated as dialogue in the Essential Sound panel, so the dialogue audio options are displayed.

4   If it's not already open, click the Repair heading in the Essential Sound panel to display the options. Select DeHum to turn it on.

5   Play the sequence to hear the difference.

The impact is significant! The electrical interference hum was loud but at a specific frequency, which makes removing it relatively straightforward.

▶ **Tip:** For more challenging audio cleanup, when the repair options in Premiere Pro don't give you a result that is clean enough, try Adobe Audition, which has advanced noise reduction features. Learn more in *Adobe Audition CC Classroom in a Book, 2nd Edition.*

If the amount of DeHum impacts the speech in the voice-over, try dragging the slider to adjust the amount.

This example clip has 60 Hz hum, so the default option of 60 Hz is suitable. If the default option doesn't work, try switching to 50 Hz.

After adjusting the DeHum control, check the start of the clip. You may discover a tiny amount of hum remains before the repair is applied. To remove this, add a short crossfade at the beginning of the clip.

Reducing noise and reverb

In addition to specific types of background noise like hum and rumble, Premiere Pro offers advanced noise and reverb reduction tools. These audio cleanup effects have simple controls in the Essential Sound panel and more advanced options when accessed via the Effect Controls panel.

Reducing noise

Let's try reducing noise first.

1   Open the sequence 04 Auto Noise and Reverb. This sequence has clips suffering from background noise *and* reverberation. Play the sequence to familiarize yourself with this challenging audio—lots of unwanted background noise and reverb because it was recorded at a noisy location.

© Copyright Maxim Jago 2018

The clips in this sequence have already been assigned the Dialogue audio type in the Essential Sound panel, and the Auto-Match option in the Loudness category has been applied.

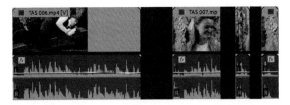

Tip: You can reset any slider in the Essential Sound panel to its default value by double-clicking the control.

2 Select the first clip in the sequence. In the Repair section of the Essential Sound panel, select Reduce Noise. The default setting for the effect intensity is 5.0.

3 Play the clip in the sequence to hear the difference. The loud rumble that begins at about 00:00:10:00 is immediately much quieter.

4 As with many effects, trial and error will usually yield the best results. Try adjusting the effect intensity during playback. If the effect is too strong, speech might begin to sound distorted. If the effect is not strong enough, too much of the unwanted background sound might remain. When you finish experimenting, leave the setting on 5.0.

Part of the challenge in working with this audio is that some of the low-frequency background sound is close to some of the frequencies of the speech, making it harder to automatically remove. Let's use more advanced settings.

5 Make sure the first clip is still selected in the Timeline panel, and open the Effect Controls panel. Click the Edit button to access the advanced controls for the DeNoise effect, which Premiere Pro applied to the clip when you enabled Reduce Noise in the Essential Sound panel.

The Essential Sound panel and the Effect Controls panel

As soon as you enable Reduce Noise in the Essential Sound panel, Premiere Pro applies a DeNoise effect to the selected sequence clip, which you'll see in the Effect Controls panel. In

fact, every adjustment you make in the Essential Sound panel will result in a new effect or adjustments to existing effects accessible in the Effect Controls panel.

You can think of the Essential Sound panel as an intelligent shortcut to ideal audio effects with optimized settings that you can adjust in the Effect Controls panel. If you can't see the Effect Controls panel, you can access it via the Window menu.

The Clip Fx Editor - DeNoise window opens. During playback, the DeNoise effect graph shows the originally detected noise (in blue at the bottom) and the cleanup adjustment applied (in red at the top). While the effect controls are open, you can still interact with the Timeline panel, placing the playhead and playing the sequence.

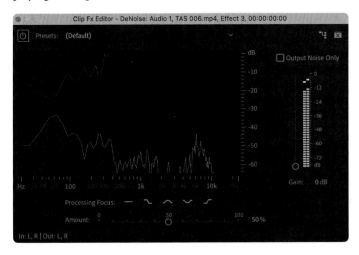

The left end of the graph shows low frequencies, and the right end shows high frequencies.

6 Play the clip again and pay particular attention to the activity in the graph when there is no speech, only rumble.

It's clear that the unwanted rumble is in the low frequencies.

Take a look at the controls:

- **Presets:** You can choose Heavy or Light Noise Reduction; these two options adjust the Amount setting.

- **Amount:** Use this to adjust the intensity of the effect.

- **Output Noise Only:** Enable this option to hear only the noise that is being removed. This is helpful when assessing whether you're removing too much of the desired audio.

- **Gain:** When reducing noise, you'll naturally be reducing the overall level of the audio. You can adjust the overall gain here to compensate. By looking at the level meter before and after applying the effect, you can see how much gain to apply to keep the overall audio at the original level.

The Processing Focus control is a little less self-explanatory.

By default, Premiere Pro applies the DeNoise effect to the full frequency range of a clip—that means it applies equally to low, medium, and high tone sounds. Using the Processing Focus control, you can selectively apply the effect to particular frequencies. If you hover your pointer over an option, a tool tip describes it, but you'll probably be able to guess which is which from the shape of the button icons.

7   Click to select the Focus On Lower Frequencies option, and play the clip again. This sounds good, but let's push the effect a little harder.

8   Drag the Amount slider up to around 80%, and play the clip again. Next, try setting the slider to 100%, and play the clip.

   ● **Note:** When you modify effect settings, related options in the Essential Sound panel are marked with ▲ as a reminder that you customized the settings. You may need to close the effect editor before a triangle will be displayed.

With the focus on the lower frequencies, even setting the effect to full allows the speech to be audible, and the rumble is almost gone. Even with this more advanced control, you will need to experiment to get the ideal result.

9   For now, set the amount to 80%, and close the Clip Fx Editor - DeNoise window.

Reducing reverb

The Reduce Reverb option works in a similar way to the Reduce Noise option.

Let's try it.

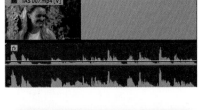

1   Listen to the second clip in the sequence. The audio has strong reverb caused by the hard surfaces at the recording location bouncing audio back to the microphone.

    The background noise is less of a challenge in this clip, but the reverb is quite intense.

2   Select the clip, and select Reduce Reverb under the Repair heading in the Essential Sound panel.

    The difference is dramatic! Just as you finessed the Reduce Noise setting, you should experiment with the Reduce Reverb setting to get the optimum balance between the effect being applied with enough intensity and the speech sounding natural.

    When you selected Reduce Reverb, Premiere Pro applied a DeReverb effect to the clip. You can access the effect controls in the Effect Controls panel.

3   Click the Edit button for the effect in the Effect Controls panel, and play a little of the second clip in the Timeline panel to update the graph in the Clip Fx Editor - DeReverb window.

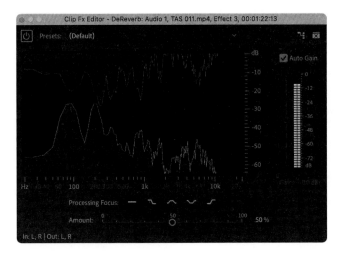

Although the colors are a little different, the DeReverb settings are otherwise almost identical to the DeNoise settings. However, you'll notice the Auto Gain option in the upper-right corner.

When reducing reverb, a reduced overall level is inevitable. Auto Gain automatically compensates, making this effect even easier to set up.

4 Make sure Auto Gain is selected, and play the clip to compare the result; then close the DeReverb settings window.

5 There are two more clips in this sequence for you to experiment with. Try combining the Reduce Noise and Reduce Reverb options for these clips, with lower values for subtler results.

Enhancing Speech

The Enhance Speech section of the Essential Sound panel has just two controls: an Enhance button and a Mix Amount slider, which allows you to blend the enhanced audio with the original audio to achieve a mix that works best for your media.

This remarkable audio cleanup feature uses Adobe Sensei GenAI technology to generate new, original audio that is separate from but inspired by the audio in your clip. The result is intended to be the audio you *would have wanted* to record.

There are no other controls, and the process is fully automated. The audio processing is also performed on your computer, so there is no need for an internet connection to upload or download the audio for processing on a server.

To try this feature with the first clip in the current sequence, first turn off Reduce Noise in the Repair section of the Essential Sound panel. Next, click Enhance in the Enhance Speech section and wait for the processing to complete.

To compare the results with the original clip audio, experiment with the Mix Amount slider.

Improving clarity

The Clarity category in the Essential Sound panel gives you three quick and easy ways to improve the quality of spoken audio:

- **Dynamics:** Increases or decreases the dynamic range of the audio—that is, the range of volume between the quietest and loudest parts of the recording.

- **EQ:** Applies amplitude (volume) adjustments at specific frequencies. A list of presets makes selecting useful settings easy.

- **Vocal Enhancer:** Improves clarity at specific frequencies, depending on your selection of a high-tone or low-tone voice.

Experiment with all three controls, as you'll find different dialogue recordings will benefit from different combinations of settings.

Let's try these settings.

1 Open the sequence 05 Clarity.

This sequence has the same content as the 03 Noise Reduction sequence, but there are two versions of the voice-over. The first version is cleaner than the second.

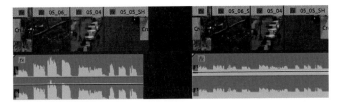

2 Listen to the first voice-over clip.

3 Select the first voice-over clip, and in the Essential Sound panel, scroll down to the Clarity options. You may need to click the Clarity heading to expand the options.

4 Select Dynamics, and experiment with different levels of adjustment. You can play the sequence while making adjustments in the Essential Sound panel, and the effect will be applied "live." Disable Dynamics when you have tried a few settings.

5 Select EQ and experiment with the Preset options. Some presets, like Old Radio, produce dramatic results!

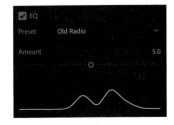

When you apply an EQ preset, a diagram illustrating the adjustment appears. This diagram is based on a Parametric Equalizer effect (see "Using the Parametric Equalizer effect" later in this lesson for more on this effect). You can adjust the Amount slider to add more or less of the effect.

6 Play the second voice-over clip.

7 Select the second voice-over clip, and in the Clarity section of the Essential Sound panel, select Enhance Speech and make sure High Tone is selected.

8 Play the second voice-over clip. Try selecting and deselecting Enhance Speech during playback.

The difference is subtle. In fact, you may need headphones or good-quality studio monitors to clearly detect the improvement. This option clarifies speech to make it more apprehensible, and in some cases, this means reducing the power in the lower frequencies.

Making creative adjustments

Below the Clarity section of the Essential Sound panel is the Creative section.

This has just one adjustment, Reverb. The effect can be similar to recording in a large room with lots of reflective surfaces, or it can be subtler.

Experiment with this effect on the first voice-over clip in the 05 Clarity sequence.

Just a small amount of reverb can "thicken" a voice to give it more presence.

Adjusting volume

In addition to adjusting the gain for clips in the Project panel, setting the volume level for clips in a sequence, and applying an automated Loudness adjustment, you can also set clip volume using the option at the bottom of the Essential Sound panel.

It's curious that this additional option exists—especially considering the number of ways you can already adjust the volume of your clips.

But there's something special about this volume control: No matter how much you change the volume of your clips using this control, the level will not distort. That is, the clips won't *override* (become so loud that the loudest parts of the audio cannot be played).

Try this now.

1 Open the sequence 06 Level.

This sequence contains just one clip—a reasonably loud version of the voice-over clip you have heard already.

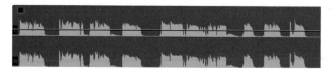

2 Select the clip and play the sequence. While the sequence plays, use the Clip Volume Level adjustment to increase and decrease the playback level.

3 Try increasing the level to the maximum, +15 dB.

No matter how much you adjust the audio level, it won't override. Even if you combine a clip gain increase with a clip volume increase (using the rubber band) and then apply this adjustment, the clip will not override.

4 Reset the Clip Volume Level adjustment by double-clicking the slider.

Note: It's a good idea to reset controls in the Essential Sound panel to their default values before making adjustments. You can do this quickly by double-clicking a control.

Using additional audio effects

As mentioned at the beginning of this lesson, there are many audio effects available in the Effects panel.

The adjustments you have made with the Essential Sound panel have resulted in regular audio effects being added to clips automatically as you worked.

Setting up effects in this way is quicker because all of the Essential Sound panel adjustments work like presets—as soon as you have set things the way you want them in the Essential Sound panel, the effects are set up appropriately in the Effect Controls panel.

Take a look now at the Effect Controls panel, with the clip you worked on in the 06 Level sequence selected.

When you made a Clip Volume Level adjustment in the Essential Sound panel, Premiere Pro applied a Hard Limiter effect to the clip, with settings to match the adjustment you applied.

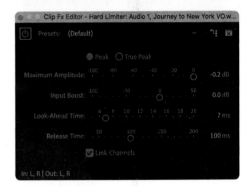

Click the Edit button for the Hard Limiter effect in the Effect Controls panel, and you'll discover all of the settings for this advanced effect are available in case you'd like to change them. If you make changes in the Essential Sound panel, you can even watch the controls update dynamically in the Effect Controls panel.

In most cases, the settings applied by the Essential Sound panel will be suitable, but the option to make further subtle changes will always be available.

Using Essential Sound panel presets

If you expect to use a combination of Essential Sound panel settings often, consider creating a preset. To create a preset, select an audio type, apply some settings, and click the Save Settings As A Preset button at the top of the Essential Sound panel. Once created, you can apply a preset without first assigning the audio type.

Essential Sound panel presets are not fixed—you can apply a preset, make changes to the settings, and even create a new preset based on the adjustments you have made.

Using the Parametric Equalizer effect

The Parametric Equalizer effect offers a nuanced and intuitive interface for precise audio level adjustment at specific frequencies.

It includes a graphic interface you can use to drag level adjustment controls that are linked together to achieve nuanced, natural-sounding audio.

Let's try this effect.

1   Open the sequence 07 Full Parametric EQ. This sequence has one musical clip and one voice-over clip.

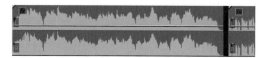

2   Locate the Parametric Equalizer effect in the Effects panel (try using the Search box at the top of the window), and drag the effect onto the first clip.

3   Make sure the clip is selected, and in the Effect Controls panel, click the Edit button to access the Custom Setup controls for the Parametric Equalizer effect.

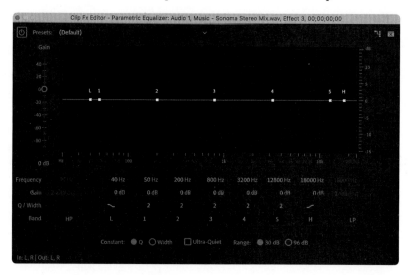

The horizontal axis of the graphic control area indicates frequency, while the vertical axis shows amplitude. The blue line across the middle of the graph represents any adjustments you have made.

Wherever the blue line is higher or lower in the display, adjustments are made to the audio level at those frequencies. You can reshape the line by dragging any of the five main control points directly, as well as the Low Pass (labeled *L*) and High Pass (labeled *H*) controls at the ends.

On the left is an overall Gain level adjustment, which offers a quick fix if the changes you make result in audio that is too loud or too quiet overall.

4 Play the clip to get familiar with its sound. The graphic control area displays the level throughout the frequency range, just as the DeHum and DeReverb effects did.

At the bottom of the dialog box, there's a Range option. By default, the Parametric Equalizer effect graph allows adjustments up to +/−15 dB.

Change Range to 96 dB now, so you can make adjustments up to +/−48 dB.

5 Drag Control Point 1 on the blue line quite a long way down in the graph to reduce the audio level at low frequencies. Listen to the music again.

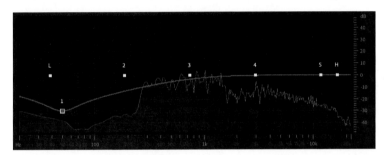

Changes you make to a specific frequency reshape the blue line, impacting surrounding frequencies and resulting in a more natural sound.

The control points you drag have a range of influence that is defined by their Q setting.

Adjustments made to the blue line update the detailed controls below. These two areas of the dialog box are connected—adjust one and the other updates automatically.

The control point numbers are at the bottom of each column of settings, and they double up as an enable/disable toggle for the control point.

In the previous example, Control Point 1 was set to 50 Hz (which is very low frequency), with a gain adjustment of −29.8 dB (which is a big gain reduction) and a Q of 2 (which is quite a wide curve for the blue line).

6 Change the Q factor for Control Point 1 from 2 to 7. You can click the 2 and type in a new setting directly.

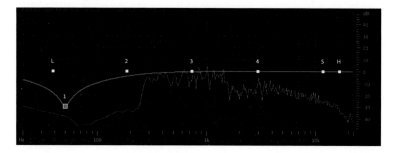

The line has a much sharper curve, so the adjustment you are making now applies to fewer frequencies.

7 Play the sequence to hear the changes.

Let's refine the vocals.

▶ **Tip:** Another way to use the Parametric Equalizer effect is to target a specific frequency and either boost it or cut it. You can use this effect to cut a particular frequency, like a high-frequency noise or a low hum.

8 Voices are mostly in the range of 100–1000 Hz. Control Point 3 is at 800 Hz by default, which is in the most prominent portion of the vocal range. Drag Control Point 3 down to about –20 dB, and set the Q factor to **1** for a very broad adjustment. You can also click the blue numbers to add these settings.

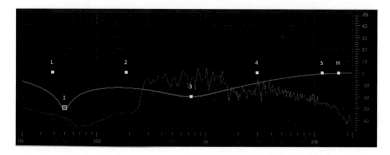

9 Play the sequence to hear the changes. The vocals are much quieter.

● **Note:** Avoid setting the volume too high (the Audio Meters will show some red, and the peak monitors will light up). This can lead to distortion.

10 Drag Control Point 4 to around 1500 Hz, with a gain of +6.0 dB. Adjust the Q factor to **3** for more precise adjustment on the EQ adjustment.

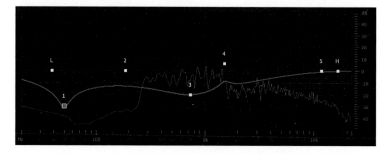

11 Play the sequence to hear the changes.

12 Drag the High Pass control (the H control) down, setting its gain to around −8.0 dB to make the highest frequencies quieter.

13 Use the Gain control to adjust the overall level. You may need to see your audio meters to find out whether your mix is right.

14 Close the Parametric Equalizer settings.

15 Play the sequence to hear the changes.

▶ **Tip:** If your audio meters are not displayed, you can access them by choosing Window > Audio Meters.

These are dramatic changes intended to illustrate a technique. Of course, you'll usually make subtler adjustments.

One of the most common uses for the Parametric Equalizer effect is for improving the quality of vocals. The second clip in the sequence is a voice-over clip. Use this to experiment with the Parametric Equalizer effect. The quality of the audio is already acceptable, but you should be able to add nuance and power to the speech with subtle adjustments using this effect.

Audio adjustments and effects can be modified during playback. You might want to enable looping playback in the Program Monitor rather than clicking repeatedly to play a clip or sequence.

You can enable looping playback by choosing Loop from the Program Monitor Settings menu.

There are also useful additional buttons available in the Program Monitor Button Editor ➕.

- Loop 🔁: This toggles looped playback on and off. If you have set In and Out points, playback will loop between them.

- Play Video In To Out ⏮: If you have set In and Out points, the sequence will play between them and stop.

Audio Plug-in Manager

It's easy to install third-party plug-ins. Choose Premiere Pro > Settings > Audio (macOS) or Edit > Preferences > Audio (Windows). Then click Manage Audio Plug-ins.

1 If you would like to add a directory that contains AU (macOS only) or VST plug-ins, click the Add button.

2 If needed, click the Scan For Plug-Ins button to find all available plug-ins.

3 Click the Enable All button to activate all of the plug-ins, or select individual plug-ins to activate them alone.

4 Click OK to apply your changes.

Using the Notch effect

The Notch effect removes frequencies near a specified value. The effect targets a frequency range and eliminates those sounds. The effect works well for removing radio interference hum and other electrical interference.

1 Open the sequence 08 Notch Filter.

2 Play the sequence and listen for the electrical hum. You can hear fluorescent light bulbs buzzing.

3 In the Effects panel, locate the Notch Filter effect (not the Simple Notch Filter effect) and apply it to the clip in the sequence. When you do, the clip is automatically selected, so the effect controls will appear in the Effect Controls panel.

4 In the Effect Controls panel, click the Edit button for the Notch Filter effect.

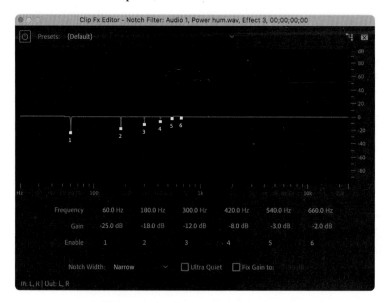

The Notch Filter effect looks a lot like the Parametric Equalizer effect and functions in a similar way. However, you will notice there's no Q control, which sets the sharpness of the curves. By default each adjustment is extremely acute, and a Notch Width menu allows you to adjust the curves.

5 While playing the sequence, experiment with presets and listen to the results.

The presets usually apply multiple adjustments. This is because signal interference is often found in multiple harmonic frequencies.

6 Choose 60 Hz And Octaves from the Presets menu and then listen to the sequence again to find out whether it's improved.

7   Often, when working with the Notch Filter effect, you'll listen, adjust, and listen again until you get the settings you need.

This audio has hum at 60 Hz, 120 Hz, and 240 Hz. These and more have been targeted by the preset you chose. Click the Enable buttons for Control Points 4, 5, and 6 to turn them off.

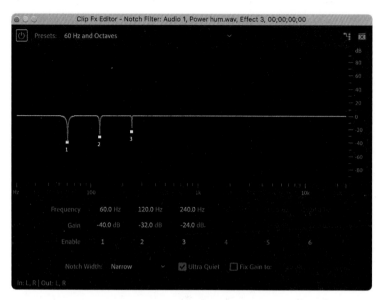

Now play the sequence again to review the effect. Even though the interference was at precise frequencies, it made hearing the vocals difficult. Now it's removed, and everything sounds clearer.

8   Close the effect settings.

When you used the Essential Sound panel to apply DeHum, a similar effect was applied to the clip—the DeHummer.

The Notch Filter effect has slightly more advanced controls, so if you don't get the result you need using the Essential Sound panel, try this next.

Close this project by choosing File > Close Project. If you are asked if you would like to save, do so.

Removing background noise with Adobe Audition

Adobe Audition offers advanced mixing and effects to improve your overall sound. You can send a whole sequence or an individual clip to Audition, directly from Premiere Pro.

If you have Audition installed, you can try the following:

1   In Premiere Pro, re-open your Lesson 11 Working.prproj file, and open the sequence 09 Send to Audition from the Project panel.

2   Right-click the Noisy Audio.aif clip in the Timeline panel and choose Edit Clip In Adobe Audition.

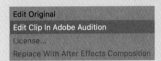

A new copy of the audio clip is created (with "Audio Extracted" appended to the name) and added to your project, both in the same bin as the original clip and replacing the original clip in the sequence. Audition opens, along with the new clip.

3   In Audition, the stereo clip should be visible in the Editor panel. Audition shows a large waveform for the clip. To use Audition's advanced noise reduction tools, you need to identify part of the clip that's just the noise so Audition knows what to remove.

4   If you don't see Spectral Frequency Display under the waveform, click the Show Spectral Frequency Display button ■ at the top of the application window. Play the clip. The beginning contains a few seconds of just noise, which is perfect for making a selection.

5   Using the Time Selection tool (the I-bar tool ▮ in the toolbar), drag to select a quiet area at the beginning of the waveform to highlight a section of noise you just identified.

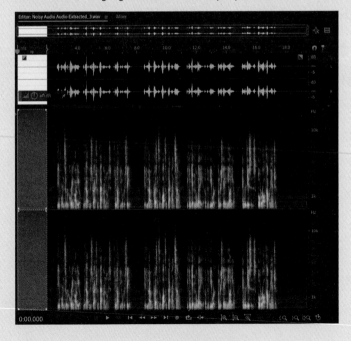

6   With the selection active, choose Effects > Noise Reduction/Restoration > Capture Noise Print. You can also press Shift+P. Click OK in the confirmation dialog.

7   Choose Effects > Noise Reduction/Restoration > Noise Reduction (process). You can also press Shift+Command+P (macOS) or Shift+Ctrl+P (Windows). A new panel opens so you can process the noise.

8   Click Select Entire File to select the entire clip.

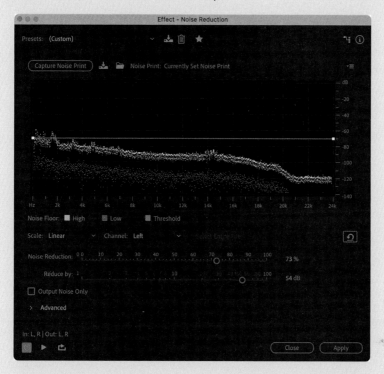

9   Select Output Noise Only. This allows you to hear only the noise you're removing, which helps you make an accurate selection so you don't accidentally remove too much of the audio you want to keep.

10 Click the Play button at the bottom of the window, and adjust the Noise Reduction and Reduce By sliders to remove noise from the clip. Try not to pull down much or any of the voice.

11 Deselect Output Noise Only, and listen to your cleaned-up audio. You may decide to begin again, selecting a different section of the audio when capturing the noise print to achieve a cleaner result.

12 When you're happy with the results, click the Apply button to apply the cleanup.

13 Choose File > Close, and save your changes.

14 Saving in Audition automatically updates the clip in Premiere Pro. Switch back to Premiere Pro, where you can listen to the cleaned-up audio clip. You can quit Audition.

Review questions

1 How would you use the Essential Sound panel to set an industry-standard audio level for broadcast television dialogue clips?

2 What's a quick, easy way to remove electrical interference hum from clips?

3 Where can you find the more detailed controls for the options you set using the Essential Sound panel?

4 How can you send a clip to Adobe Audition directly from the Premiere Pro timeline?

Review answers

1 Select the clips you want to adjust. In the Essential Sound panel, choose Dialogue as the audio type. Then, in the Loudness section, click Auto-Match.

2 Use DeHum in the Essential Sound panel to remove electrical interference hum. Try the 60 Hz or 50 Hz option, depending on the origin of your source footage.

3 Adjustments you make using the Essential Sound panel are applied as effects to clips. You can find the detailed controls by selecting a clip and looking in the Effect Controls panel.

4 Right-click the clip and choose Edit Clip In Adobe Audition.

12 ADDING VIDEO EFFECTS

Lesson overview

In this lesson, you'll learn how to do the following:

- Work with fixed effects.
- Browse effects with the Effects panel.
- Apply and remove effects.
- Mask and track video effects.
- Use keyframing effects.
- Use effect presets.
- Explore frequently used effects.
- Render effects.

 This lesson will take about 120 minutes to complete. To get the lesson files used in this chapter, download them from the web page for this book at *peachpit.com/PremiereProCIB2024*. For more information, see "Accessing the lesson files and Web Edition" in the "Getting Started" section at the beginning of this book. Store the files on your computer in a convenient location.

Adobe Premiere Pro features more than 80 video effects. In this lesson, you'll learn the main skills you need to work with all kinds of effects, as well as some of the more advanced workflows. Most effects come with an array of controls, almost all of which you can change over time using keyframes.

Starting the lesson

Note: To ensure that the tools function and the defaults are set exactly as described in this lesson, reset the Premiere Pro preferences by holding Option (macOS) or Alt (Windows) while launching the application and then clicking Continue in the Reset Options dialog box.

You might use video effects for many reasons. They can solve problems with image quality, such as under exposure or a color balance offset. They can create complex composite video effects using techniques such as chromakey. They can also help solve a number of production problems, such as camera shake or a poorly lit subject.

1 Open Lesson 12.prproj.

2 Save the project as **Lesson 12 Working.prproj**.

3 Switch to the Effects workspace by choosing Effects from the Workspaces menu.

4 Reset the workspace by returning to the Workspaces menu and choosing Reset To Saved Layout.

Effects can also serve stylistic purposes. You can distort footage or alter its color, and you can animate the size and position of a clip within the frame. The exciting challenge is in knowing when to use an effect and when to keep it simple.

Standard effects can be constrained within elliptical or polygon masks, and these masks can automatically track your footage. For example, you might blur someone's face to hide their identity and have the blur follow them as they move through the shot. You can use the same feature to relight a scene in post-production.

Working with video effects

You already know how to apply effects and change their settings. You can drag a video effect onto a clip, as you have already done with audio effects, or you can select the clip (or multiple clips) and double-click the effect in the Effects panel. You can combine as many effects as you want on a single clip, which can produce surprising results. You can use an adjustment layer to add effects to a collection of clips.

When it comes to deciding which video effects to use, the number of choices in Premiere Pro can be a little overwhelming. Plus, *many* additional effects are available from third-party manufacturers for sale or free of charge.

Although the range of effects and their controls can be complex, the techniques you'll use to apply, adjust, and remove effects are straightforward and consistent.

Modifying fixed effects

When you add a clip to a sequence, it will automatically have a few effects applied. These effects are called *fixed* effects, or *intrinsic* effects, and you can think of them as controls for the usual geometric, opacity, speed, and audio properties that every clip should have.

Although fixed effects are applied automatically, they don't change the appearance of clips until you modify their settings. The effects include:

- **Motion:** The Motion effect allows you to animate, rotate, and scale a clip. You can also use the Anti-flicker Filter control to decrease shimmering edges for an animated object. This comes in handy when you scale down a high-resolution or interlaced source and Premiere Pro must resample the image.

- **Opacity:** The Opacity effect lets you control how opaque or transparent a clip is. You can also access special blend modes to create visual effects from multiple layers of graphics or video. You'll explore this more in Lesson 14.

- **Time Remapping:** This effect lets you slow down, speed up, or reverse playback, and it even lets you freeze a frame. Think of it as a more advanced version of the Clip Speed/Duration options in the Timeline panel. In fact, the two controls are linked.

- **Audio Effects:** If a clip has audio, Premiere Pro displays its Volume, Channel Volume, and Panner controls. You learned about these in Lesson 10.

You can modify all fixed effects using the Effect Controls panel.

1   If it's not already in the Timeline panel, open the sequence 01 Fixed Effects. Scrub through the sequence to familiarize yourself with the content.

▶ **Tip:** To expand or collapse all items in the Effect Controls panel or the Project panel, hold Option (macOS) or Alt (Windows) when you click a disclosure triangle.

2   Click the first clip in the sequence to select it. In the Effect Controls panel, review the fixed effects applied to this clip.

3   Click the disclosure triangles ❯ next to headings or individual controls to display their properties.

4   Click to select the second clip in the sequence, and look at the Effect
    Controls panel.

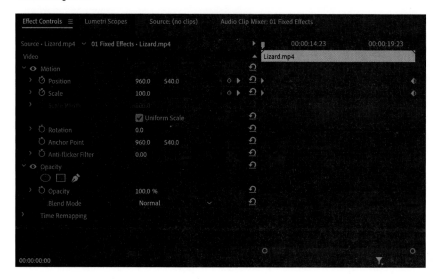

These Position and Scale controls under the Motion effect heading have keyframes, so the settings can change over time. In this case, a slow Scale and Position animation was applied to the clip to create a digital zoom that didn't exist
before and to recompose the shot.

When people fix attention on an object, they tend to experience subtle tunnel
vision. A slow zoom-in effect can feel the same way for your audience, enhancing
the viewer's focus and adding tension in a dramatic moment.

5   Play the current sequence to compare the two clips and view the animation at
    normal playback speed.

Navigating the Effects panel

In addition to the fixed video effects, Premiere Pro has standard effects that change
a clip's appearance. Because there are so many to choose from, effects are organized
into categories, such as Distort, Keying, and Time, so you can more easily navigate
them. If you install third-party effects, you will have even more choices.

The Obsolete category is a special case.

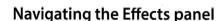

Many of the effects in the Obsolete category have been replaced with newer, better-
designed, or alternative versions, but Adobe keeps them in Premiere Pro to ensure
compatibility with older project files. It is best not to use these effects when working
on new projects as they may be removed in future versions.

Each category has its own bin in the Effects panel. Like the Project panel, the Effects panel includes the option to create new bins to store copies of effects to make it easier to locate them.

Tip: The keyboard shortcut to display the Effects panel is Shift+7.

1   Open the Effects panel, and expand the Video Effects category.

2   Click the New Custom Bin button at the bottom of the panel.

The new custom bin appears in the Effects panel at the bottom of the list (you may need to scroll down to see it). Let's rename it.

Note: When you add an effect to a custom bin in the Effects panel, the original effect remains in its original folder. You can use custom bins to create your own additional effect categories.

3   The bin name should be selected, ready to rename. If not, click once to select the bin, and click once more, directly on the bin's name (Custom Bin 01), to select that.

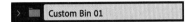

4   Change its name to **Favorite Effects**.

5   Expand a few video effects categories and drag several effects into your new Favorite Effects bin to copy them. You may need to resize the panel to make it easier to drag effects. Choose any effects that sound interesting to you. You can add or remove effects from a custom bin whenever you like. You can also click the Delete Custom Items button 🗑 to remove copied effects.

Tip: With so many video effect categories, it's sometimes tricky to locate the effect you want. If you know part or all of an effect's name, start typing it in the search box at the top of the Effects panel. Premiere Pro will display all effects and transitions that contain that letter combination, narrowing the search as you type.

Effect types

If you are working on a smaller computer monitor, some additional useful icons may be hidden in the Effects panel.

If necessary, resize the Effects panel until you can see all of the Effect Type buttons next to the search box.

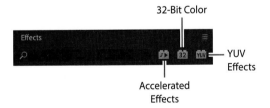

If you widen the Effects panel a little more, you'll notice icons next to many of the effect names (you may need to resize the Effects panel to see the icons). Understanding these icons should influence your choices when working with effects.

Only some effects have all three icons. Click the effect type buttons at the top of the Effects panel to display only effects with those features.

Accelerated effects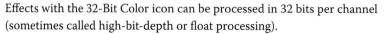

The Accelerated Effect icon indicates that the effect can be accelerated by your graphics processing unit (GPU). The GPU (often called the video card or graphics card) can greatly enhance the performance of Premiere Pro. The range of cards supported by the Mercury Playback Engine is broad, and with the right card installed, these effects offer accelerated or even real-time performance and need rendering only on final export (which is also hardware accelerated). You'll find a list of recommended cards on the Premiere Pro product page.

32-bit color (high-bit-depth) effects

Effects with the 32-Bit Color icon can be processed in 32 bits per channel (sometimes called high-bit-depth or float processing).

For maximum quality, use 32-bit color effects.

If you are editing without GPU acceleration, in Software mode, Premiere Pro will render effects in 8-bit color by default. To take advantage of 32-bit color effects, make sure your sequence settings have the Maximum Bit Depth video-rendering option selected. If your project is set to use a hardware-accelerated renderer (in the Project settings), supported accelerated effects will automatically be rendered in 32-bit.

> **Note:** When using 32-bit color effects on a clip, try to use only combinations of 32-bit effects for maximum quality. If you mix and match effects on a single clip, the non-32-bit effects force processing back to 8-bit color for that clip.

Understanding bit depth

Bit depth is the number of steps from one end of a scale to another. A good example is the brightness of a pixel. How many steps should there be between 0% brightness and 100% brightness?

Many video cameras record 8-bit video by default. Without getting into how it's calculated, 8-bit video gives 256 steps per color channel from one end of the scale to the other.

For every 1 bit you add, the number of steps doubles. So, 10-bit video (a popular option) has 1,024 steps.

Because these scales begin at 0 (not 1), they are really:

    8-bit: 0–255

    10-bit: 0–1,023

32-bit processing allows more than 4 billion possible steps—that's a lot of doubling! When rendering effects in 32-bit color, the result is as good as lossless—no quality is lost when calculating the effect.

YUV effects

Effects with the YUV icon process color in YUV (processed in Premiere Pro as Luminance, Color-Blue, Color-Red channels). This is particularly important if you're applying color adjustments.

Effects with the YUV icon process color in YUV color mode. YUV effects break down the video into a Y (or luminance) channel and two channels for color information, which is how most video footage is structured natively. Because the brightness of the image is separate from the colors, it's easy to adjust contrast and exposure without shifting the colors.

Effects without the YUV icon are processed in the computer's native RGB space, which might make adjusting exposure and color less accurate.

Note: To learn more about YUV effects, be sure to read the article at *www.providecoalition .com/what_is_yuv.*

Applying effects

Once you have applied an effect, the video effect settings are accessible in the Effect Controls panel. You can add keyframes to nearly every control to apply changes over time (just look for controls with a stopwatch icon). In addition, you can use Bezier curve handles on those keyframes to adjust the velocity and acceleration of those changes.

1 Open the sequence 02 Browse.

2 Type **white** into the Effects panel search box to narrow the results. Locate the Black & White video effect.

Tip: If you type the word **black** instead of **white** into the Effects panel search box, you'll see a fantastic list of Lumetri presets for Blackmagic Cameras. Typing the word **white** instead displays a shorter list of effects to scroll through.

3 Drag the Black & White video effect onto the Run Past clip in the Timeline panel.

This effect immediately converts your full-color footage to black and white, or, more accurately, grayscale.

4 Make sure the Run Past clip is selected in the Timeline panel, and open the Effect Controls panel.

5 Toggle the Black & White effect off and on by clicking the FX button  next to the effect name in the Effect Controls panel. Be sure the sequence playhead is over the clip to view the result.

Toggling an effect on and off is a good way to see how it works with other effects.

6 Make sure the clip is selected. In the Effect Controls panel, click the Black & White effect heading to select it, and press Delete (macOS) or Backspace/Delete (Windows). This removes the effect.

7 Type **direction** into the Effects panel search box to locate the Directional Blur video effect.

● **Note:** If you have a clip selected, you can apply effects by double-clicking them in the Effects panel or by dragging them into the Effect Controls panel directly.

8 In the Effects panel, double-click the Directional Blur effect to apply it to the selected clip.

9 In the Effect Controls panel, expand the Directional Blur effect's controls if they are not already expanded.

10 Set Direction to **75.0** degrees and Blur Length to **45**.

▶ **Tip:** The upper limit for a slider may be smaller than the number you can enter by typing.

11 It's an interesting result, but now it's impossible to tell what's going on in the image. This might work well if you were simulating a very fast pan effect (a so-called *whip pan*), but let's tone down the intensity. Click the disclosure triangle to expand the Blur Length control, and move the slider to reduce the strength of the effect.

As you change the setting, the result is displayed in the Program Monitor.

● **Note:** You won't always use video effects to achieve dramatic results for visual impact. Sometimes effects are intended to look natural.

12 Click the panel menu ☰ for the Effect Controls panel, and choose Remove Effects. The Remove Attributes dialog box opens.

13 The Remove Attributes dialog box lets you select which effects to remove and deselect which effects you want to keep. By default, everything is selected. You want to remove them all, so click OK. This is an easy way to start fresh.

▶ **Tip:** You can also access the Remove Attributes dialog box by right-clicking one or more selected clips in the Timeline panel and choosing Remove Attributes from the contextual menu or by selecting one or more clips and choosing Edit > Remove Attributes.

Premiere Pro processes effects in a particular order, which can lead to unwanted scaling or resizing. You can't reorder fixed effects, but you can bypass them and use other, similar effects. For example, you can use the Transform effect to achieve similar results to the Motion effect, or you can use the Alpha Adjust effect instead of the Opacity effect. These effects are not identical, but they're a close match, they behave similarly, and they can be placed in any order you choose.

Other ways to apply effects

There are multiple ways to reuse an effect you have already configured:

- You can select an effect name from the Effect Controls panel, choose Edit > Copy, select a destination clip (or several clips) in the Timeline panel, and choose Edit > Paste.

- You can copy all the effects from one clip so you can paste them onto another clip: Select a clip and choose Edit > Copy; then select the destination clip (or clips) and choose Edit > Paste Attributes.

- You can create an effect preset to store an effect (or multiple effects) with pre-selected settings for reuse later. You'll learn about this advanced technique later in this lesson.

Using adjustment layers

Adjustment layers offer a convenient way to apply effects to multiple clips. The concept is straightforward: Create an adjustment layer clip that can hold effects, and position it above other clips on the timeline, on a higher video track. Everything beneath the adjustment layer clip is viewed through it, receiving any effects it contains.

You can easily adjust the duration and opacity of an adjustment layer clip, as you would adjust any graphics clip, making it easy to control which other clips on lower tracks are seen through it. An adjustment layer makes it faster to work with effects because you can change the settings on the layer (a single item) to influence the appearance of several other clips.

Let's add an adjustment layer to a sequence.

1   Open the sequence 03 Multiple Effects.

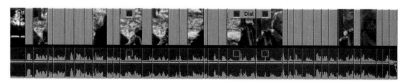

2   At the bottom right of the Project panel, click the New Item button, and choose Adjustment Layer. You may need to resize the Project panel to see the New Item button .

The Adjustment Layer dialog box allows you to specify settings for the new item you're creating. The settings in the dialog box will reflect the settings in the current sequence.

3   Click OK. Premiere Pro adds a new adjustment layer to the Project panel.

4   Drag the adjustment layer from the Project panel to the beginning of the Video 2 track in the Timeline panel.

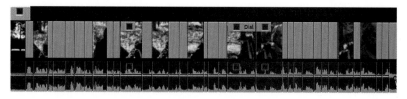

5   Click the right edge of the adjustment layer clip in the Timeline panel to select just the Out point. A red trim handle icon appears on the end of the clip.

Next, position the playhead at the end of the sequence, just after the last clip. You can achieve this quickly by pressing the End key.

Press E to perform an Extend edit. This extends the selected trim handle to the location of the playhead.

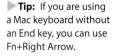 **Tip:** If you are using a Mac keyboard without an End key, you can use Fn+Right Arrow.

Now that the adjustment layer is in place, let's apply an effect to it. Once the effect is set up, you can change the adjustment layer's opacity to alter the intensity of the effect.

6   In the Effects panel, search for and locate the Gaussian Blur effect.

7   Drag the effect onto the adjustment layer clip in the sequence.

8   Move the playhead to 27:00 to have a good close-up shot to use when designing the effect. Audiences pay particular attention to the eyes of your subjects, so it can be helpful to use a close-up as a reference when applying effects.

9   By default, the Gaussian Blur effect doesn't change the image. Make sure the adjustment layer clip is selected. In the Effect Controls panel, set Blurriness to a high value, around 25.0. Make sure Repeat Edge Pixels is selected to apply the effect evenly.

The effect is too strong. Let's blend the adjustment layer with the clips beneath it using a blend mode to create a film look. *Blend modes* let you mix two layers together based on their brightness and color values. You'll learn more about them in Lesson 14.

10 With the adjustment layer still selected in the sequence, click the disclosure triangle next to the Opacity control in the Effect Controls panel to view the settings.

11 Choose Soft Light from the Blend Mode menu to create a gentle blend with the footage.

12 Set Opacity to **75%** to reduce the effect.

Your eyes will quickly adjust to the new appearance of the clip. So, to compare the before and after states, enable and disable the Track Output for the Video 2 track in the Timeline panel using the Toggle Track Output button ⬤.

Adjustment layers are a great way to apply a look to a whole scene. Once you have adjusted the colors for individual clips so they match, you can give the overall scene a particular look with an adjustment layer. The same is true of your entire sequence: You can place an adjustment layer above the clips and below graphics to give all clips the same look.

Sending a clip to Adobe After Effects

If you're working with a computer that also has Adobe After Effects installed, you can easily send clips back and forth between Premiere Pro and After Effects. Thanks to the close relationship between the two applications, you can seamlessly integrate them more easily than with any other editing platform. This is a useful way to significantly extend the effects capabilities of your editing workflow.

You don't need to learn to use After Effects to get the most out of Premiere Pro. Still, many editors find working with both applications expands their creative toolset in exciting ways. The process you use to share clips is called *Dynamic Link*. With Dynamic Link you can seamlessly exchange clips with no unnecessary rendering. When a clip is sent from Premiere Pro to After Effects, it is put into a new *composition* (After Effects compositions are similar to sequences in Premiere Pro). The new composition has settings that match the original Premiere Pro sequence, with a composition name based on the Premiere Pro project name, followed by *Linked Comp*. If you'd like to try this, follow the steps in this sidebar.

For After Effects to complete installation, it needs to be started at least once. You'll also need to restart Premiere Pro after installing After Effects so that the installation is recognized. If restarting Premiere Pro after installing After Effects does not enable Premiere Pro to detect the After Effects installation, try restarting your computer. Do this before you perform the following workflow.

1   Open the sequence AE Dynamic Link, and scrub through the sequence to familiarize yourself with the content.

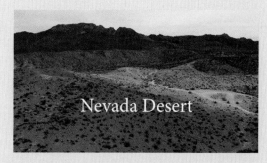

This sequence has several drone shots of the Valley of Fire State Park in Nevada, with an opening title placed above the second clip. The title would benefit from the advanced text animation features offered by After Effects.

2   Right-click the Nevada Desert clip on the Video 2 track in the sequence and choose Replace With After Effects Composition.

3   If it's not running already, After Effects launches. If the After Effects Save As dialog box appears, enter a name and location for the After Effects project. Name the project **Lesson 12-01.aep**, and save it to a new folder inside the Lessons folder.

Clips become layers in After Effects compositions to make it easier to work with advanced controls in the Timeline panel.

There are lots of ways to apply effects with After Effects. To keep things simple, let's work with animation presets (these are similar to effect presets in Premiere Pro). For more on effects workflows, see *Adobe After Effects Classroom in a Book 2024 Release*.

4   The composition should be open in the Timeline panel already. If not, look for it in the After Effects Project panel, and double-click to load it. It should be called Lesson 12 Working Linked Comp 01 (the number may be higher if you have tried this workflow before). There's just one layer, called Nevada Desert. The layer contains the text that you'll work on next.

5   Double-click the Nevada Desert layer, under the Source Name heading, to open it in a new Timeline panel.

6   Locate the Effects & Presets panel (you can find this in the Window menu if it's not onscreen already). Click the disclosure triangle to expand the *Animation Presets category. If the category is not displayed, check that it is enabled in the Effects & Presets panel menu.

Animation presets in After Effects use standard built-in effects to achieve impressive results. They are an excellent shortcut to producing a professional finish for your work.

continues on next page

7   Expand the Text category and then the Animate In group. You may need to resize the panel a little to read the full preset names.

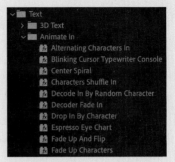

8   Make sure the playhead is at the beginning of the composition. Drag the Decoder Fade In preset onto the Nevada Desert layer in the Timeline panel.

9   Press the spacebar to play the animation—a cool animated effect as the text appears.

The green line at the top of the Timeline panel indicates After Effects created a temporary preview. Only playback of the highlighted section of the timeline is likely to be smooth.

10 This looks great, but it's hard to know what the effect looks like against the desert background. Switch back to Premiere Pro to check.

In Premiere Pro, the title has been replaced with the dynamically linked After Effects composition you just created. The new animation plays right away in Premiere Pro. Any changes made in After Effects appear automatically in Premiere Pro.

11 Switch back to After Effects, and choose File > Save. Then quit After Effects.

The frames are processed in the background and handed off from After Effects to Premiere Pro. As Premiere Pro has the After Effects playback engine built in, the result continues to display properly.

12 Preview your sequence in Premiere Pro. To improve preview playback performance, you can select the clip in the Timeline panel and choose Sequence > Render Effects In To Out.

You're not limited to sending single clips from Premiere Pro into new After Effects projects. If an After Effects project is already open when you send a clip, the clip will be added as a new composition to the existing project, rather than needing a new project. You can also select multiple clips to send to After Effects in a single step, making it easier to check compositions and set up more complex animated compositions.

Applying source clip effects

You can also apply video effects to clips in the Project panel. You use the same effects and work with them in the same way. Clips in the Project panel are called *source clips* (to distinguish them from *sequence clip instances)*, and effects applied to them are called *source clip effects*. With source clip effects, any instance of a clip, or part of a clip, you add to a sequence will inherit the effects you have applied. You can even apply source clip effects *after* adding clips to sequences, and the sequences will update—a powerful way to make adjustments to multiple clip segments in a single step.

For example, you could add a color adjustment to a clip in the Project panel so that it matches other camera angles in a scene. Each time you use that clip or part of that clip in a sequence, the adjustment will already be applied. Even if you don't make the adjustment until after the scene is edited, you can use a source clip effect to quickly match the colors.

Let's add a source clip effect now.

1   Open the sequence 04 Source Clip Effects.

    This has one clip, Laura_02, edited five times into the same sequence. The copies of the clip are separated by a number of other, similar shots.

2   Position the Timeline panel playhead somewhere over the first instance of the Laura_02 clip. You want to open this sequence clip's original source clip in the Source Monitor so you can apply an effect to it. It's no good double-clicking the clip in the sequence because it will open that instance.

    Select the clip and press the F key. This is the shortcut for Match Frame, which opens the original source clip in the Source Monitor at the frame that is displayed in the Program Monitor.

    This is a useful shortcut to remember, as you will often want to check source clips when reviewing sequences, either to see a version of a clip without effects applied or to check for alternative content.

    You now have the same clip open in the Source Monitor (the source clip) and displayed in the Program Monitor (the sequence segment), so you can see how the changes affect the sequence as you apply them.

3   In the Effects panel, type **100** in the search box to quickly locate the Lumetri Look effect preset named Cinespace 100.

4 Drag the Cinespace 100 effect into the Source Monitor.

This applies the effect to the source clip.

● **Note:** Selection is important in Premiere Pro. Clicking to activate the Source Monitor before going to the Effect Controls panel is necessary to see the correct options.

5 Click the Source Monitor to make sure it's the active panel, and then open the Effect Controls panel to see the effect options.

▶ **Tip:** You can also apply an effect to a source clip by dragging the effect onto the clip directly in the Project panel or by selecting a clip in a sequence and clicking the source clip name at the top left of the Effect Controls panel and then dragging the effect into that panel.

Because you applied the effect to the clip in the Source Monitor and then selected the Source Monitor to make it active, the Effect Controls panel shows the effect applied to the source clip, rather than the instance in the sequence.

This is a Lumetri Color effect, and you will be learning a lot more about these effects in Lesson 13, "Applying Color Correction and Grading."

6 Because the effect has been applied to the source clip, every instance of the clip in the sequence shows the results. Play the sequence to see that the effect is applied to every copy of the Laura_02 clip. You can tell a source clip effect is applied to a clip because the FX badge has a red underline .

The result of the effect is displayed in the Source Monitor *and* the Program Monitor because sequence clips inherit their source clip effects dynamically.

From now on, anytime you use this clip, or part of it, in a sequence, Premiere Pro will include the effect.

However, while the source clip has the effect applied, none of the timeline instances of the clip (the sequence clips) has the effect applied.

7 Single-click any of the sequence instances of the Laura_02 clip on the timeline to select it, and look in the Effect Controls panel—no Lumetri Color effect, just the usual fixed effects (which are applicable only to sequence clips, not clips in the Project panel).

At the top of the Effect Controls panel there are two tabs. The tab on the left shows the name of the source clip, Source • Laura_02.mp4.

Source • Laura_02.mp4 ⌄ 04 Source Clip Effects • Laura_02.mp4 ▶

Video ▲

The tab on the right shows the name of the sequence followed by the name of the sequence clip, 04 Source Clip Effects • Laura_02.mp4.

Because you selected the clip in the sequence, the tab on the right is highlighted in blue, showing that you're working on that instance of the clip.

There's no Lumetri Color effect displayed because you haven't applied the effect to the Timeline panel's instance of the clip.

8   In the Effect Controls panel, click the tab at the top that shows the source clip name. Now you'll see the source clip effect options.

9   Experiment with the controls for the Lumetri Color effect, and then play the sequence. You'll see the changes are applied to every instance of the clip.

Source clip effects provide a powerful way to manage effects in Premiere Pro. You may need to experiment a little to make the most of them. You use the same video effects as you would use on the timeline, so the techniques you're learning in this book will work the same way, but the planning is a little different.

Masking and tracking video effects

All standard video effects can be constrained within elliptical, polygonal, or custom masks, which you can manually animate using keyframes. These masks can motion track your shots to animate their position, following the action with the constrained special effect.

Masking and tracking effects are great ways to hide a detail like a face or logo behind a blur. You can also use the technique to apply subtle creative effects or modify the lighting in a shot.

Note: This example uses a vivid adjustment to illustrate a technique. You will usually make subtler adjustments.

Continue working with the 04 Source Clip Effects sequence.

1   Position the playhead over the first frame of the second clip in the sequence, Evening Smile.

It looks good, but it would benefit from a stronger light on the subject to help separate the foreground from the background.

2   Search the Effects panel for the Brightness & Contrast effect.

3   Apply this effect to the clip.

4   In the Effect Controls panel, scroll down to the Brightness & Contrast controls.

Choose the following settings:

- Brightness: **35**

- Contrast: **25**

You can set these levels by clicking the blue numbers and typing the new setting, by scrubbing the blue numbers, or by expanding the controls and using the sliders.

This effect changes the entire picture. You're going to constrain the effect to just one area of the shot.

   Just under the name of the Brightness & Contrast effect in the Effect Controls panel, you'll see three buttons that allow you to add a mask to the effect.

5   Click the first button to add an elliptical mask.

A mask is added to the Brightness & Contrast effect in the Effect Controls panel, and, in the Program Monitor, the effect is constrained to the new mask region.

You can add multiple masks to an effect. If you select a mask in the Effect Controls panel, you can modify the shape in the Program Monitor.

6   Make sure the playhead is at the start of the clip, and use the mask control points (the small squares on the mask shape) in the Program Monitor to reshape the mask so it covers the subject's face and hair. You may find it helpful to adjust the Zoom level for the Program Monitor to see beyond the edges of the image.

If you deselect the mask, the controls will disappear in the Program Monitor. To bring them back, select the name of the mask in the Effect Controls panel. In this case, select Mask (1) to display the controls again.

7   Feathering softens the edge of the mask. In the Effect Controls panel, set Mask Feather to **240**.

You have brightened the area around the subject's face, with a natural return to regular lighting in the rest of the picture. Now you just need the mask to follow the moving video.

8   In the Effect Controls panel, to the right of the Mask Path item, there are several mask-tracking controls.

Click the Track Selected Mask Forward button ▶. Premiere Pro tracks the contents of the clip to reposition and resize the mask to continue covering the subject's face as it moves in the frame.

The movement is quite subtle, so it's easy for Premiere Pro to follow the action.

9   Scrub the Effect Controls panel playhead to see the movement of the mask.

10 Deselect the mask by clicking away from the mask name in the Effect Controls panel or by clicking an empty track in the Timeline panel. The mask handles in the Program Monitor will be removed.

Premiere Pro can also track backward so that you can select an item partway through a clip and then track in both directions to create a natural path for the mask to follow.

In this example you're making a subtle lighting adjustment, but almost any video effect can be constrained to a mask in this way.

Keyframing effects

When you add keyframes to an effect, you're setting particular values for controls at precise moments in time. Each keyframe will store a setting for one control. If, for example, you were intending to keyframe Position, Scale, and Rotation, you would need three separate keyframes.

Set keyframes at precise moments where you need a particular setting and let Premiere Pro work out how to animate the controls between them.

Adding keyframes

You can change almost all parameters for all video effects over time using keyframes. For example, you can have a clip gradually become out of focus, change color, or lengthen its shadow.

Note: Be sure to move the playhead over the clip you're working with when applying effects so you can view your changes as you work. Selecting the clip alone will not make it visible in the Program Monitor.

1 Open the sequence 05 Keyframes.

2 View the sequence to get familiar with the footage, and then position the Timeline playhead over the first frame of the clip.

3 In the Effects panel, locate the Lens Flare effect and apply it to the clip in the sequence. This is not a subtle effect, but it illustrates Motion keyframes beautifully.

4 In the Effect Controls panel, select the Lens Flare effect heading. With the effect selected, the Program Monitor displays a small control handle. Use the handle to reposition the lens flare to match the following figure so that the center of the effect is near the top of the waterfall, as seen in the frame.

5 Make sure the Effect Controls panel timeline is visible. If it isn't, click the Show/ Hide Timeline View button ![icon] next to the clip name at the top right of the panel to toggle the display.

6 Click the stopwatch icons ![icon] to toggle animation on ![icon] for the Flare Center and Flare Brightness properties. Clicking the stopwatch icon enables keyframing and adds a keyframe at the current location with the current settings.

7 Set the Flare Brightness to **50%**.

8 Move the playhead to the last frame of the clip.

To do this, you can drag the playhead directly in the Effect Controls panel. Make sure you see the last frame of video and not black (which would be the first frame of the next clip if there were one).

9 Adjust Flare Center and Flare Brightness settings so the flare drifts across the screen with the camera pan and gets brighter. With the Lens Flare effect selected in the Effect Controls panel, you can drag the lens flare center to a new position directly in the Program Monitor.

Use the following figures for guidance.

10 Deselect the Lens Flare effect to hide the controls in the Program Monitor, and play the sequence to watch the effect animate over time. You may need to render the sequence for full-frame-rate playback, by choosing Sequence > Render Effects In To Out.

Adding keyframe interpolation and velocity

Keyframe interpolation changes the behavior of an effect setting as it moves between keyframes with different settings. The default behavior you've seen so far is linear; in other words, it produces a constant change between keyframes. What generally works better is something that mirrors your real-world experience or exaggerates it, such as gradual acceleration or deceleration.

Premiere Pro offers a way to control those changes: keyframe interpolation and the Velocity graph. Keyframe interpolation is easy and simplified, whereas adjusting the Velocity graph can be complex but more precise.

Velocity graphs appear in the timeline on the right side of the Effect Controls panel, along with the keyframes, when you expand a property by clicking its disclosure triangle ⟩.

1 Open the sequence 06 Interpolation. Play the sequence to view the action.

A Lens Flare effect has been applied to this clip and animated. However, the movement begins before the camera, which isn't very natural-looking.

2 Position the playhead at the beginning of the clip, and select the clip.

3 In the Effect Controls panel, toggle the Lens Flare effect off and on by clicking the FX button 👁 next to the effect name in the Effect Controls panel so you can see the result.

▶ **Tip:** Be sure to use the Next Keyframe and Previous Keyframe buttons to move between keyframes efficiently. This will keep you from adding unwanted keyframes.

4 In the Effect Controls panel time-line, right-click the first keyframe for the Flare Center property. Choose Temporal Interpolation > Ease Out to create a gentle transition into the move from the keyframe that more closely matches the camera movement.

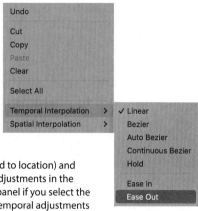

| Undo |
| Cut |
| Copy |
| Paste |
| Clear |
| Select All |
| Temporal Interpolation > |
| Spatial Interpolation > |

✓ Linear
Bezier
Auto Bezier
Continuous Bezier
Hold
Ease In
Ease Out

Note: When working with position-related parameters, the context menu for a keyframe will offer two types of interpolation: spatial (related to location) and temporal (related to time). You can make spatial adjustments in the Program Monitor as well as in the Effect Controls panel if you select the effect in the Effect Controls panel. You can make temporal adjustments on the clip in the Timeline and Effect Controls panels. These motion-related topics were covered in Lesson 9, "Putting Clips in Motion."

5 Right-click the second keyframe for the Flare Center property and choose Temporal Interpolation > Ease In. This creates a gentle transition from the stationary position of the last keyframe.

6 Let's modify the Flare Brightness property. Click the first keyframe for Flare Brightness, and then hold down the Shift key and click the second keyframe so both are active, highlighted in blue.

You could also click the Flare Brightness property name, which selects all exist-ing keyframes for the property. However, there will be occasions when you'll want to select specific keyframes, so it's worth remembering the Shift key.

Keyframes

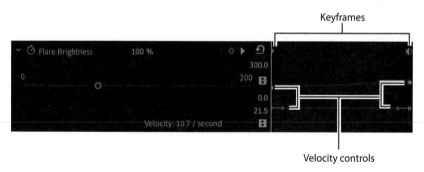

Velocity controls

7 Right-click either one of the Flare Brightness keyframes and choose Auto Bezier to create a gentle animation between the two properties. Because both key-frames were selected, both are changed.

8 Play back the animation to watch the changes you've made.

When you animate position, a clip anchor point or effect center (in this example, the Flare Center control) follows a path across the frame. This path is called the *motion path*.

9 In the Effect Controls panel, select the Lens Flare effect name. Scrub through the clip to see the animation with the effect motion path displayed.

Let's refine the keyframes with the Velocity graph.

10 Hover the pointer over the Effect Controls panel, and then, if your keyboard has the key, press ` (accent grave) to maximize the panel; or double-click the panel name. This will give you a clearer view of the keyframe controls.

11 If necessary, click the disclosure triangles next to the Flare Center and Flare Brightness controls to show the adjustable properties.

The Velocity graph shows the velocity between keyframes. Any sudden drops or jumps represent sudden changes in velocity. The farther the point or line is from the baseline, the greater the velocity.

Understanding interpolation methods

Here's a rundown of the keyframe interpolation methods available in Premiere Pro:

- **Linear:** This is the default behavior and creates a uniform rate of change between keyframes.
- **Bezier:** This lets you manually adjust the shape of the graph on either side of a keyframe. Beziers allow for sudden or smooth acceleration into or out of a keyframe.
- **Continuous Bezier:** This method creates a smooth rate of change through a keyframe. Unlike with regular Bezier keyframes, if you adjust one handle of a Continuous Bezier keyframe, the handle on the other side moves equally to maintain a smooth transition through the keyframe.
- **Auto Bezier:** This method creates a smooth rate of change through a keyframe even if you change the keyframe value. If you choose to manually adjust the keyframe's handles, it changes to a Continuous Bezier point, retaining the smooth transition through the keyframe. The Auto Bezier option can occasionally produce unwanted motion, so try one of the other options first.
- **Hold:** This method holds a setting until the next keyframe. The graph following a keyframe with the Hold interpolation applied appears as a horizontal straight line.
- **Ease In:** This method slows down the value changes entering a keyframe and converts it to a Bezier keyframe.
- **Ease Out:** This method gradually accelerates the value changes leaving a keyframe and converts it to a Bezier keyframe.

12 Select a keyframe, and then adjust its extended handle to change the steepness of the velocity curve.

13 Press the ` (accent grave) key, or double-click the panel name, to restore the Effect Controls panel, and play back your sequence to see the impact of your changes. Experiment some more until you have the hang of keyframes and interpolation.

Perhaps the change to the velocity of the keyframes for the Flare Center isn't enough to make the movement appear perfectly natural. Try dragging the first keyframe later to better match the camera movement and adjust the velocity keyframes.

Using effect presets

There are several prebuilt presets included for specific tasks, but the true power of effects lies in creating your own presets, particularly when you know you'll need an effect configuration again in the future. A single preset can contain more than one effect and can even include keyframes for animation.

Using built-in presets

The effect presets provided with Premiere Pro give you a head start when performing common tasks, such as setting up a picture-in-picture effect or creating a stylized transition.

1 Open and preview the sequence 07 Presets.

This sequence has a single clip with a slow start—the emphasis is on the texture of the background. Let's use a preset to add visual interest to the beginning of the shot.

2 In the Effects panel, click the X to clear the search box at the top of the panel. Browse inside the Presets > Solarizes category to find the Solarize In preset.

3 Drag the Solarize In preset onto the clip in the sequence.

4 Play back the sequence to watch the Solarize effect transform the opening.

5   Select the clip in the Timeline panel, and view its controls in the Effect Controls panel.

6   There are two keyframes, relatively close together. Zoom in by adjusting the navigator at the bottom of the Effect Controls panel timeline to see them more clearly.

Experiment with adjusting the position of the second keyframe in the Effect Controls panel to customize the effect. If you extend the timing of the effect, it creates a gentler start to the shot.

7   Remove the Solarize effect and experiment with other presets in the Effects panel—or combine multiple presets.

Saving effect presets

Although there are several built-in effect presets to choose from, you can easily create your own. You can also import and export presets to share them between editing systems.

1   Open the sequence 08 Creating Presets.

This sequence has two clips, each with an adjustment layer on the V2 track and a title on the V3 track.

2   Play the sequence to watch the opening animation.

3   Select the first instance of the "Laura in the snow" title clip on the V3 track and look in the Effect Controls panel. A Fast Blur effect has been applied to the title, and there are keyframes animating several controls.

4   In the Effect Controls panel, click the Vector Motion effect heading to select it. Next, hold Command (macOS) or Ctrl (Windows) while you click the effect headings for the Fast Blur effect and then the Opacity effect. Now all three effects are selected.

5　Right-click any of the selected effects and choose Save Preset.

6　In the Save Preset dialog, name the effect **Title Animation**. Click in the Description box, and type **Title blurs into view**.

When you apply an animated preset to a clip with a different duration, Premiere Pro needs to know how to distribute the keyframes.

There are three options.

- **Scale:** Redistributes the original preset keyframes to the duration of the new clip proportionally.

- **Anchor To In Point:** Preserves the position of the first keyframe as well as the relationship of other keyframes in a clip relative to its In point.

- **Anchor To Out Point:** Preserves the position of the last keyframe as well as the relationship of other keyframes in a clip relative to its Out point.

7　For this preset, select Anchor To In Point so the timing matches at the start of each clip the preset is applied to.

8　Click OK to store the effects and keyframes as a new preset.

9　In the Effects panel, locate the Presets category and your newly created Title Animation preset. Hover the pointer over the preset to see the description you added appear as a tool tip.

Tip: Effect presets can be exported and imported so they can be shared. You'll find the Import and Export options in the Effects panel menu. You can select and export an individual preset or a whole custom bin containing multiple presets. You'll find a number of free presets at *premierepro.net/ presets*.

10　Drag the new Title Animation preset from the Effects panel onto the second instance of the "Laura in the snow" title clip on the V3 track in the Timeline.

11　Watch the sequence play back to see the newly applied title animation.

12 Select the second title clip on the V3 track and look in the Effect Controls panel. All three effects included in the preset have been added to the clip. The name of the preset is included in parentheses after each effect name, so you know the way the effect has been configured. You can still edit the effect controls, but it's a useful way to check which preset you used in the first place.

You can change the configuration of a preset by right-clicking it in the Effects panel and choosing Preset Properties or by double-clicking it. Double-clicking an effect (rather than a preset) will apply the effect to a selected clip.

Using multiple GPUs

If you'd like to speed up the rendering of effects or the export of clips, consider adding an internal GPU card or external GPU. If you're using a tower or workstation, you may have an additional internal slot that can support a second graphics card. An additional GPU won't improve playback performance when previewing real-time effects or displaying multiple layers of video, but Premiere Pro takes full advantage of computers with multiple GPU cards to significantly accelerate render and export times. You can find additional details about supported cards on the Adobe website.

Exploring frequently used effects

Although it's beyond the scope of this book to explore all the effects available, here are a few that are useful in many editing situations. You'll learn about color adjustments in the next lesson.

Applying image stabilization and rolling shutter reduction

The Warp Stabilizer effect can remove jitter caused by camera movement (which is increasingly common with today's lightweight cameras). The effect is useful because it can remove unstable parallax-type movements, where images appear to shift on planes.

The result is achieved by zooming into the image by just enough to automatically animate the clip position within the frame to compensate for unwanted camera movement.

Let's explore the effect.

1 Open the sequence 09 Warp Stabilizer.

2 Play the first clip in the sequence to see the wobbly shot.

Stabilizing

3 In the Effects panel, locate the Warp Stabilizer effect and apply it to the shot.

As Premiere Pro analyzes the clip, a banner across the footage lets you know you'll need to wait before working with the effect. The Effect Controls panel also displays a detailed progress indicator. The analysis takes place in the background, so you can carry on working while waiting for it to complete.

4 Once the analysis has completed, you can adjust settings in the Effect Controls panel to improve results by choosing options that better suit the shot.

- **Result:** You can choose Smooth Motion to retain the general camera movement (albeit stabilized), or you can choose No Motion to attempt to remove all camera movement. For this exercise, choose Smooth Motion.

- **Smoothness:** This option specifies how much of the original camera movement should be retained for Smooth Motion. Use a higher value to smooth out the shot the most. Experiment with this shot until you're happy with its stability.

- **Method:** You can use the four methods available. The two most powerful, because they warp and process the image more heavily, are Perspective and Subspace Warp. If either method creates too much distortion as the effect compensates for camera movement, try switching to Position, Scale, Rotation, or just Position. More of the image will probably be cropped using these alternative methods, but it may be worth it when working with very shaky footage.

▶ **Tip:** If you notice that some of the details in the shot appear to wobble, you may be able to improve the overall effect. In the Advanced section, select Detailed Analysis. This makes the Analysis phase do extra work to find elements to track. You can also use the Enhanced Reduction option from the Rolling Shutter Ripple option in the Advanced category. These options are slower to render but often do produce better results.

5 Play the clip. The impact is pretty dramatic.

6 Play the second clip in the sequence to review it. This shot should be static, but it's handheld, so there's a little movement. Apply the Warp Stabilizer effect to this clip. Choose No Motion from the Warp Stabilizer Result menu.

© Maxim Jago 2016

The Warp Stabilizer effect is amazingly effective at locking these kinds of shots into position.

Because the results are achieved by moving the image to compensate for camera wobble, the copyright notice that is burned into this footage now appears to move. This is a good reason to avoid using footage with burned-in graphics or text.

The Warp Stabilizer effect adds quite a lot of data to the Premiere Pro project file. If you plan to stabilize lots of clips, consider performing the stabilization in a separate project and exporting new media files for use in your main project. Large project files take longer to open and to save.

Use an adjustment layer with the Clip Name effect

If you intend to send a review copy of a sequence to a client or colleague, you can apply the Metadata & Timecode Burn-in effect to an adjustment layer and have it generate visible clip names for the entire sequence.

This is helpful because it allows others to give feedback based on a particular clip. You can control the clip name format position, size, and opacity.

You can enable a similar timecode overlay when exporting media, but this clip effect has more options.

1 Open the sequence 10 Clip Names.

2 At the lower right of the Project panel, click the New Item button ⬚ (you may need to resize the Project panel to see it), and choose Adjustment Layer from the menu. Click OK in the Adjustment Layer dialog box.

   A new adjustment layer is added to the Project panel, with settings that match your current sequence.

3 Drag the new adjustment layer to the beginning of track V2 in the current sequence.

4 Position the Timeline playhead at the end of the sequence. Click once to select the right edge of the new adjustment layer clip, and press E. Then press Esc to deselect the edit.

   This useful shortcut performs an Extend edit, which trims the selected edit to the current position of the playhead.

> **Tip:** If you work with multiple sequences with different format settings in a single project, it's worth naming adjustment layers to make it easier to identify their resolution. You can rename adjustment layers in the Project panel just as you would any other item.

5   You can add most video effects to an adjustment layer. Let's try an example effect.

In the Effects panel, locate the Horizontal Flip effect. Drag it onto the adjustment layer to apply it. This switches the video horizontally, giving the effect of changing the direction of movement.

There are no controls for the Horizontal Flip effect. You can still use masks to constrain the effect, which produces interesting results where there is movement in the shot.

This effect works well with this kind of content but may not work if there is visible text or a recognizable logo in the picture.

Let's add the Metadata & Timecode Burn-in effect.

6   In the Effects panel, search for the Metadata & Timecode Burn-in effect.

7   Apply the Metadata & Timecode Burn-in effect to the adjustment layer clip.

By default, the effect shows the timecode of the clip you applied it to, which in this case is Adjustment Layer—not very useful!

8   In the Effect Controls panel, in the Metadata & Timecode Burn-in effect controls, use the Metadata menu to choose Sequence Clip Name, and use the Source Track menu to choose Video 1. Now the clip names from the V1 track are displayed.

9   Clear the Effects panel search box by clicking the X.

▶ **Tip:** You can click the Clip Name effect heading in the Effect Controls panel and then drag the anchor point for the name displayed in the Program Monitor to reposition it.

Rendering all sequences

If you have several sequences with effects you want to render, you can render them all as a batch, without opening each sequence to render it individually.

Select the sequences you would like to render in the Project panel, and choose Sequence > Render Effects In To Out.

All effects that need to render in the selected sequences will be rendered.

Using the Render And Replace command

If you are working on a low-powered system and your media is high resolution, you may find media tends to drop frames routinely when previewing. You may also see dropped frames when working with dynamically linked After Effects compositions or complex third-party video effects that don't support GPU acceleration.

If all your media is high resolution, you may decide to use the proxy workflow, which allows you to switch between full-resolution and lower-resolution media file playback.

However, if just one or two clips are difficult to play back, you also have the option to render just those clips as new media files and replace the original item in a sequence quickly and easily.

To replace a sequence clip segment with a version that's easier to play back, right-click the clip and choose Render And Replace.

The Render And Replace dialog box has similar options to the proxy work-flow. Here are the main settings:

- **Source:** Choose whether the new media file that will be created will match the frame rate and frame size of the sequence, the original media, or a preset.

- **Format:** Specify your preferred file type. Different formats give access to different codecs.

- **Preset:** Choose a preset here. You can use a custom preset created with Adobe Media Encoder or one of the several built-in options.

> **Tip:** Another benefit of using the Render And Replace command is that clips do not need to be re-rendered if you move them to a different part of your sequence or combine them with other clips in a layered composition. This can be a huge time-saver.

If you enable Include Video Effects for an option, Premiere Pro will incorporate the effects into the new file, which means you will no longer be able to adjust those effects' settings in the Effect Controls panel.

Once you have chosen a preset and a location for the new file, click OK and the sequence clip is replaced.

A rendered and replaced clip is no longer directly linked to the original media—it's linked to a new media file. This means, for example, changes that you make to a dynamically linked After Effects composition will not update in Premiere Pro. To restore the link to the original item, right-click the clip and choose Restore Unrendered.

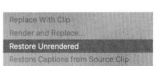

If you had chosen the option to include video effects, they would be restored along with the original file and fully editable again.

Review questions

1 What are two ways to apply an effect to a clip?

2 List three ways to add a keyframe.

3 Dragging an effect onto a clip turns on its parameters in the Effect Controls panel, but you don't see the effect in the Program Monitor. Why not?

4 Describe how you can apply one effect to a range of clips.

5 Describe how to save multiple effects to a custom preset.

Review answers

1 Drag the effect to the clip, or select the clip and double-click the effect in the
   Effects panel.

2 Move the playhead in the Effect Controls panel to where you want a keyframe and
   activate keyframing by clicking the stopwatch icon to toggle animation on; move the
   playhead and click the Add/Remove Keyframe button; and with keyframing activated,
   move the playhead to a position and change a parameter. You could also set up and use
   a custom keyboard shortcut.

3 You need to move the Timeline panel playhead to the selected clip to see it in the
   Program Monitor. Selecting a clip does not move the playhead to that clip. Also, many
   effects do not produce visible changes until you adjust the controls.

4 You can add an adjustment layer above the clips you want to affect. You can then apply
   an effect to the adjustment layer that will modify all the clips below the layer. You can
   also select the clips you would like to apply the effect to and then drag the effect onto
   the group or double-click the effect in the Effects panel.

5 With the Effect Controls panel active, you can choose Edit > Select All. You can also
   hold Command (macOS) or Ctrl (Windows) while you select multiple effect headings
   in the Effect Controls panel. Once the effects are selected, right-click the selection and
   choose Save Preset. You can also choose Save Preset in the panel menu.

13 APPLYING COLOR CORRECTION AND GRADING

Lesson overview

In this lesson, you'll learn how to do the following:

- Work in the Color workspace.

- Use the Lumetri Color panel.

- Use vectorscopes and waveforms.

- Compare and match clip colors.

- Use color correction related effects.

- Fix exposure and white balance problems.

- Work with special color effects.

- Create a look.

 This lesson will take about 150 minutes to complete. To get the lesson files used in this chapter, download them from the web page for this book at *peachpit.com/PremiereProCIB2024*. For more information, see "Accessing the lesson files and Web Edition" in the "Getting Started" section at the beginning of this book. Store the files on your computer in a convenient location.

Editing your clips together is just the first part of the creative process. Now it's time to work with color. In this lesson, you'll learn some key techniques for improving the look of your clips to give them a distinctive atmosphere.

Starting the lesson

So far, you've organized your clips, built sequences, and applied special effects. All of these skills come together when working with color correction.

● **Note:** To ensure that the tools function and the defaults are set exactly as described in this lesson, reset the Premiere Pro preferences by holding Option (macOS) or Alt (Windows) while launching the application and then clicking Continue in the Reset Options dialog box.

Consider the way your eyes register color and light, the way cameras record it, and the way your computer screen, a television screen, a video projector, a phone, a tablet, or a cinema screen displays it. There are a great many factors when considering the final look of your production.

Premiere Pro has multiple color correction tools and makes it easy to create your own presets. In this lesson, you'll begin by learning some fundamental color correction skills and then explore some of the most popular color correction special effects, before using them to deal with common color correction challenges.

1 Open Lesson 13.prproj in the Lessons folder.

2 Save the project as **Lesson 13 Working.prproj**.

3 Choose Color from the Workspaces menu to switch to the Color workspace.

4 Open the Workspaces menu again, and choose Reset To Saved Layout.

   This changes the workspace to a preset that was created to make it easier to work with color correction effects and, in particular, the Lumetri Color panel and Lumetri Scopes panel.

Understanding display color management

Computer monitors generally use a different system for displaying color than do TV screens and cinema projectors (see the sidebar "About 8-bit video" for more on this).

If you're producing video for online distribution, you can be reasonably confident your audience will be using a computer monitor similar to yours to view your content, and you can be confident the colors and brightness levels of your images will be comparable. If you're delivering video for TV or the cinema screen, you'll need a way to view video that matches the type of screen it's intended for.

Professional colorists have multiple display systems to check their work on. If they're working on a film intended for theaters, they'll use the same kind of projector a theater would use—projecting the image onto a screen for review purposes.

Some computer monitors offer excellent color reproduction—better than television screens. If you have enabled GPU acceleration (see Lesson 2, "Setting Up a Project") and you are using a computer monitor of this kind, Premiere Pro can adjust the way video is displayed in the Source Monitor and Program Monitor to match the colors a television screen would display.

Premiere Pro automatically detects if you have the right kind of monitor. To enable this feature, choose Premiere Pro > Settings > Color (macOS) or Edit > Preferences > Color (Windows), and select Display Color Management (Requires GPU Acceleration).

If you are working with high dynamic range (HDR) media and have a monitor that can display in HDR, you can also enable the Extended Dynamic Range Monitoring option to display the full contrast range.

These options are also available in the Lumetri Color panel under the Settings tab, which you'll learn about in this lesson.

For more information about these color management features, check out *helpx.adobe.com/premiere-pro/using/color-management.html*.

About 8-bit video

As mentioned earlier, 8-bit video works on a scale from 0 to 255 for each of the three color channels. That means, for RGB color, each pixel has red, green, and blue (RGB) values somewhere on that scale, which combine to produce a particular color. You can think of 0 as 0% and 255 as 100%. A pixel that has a red value of 127 is equivalent to having a red value of 50%.

Broadcast video uses a similar but different range, with a color system called YUV.

Although YUV color uses the three color channels differently, it still uses 8 bits per channel. However, if you were to compare the YUV scale with the 0 to 255 RGB scale, you'd find that the 8-bit YUV scale ranges from 16 to 235.

TVs usually use YUV color, not RGB. However, your computer screen is RGB. If you are producing video for broadcast television, you may encounter issues because you are looking at your video footage on a different kind of screen than the kind it will ultimately be viewed on. There is only one sure way of overcoming the uncertainty this creates: Connect a TV or calibrated broadcast monitor to your editing system and view your footage on that screen.

The difference is a little like comparing a photograph you view onscreen in Photoshop with a printed version. The printer and your computer screen use different color systems, and it's an imperfect translation from one to the other.

Sometimes you will view footage with visible detail in the brightest and darkest pixels on an RGB screen (like your computer display) that disappears when viewed on a TV screen. You'll need to make adjustments to the color to bring those details into the TV screen color range.

Some TVs give you the option to display color as RGB, using a range of names such as Game Mode or Photo Color Space. If your screen is set up this way, you may see the full 0 to 255 RGB range, and the only way to know is to check the settings—confusing!

With some computer screens, Premiere Pro can adjust the way video colors are displayed to more accurately mimic other screens (see "Understanding display color management").

Following the color adjustment workflow

Now that you've switched to the Color workspace, it's a good time to switch to a different kind of thinking too. With your clips in place, it's time to look at them less in terms of the action, events, and continuity of movement, and more in terms of whether they fit together aesthetically and have the right look.

There are two main phases to working with color.

- Make sure clips in each scene have matching colors, brightness, and contrast so they look like they were shot at the same time, in the same place, and with the same camera.

- Give everything a "look"—in other words, a particular tonality or color tint.

You'll use the same tools to achieve both of these goals, but it's common to approach them in this order, separately. If two clips from the same scene don't have matching colors, it creates a jarring continuity problem that will distract the audience. This might be your goal, but most of the time you will want your audience to focus on the story.

Color correction and color grading

You've probably heard of both color correction and color grading. There is often confusion about the difference. In fact, both types of color work use the same tools, but there's a difference of approach.

Color correction is usually aimed at standardizing the shots to make sure they fit together and to improve the appearance in general—to give brighter highlights and stronger shadows or to correct a color bias captured in-camera. This is more craft than art.

Color grading is aimed at achieving a look that conveys the atmosphere of the story more completely.

This is more art than craft. There is, of course, a debate about where one ends and the other begins, and you will sometimes alternate between the two approaches.

Exploring the Color workspace

The Color workspace includes the Lumetri Color panel, which has a number of sections offering color adjustment controls, and places the Lumetri Scopes panel in the same group as the Source Monitor. The Lumetri Scopes panel contains a set of image analysis tools.

The remaining screen area is devoted to the Program Monitor, Timeline panel, Project panel, Tools panel, and Audio Meters. The Timeline panel shrinks to accommodate the Lumetri Color panel.

If it's not already visible, select the Lumetri Scopes panel to bring it into view. Here, the panel is shown with more display options enabled than the default.

The Lumetri Scopes panel contains a set of image analysis tools, called *scopes*. To view the scopes shown in the example, right-click in the middle of the Lumetri Scopes panel and choose Presets > Vectorscope YUV/Parade RGB/Waveform YC. You'll learn more about these important tools later in this lesson.

You can open and close any panel at any time, but this workspace focuses on finishing work, rather than organizing or editing your project.

While the Lumetri Color panel is displayed, sequence clips on tracks that have track targeting enabled are selected automatically as you scrub the playhead over them.

Tip: If more than one track-targeted track has a clip under the playhead, the clip on the highest targeted track is selected.

This feature is important because adjustments made with the Lumetri Color panel, like other effects, are always applied to the selected clip. You can apply an adjustment and quickly move the Timeline panel playhead over the next clip to automatically select it, and then you can work on it.

You can enable or disable automatic clip selection by choosing Sequence > Selection Follows Playhead.

Getting an overview of the Lumetri Color panel

There is an effect available in the Effects panel called Lumetri Color, which provides all the controls and options available in the Lumetri Color panel. Like any other effect, its controls are displayed in the Effect Controls panel.

The first time you make an adjustment using the Lumetri Color panel, a Lumetri Color effect is applied to the selected clip. If there is a Lumetri Color effect already applied to the clip, the settings for that existing effect are updated as you make adjustments.

In a sense, the Lumetri Color panel is a kind of remote control for the Lumetri Color effect settings in the Effect Controls panel. As with any other effect, you can create presets, copy and paste Lumetri Color effects from one clip to another, and change the settings in the Effect Controls panel.

You can apply more than one Lumetri Color effect to the same clip, each making different types of adjustments to produce a combined result. This can make it easier to stay organized when working on complex projects. For example, you might use one Lumetri Color effect to match the colors between clips, and another to add a particular color tint. Keeping the effects separate makes it easier to apply precise adjustments later.

At the top of the Lumetri Color panel, you can choose which Lumetri Color effect you're currently working on. You can also add a new Lumetri Color effect.

The same menu allows you to rename the current Lumetri Color effect to make it easier to navigate your effects. You can also rename effects in the Effect Controls panel by right-clicking the effect name and choosing Rename.

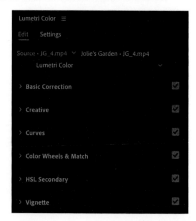

The Lumetri Color panel contains an Edit tab divided into six sections, and a Settings tab divided into five.

Each section provides a group of controls with different approaches to color adjustment. You can use any or all of the sections to achieve the result you want. You can expand or collapse a section in the Lumetri Color panel by clicking its heading. Let's take a look at each section.

Basic Correction

The Basic Correction section provides you with simple controls to apply quick fixes to your clips.

At the top of the section, the Input LUT menu allows you to apply a preset adjustment to your media in the form of an Input LUT (Lookup Table), which makes standard adjustments to media that might otherwise look quite flat.

A LUT is actually a file, a little like an effect preset, intended to adjust the appearance of clips. LUTs can be imported and exported for advanced collaborative color grading workflows.

If you're familiar with Adobe Photoshop Lightroom, you'll recognize the controls in the Basic Correction section. You can work your way down the list making adjustments to improve the look of your footage, or you can click the Auto button to let Premiere Pro work out some settings for you.

Creative

As the name suggests, the Creative section allows you to go a little further into developing a look for your media.

A number of creative Looks are included, with a preview based on your current clip. Click the arrows on the preview to review different Looks, and then click the image to apply a Look to the clip.

You can make subtle adjustments to the color intensity, and there are color wheels configured to adjust the color for the shadow (darker) pixels or highlight (lighter) pixels in the image.

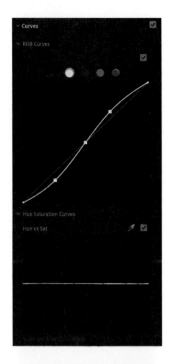

Curves

With curves you can make precise adjustments to visuals. They make it easier to achieve natural-looking results with just a few clicks.

These are some of the more advanced controls, providing nuanced adjustments to the luminance, red, green, and blue pixels.

Adjustments are made in a similar way to those you applied to the Parametric Equalizer effect graph or the audio rubber bands on clips. The position of the line in the graph indicates the adjustment.

In addition to traditional RGB curves, the Curves section contains multiple controls for hue, saturation, and luma curves. Each of these gives precise control over a specific adjustment.

For example, the first control, Hue Vs Sat, allows you to add (by clicking) and position (by dragging) control points to increase or decrease color saturation for specific hues.

The next, Hue Vs Hue, allows you to change one hue into another. For an exploration of these controls, check out *blog.frame.io/2017/11/06/ advanced-curves-techniques*.

▶ **Tip:** You can reset most controls in the Lumetri Color panel by double-clicking the control.

Color Wheels & Match

The Color Wheels & Match section provides precise control over the shadow, midtone, and highlight pixels in the image. Drag the control puck from the center of a wheel toward the edge to apply an adjustment.

Each color wheel has a luminance control slider on the left, which allows you to make adjustments to the brightness for each of the three types of pixels.

There's also a button that opens the Program Monitor Comparison view and another button to automatically color match clips.

HSL Secondary

The HSL Secondary settings enable you to make color adjustments to precisely selected areas of an image, defined by selecting Hue, Saturation, and Luminance ranges.

Using this section of the Lumetri Color panel, you could selectively make a blue sky even bluer, or make a field of grass a deeper green, without affecting other areas of the picture.

The Hue Saturation Curves controls (in the Curves section of the Lumetri Color panel) can provide similar results, and you are likely to choose one method or the other based on personal preference.

Vignette

It's surprising how much difference a simple vignette effect can make to a picture.

A classic vignette is caused by camera lenses darkening the edge of the frame. Modern lenses produce a subtler effect than older lenses.

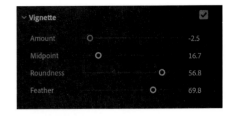

Instead, a vignette is commonly used to bring attention to the center of an image, and it can be highly effective, even when the adjustment is subtle.

Adjusting the Lumetri Color settings

The Lumetri Color panel Settings tab includes several important settings that impact the way color is interpreted and displayed.

Many of these settings are repeated in other menus, but it's convenient to have them all in one place as part of the Lumetri Color panel. Here you'll find settings for your general user preferences, your project, the source clip for a currently selected clip, the currently active sequence, and the currently selected sequence clip. For example, the Display Color Management and Extended Dynamic Range Monitoring options you explored earlier are also available here. Changing any of these settings in one place changes them everywhere.

By default, clips that have no defined color space are interpreted as having Rec.709 color (the industry standard for HD video) and automatically adjusts clip tones to display them correctly in newly created sequences (this is described as *tone mapping*). Sequences created using previous versions of Premiere will not have automatic tone mapping enabled, but you can enable it in the Sequence section of the Lumetri Color panel settings by selecting the Auto Tone Map Media option.

In most cases, all the default settings on this tab will work well and there should be no need for you to change anything.

If you are working with high dynamic range (HDR) video shot on a phone, you will probably get acceptable results by setting the sequence working color space to Rec. 709 and selecting Auto Tone Map Media.

For now, switch back to the Edit tab.

The Lumetri Color panel in action

Because adjustments made using the Lumetri Color panel are added collectively as a regular Premiere Pro effect, you can also enable and disable the effect in the Effect Controls panel or create an effect preset.

Let's start with some prebuilt Looks.

1   If it's not already open, open the sequence Jolie's Garden in the Sequences bin. This simple sequence has a series of clips that have a good range of color and contrast.

2   Position the playhead over the first clip in the sequence. The clip should highlight automatically in the Timeline panel.

3   Click the Creative section heading in the Lumetri Color panel to reveal its controls.

4   Browse through several prebuilt Looks by clicking the arrows on the right and left sides of the preview display. When you see a Look you like, click the preview image to apply it.

5   Try adjusting the Intensity slider to vary the amount of adjustment.

This is a good time to experiment with the other controls in the Lumetri Color panel. Some controls will make sense immediately, while others will take time to master. Use the clips in this sequence as a testing ground to learn about the Lumetri Color panel through experimentation; drag all the controls from one extreme to the other to see the result. You'll learn about many of these controls in detail later in this lesson.

Understanding Lumetri Scopes essentials

You might have wondered why the Premiere Pro interface is dark gray. There's a good reason: Human vision is subjective. In fact, it's also highly relative.

If you see two colors next to each other, the way you see one is changed by the presence of the other. To prevent the Premiere Pro interface from influencing the way you perceive colors in your projects, Adobe has made the interface almost entirely gray. If you've ever seen a professional color-grading suite, where artists provide the finishing touches to films and television programs, you've probably noticed that most of the room is gray. Colorists sometimes also have a large gray piece of card, or a section of a wall, that they can look at for a few moments to "reset" their vision before checking a shot.

The combination of your subjective vision and the variations in the way computer monitors and television monitors display color and brightness means we need a way to objectively measure color and brightness.

Video scopes provide exactly that. And they're used throughout the media industry; learn them once, and you'll be able to use them everywhere!

1 Open the sequence Lady Walking.

2 Position the Timeline playhead so that it's over the clip in the sequence.

3 The Lumetri Scopes panel should be sharing the panel group with the Source Monitor. Click to select the panel and make it active, or select it in the Window menu.

4 Open the Lumetri Scopes panel Settings menu ![icon], and choose Presets > Premiere 4 Scope YUV (float, no clamp).

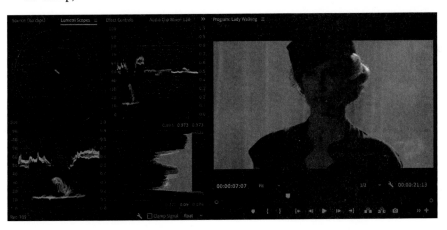

▶ **Tip:** You can also access the Lumetri Scopes Settings menu by right-clicking anywhere in the panel.

You should see the lady walking in the street in the Program Monitor, along with the synchronized display in the Lumetri Scopes panel. For an exploration of the Lumetri Scopes panel, see *blog.frame.io/2017/09/27/introduction-to-video-scopes.*

Working with the Lumetri Scopes panel

The Lumetri Scopes panel displays an array of industry-standard meters to get an objective view of your media.

The full complement of displays can be a little overwhelming at first, plus you'll have smaller graphs because they are all sharing one panel. You can turn individual items off and on by opening the Settings menu and choosing items on the list.

In the Settings menu, you can specify which professional color space you are working to. If you're producing content for broadcast television, you will almost certainly be working to one of these standards. If you're not sure, choose Automatic.

At the bottom right of the Lumetri Scopes panel, you can choose to display the scopes in 8 Bit, 10 Bit, Float (which is 32-bit, floating-point color), or HDR.

The option you choose does not change the clip or the way effects are rendered, but it does change the way the scopes display the information. You'll want to choose an option that matches the color space you're working in or choose Automatic.

The HDR option refers to High Dynamic Range, which has a much bigger range between the darkest and brightest parts of the picture than SDR (Standard Dynamic Range). Though HDR is beyond the scope of these lessons, it's an important technology that is increasingly supported by cameras and displays.

The Clamp Signal option constrains the scopes to standard legal levels for broadcast television. Again, this doesn't impact the image or the result of your effects—it's a matter of personal preference if you would like to limit the range of the scopes in this way to see the scales more clearly.

Let's simplify the view and take a look at two of the main components in the Lumetri Scopes panel.

Begin by using the Lumetri Scopes settings menu to click each of the selected items to deselect them and remove them from the display, keeping only the Waveform (YC).

Waveform

Right-click in the panel and choose Waveform Type > RGB.

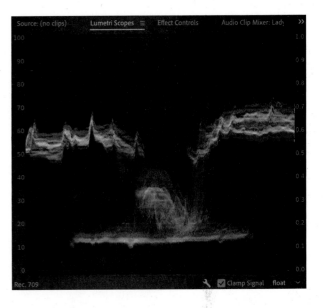

If you're new to waveforms, they can look a little strange, but they're actually a relatively simple graph. They show you the brightness and color intensity of your images.

Every pixel in the current frame is displayed in the waveform. The brighter the pixel, the higher it appears on the graph. The pixels have their correct horizontal position (that is, a pixel half-way across the screen will be displayed halfway across the waveform), but the vertical position is not based on the pixel's position in the image.

Instead, the vertical position indicates bright-ness or color intensity; the brightness and color intensity waveforms are displayed together in this version of the waveform, using different colors.

- 0, at the bottom of the scale, represents no luminance at all and/or no color intensity.

- 100, at the top of the scale, represents a pixel that is fully bright. On the 8-bit RGB scale, this value would be 255 (if you set the Scope to 8 Bit, you can see this scale on the right side of the waveform display).

This all might sound rather technical, but in practice it's straightforward. There's a visible baseline that represents "no brightness" and a top level that represents "fully bright." The numbers on the edge of the graph might change depending on your set-tings, but the use is essentially always the same.

You can view the waveform in several ways. To access a type, open the Lumetri Scopes Settings menu and choose Waveform Type, followed by one of these options:

- **RGB:** Shows the Red, Green, and Blue pixels in their own colors.

- **Luma:** Shows the brightness (luminance) value of pixels against a scale of −20 to 120, called IRE (Institute of Radio Engineers). This allows for precise analysis of bright spots and contrast ratio.

- **YC:** Shows the image luminance (brightness) in green and the chrominance (color intensity) in blue.

- **YC No Chroma:** Shows the luminance only, with no chrominance.

Let's try this display a little.

1   Continue using the Lady Walking sequence. Set the Timeline playhead to 00:00:07:00 so you can see the subject against the smoky background.

2   Set the waveform display to YC No Chroma. This is a brightness-only waveform.

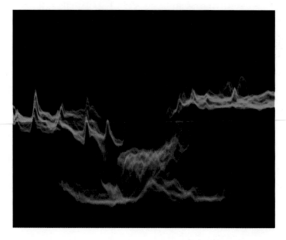

The smoky parts of the image have little contrast and are displayed as a relatively flat line in the waveform display. The lady's head and shoulders are darker than the smoky background. They're around the middle of the image, and they are clearly visible in the middle area of the waveform display.

3   Expand the Basic Correction section of the Lumetri Color panel.

4 Experiment with the Exposure, Contrast, Highlights, Shadows, Whites, and Blacks controls. As you adjust the controls, watch the waveform display to see the result.

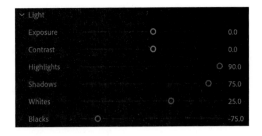

If you make an adjustment to the image and then wait a few seconds, your eyes will adjust to the new appearance, and it will seem normal. Make another adjustment, and a few seconds later the new appearance seems normal too. Which is correct?

Ultimately, the answer is based on perceived quality. If you like what you see, it's right. However, the waveform display will give you objective information about how dark or bright pixels are or how much color is in the shot, which is useful when attempting to meet delivery standards.

If you scrub through the sequence or play the sequence, you'll see the waveform display update live.

The waveform display is useful for showing how much contrast you have in your images (the difference between the bright and dark areas of the image) and for checking whether you are working on video that has "legal" levels (that is, the minimum and maximum brightness or color saturation permitted by a broadcaster). Broadcasters adopt their own standards for legal levels, so you will need to find out for each case where your work will be broadcast.

You can see right away that you do not have great contrast in this shot. There are some strong shadows but few *highlights* in the upper part of the waveform display. Any time you see perfectly flat horizontal lines in the waveform display, it means there's no visible detail. In the following example, the shadows have been darkened so much, they're flattened at the bottom of the waveform.

The flattening may not be visible until you select Clamp Signal to limit the waveform display to the visible part of the output.

▶ **Tip:** It can sometimes seem as if the waveform display is showing an image. Remember, the vertical position of the pixels in your images is not indicated in a waveform display.

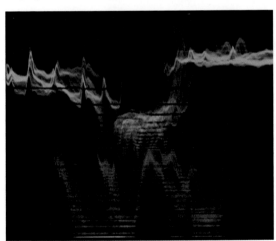

The result is not necessarily bad and might be exactly the look you are seeking—it's certainly dramatic! It's just important to know when adjustments are so extreme that detail is being lost.

Reset the Lumetri Color panel by clicking the Reset Effect button  at the upper-right corner of the panel.

YUV vectorscope

Whereas the Luma waveform shows luminance in terms of the vertical position of pixels displayed, with brighter pixels displayed at the top and darker pixels displayed at the bottom, the vectorscope shows only color.

1   Open the sequence Skyline.

2   Open the Lumetri Scopes Settings menu, and choose Vectorscope YUV; then open the Settings menu again, and choose Waveform (YC No Chroma) to deselect it.

Pixels in the image are displayed in the vectorscope. If a pixel appears in the center of the circle, it has no color saturation. The closer to the edge of the circle, the more color a pixel has.

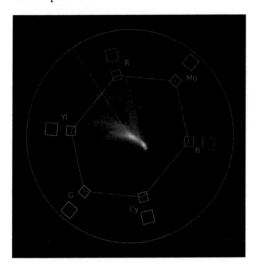

If you look closely at the vectorscope, you'll see a series of targets indicating primary colors.

- R = Red
- G = Green
- B = Blue

There are two boxes for each target. The smaller, inner box is at 75% saturation, the YUV color limit, while the larger, outer box is at 100% saturation, the RGB color limit. RGB color extends to a greater level of saturation than YUV. The thin line connecting the inner boxes shows the YUV color gamut (the range of YUV colors).

You'll also see a series of targets indicating secondary colors.

- Yl = Yellow
- Cy = Cyan
- Mg = Magenta

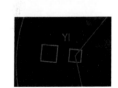

The closer a pixel is to one of these targets, the more of that color it has. Unlike the waveform display, which indicates the horizontal position of each pixel, no position information is indicated in the vectorscope.

It's clear enough to see what's happening in this shot of Seattle. There's a lot of blue, and there are a few spots of red and yellow. The small amount of red is indicated by the streak of peaks reaching out toward the R marking in the vectorscope.

The vectorscope is helpful because it gives you objective information about the colors in your sequence. If there's a color cast, perhaps because the camera was not calibrated properly, it's often obvious in the vectorscope display. You can use one of the Lumetri Color panel controls to reduce the amount of the unwanted color or add more of the opposite color.

Some of the controls for color correction adjustments have the same color wheel design as the vectorscope, making it easy to see what you need to do.

About primary and secondary colors

Computer screens and televisions use additive color, which means the colors are created by generating light in different colors and combining them to produce a precise mix.

When you draw with color on paper, it is usually white paper, which reflects a full spectrum of colors. You subtract from the white of the paper by adding pigment. Because the pigment absorbs light in a portion of the spectrum and prevents those parts of the light from being reflected, this is called *subtractive color*.

Red, green, and blue are the primary colors used by video displays. Television screens and your computer monitor combine these three colors in varying relative amounts to produce the colors you see. You produce white by combining equal amounts of red, green, and blue.

There's a beautiful symmetry to the way a standard color wheel works, and a color wheel is essentially what the vectorscope displays.

Any two primary colors will combine to produce a secondary color. The secondary colors for additive color (yellow, cyan, and magenta) appear opposite the remaining primary color on a color wheel.

For example, red and green (two of the primary colors) combine to produce yellow, which is the opposite of blue (the third primary color).

The secondary colors used in additive color are equivalent to the primary colors used in subtractive color. It's an elegant symmetry!

For a more detailed explanation of color, see *helpx.adobe.com/photoshop/using/color.html*.

Let's make an adjustment and observe the result in the vectorscope display.

Tip: You can jump to 00:00:01:00 by clicking the timecode in the Source Monitor, Program Monitor, or Timeline panel; typing **1.** (that's 1 followed by a period); and then pressing Return (macOS) or Enter (Windows). Each period (.) adds one pair of zeros.

1 Continue working with the Skyline sequence. Position the Timeline playhead at 00:00:01:00, where the colors are more vivid than at the end of the clip.

2 In the Lumetri Color panel, expand the Basic Correction section.

3 While watching the result in the vectorscope display, drag the Temperature slider from one extreme to the other. Try making an extreme blue adjustment.

Temperature ○──────────────── -100.0

The pixels displayed in the vectorscope move away from the orange area of the display toward the blue.

4   The adjustment enhances the existing blue tint. Now try an extreme orange adjustment.

Shifting the color temperature to the orange compensates for the original tint and makes the shot look more natural.

5   Double-click the Temperature slider to reset it.

6   In the Lumetri Color panel, drag the Tint slider from one extreme to the other.

The pixels displayed in the vectorscope move between the green and magenta areas of the display.

7   Double-click the Tint slider to reset it.

By making adjustments while checking the vectorscope, you can give an objective indication of the change you're making.

RGB parade

Open the Lumetri Scopes Settings menu and choose Presets > Parade RGB.

The RGB parade provides another form of waveform-style display. The difference is that the red, green, and blue levels are displayed separately. To fit all three colors in, each display is squeezed horizontally to one-third of the total width.

You can choose which kind of parade you see by clicking the Lumetri Scopes Settings menu or by right-clicking in the Lumetri Scopes panel and choosing Parade Type.

The three parts of the parade have similar patterns in them, particularly where there are white or gray pixels, because these parts will have equal amounts of red, green, and blue. The RGB parade is one of the most frequently used tools in color correction because it clearly shows the relationship between the primary color channels.

To see the dramatic impact color adjustments can have on the parade, go to the Basic Correction section of the Lumetri Color panel and try adjusting the White Balance using the Temperature and Tint controls. Be sure to reset them when you finish by double-clicking each control.

Using Comparison view

Let's take a moment to consider two important stages in the process when adjusting colors.

- **Color correction:** Correcting for color cast or brightness issues and matching shots in the sequence to ensure they look like part of content that was shot at the same time in the same location or that they match an in-house standard for final delivery.

- **Color grading:** Establishing a creative look for shots on a shot-by-shot, scene-by-scene, or sequence-wide basis.

When color correcting, it's helpful to compare one shot with another to achieve a match. This is especially helpful when the two shots come from different scenes, meaning some color variation is expected even if the overall tone should be similar.

You can drag your current sequence from the Project panel into the Source Monitor to use that monitor as a reference for side-by-side comparison, but there's an easier way: You can set the Program Monitor to Comparison view.

Let's explore the controls:

1 Open the Jolie's Garden sequence, and position the Timeline playhead over the last clip in the sequence.

2 Click the Comparison View button 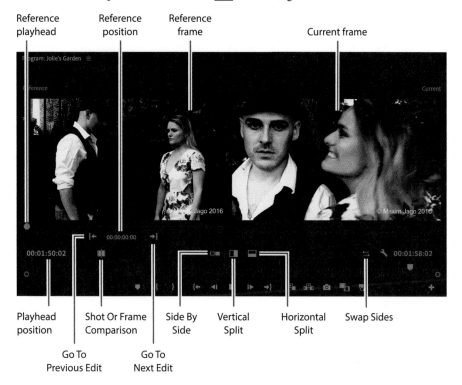 in the Program Monitor.

Note: The Comparison View button may not be visible on smaller displays. In the Program Monitor click the double arrow in the lower-right corner and choose Comparison View from the menu. You can also choose Comparison View from the Program Monitor Settings menu.

Let's take a look at the new controls.

- **Reference frame:** The frame in the current sequence you are using as a reference or for color matching.

- **Reference position:** The timecode for the reference frame.

- **Playhead position:** The timecode for the current frame.

- **Shot Or Frame Comparison:** Toggle between using another frame as a reference and using the current state of the current frame. The latter option is useful when working on effects, as it allows a constant before-and-after view when working with effects so your eyes can't adjust to the finished version.

- **Side By Side:** View the two images separately, side by side.

- **Vertical Split:** View the two images as a single vertically split screen, with a divider you can drag to reposition.

- **Horizontal Split:** The same as the Vertical Split option but now with a horizontal divider.

- **Swap Sides:** Switch the sides displayed of the reference and current frame images.

- **Current frame:** The frame you're working on now.

Tip: Whenever the Program Monitor is not already set to Comparison view, you can click the Lumetri Color panel's Comparison View button in the Color Wheels & Match section, just under the heading. It has the same function as the button in the Program Monitor.

3 Make sure the last clip in the sequence is selected, and in the Lumetri Color panel, open the Color Wheels & Match section.

4 Try changing the reference frame in one of these ways:

   • Drag the mini playhead under the reference frame to a new position.

   • Click the reference position timecode, and enter a new time or scrub the timecode to choose another time.

   • Click the Go To Previous Edit or Go To Next Edit button on either side of the reference position timecode to jump between clips.

5 Try the split view options, and drag the divider between the two sides of the split.

At first, Comparison view might seem to have lots of new buttons to remember. They all work together, however, giving you precise control over the two clips you are comparing and how they are displayed.

Viewing two parts of your sequence using Comparison view is helpful, and it's the starting point for an automated color adjustment available in the Lumetri Color panel.

Now that you're familiar with Comparison view, it's time to work on these clips and match their colors.

Matching colors

One of the most powerful and time-saving features of the Lumetri Color panel is the option to automatically match colors between two clips.

To use this feature, you'll switch to Comparison view in the Program Monitor, choose a reference frame and a current frame, and click the Apply Match button in the Color Wheels & Match section of the Lumetri Color panel.

The result will not always be perfect, and you may need to experiment with different reference and current frame selections to get a closer match. However, the result *is* often close enough for you to make final adjustments that are guided by the initial automated adjustment. If Premiere Pro gets the color 80% right, it's a huge time-saver.

Let's try this with our current sequence.

1 Continuing from the previous exercise, set the reference frame to 00:00:01:00.

2 Position the Timeline panel playhead on the first frame of the last clip in the sequence, and set the comparison view to Side by Side.

3   These are clips from different scenes in the same film. They don't need to have exactly the same colors, but it would be helpful if the skin tones matched better. Make sure the Face Detection option is selected in the Lumetri Color panel. This way, Premiere Pro will automatically detect faces and prioritize matching those tones.

4   Click the Apply Match button in the Lumetri Color panel, and Premiere Pro applies a color adjustment to the selected clip.

5   The difference is clear. However, within a few moments, your eyes are likely to adjust to the new appearance of the current frame. To help see the change more clearly, toggle the Color Wheels & Match checkbox off and on repeatedly.

6   Click the Comparison View button to switch back to the regular playback view in the Program Monitor.

The automated color matching offered by the Lumetri Color panel is not likely to produce an identical color match, partly because the perception of color is so subjective and contextual. However, all of the adjustments that were applied are editable, so you can finesse the result until it's perfect.

Exploring the color-adjustment effects

As well as adjusting color using the Lumetri Color panel, there are a number of regular color adjustment effects worth familiarizing yourself with. Just as with the other effects, you can use keyframes to modify the settings over time. In fact, the same is true of the Lumetri Color effect, if you adjust the controls in the Effect Controls panel.

As you build familiarity with Premiere Pro, you may find yourself uncertain about which effect is best for a particular purpose; this is normal! There are often several ways of achieving the same outcome in Premiere Pro, and sometimes the choice comes down to which interface you prefer.

It's a good idea to experiment with effects to get to know the options available to you. Choose footage with a range of colors, highlights, and shadows, so you can see the results for different types of content.

Using the Video Limiter effect

In addition to creative effects, the color correction repertoire available in Premiere Pro includes effects used for professional video production.

When you prepare video for distribution, keep in mind that the video must not exceed specific limits for maximum luminance, minimum luminance, and color saturation. Although it's possible to confine your video levels to the limits permitted using manual controls, it's easy to miss parts of your sequence that need adjustment.

In the Effects panel, the Video Limiter effect, found in Video Effects > Color Correction, automatically limits the levels of clips to ensure they meet the standards you set.

Check the limits approved by your broadcaster before adjusting the Clip Level setting. This is the level above which the broadcaster will enforce prescribed limits and cut off luminance and/or saturation.

Next, it's simply a question of choosing the Compression Before Clipping amount. You can have Premiere Pro apply a gradual compression of the higher levels to produce a more natural-looking result before the absolute cut-off level set in the Clip Level menu.

The compression can be set to begin 3%, 5%, 10%, or 20% before the cutoff level.

If you turn on the Gamut warning, pixels that would have gone above the Clip Level setting or would be affected by the compression setting are highlighted in the Gamut Warning color. This is useful when reviewing your sequence, but be sure to deselect the Gamut Warning option before exporting your sequence, as the color highlight will be included in the exported file!

Tip: It's common to apply the Video Limiter effect to the whole sequence by using it on an adjustment layer or by enabling it as an export setting (see Lesson 16, "Exporting Frames, Clips, and Sequences").

Using Lumetri Color presets in the Effects panel

In addition to the controls available in the Lumetri Color panel, there are a number of Lumetri Color presets available in the Effects panel. These are a fantastic way to get started with advanced color adjustments, and as they are presets, you can modify the settings to achieve exactly the finish you want. If you resize the Effects panel to make it wider, you can reveal previews of the presets.

You apply a Lumetri Color preset effect in the same way that you would apply any other effect available in the Effects panel.

Lumetri Color presets are Lumetri Color effects with an input LUT applied in the Basic Correction settings or a Look applied in the Creative settings.

You can switch or remove these in the Effect Controls panel or in the Lumetri Color panel.

Fixing exposure problems

Let's look at some clips that have exposure issues and use some of the Lumetri Color panel controls to address them.

1   Make sure you are in the Color workspace, and reset it to the saved version if necessary.

2   Open the sequence Color Work.

3   In the Lumetri Scopes panel, right-click or open the Settings menu to choose Presets > Waveform RGB. This is a quick way to close any other scopes and open the waveform display on its own.

4 Again, in the Lumetri Scopes panel, right-click or open the Settings menu to choose Waveform Type > YC No Chroma. This changes the display to a waveform that uses the standard broadcast television range, which is a useful reference for most video projects.

5 Position the Timeline playhead over the first clip in the sequence. It's the shot of the lady walking. You're going to add some contrast.

This composition is smoky; 100 IRE (at the top of the scale on the left on the waveform) means fully exposed, and 0 IRE (at the bottom of the scale on the left) means not exposed at all. No part of this image comes close to these upper or lower limits. Your eye quickly adjusts to the image, and it'll soon appear fine, but it's relatively low contrast and the waveform shows it. Let's see whether you can bring it to life a little.

6 In the Lumetri Color panel, click the Basic Correction heading to display that section.

7 Use the Exposure and Contrast controls to make adjustments to the shot while checking the waveform display to make sure the image doesn't become too dark or too light.

You'll get the best perceived results if you have a frame from later in the clip on the screen. Around 00:00:07:19 there's a section of sharp focus.

Try an Exposure setting of **0.6** and a Contrast setting of **60**.

8   Your eyes are likely to adjust quickly to the new image. Use the checkbox to toggle the Basic Correction section off and on to compare the image before and after.

The subtle adjustment you made adds depth to the image, giving it stronger highlights and shadows. As you toggle the effect off and on, you'll see the waveform changing in the Lumetri Scopes panel. The image still doesn't have bright highlights, but that's fine because the colors, particularly in the fog, are mainly midtones.

Fixing underexposed images

Now let's work with an underexposed image.

1   Switch to the Effects workspace.

2   Position the Timeline playhead over the second clip in the Color Work sequence. When you first look at this clip, it might look fine. The highlights don't look strong, but there's a reasonable amount of detail throughout the image. The face, especially, is sharp and detailed.

3   Open the Lumetri Scopes panel so you can view a waveform representation of this clip. At the bottom of the waveform there are quite a few dark pixels, with some touching the 0 IRE line.

▶ **Tip:** You can create a keyboard shortcut to temporarily turn off all instances of the Lumetri Color effect. Use the Keyboard Shortcuts dialog box to assign a keyboard shortcut to the Bypass Lumetri Color Effects command. For information on assigning keyboard shortcuts, see Lesson 1, "Touring Adobe Premiere Pro."

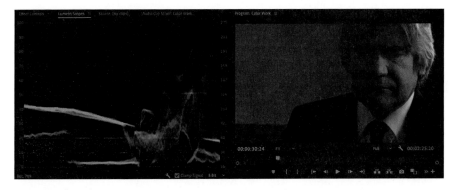

▶ **Tip:** The Lumetri Scopes panel isn't limited to the Color workspace. You can always open it from the Window menu.

For this clip, it looks like the missing detail is in the shoulder of the suit, on the left. The problem with such dark pixels is that increasing the brightness will simply change the strong shadows into gray, and no detail is likely to emerge.

4   In the Effects panel, locate the Brightness & Contrast effect. Apply the effect to the clip.

5   Drag the Lumetri Scopes panel to the right and down to move it into a new panel group on the left of the Program Monitor.

This way you can view the Effect Controls panel and Lumetri Scopes panel together with the Program Monitor.

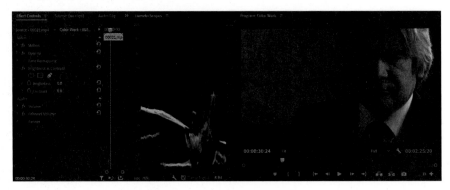

6 Use the Brightness control in the Effect Controls panel to increase the brightness. Rather than clicking the blue number and typing a new number, drag to the right so you can see the change happening incrementally.

Note: The Brightness & Contrast effect offers a quick, easy fix, but it's also easy to accidentally clip the black (dark) or white (bright) pixels, losing detail.

As you drag, notice that the whole waveform moves up. This is fine for bringing out the highlights in the image, but the shadows remain a flat line. You're changing the black shadows to gray. If you drag the Brightness control all the way to 100, clipping the highlights a little, you'll see just how flat the image still is.

7 Remove the Brightness & Contrast effect.

8 Switch back to the Color workspace. Try making an adjustment using the RGB Curves control in the Curves section of the Lumetri Color panel. Here's an example of an RGB Curves adjustment that would improve the image.

9 Experiment with the third clip in the sequence. This clip demonstrates that there are limits to what can be "fixed in post!"

That doesn't mean it's unusable, but you'd probably have to apply some significant artistic effects to create a look that seemed intentional.

10 Try the fourth clip in the sequence. This drone shot of a desert was underexposed. Drag the lowest RGB Curves control point to the right until the darkest pixels displayed in the Lumetri Scopes panel waveform touch the bottom of the range. This darkens the shadows.

11 Next, drag the top RGB Curves control point to the left, until the lightest pixels touch the top of the waveform range. This brightens the highlights.

The effect of both darkening the shadows and brightening the highlights increases the contrast overall.

12 Finally, click in the middle of the curve to add a control point to the RGB Curves control and drag up and left until you are satisfied with the result—a dramatic improvement!

Fixing overexposed images

The next clip you'll work with is overexposed.

1 Move the Timeline playhead to the fifth clip in the sequence. A lot of the pixels are burned out. Just as with the flat shadows in the second clip in the sequence, there's no detail in burned-out highlights. This means that lowering the brightness will simply make the character's skin and hair gray; no detail will emerge.

2 Notice that the shadows in this shot don't reach the bottom of the Waveform Monitor. The lack of properly dark shadows has a flattening effect on the image.

3 Try using the Lumetri Color panel to improve the contrast range. You might produce acceptable results, although the clip will definitely end up looking processed.

This footage is 8 bit, so there is less detail available to reveal when making adjustments to the image. If it had been shot in 10 bit or even 16 bit, it might have been possible to achieve an acceptable result.

Correcting color offset

Your eyes adjust to compensate for changes in the color of light around you automatically. It's an extraordinary ability that allows you to see white as white, even if objectively it's orange, for example, because it's lit by tungsten light.

Cameras can automatically adjust their white balance to compensate for different lighting in the way that your eyes do. With the right calibration, white objects look white, whether you are recording indoors (under oranger tungsten light) or outdoors (in bluer daylight).

Sometimes automatic settings are hit or miss, so professional shooters often prefer to adjust white balance manually. If the white balance is set wrong, you can end up with some interesting results. The most common reason for a white balance problem in a clip is that the camera was not calibrated properly.

When is color correction right?

Making adjustments to images is highly subjective. Though there are precise limits for image formats and broadcast technologies, whether an image should be light, dark, blue-tinted, or green is ultimately a subjective choice. The reference tools that Premiere Pro provides, such as the Lumetri Scopes panel, are a helpful guide, but only you can decide when the picture looks right.

If you're producing video for display on televisions, it's vital that you have a television screen connected to your Premiere Pro editing system to view your content. Television screens usually display color differently from computer monitors, and consumer screens sometimes have special color modes that change the appearance of video. For professional broadcast television, editors will usually have a carefully calibrated preview monitor connected to their editing system. The Display Color Management option helps to show the colors as they might be displayed on a TV, but nothing compares to a calibrated monitor.

The same rule applies if you are producing content for digital cinema projection, Ultra High Definition TV, or High Dynamic Range TV. The only way to know exactly how the picture will look is to view it using the destination medium. Thankfully, the same principle means if your ultimate destination is a computer screen, perhaps as web video or part of a software interface, you are already looking at the perfect test monitor.

Balancing with the Lumetri color wheels

Let's try using the Lumetri Color panel color wheels to adjust the last shot in the sequence.

1. Make sure you are still viewing the Color workspace, and reset it if necessary.

2. Position the Timeline playhead over the last clip in the Color Work sequence.

3. In the Lumetri Color panel, expand the Basic Correction section and click the Auto button to automatically adjust the levels.

   Premiere Pro automatically adjusts the Color and Light controls to compensate for both the luminance levels and color balance in the shot. The result is an improvement, but there's still a strong blue color cast.

   Applying an automatic adjustment in this way will usually produce results that are close to ideal, but because the shot includes mixed light sources (interior and exterior), Premiere Pro can't know which color temperature is correct.

4. If the Lumetri Scopes panel isn't at the front of its panel group, click its tab to bring it forward.

5. Right-click the middle of the Lumetri Scopes panel and choose Presets > Vectorscope YUV.

   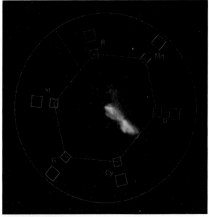

   It's clear there's a strong bias toward the blue. Though the scene has mixed lighting, the bluer daylight coming from the window dominates warmer tungsten light coming from the interior of the room.

6. In the Basic Correction section of the Lumetri Color panel, use the Temperature slider to push the colors toward the orange. You'll need to push the adjustment all the way to 100 to see a reasonable result because the color shift is so strong.

   The result is an improvement, but perhaps it could be better.

   The darker pixels in this shot are generally lit by the interior, warmer room light, while the lighter pixels are generally lit by the bluer daylight. This means different color wheels will interact with different areas of the picture in convincing and natural ways.

7. Expand the Color Wheels & Match section of the Lumetri Color panel. To emphasize the different light sources, try using the Shadows color wheel to pull the color toward the orange, use the Midtones color wheel to pull the color toward the red, and adjust the Highlights color wheel to pull the color toward blue.

8 You've adjusted the color wheels to warm up the shadows and midtones and cool down the highlights. Experiment with the midtones to obtain the most natural result possible. Use the images as a guide.

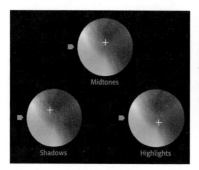 

Experiment with the other controls in the Lumetri Color panel to see whether you can improve the result further.

For more precise control of the image, you can add two Lumetri effects and mask them using the controls in the Effect Controls panel. With one effect constrained to the left side of the image and another constrained to the right, you will be able to make adjustments to suit the interior and exterior lighting in more natural ways.

Making a secondary color adjustment

The Lumetri Color panel allows you to make adjustments that are limited to a particular range of hues, a level of color saturation, or a level of brightness.

This is useful if you want to bring out the blue in a subject's eyes or give a flower a color boost. Let's try it.

1 Open the sequence Yellow Flower, and position the Timeline playhead over the first clip. This sequence has two shots, each with clearly defined areas of color.

2 Expand the HSL Secondary section of the Lumetri Color panel.

3 Click the first Set Color eyedropper to select it, and then click the yellow petals of the flower to pick that color.

If you hold Command (macOS) or Ctrl (Windows) while clicking, the sample that is captured is based on a 5×5-pixel average.

> ● **Note:** If you're using macOS, you may see an alert asking you to give Premiere Pro permission to record your computer screen. To do so, click Open System Settings and use an administrator password to unlock Security & Privacy preferences. You'll have to quit Premiere Pro and restart it to confirm the change.

The Hue, Saturation, and Luminance selection controls update based on the area of the petal you clicked.

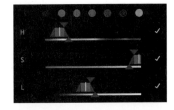

4　Drag the H, S, and L (Hue, Saturation, Luminance) color range selection controls to expand the selection. Your initial selection probably selected only a few pixels, as there is quite a lot of variation in the yellow petals.

For each control, the upper triangles represent the hard-stop range of the selection. The lower triangles extend the selection with a softening that reduces hard edges.

As you drag the controls, the image hides unselected pixels with gray. When you release the control, the image returns.

5　Experiment with the Denoise and Blur options in the Refine category. These help to smooth the selection range, rather than adjusting the image contents.

6　Once you're happy you have selected all the pixels in the petals of the flower, adjust the Temperature and Tint controls under the Correction heading.

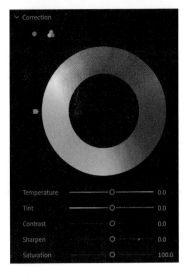

The adjustments you make will be limited to the pixels you selected.

7　Now that you have mastered these controls, experiment with the second clip in the sequence. Select the pixels in the blue sky, and then increase the color saturation and add a blue tint to the selection.

Making precise adjustments with curves

The Hue Saturation Curves controls in the Curves section of the Lumetri Color panel offer precise control when adjusting hue and luminance.

Though there are several different controls, they all work essentially the same way. Each control focuses on a different type of precise selection. Adjustments are applied to pixels that have been selected by reshaping the curve—if this feels a little like adjusting the Parametric Equalizer audio effect, you're right!

The result is similar to the HSL Secondary adjustment you just made but with simplified, faster controls.

Curves start as a straight line but become curved when you add control points to them by clicking. The position of the control points can be set by dragging, and this determines the type of adjustment applied.

The first part of the name of a curve indicates its horizontal axis, while the second part of the name indicates the vertical axis.

Let's take a look at each one.

- **Hue Vs Sat:** Select pixels with a particular hue, and change their level of saturation.
- **Hue Vs Hue:** Select pixels with a particular hue, and change that hue.
- **Hue Vs Luma:** Select pixels with a particular hue, and change their brightness (luma).
- **Luma Vs Sat:** Select pixels with a particular brightness (luma), and change their color saturation.
- **Sat Vs Sat:** Select pixels with a particular level of color saturation, and change their level of color saturation. This is particularly useful for reducing the impact of highly color-saturated parts of an image while leaving the rest of the image untouched.

As with so many effects, the quickest way to learn what the controls can do is to try them with extreme adjustments and then experiment to achieve subtler results.

Let's try these controls on some clips.

1 Open the sequence The Ancestor Simulation. Play the sequence to familiar-ize yourself with the shots. These images have muted colors with some specific regions with distinguishable colors, such as the flowers on the table.

2 Expand the Curves section of the Lumetri Color panel, and position the Timeline playhead over the second clip, at 00:00:06:00.

© Copyright Maxim Jago 2018

At the top right of each Hue Saturation Curves control, there's an eyedropper . When you use the eyedropper to click the image, Premiere Pro adds three control points to the curve control: One matches the part of the image you clicked, and the other two (one on either side) separate the adjustment you'll make from the rest of the curve.

3   Click the eyedropper for the Hue Vs Sat curve to select it, and then click the petals of the reddish flower closest to the camera on the table to sample the color.

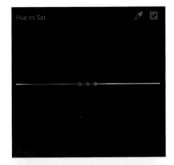

4   If the selection is right at the edges of the hue graph, drag the scroll bar at the bottom of the curve control to access the control points more easily.

5   Drag the middle control point up to dramatically increase the saturation for the flower.

The shape of the curve produces a smoothing effect for the selection. Even so, you may want to reduce the intensity of the adjustment for a more natural result.

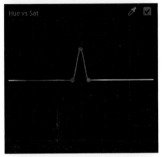

6   Place the Timeline playhead at the beginning of the sequence, on the first frame. Use the eyedropper for the Sat Vs Sat curve to select the pale beige color of the sofa. This selects pixels that have little color saturation. Drag the left control point up, quite high in the graph, to bring some life to the sofa and similar pale areas of the image.

Because you exclusively selected pixels that originally had little color saturation, other areas of the image with more saturation are unaffected. The result is a natural-looking adjustment.

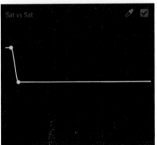

● **Note:** The example video clips are low resolution and are compressed to keep file sizes small. The result is softer edges in images than you can expect when working with your original media files.

7   Experiment with the other clips in this sequence. For example, for the sixth clip, showing the castle with trees, try using the Hue Vs Sat curve to increase the saturation of the green in the trees and then use the Hue Vs Luma curve to darken the leaves. This adds more visual interest and contrast without making an adjustment to the whole clip.

Using special color effects

Several effects available in the Effects panel give you great creative control over the colors in your clips.

Using Gaussian Blur

While it's not technically a color adjustment effect, adding a tiny amount of blurring can soften the results of your adjustments, making an image look more natural. Premiere Pro has a number of blur effects. The most popular is Gaussian Blur, which has a natural-looking, smoothing effect on an image.

Using Stylize effects

The Stylize category of effects includes some dramatic options, some of which, like the Mosaic effect, you'll use for more functional applications in combination with an effect mask, such as hiding someone's face.

The Solarize effect, which you worked with in Lesson 12, gives vivid color adjustments that can be used to create stylized back plates for graphics or intro sequences.

Adding color adjustments from a file

The Lumetri Color panel includes the list of built-in Looks you experimented with earlier, and as you have found, there are a number of Lumetri color presets in the Effects panel to get you started.

These effects all make use of the Lumetri Color effect.

In addition to using the built-in presets, the Lumetri Color effect allows you to browse to an existing LOOK, LUT, or CUBE file to apply nuanced, subtle color adjustments to your footage.

It's possible you will be given a LOOK or LUT file to use as a starting point for your color adjustments. It's increasingly common for cameras and location monitors to employ a color reference file of this kind. It helps to use the same reference when you are working on footage in post-production.

To apply an existing LOOK, LUT, or CUBE file, open the Input LUT menu in the Basic Correction section, at the top of the Lumetri Color panel, and choose Browse.

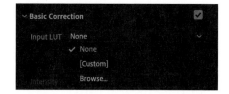

Creating a distinctive look

Once you've spent a little time with the color correction effects available in Premiere Pro, you should have a feel for the kinds of changes you can make and the impact those changes have on the overall look and feel of your footage.

You can use effect presets to create a distinctive look for your clips. You can also apply an effect to an adjustment layer to give your sequence, or part of a sequence, an overall look.

Let's try using an adjustment layer to apply a color adjustment to a scene.

1   Open the Theft Unexpected sequence.

2   Click into the Project panel to make it active, and choose File > New > Adjustment Layer. The settings automatically match the current sequence, so click OK.

3   Drag the new adjustment layer to the beginning of the Video 2 track in the sequence. If snapping is enabled in the Timeline panel, the clip should snap to the beginning of the sequence. If snapping is disabled, you can enable it while still dragging the clip by pressing S.

   The default duration for adjustment layers is the same as the duration of still images. It's too short for this sequence.

4   Trim the adjustment layer until it stretches from the beginning to the end of the sequence.

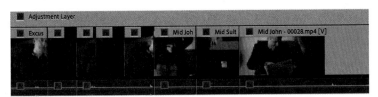

Note: If you use adjustment layers in this way on a sequence that has graphics, such as titles, you may want to ensure that the adjustment layer is on a track between the titles and the video. Otherwise, you will adjust the appearance of your titles too.

5   In the Effects panel, browse to Lumetri Presets > SpeedLooks > Universal. Drag one of these SpeedLooks onto the adjustment layer. The example uses the SL Gold Heat (Universal) preset.

Tip: SpeedLooks available in the Effects panel are applied as regular effects, so it's easy to combine them—just apply another.

The Look will apply to every clip in the sequence, and you can modify it using the controls in the Effect Controls panel or in the Lumetri Color panel.

You can apply any standard visual effect this way and use multiple adjustment layers to apply different looks to different scenes.

The Lumetri Color panel controls will adjust whichever Lumetri Color effect is selected at the top of the panel.

This is just a brief introduction to color adjustment, and there's an enormous amount more to explore. It's worth investing the time to familiarize yourself with the advanced controls in the Lumetri Color panel. There are a great many visual effects that can add nuance or a striking look to your footage. Experimentation and practice are key to developing your understanding in this important and creative aspect of post-production.

For an exploration of the Lumetri Color panel controls, check out *blog.frame.io/2018/05/21/premiere-lumetri-guide.*

Review questions

1 How do you change the display in the Lumetri Scopes panel?

2 How do you access the Lumetri Scopes panel when not viewing the Color workspace?

3 Why should you use the vectorscope rather than depending on your eyes?

4 How can you apply a look to a whole sequence?

5 Why might you need to limit your luminance or color levels?

Review answers

1 Right-click in the panel, or open the Settings menu, and choose the display type you would like.

2 You can choose the Lumetri Scopes panel from the Window menu.

3 Color perception is subjective and relative. Depending on the colors you have just seen, you will see new colors differently. The vectorscope display gives you an objective reference.

4 You can use effect presets in the Effects panel to apply the same color correction adjustments to multiple clips, or you can add an adjustment layer and apply the effects to that. Any clips on lower video tracks covered by the adjustment layer will be affected.

5 If your sequence is intended for broadcast television or professional online distribution, you'll need to ensure you meet the stringent requirements for maximum and minimum levels. The broadcasters you work with will be able to tell you their required levels.

14 EXPLORING COMPOSITING TECHNIQUES

Lesson overview

In this lesson, you'll learn how to do the following:

- Use the alpha channel.

- Use compositing techniques.

- Work with opacity.

- Work with a greenscreen.

- Use mattes.

- Use the Track Matte Key effect to combine layers.

 This lesson will take about 60 minutes to complete. To get the lesson files used in this chapter, download them from the web page for this book at *peachpit.com/PremiereProCIB2024*. For more information, see "Accessing the lesson files and Web Edition" in the "Getting Started" section at the beginning of this book. Store the files on your computer in a convenient location.

Anything that combines two images is compositing, including blending, layering, keying, masking, and cropping. Premiere Pro has powerful tools that enable you to combine layers of video, photos, graphics, and titles in your sequences. In this lesson, you'll learn about the technologies that make compositing work, as well as ways to prepare for and perform compositing.

Starting the lesson

Until now, you have been mainly working with single, whole-frame visuals. You have created edits in which you have transitioned between one image and another or edited clips onto upper video tracks to have them appear in front of clips on lower video tracks.

In this lesson, you'll learn about ways to combine those layers of video. You'll still use clips on upper and lower video tracks, but now they will become foreground and background elements in one combined composition.

You might combine layers by cropping part of the foreground image, masking, or *keying*—setting pixels with a specific color to become transparent—but whatever the method, the way you edit clips onto a sequence is the same as ever.

● **Note:** To ensure that the tools function and the defaults are set exactly as described in this lesson, reset the Premiere Pro preferences by holding Option (macOS) or Alt (Windows) while launching the application and then clicking Continue in the Reset Options dialog box.

Let's begin by learning about the important concept of *alpha*, which explains the way pixels are displayed, and then try several compositing techniques.

1 Open Lesson 14.prproj in the Lessons folder.

2 Save the project as **Lesson 14 Working.prproj**.

3 Use the Workspaces menu to switch to the Effects workspace.

4 Reset the workspace by opening the Workspaces menu and choosing Reset To Saved Layout.

What is an alpha channel?

Cameras record the red, green, and blue parts of the light spectrum as separate color *channels*. Because each channel has a single color, the channels are commonly described as *monochrome*.

Adobe Premiere Pro uses these three monochromatic (single-color) channels to produce the corresponding primary color channels. They are combined using what's called *additive color* to create a complete RGB image. Your eyes perceive the three channels combined as full-color video.

This approach of combining multiple monochromatic colors to produce a full color range is a little like combining two mono audio channels to produce a stereo mix.

Finally, there is a fourth monochromatic channel: *alpha*. The fourth channel defines no colors at all. Instead, it defines *opacity*—how visible each pixel is. The opacity of pixels is independent of their colors because the alpha channel is separate from the color channels. This fourth channel has several different names, including *visibility*, *transparency*, *mixer*, and *opacity*. The name is not particularly important as long as you can find the setting.

Just as you might use color correction to adjust the amount of red in a clip, you can use Opacity controls to adjust the amount of alpha. By default, the alpha channel, or opacity, of clips is 100%, or fully visible. On the 8-bit video scale of 0 to 255, this means it will be at 255. Not all media will include an alpha channel. Video cameras do not record an alpha channel, for example. In fact, most codecs (methods for storing image and sound information) cannot store an alpha channel.

Animation clips, titles, or graphics will often include alpha channels to define which parts of an image are opaque or transparent.

You can set the Source Monitor and Program Monitor to display a checkerboard background instead of black, just as in Adobe Photoshop, to make it easier to identify transparent pixels. Let's compare views:

1   From the Graphics bin, open the clip Theft_Unexpected.png in the Source Monitor (be sure to open the PNG clip).

2   Open the Source Monitor Settings menu ![icon], and make sure Transparency Grid is *not* selected.

It looks as if the graphic has a black background, but those black pixels are actually the background of the Source Monitor. If you were to export this as a media file with a codec that does not support an alpha channel, the new file would indeed have a black background.

3 Open the Source Monitor Settings menu again and choose Transparency Grid to turn it on.

Now you can clearly see which pixels are transparent. However, for some kinds of media, the transparency grid is an imperfect solution, and this is a good example. It's a little difficult to see the edges of the text against the grid.

▶ **Tip:** If there are any specialist words in this lesson that you are not familiar with, check out "Understanding essential terminology," later in the lesson.

4 Open the Source Monitor Settings menu, and choose Transparency Grid again to turn it off.

Media files that are created using a codec that does not support an alpha channel will always have a black background rather than transparent areas.

The Source Monitor and Program Monitor can also display the alpha channel as a grayscale image. To enable or disable this view, choose Alpha from the Source Monitor or Program Monitor Settings menu.

Making compositing part of your project

Using compositing effects and controls can take your post-production work to a whole new level. Once you begin working with the compositing effects available in Premiere Pro, you'll find yourself discovering new ways of filming and new ways of structuring your edit to make it easier to blend images together.

A combination of pre-production planning, filming techniques, and precise effects setup will produce the most powerful results when compositing. You can combine still images of environments with complex, interesting patterns to produce extraordinary textured moods. Or you can cut out parts of an image that don't fit and replace them with something else.

Compositing is one of the most creative, flexible, and fun parts of nonlinear editing with Premiere Pro.

Shooting videos with compositing in mind

Much of the most effective compositing work begins in pre-production, when you are planning your shoot. Right at the start, you can think about how to help Premiere Pro identify the parts of the image you'd like to be transparent, and there are a number of ways to do this. Consider *chroma keying*, for example, a standard special effect used by major feature film productions to allow action to take place in environments that would otherwise be too dangerous or physically impossible—like the inside of a volcano!

The actors are actually standing in front of a screen that is solid green. The green color is used to identify which pixels should be transparent. The video image of the actors is used as the foreground of a composition, with some visible pixels (the actors) and some transparent pixels (the green background).

Next, it's just a question of putting the foreground video image in front of another background image. In an epic action feature film, it's the prebuilt set, a real-world location, or a composite created by visual effects artists; it could be anything.

The result is a combined composition.

Planning ahead makes a big difference to the quality of your compositing. For the greenscreen effect to work well, the background needs to be a consistent color. It also needs to be a color that does not appear anywhere on your subject. Green-colored jewelry, for example, might turn transparent when a chroma key effect is applied.

> **Note:** Sometimes chroma key effects are achieved using a blue background. Many of the reasons in favor of using green also apply to blue; it was a more popular background color in the past. Recent developments in camera technology allow green backgrounds to produce better results, which is why green has become the standard.

When shooting greenscreen footage, the way you film can make a big difference to the finished result. Try to match the lighting for your subject to the replacement background you intend to use, in particular when considering the direction of shadows.

Capture the greenscreen background with soft, evenly distributed light, and try to avoid *spill*, where light reflected from the greenscreen in the background bounces onto your subject. If this happens, you'll be in danger of *keying out*, or making transparent, parts of your subject because they will be in the same green color that you are removing.

> **Note:** Heavily compressed media files will generally not give the same high-quality result as a raw or lightly compressed file (such as ProRes 4:4:4:4) captured using a high-end camera.

Preprocessing footage

In a perfect world, every greenscreen clip would have a flawless green background and nice, clean edges on your foreground elements. In reality, there are lots of reasons why you might face less-than-perfect material.

There are often problems caused by poor lighting when the video is created. However, there's a further problem caused by the way many video cameras store image information.

Because our eyes do not register color as accurately as they do brightness information, it's common for cameras to reduce the amount of color information stored. This saves storage space and is rarely immediately visible.

The approach varies from system to system. Sometimes color information is stored for every other pixel; other times it might be recorded for every other pixel on every second line. This type of file-size reduction is usually a good idea because otherwise the storage required would be *huge*. However, it can make keying more difficult because there isn't as much color detail.

If you find that your footage is not keying well, try the following:

- Consider applying a light blur effect before keying a foreground clip. This blends pixel detail, softening the edges and often giving a smoother-looking result. If the amount of blur is light, it should not dramatically reduce the quality of your image. You can apply a blur effect to the clip, adjust the settings, and then apply a chroma key effect on top of the blur.

- Consider color correcting your shot before you key it. If your shot lacks good contrast between your foreground and background, you can sometimes help the key by adjusting the picture first using the Lumetri Color panel.

Understanding essential terminology

In this lesson, you'll encounter some terms that might be new to you. Let's run through the important ones.

- **Alpha/alpha channel:** The fourth channel of information for each pixel. An alpha channel defines transparency for a pixel. It's a separate channel, and it can be created and adjusted entirely independently of the content of the image. Whether or not your original media file includes an alpha channel, you can work with it in sequences in Premiere Pro.

- **Matte:** An image, shape, or video clip used to identify a region of your image that should be transparent or semitransparent. Premiere Pro allows multiple types of mattes, and you'll work with them in this lesson. You can use an image, another video clip, or a visual effect like a chroma key to generate a matte dynamically based on pixel colors.

When you made a secondary color adjustment in Lesson 13, "Applying Color Correction and Grading," Premiere Pro dynamically generated a matte that was applied only to the color adjustment based on the selection you made.

This limited the pixels that were changed by the color adjustment. In contrast, a chroma key effect applies its matte to the alpha channel, selectively making pixels transparent.

- **Opacity:** The overall alpha channel value for clips in a sequence in Premiere Pro. The higher the value, the more opaque the clip is—the inverse of transparency. You can adjust the opacity for a clip over time using keyframes, just as you adjusted audio level in a previous lesson.

- **Blend mode:** A technology originally seen in Adobe Photoshop. Rather than simply placing foreground images in front of background images, you can select one of several blend modes that cause the foreground to interact with the background in various ways. You might, for example, choose to view only pixels that are brighter than the background or to apply only the color information from the foreground clip to the background. You used a blend mode in Lesson 12, "Adding Video Effects." Experimentation is a good way to learn about the many blend modes available. You'll find them on the Effect Controls panel, under the Opacity effect.

- **Key/keying:** The process of selectively making pixels transparent based on their color or brightness. Chroma key effects use color as a reference to generate transparency (that is, to modify the alpha channel). Luma key effects use brightness.

- **Greenscreening or bluescreening:** The process of filming a subject in front of a screen that is solid green and then using a special effect to selectively turn green pixels transparent. The clip is then combined with a background image. Greenscreening is a type of chroma key effect.

Tip: For more information on blend modes in Adobe software, see *The Hidden Power of Adobe Photoshop: Mastering Blend Modes and Adjustment Layers for Photography*, by Scott Valentine (Adobe Press).

Working with the Opacity effect

You can adjust the overall opacity of a clip using keyframes in the Timeline panel or in the Effect Controls panel.

1 If it's not already open in the Timeline panel, open the sequence Desert Jacket. This sequence has a foreground image of a man putting on a jacket, with a background image of a desert. The composition was created using the Ultra Key effect. You'll learn how to use this effect later in this lesson.

2 Increase the height of the Video 2 track so the thumbnail is easily visible. You can do this by dragging the dividing line in the track header (at the far left of the Timeline panel) between Video 2 and Video 3. You can also hover the pointer over the Video 2 track header, hold Option (macOS) or Alt (Windows), and scroll with your mouse wheel or trackpad.

3 Open the Timeline panel Display Settings menu 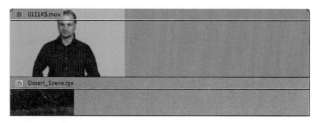, and make sure Show Video Keyframes is enabled.

Now you can use the rubber band (the thin horizontal black-and-white line on clips) to adjust the settings and keyframe effects. There is only ever one rubber band per clip, and it allows the adjustment of one control at a time.

By default, the rubber band on visual clips controls the Opacity setting. The default for audio clips is the Volume setting.

The small FX badge in the upper-left corner of a clip changes color if an effect is applied to a clip or if an intrinsic effect is adjusted. The FX badge for the foreground clip in this sequence is purple because a non-intrinsic effect (the Ultra Key chroma key effect) has been applied.

If you want to specify that the rubber band adjust a different effect parameter, right-click the FX badge, and choose an effect and parameter from the menu.

4 Try dragging the rubber band up and down using the Selection tool on the clip on Video 2. Try to set it to exactly 50%. The clip FX badge turns green to indicate that you have combined a non-intrinsic effect with an intrinsic effect adjustment.

You can make more precise adjustments by holding Command (macOS) or Ctrl (Windows) after you have begun dragging. Be careful not to press the modifier key before clicking or you'll add a keyframe instead.

When you use the Selection tool in this way, the entire rubber band is moved without additional keyframes being added.

FX badge colors

There are several colors you'll see on clip FX badges in the Timeline panel. Here's what they all mean:

- **Gray:** No effect applied (default badge color).
- **Purple:** Non-intrinsic effect applied (for example, color correction or a blur).
- **Yellow:** Intrinsic effect modified (for example, Motion and Opacity).
- **Green:** Intrinsic effect modified and additional effect applied (from the Effects panel).
- **Red underline:** Source Clip effect applied.

Keyframing opacity

Keyframing opacity in the Timeline panel is similar to keyframing volume. You use the same tools and keyboard shortcuts, and the results are likely to be exactly as you expect: The higher the rubber band, the more visible a clip will be.

1 Open the Theft Unexpected sequence in the Sequences bin. Scrub through the sequence to familiarize yourself with the content.

This sequence has a title in the foreground, on the V2 track. It's common to fade titles up and down at different times and with different durations. You can do so using a transition effect, just as you would add a transition to a video clip; or, for more control, you can use keyframes to adjust the opacity.

2 Make sure track Video 2 is expanded so you can see the rubber band for the foreground title, Theft_Unexpected.png. Zoom in enough to be able to make precise adjustments to the title graphic's rubber band.

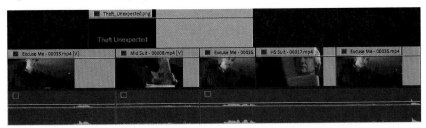

3 Command-click (macOS) or Ctrl-click (Windows) the rubber band for the title graphic four times to add four keyframes—two near the beginning and two near the end. Don't worry about the precise positions of the new keyframes; you'll adjust them in a moment.

▶ **Tip:** It's sometimes easier to add the keyframe markers to set the timing first and then drag them vertically to adjust them.

Tip: Once you've added a keyframe by Command-clicking (macOS) or Ctrl-clicking (Windows), you can release the key and start dragging to set the keyframe position.

4 Adjust the keyframes so the title fades up and down, just as you would with audio keyframes.

5 Play through the graphic clip in the sequence, and watch the results of your keyframing.

You can also use the Effect Controls panel to add keyframes to the opacity for a clip. If you select the title clip in the Timeline panel, you'll see that the keyframes you just added are also displayed in the Effect Controls panel.

Combining tracks using a blend mode

Blend modes are special ways for foreground pixels (in clips on upper tracks) to combine with background pixels (in clips below them). Each blend mode applies a different calculation to combine the foreground red, green, blue, and alpha (RGBA) values with those of the background. Each pixel is calculated in combination with the pixel directly behind it.

The default blend mode is called Normal. In this mode, the foreground image has a uniform alpha channel value across the entire image. The more opacity the fore-ground image has, the more strongly you will see those pixels in front of the pixels in the background.

The best way to find out how blend modes work is to try them.

1 Replace the current title in the Theft Unexpected sequence with the more complex title Theft_Unexpected_Layered.psd in the Graphics bin.

You can replace the existing title by dragging the new item onto it while holding Option (macOS) or Alt (Windows). Notice that replacing a clip this way retains the sequence clip keyframes you added.

2 Select the new title in the sequence, and take a look at the Effect Controls panel.

3 In the Effect Controls panel, expand the Opacity controls, and browse through the Blend Mode menu options.

4 Right now, the blend mode is set to Normal. Try a few different options to see the results. Each blend mode calculates the relationship between the foreground layer pixels and the background pixels differently. See Premiere Pro Help for a description of the blend modes.

To quickly browse through the modes, hover the pointer over the Blend Mode menu, without clicking to open it, and scroll with your mouse wheel or trackpad.

Try the Lighten blend mode, for instance. In this mode, a pixel is visible only if it is lighter than the pixel behind it.

5 Choose the Normal blend mode when you have finished experimenting.

Adjusting alpha channel transparencies

Many types of media will already have an alpha channel. A title graphic is an obvious example: Where text exists, pixels generally have 100% opacity, and where there is no text, pixels usually have 0% opacity. Elements such as drop shadows around text typically have a value somewhere in between. Keeping some transparency in a drop shadow helps it look a little more realistic.

Premiere Pro sees pixels with higher values in the alpha channel as being more visible. This is the most common way to interpret alpha channels, but occasionally you might come across media that is configured in the opposite way. You will immediately recognize the problem because you'll see a cutout in an otherwise black image. This is easy to address because, just as Premiere Pro can interpret the audio channels on a clip, it's also possible to choose a different interpretation of an alpha channel.

You can see the results using a title in the Theft Unexpected sequence.

1. Locate Theft_Unexpected_Layered.psd in the Project panel.

2. Right-click the clip and choose Modify > Interpret Footage. In the lower half of the Modify Clip dialog box, you'll find the Alpha Channel interpretation options.

- **Alpha Premultiplication options:** Relate to the way semitransparent areas are interpreted. If you find that soft semitransparent image areas are blocky or poorly rendered, try selecting Premultiplied Alpha and compare the results.

- **Ignore Alpha Channel:** Treats all pixels as having 100% alpha, with no transparency. This can be useful if you don't intend to use a background clip in your sequence and would prefer black pixels.

- **Invert Alpha Channel:** Reverses the alpha channel. This means that pixels that were fully opaque will become fully transparent, and pixels that were transparent will become opaque.

3. Try selecting Ignore Alpha Channel, and click OK; then open the Modify Clip dialog box again, deselect Ignore Alpha Channel, and then select Invert Alpha Channel. Compare the results in the Program Monitor.

   Note: Blend modes still apply when changing the interpretation of the alpha channel. For example, if you invert the alpha channel and use a blend mode like Lighten, the black background won't be visible.

4. When you have finished experimenting, make sure the Alpha Channel option is set to Use Alpha Premultiplication From File and Invert Alpha Channel is deselected. You can use Undo to restore the clip interpretation.

Color keying a greenscreen shot

When you change the opacity level of a clip using the rubber band or the Effect Controls panel, you adjust the alpha for every pixel in the image by the same amount. There are also ways to selectively adjust the alpha for pixels, based on their position on the screen, their brightness, or their color.

Chroma key effects adjust the opacity for specific pixels, selected based on their luminance, hue, and saturation level.

The principle is straightforward: Select a color or range of colors, and the more similar a pixel is to the selection, the more transparent it becomes. That is, the more closely a pixel matches the selection, the more its alpha channel value is lowered, until it becomes fully transparent.

Let's create a chroma key composition.

1   If necessary, resize the Project panel to display the New Item button. Drag the clip Timekeeping.mp4, in the Greenscreen bin, onto the New Item button in the Project panel. This creates a sequence with settings that match the media. The clip will be added to the Video 1 track.

> **Tip:** To create a new sequence with matching settings, you can also right-click a clip in the Project panel and choose New Sequence From Clip. Both options work with multiple selected clips too. If you select clips with multiple formats, the first item selected will be used to configure the new sequence.

2   In the sequence, drag the Timekeeping.mp4 clip up to Video 2—this will be the foreground. You may need to resize the Video 2 track to see the thumbnail for the clip. You can do this quickly by double-clicking the blank part of the Video 2 track header.

3   Drag the clip Seattle_Skyline_Still.tga from the Shots bin to track Video 1, under the Timekeeping.mp4 clip on the Timeline panel.

Because this is a single-frame graphic, its default duration is too short.

4   Trim the Seattle_Skyline_Still.tga clip so that it's long enough to be a background for the full duration of the foreground clip on Video 2.

A quick way to extend the background clip is to position the playhead at the end of the Timekeeping.mp4 clip, select the outpoint of the Seattle_Skyline_Still.tga clip (the right edge of the clip in the sequence), and press E—this is the default keyboard shortcut for Extend.

5   In the Project panel, your sequence is still named after the Timekeeping.mp4 clip, and it's stored in the same Greenscreen bin. Rename the sequence **Seattle Skyline,** and drag it into the Sequences bin.

   This kind of on-the-fly organization is worth the extra effort, as it helps you stay in control of your project.

You now have foreground and background clips. All that remains is to make the green pixels transparent.

Using the Ultra Key effect

Premiere Pro includes a powerful, fast, and intuitive chroma key effect called Ultra Key. To apply a key, you'll choose a color that should be transparent and then adjust settings to improve the color selection.

The Ultra Key effect generates a matte (defining which pixels should be transparent) dynamically based on the color selection. The matte is adjustable using the detailed settings in the Effect Controls panel. Let's try using the Ultra Key effect on the Timekeeping clip.

1   Apply the Ultra Key effect to the Timekeeping.mp4 clip in the new Seattle Skyline sequence. You can find the effect by typing **Ultra** in the Effects panel search box.

2   In the Effect Controls panel, click the Key Color eyedropper (not the color swatch) to select it.

▶ Tip: Avoid using too much in-camera sharpening when filming greenscreen footage as it can make it difficult to get a clean edge when configuring a chroma key effect.

3   Holding the Command key (macOS) or Ctrl key (Windows), use the eyedropper to click a green area in the Program Monitor. This clip has a consistent green background, so it's not too important where you click. With other footage, you may need to experiment to find the best spot.

   ⬤ **Note:** If you're using macOS, you may see an alert asking you to give Premiere Pro permission to record your computer screen. To do so, click Open System Settings and use an administrator password to unlock Security & Privacy settings. You may have to quit Premiere Pro and restart it to confirm the change.

If you hold Command (macOS) or Ctrl (Windows) when you click with the eyedropper, Premiere Pro takes the average of a 5×5-pixel sample, rather than a single-pixel selection. This often captures a better color for keying.

The Ultra Key effect identifies all pixels that have the green you selected and sets their alpha to 0%.

4 In the Effect Controls panel, under the Ultra Key effect, choose Alpha Channel from the Output menu. In this mode, the Ultra Key effect displays the alpha channel that has been generated as a grayscale image, where dark pixels will be transparent and light pixels will be opaque.

It's a pretty good key, but there are a few areas of gray where the pixels will be partially transparent, which you don't want. Where there's naturally semitransparent detail, like hair or the soft edges of clothing, there should be some gray, and the right and left sides of the image don't have any green, so none of those pixels can be keyed. We'll fix that later. Still, the main areas of the alpha channel should be solid black or white.

5 In the Effect Controls panel, under the Ultra Key effect, choose Aggressive from the Setting menu. This cleans up the selection a little. Scrub through the shot to see whether it has clean black areas and white areas. If you see gray pixels in this view, the result will be partially transparent parts in the picture. This might be desirable if the image area should be partially transparent. Expect to switch back and forth between viewing the composite image and the alpha channel often when setting up the Ultra Key effect.

▶ **Tip:** You may notice the image looks cleaner when paused than during playback. If so, this may be because you have the Program Monitor playback resolution set to 1/2 (which is the default). Try setting it to full quality. You may also want to try enabling High Quality Playback in the Program Monitor Settings menu.

6 Choose Composite from the Ultra Key effect Output menu to see the result.

The Aggressive setting works better for this clip.

The Default, Relaxed, and Aggressive settings actually modify the Matte Generation, Matte Cleanup, and Spill Suppression settings. You can also modify these manually to get a better key with more challenging footage.

Here's an overview of those settings:

- **Matte Generation:** Once you've chosen your key color, the controls in the Matte Generation category change the way it's interpreted. Even with challenging footage, you'll often get positive results by adjusting these settings.

In the example you are working on, there are issues with the original media, particularly around the edge of the subject. These are more visible during fast motion, such as when the jacket is moving quickly. Try matching the settings in the figure shown here.

When adjusting settings, try dragging each control to its extremes first, then find the middle ground to discover the best configuration possible. You will often find you will need to re-adjust a parameter as you finesse the settings.

- **Matte Cleanup:** Once your matte is defined, you can use these controls to adjust it:

  - **Choke** shrinks the matte, which is helpful if your key selection misses some edges. Be careful not to choke the matte too much because you'll begin to lose edge detail in the foreground image, often applying a *digital haircut* in the vernacular of the visual-effects industry.

- **Soften** applies a blur to the matte, which often improves the apparent "blending" of the foreground and background images for a more convincing composite.

- **Contrast** increases the contrast of the alpha channel, making that black-and-white image a stronger black-and-white version and more clearly defining the key. You will often get cleaner keys by increasing the contrast, at the risk of producing unwanted hard edges.

- **Mid Point** is the level from which contrast is adjusted—a kind of anchor point for contrast. Adjust contrast around a different level for more subtle control.

Note: In this example, you're using footage with a green background. If you have footage with a blue background, the workflow is the same.

- **Spill Suppression:** Spill Suppression compensates for color that bounces from the green background onto the subject. When this happens, the reflected green color does not affect the subject's own colors enough to cause them to be keyed out (made transparent). However, it does not look good when the edges of your subject are green!

  Spill Suppression automatically compensates by adding color to the foreground element edges that are positioned opposite, on a color wheel, to the key color. For example, Spill Suppression adds magenta when you're green-screen keying and yellow when you're bluescreen keying. This neutralizes the color "spill" in the same way that you'd fix a color cast.

- **Color Correction:** The built-in Color Correction controls give you a quick and easy way to adjust the appearance of your foreground video to help it blend in with your background more naturally. For more comprehensive color adjustment controls, use the Lumetri Color panel.

These color adjustment controls are often enough to make a more natural match. The adjustments are applied after the key, so you won't cause problems for the key by adjusting the colors with these controls. You can use any color adjustment tools in Premiere Pro, including the Lumetri Color panel.

Partially masking clips

The Ultra Key effect generates a matte dynamically, based on the colors in your shot. You can also create your own custom-shaped matte or use another clip as the basis for a matte.

Earlier, you used a mask to constrain an effect to a region in the image. The Opacity setting can be combined with a mask in the same way, allowing you to set regions in an image that should be transparent with great precision.

Let's create a matte to remove the unwanted edges from the Timekeeping.mp4 clip.

1 Return to the Seattle Skyline sequence.

As you discovered earlier, the foreground clip has an actor standing in front of a greenscreen, but the screen does not reach the edge of the picture. It's common to shoot greenscreen footage this way, particularly when filming on location, where full studio facilities may not be available.

2 Turn off the Ultra Key effect, without removing it, by clicking the Toggle Effect button ⬤ in the Effect Controls panel ⬤. This allows you to clearly see the green areas of the picture again.

▶ **Tip:** If you deselect the mask, the control points displayed in the Program Monitor will disappear. Select the mask in the Effect Controls panel to reactivate them.

3 Still in the Effect Controls panel, expand the Opacity controls and click the Create 4-Point Polygon Mask button ▦ just under that heading. Premiere Pro applies a mask to the clip's opacity setting, making most of the image transparent.

Note: A rough mask of this kind, used to remove unwanted image elements, is often referred to as a garbage matte.

4 Resize the mask so that it reveals the central area of the shot but hides the black edges. You will almost certainly need to reduce the Program Monitor zoom to 50% or 25% to see beyond the edges of the image.

As long as you have the mask selected in the Effect Controls panel, you can click directly in the Program Monitor to reposition the corner control points for the mask. Don't worry about precisely matching the edges of the frame. Instead, focus on selecting the areas in the picture the subject moves into.

5   Set the Program Monitor zoom option to Fit.

6   Toggle the Ultra Key effect back on in the Effect Controls panel, and deselect the
    clip to hide the visible mask handles.

> **Tip:** You can add control points for a more precise shape by clicking the mask outline. Hold
Command (macOS) or Ctrl (Windows) when you click a control point to remove it.

> **Tip:** If you have dif-
ficulty clicking the right
part of the image in the
Program Monitor, it may
be because the screen
scaling applied by your
operating system is
causing an offset. Try
adjusting your operat-
ing system settings
to make sure screen
scaling is set to 100% or
200%. This is easier to
set in Windows, which
displays a percentage in
the setting. On macOS,
you may find it easier to
keep your monitor set
to the default scaling.
There are third-party
apps that can help
with this.

This is challenging footage to key because the original camera recording includes
adjustments to the edges of the subject, and it uses a color compression system that
reduces color fidelity. With patience and precise adjustments, you can still achieve a
reasonable result.

Using the Track Matte key effect

Adding a mask to the Opacity effect in the Effect Controls panel sets a user-defined
region that should be visible or transparent. Premiere Pro can also use another
sequence clip, positioned above the clip to be affected, to generate a custom matte.

The Track Matte Key effect uses the luminance information or existing alpha channel information from clips placed on one track to define a transparency matte for
a clip on another track. With a little planning and preparation, this simple effect
can produce powerful results because you can use any clips as a reference and even
apply effects to them, changing the resulting matte.

Let's use the Track Matte Key effect to add a layered title to the Seattle Skyline
sequence.

1   Trim the Seattle_Skyline_Still.tga clip longer so you can use it as the background
    for another foreground clip. Trim it to a duration of around 50 seconds.

2 Edit the clip Laura_06.mp4, from the Shots bin, onto the Video 2 track, lined up with the end of the background clip.

3 Drag the graphic clip SEATTLE from the Graphics bin onto the Timeline V3 track, directly above the Laura_06.mp4 clip. This clip has an alpha channel that defines the non-text portion of the image as transparent, allowing you to see the background.

4 Trim the SEATTLE graphic clip to match the duration of the Laura_06.mp4 clip.

5 Find the Track Matte Key effect in the Effects panel, and apply it to the Laura_06.mp4 clip on the Video 2 track. The effect is applied to the clip you want to change (not the clip or clips you are using as a reference for the effect).

6 Make sure the Laura_06.mp4 clip is selected. In the Effect Controls panel, choose Video 3 from the matte menu in the Track Matte Key controls. Any clips on the chosen track will be used as the reference for the newly generated matte.

Tip: In this example, you're using a still image as a reference for the Track Matte Key effect. You can use any type of visual clip, though, including video clips.

7 Scrub through the sequence to see the result. The white text in the title clip on Video 3 is no longer visible. Instead, it's being used as a guide to define the visible and transparent regions of the clip on V3.

By default, the Track Matte Key effect uses the alpha channel from clips on the selected track to generate a key. If your reference clips don't use an alpha channel, change the Composite Using menu to Matte Luma, so the Track Matte Key effect uses the brightness of the reference clips instead.

The Track Matte Key effect is an unusual effect because most other effects exclusively change the clip they are applied to. The Track Matte Key effect changes both the clip it's applied to *and* the clip used as a reference, which is made transparent for the duration of the effect.

The colors in the Laura_06.mp4 clip work well against the blue in the background clip, but they could be more vivid. You might want to experiment with color correction tools to make the red stronger and brighter so it's a more compelling composition.

You could animate the SEATTLE title too, having it move on-screen or gradually increase in size.

You could also add a blur effect to the Laura_06.mp4 clip before adding the Track Matte Key effect and change the playback speed to create a softer, slower-moving texture.

Review questions

1 What is the difference between the RGB channels and the alpha channel?

2 How do you apply a blend mode to a clip?

3 How do you keyframe clip opacity?

4 How do you change the way a media file's alpha channel is interpreted?

5 What does it mean to key a clip?

6 Are there any limits to the kinds of clips you can use as a reference for the Track Matte Key effect?

Review answers

1 RGB channels contain color information; the alpha channel describes opacity.

2 Choose a blend mode from the Blend Mode menu in the Opacity category in the Effect Controls panel.

3 You adjust clip opacity in the same way you adjust clip volume, in the Timeline panel or in the Effect Controls panel. To make an adjustment in the Timeline panel, make sure you're viewing the Opacity rubber band for the clip you want to adjust and then drag with the Selection tool. If you hold Command (macOS) or Ctrl (Windows) while clicking, you'll add keyframes. You can also work with keyframes in more advanced ways using the Pen tool.

4 Right-click the file in the Project panel and choose Modify > Interpret Footage.

5 A key is usually a special effect where the color or brightness of pixels is used to define which part of the image should be transparent and which part should be visible.

6 You can use just about anything visual to create your key with the Track Matte Key effect, as long as it is positioned on a track above the clip you apply the effect to. You can apply special effects to the reference clip, and the results of those effects will be reflected in the matte. You can even use multiple clips because the setting is based on the whole track, rather than a particular clip.

15 CREATING NEW GRAPHICS

Lesson overview

In this lesson, you'll learn how to do the following:

- Use the Essential Graphics panel.

- Work with video typography.

- Create graphics.

- Work with shapes and logos.

- Make text roll and crawl.

- Work with Motion Graphics templates (MOGRTs).

- Create captions.

 This lesson will take about 90 minutes to complete. To get the lesson files used in this chapter, download them from the web page for this book at *peachpit.com/PremiereProCIB2024*. For more information, see "Accessing the lesson files and Web Edition" in the "Getting Started" section at the beginning of this book. Store the files on your computer in a convenient location.

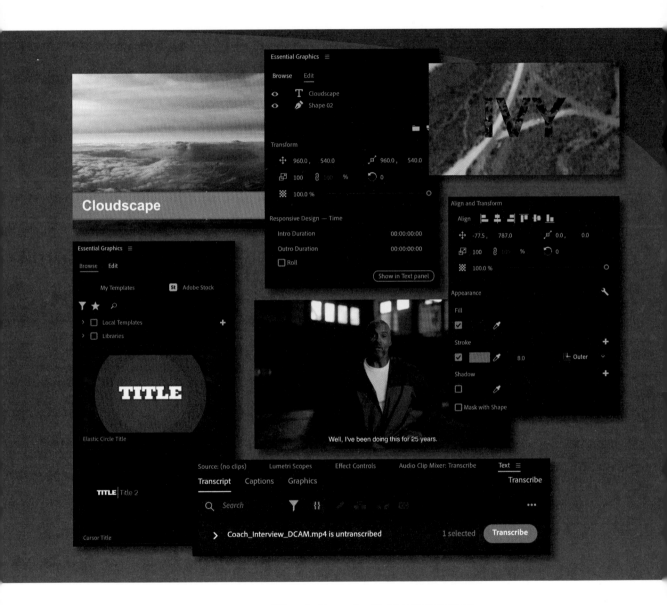

Although video and audio clips are the primary ingredients in a sequence, you will also often choose to incorporate text and graphics into your project. Adobe Premiere Pro includes powerful title and graphic-creation tools you can work with right in the Program Monitor; or you can browse editable templates in the Essential Graphics panel.

Starting the lesson

Text can help to convey information quickly to your audience. For example, you can identify a speaker in your video by superimposing their name and title during the interview (often called a *lower third*). You can also use text to identify sections of a longer video (often called *bumpers*) or to acknowledge the cast and crew (with *credits*).

Text can be clearer than a narrator's voice and allows for additional information to be presented in the middle of dialogue. Text can also reinforce key information.

In the Program Monitor, the Essential Graphics panel, and the Text panel, you'll find a range of text-editing and shape-creation tools that you can use to design graphics. You can use the fonts loaded on your computer (and those available via Adobe Fonts as part of your Creative Cloud membership).

You can also control opacity and color and insert graphic elements or logos.

Let's try a few graphic and titling techniques.

1 Open Lesson 15.prproj in the Lessons folder.

2 Save the project as **Lesson 15 Working.prproj**.

3 Switch to the Captions and Graphics workspace by choosing Captions And Graphics from the Workspaces menu or by choosing Window > Workspaces > Captions And Graphics.

4 Reset the workspace by opening the Workspaces menu and choosing Reset To Saved Layout, or by choosing Window > Workspaces > Reset To Saved Layout.

The Captions And Graphics workspace reveals the Essential Graphics panel and positions the Tools panel next to the Program Monitor to give quick access to text and shape tools.

● **Note:** To ensure that the tools function and the defaults are set exactly as described in this lesson, reset the Premiere Pro preferences by holding Option (macOS) or Alt (Windows) while launching the application and then clicking Continue in the Reset Options dialog box.

Exploring the Essential Graphics panel

The Essential Graphics panel has two tabs.

• **Browse:** Select built-in or imported title templates and Motion Graphics templates, many of which include animation.

• **Edit:** Adjust titles and graphics in a sequence.

When using the Browse tab, you can look for templates you own in the My Templates area or switch to searching Adobe Stock. There are free and paid templates available from Adobe Stock. For these lessons, we'll focus on templates available in My Templates.

In addition to starting with an editable built-in template, you can use the Type tool , Pen tool , Rectangle tool , Ellipse tool , or Polygon tool to create new graphics by clicking in the Program Monitor with no clips selected (if a graphic clip is selected, you'll add to that clip).

If you click and hold the Type tool, you'll reveal the Vertical Type tool, which allows you to type text in a column, instead of a row.

You can also use the Pen tool directly in the Program Monitor to create custom shapes to use as graphic elements in titles.

You can click and hold the Rectangle tool to reveal the Ellipse tool and the Polygon tool.

You can select, reposition, and resize graphic and text elements using the Selection tool .

You perform all of this creative work directly in the Program Monitor. As soon as you click to add text or a shape, Premiere Pro creates a new clip in the Timeline panel. You apply adjustments in the Essential Graphics panel.

Let's start with some preformatted text and modify it. This is a good way to get an overview of the powerful features of the Essential Graphics panel. Later in this lesson, you'll build a new title.

1. If it's not open already, open the sequence 01 Clouds.

2. Position the playhead over the Cloudscape title on the V2 track and select it.

3. If the Essential Graphics panel is open, selecting the title in the Timeline panel should automatically switch the view to the Edit tab. If not, click Edit at the top of the Essential Graphics panel.

Like the Effect Controls panel, the Edit tab of the Essential Graphics panel shows options for whichever clip is selected in the Timeline panel.

Also, just as with the Effect Controls panel, the Essential Graphics panel displays options for only one clip at a time.

Like the Lumetri Color panel, changes made in the Essential Graphics panel actually appear as effects in the Effect Controls panel, with the full range of settings available, including the options to create effect presets and to animate graphic elements with keyframes.

Graphics and titles use a vector-based version of the Motion effect, which works the same way as the video version you are familiar with but which maintains the clean edges of fonts and shapes.

Notice there are two items listed at the top of the Essential Graphics panel: Cloudscape and Shape 02.

If you are familiar with Adobe Photoshop, you'll recognize these as layers. Every item in a graphic is displayed as a *layer* in the Essential Graphics panel, a little like tracks in the Premiere Pro Timeline panel.

The layers at the top are in front of the layers at the bottom, and you can drag items up and down the list.

You'll also recognize the familiar eye button for making layers visible 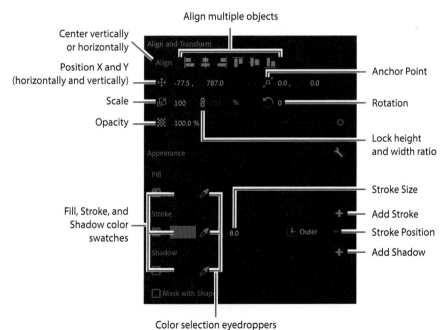 or invisible .

Provided no layers are selected in the Essential Graphics panel and no graphic or text items are selected in the Program Monitor, below these layers you'll see the transform controls for the entire graphic and the Responsive Design controls. These allow you to specify a time duration at the start and end of the graphic clip that will not be adjusted if you change the duration of the clip in the sequence. This protects the timing of animation keyframes at the start and end of the graphic.

4 Click to select the Shape 02 layer at the top of the Essential Graphics panel. This is the red band that goes across the screen.

Now the Essential Graphics panel displays alignment, transform, and appearance controls for the shape.

Although the controls do not display a name, you can hover over an icon to see a tool tip that includes a description of the control. Most of the icons are actually buttons, some of which enable keyframe animation in the same way that the stopwatch icons in the Effect Controls panel do.

Many of the options will be familiar to you from the Motion effect in the Effect Controls panel.

Align multiple objects

Center vertically or horizontally

Position X and Y (horizontally and vertically)

Scale

Opacity

Fill, Stroke, and Shadow color swatches

Anchor Point

Rotation

Lock height and width ratio

Stroke Size

Add Stroke

Stroke Position

Add Shadow

Color selection eyedroppers

In the Appearance section you can set a color for shape fill, stroke (a colored line on the edges of a shape or text), background (directly behind the text), and shadow (see "Text styles" later in this lesson for more information about them).

Perhaps these color swatches are already familiar to you. They work in an intuitive way.

5   Click the Fill color swatch.

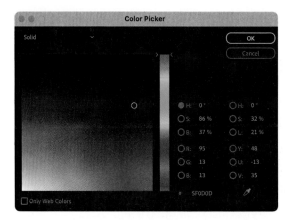

A Color Picker appears that allows you to choose a precise color. There are a number of color models to choose from, or you can move your pointer over a sample of the color you want and click to select it directly.

6   Click Cancel, and then click the eyedropper  for the fill color, on the right side of the Essential Graphics panel.

The eyedropper allows you to pick a color from anywhere in the image. In fact, you can pick colors from anywhere on your computer screen! This is particularly useful if you have a range of colors you always want to use. For example, you may need to be certain that you match a logo or branding color.

7   In the Program Monitor, click the thin blue band of sky between the clouds. The shape fill changes color to match the sky.

8 Make sure you have selected the Selection tool in the Tools panel and that the Shape 02 layer is still selected in the Essential Graphics panel.

> **Tip:** With all the clicking and testing, it's easy to accidentally deselect layers. If there's no bounding box with handles around the text or shape, select it using the Selection tool.

Notice the tiny control handles visible on the midpoint of the shape in the Program Monitor. You can use the Selection tool to change the shape directly.

For now, you're going to use the Selection tool to select another layer in the title.

To select a layer in the Program Monitor, you may need to first deselect the layer that's already selected. You can do this by clicking the background of the Program Monitor or by deselecting the title clip in the Timeline panel.

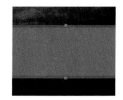

9 Use the Selection tool to click the word *Cloudscape* in the Program Monitor.

The familiar Align And Transform and Appearance controls are displayed in the Essential Graphics panel, but now there are additional controls for the text.

> **Note:** You may have to expand the window or scroll to see all the Essential Graphics panel options.

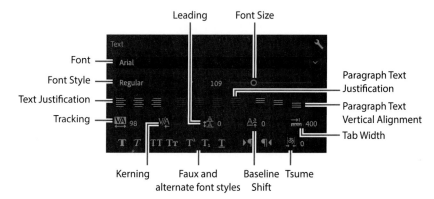

> **Tip:** If you're unsure about the purpose of a control, hover the pointer over an icon and a tool tip will tell you the name.

10 Try a few fonts and font styles to experiment with the controls. Anywhere you see blue numbers, you can scrub to update the setting. You can also click a blue number to select it and use the Up Arrow and Down Arrow keys to change a setting incrementally. If you hold Shift while using the arrow keys, you'll change the settings by 10 at a time.

This is a quick way to find out what a control is for—make an extreme adjustment to view the result; then undo.

The specific fonts loaded on each system will vary, and your Adobe Creative Cloud membership includes access to many more fonts than you will have available to begin with.

To add fonts, click the Add Adobe Fonts button that  appears while browsing fonts (or choose Graphics And Titles > Add Fonts From Adobe Fonts). This will open the Adobe Fonts website in your default internet browser, where you will find thousands of fonts to use.

> **Note:** When working with Chinese, Japanese, and Korean fonts, Tsume adjusts the spacing around characters without adjusting the vertical or horizontal scaling of the characters.

> **Note:** Premiere Pro saves your titles in the project file. They do not show up as separate files on your hard drive.

Learning video typography essentials

When you design text for video, it's helpful to follow typography conventions. If text is composited over a moving video background with multiple colors, it can take some adjustment to create a clear design.

Find a balance between legibility, style, and making sure enough information is on the screen. The more text there is, the harder it is to read, particularly if the words are moving.

Choosing a font

▶ **Tip:** If you'd like to learn more about typography, consider the book *The Complete Manual of Typography: A Guide to Setting Perfect Type, 2nd Edition* (Adobe Press, 2011), by Jim Felici.

Your computer has many fonts, which can make choosing a good option for video work time-consuming. To simplify the selection process, try using a triage approach and consider these factors:

- **Readability:** Is the font easy to read at the size you're using? Are all the characters readable? If you look at it quickly and then close your eyes, what do you remember about the text?

- **Style:** Using adjectives only, how would you describe the font you've chosen? Does the font convey the right emotion? Type is a little like a wardrobe or a haircut; picking the right font is essential to the overall success of the design.

- **Flexibility:** Does the font mix well with others? Does it come in various weights (such as bold, italic, and semibold) that make it easier to convey significance? Can you create a hierarchy of information that conveys different kinds of information, such as a name and title for a speaker's lower-third name graphic?

- **Language compatibility:** Does the font include all the characters required for the language you are using? Some fonts have limited character sets.

The answers to these guiding principles should help steer you toward better-designed titles. You may need to experiment to find the best font. Fortunately, you can easily modify an existing title or duplicate it and change the copy for a side-by-side comparison.

When creating text for use in a video, you will often find yourself placing it over a background that has many colors present. This will make it difficult to achieve proper contrast (which is essential to preserving legibility). To help in this case, you may need to add a stroke or shadow to get a contrasting edge. For more information about adding a stroke or shadow, see "Text styles" later in this lesson.

Choosing a color

Although you can create a near-infinite number of color combinations, choosing the right colors to use in a design can be surprisingly tricky. This is because only a few colors work well for text while remaining clear for the viewer. This task becomes even more difficult if you're editing your video for broadcast television or if your design must match the style and branding of a show, product, or company. The text may also need to work when placed over a busy moving background.

While it may feel a little conservative, the most common choices for text in video are black and white. If colors are used, they tend to be very light or very dark shades or have a thick, strongly colored stroke.

Note: The Adobe Color service helps you choose harmonious and appealing color combinations for your design projects. For more information, visit *color.adobe.com*.

The color you choose must provide suitable contrast with its background, which means you'll be making constant assessments about ideal colors, which often include factors such as branding requirements or a consistent color palette for your sequence.

Consider a positive example with clear light text over a dark background.

And now here's a less positive example. The text is similar in color and tone to parts of the sky.

Adjusting the kerning

It's common to adjust the spacing between the letters in a title to improve the appearance of text and help match it to the design of the background. This process is called *kerning*. Taking the time to manually adjust text becomes more important the larger the font gets (because it makes improper kerning more visible). The goal is to improve the appearance and readability of your text while creating visual flow.

Note: It's common to begin kerning by adjusting the spacing between an initial capital letter and the succeeding lowercase letters, particularly in the case of a letter with very little "base," such as T, which creates the illusion of excessive space along the baseline.

You can learn a lot about kerning by studying professionally designed materials such as posters and magazines. Kerning is applied letter by letter, allowing for creative use of spacing.

Try kerning an existing title.

1 Locate the title clip White Cloudscape in the Assets bin.

2 Edit the clip into the 01 Clouds sequence after the first title on the Video 2 track.

Make sure the title is positioned over the background video clip so you can use it as a reference for positioning.

3 Select the Type tool **T** (the keyboard shortcut is T), and click to place the insertion point between the *D* and the *S* of the word *CLOUDSCAPE*.

4 In the Edit tab of the Essential Graphics panel, in the Text section, set Kerning to **300**.

The Kerning option is available only when you select a single letter or place the text cursor between two letters.

CLOUD SCAPE

5 Repeat this process for the other letters to the right, adjusting kerning between each pair of letters.

Note: After using a different tool, it's a good idea to return to the Selection tool to avoid accidentally adding new text or making unwanted changes to your sequence.

6 Click the Align Center Horizontally button ▦ in the Align And Transform section of the Essential Graphics panel to reposition the text. Then deselect the text by clicking an empty track in the Timeline panel.

7 Select the Selection tool.

Setting the tracking

Another important text property is *tracking* (which is similar to kerning). This is the overall control of spacing between multiple selected letters. You can use tracking to globally condense or expand selected text.

Here are some common scenarios:

- **Tighter tracking:** If a line of text is too long (such as a lengthy title for a speaker's lower third), you might tighten the tracking slightly. This keeps the font size the same but fits more text into the available space.

- **Looser tracking:** When using all uppercase letters or a more complex font, it can help readability to spread out the letters. It's used often for large titles or when text is used as a design or motion-graphics element.

You can adjust tracking for a selected layer (or item in the Program Monitor) in the Text section of the Essential Graphics panel. Let's try it.

1 Drag the clip Cloudscape Tracking from the Assets bin onto the clip White Cloudscape in the 01 Clouds sequence to overwrite one clip with the other.

  If Snap is turned on in the Timeline panel, the new clip will snap to the beginning of the existing title in the sequence. They have the same duration, so the new clip will perfectly replace the old one.

2 Make sure the clip is selected, and use the Selection tool to select the text.

3 In the Edit tab of the Essential Graphics panel, experiment with the tracking control. As you increase the tracking, the letters expand to the right, away from the anchor point.

4 Set the tracking to **530**.

5 In the Text section of the Essential Graphics panel, click the Center Align Text button ![icon] to center the text object on its anchor point.

  This moves the text object too far to the left.

6 Click the Align Center Horizontally button ![icon] to align the object's anchor point with the center of the frame. This will also center the text object in the frame.

7 Now that the text is centered, try adjusting the tracking to **700**. Notice that the text stays centered.

  Tracking adjustments tend to look neater and more intentional than individual kerning adjustments.

8 Restore the tracking to **530** to continue working on this design.

Adjusting the leading

Kerning and tracking control the horizontal space between characters. *Leading* (pronounced "led-ing") controls the vertical space between lines of text. The name comes from a time when strips of lead were used on a printing press to create space between lines of text.

You adjust the leading in the Text section of the Essential Graphics panel Edit tab. Let's add another line of text.

1 Continue to work with the Cloudscape Tracking clip in the 01 Clouds sequence.

2 With the Cloudscape Tracking clip selected in the Timeline panel, use the Selection tool to double-click the CLOUDSCAPE text in the Program Monitor.

   This highlights the text, ready for editing, and changes the Selection tool to the Type tool.

3 Press the Right Arrow key to move the cursor to the end of the text.

4 Press Return (macOS) or Enter (Windows) to enter a second line of text. Type (in all capital letters) **A NEW LAND**.

5 Triple-click the new second line of text to select the whole line. Give the new text a font size of **48**, set the tracking to **1000**, and set the leading to **40**.

6 Click an empty track in the Timeline panel to deselect the graphic.

Increasing the leading helps to separate the second line of text, but it's still a little difficult to read because of the background image.

7   Using the Selection tool, select the text in the Program Monitor. This is a quick way to access a specific element in a graphic.

At the top of the Essential Graphics panel, the text layer CLOUDSCAPEA NEW LAND is selected (the text in the layer is condensed into a single layer name).

Increase the leading to **140**. This adds space between lines and improves readability.

8   Click an empty track in the Timeline panel to deselect the clip.

In most cases, you'll find the default setting works well for leading. Adjusting leading can have a big impact on your title. Don't set the leading too tight; otherwise, descenders from the top line (such as the downward lines on *j*, *p*, *q*, and *g*) will cross ascenders from the lower line (like the upward lines on *b*, *d*, *k*, and *l*). This collision is likely to make the text more difficult to read, particularly against a moving background.

Setting the alignment

Although you may be used to seeing text left justified for things like a newspaper, there are no hard-and-fast rules for aligning text for video. Generally, text used for a lower-third title is left-aligned or right-aligned.

You'll often center text used in a rolling title sequence or segment bumper. In the Essential Graphics panel, there are buttons for aligning and justifying your text. The alignment buttons align selected text to the left, center, or right relative to the anchor point of the text.

You can create a text box by dragging with the Type tool in the Program Monitor, rather than clicking.

With text inside a box, use the justification buttons to make the text fill the width of its bounding box.

With text inside a box, you can also use the vertical alignment buttons to make the text align with the top, middle, or bottom edge of the box.

It's safe to experiment and use the Undo option if necessary, so don't worry about memorizing which alignment option is which.

You may find the position of text in the frame changes when choosing a new alignment setting. If so, manually reposition the text, or click the Align Center Vertically button ⬚ or Align Center Horizontally button ⬚ to bring the text back into the middle of the frame.

Setting the safe title margin

When creating titles, you may want to view guides to help you position text and graphic elements.

You can enable or disable these by opening the Settings menu ⬚ in the Program Monitor and choosing Safe Margins.

By default, the outer guide leaves a 10% margin on each edge of the screen. The area inside this box is considered the *action-safe area*. Things that fall outside this box may get cut off when the video signal is viewed on a television monitor. Be sure to place all critical elements that are meant to be seen (like a logo) inside this region.

By default, the inner guide leaves a 20% margin on each edge of the screen. The area inside this box is called the *title-safe area*. Just as this book has margins to keep the text from getting too close to the edge, it's a good idea to keep text inside the innermost safe margin. This will make it easier for your audience to read the information.

If text is outside the *title-safe area*, there's a chance some letters may be missed on a miscalibrated screen.

Screen technology has improved over time, and it's now common to set the *action-safe area* to 3% from the edge, and the *title-safe area* to 5% from the edge.

You can change these settings by opening the Settings menu in the Source Monitor or Program Monitor and choosing Overlay Settings > Settings.

Creating new titles

When you create a title, you'll need to make some choices about how the text is displayed. There are two approaches to creating text, each offering both horizontal and vertical text direction options.

- **Point text:** This approach builds a text bounding box as you type. The text runs on one line until you press Return/Enter. Changing the shape and size of the box changes the Scale property in the Essential Graphics panel (and the Effect Controls panel).

- **Paragraph (Area) text:** You set the size and shape of a text box before entering text inside it. Changing the box size later displays more or less text but does not change the size of the text.

When using the Type tool in the Program Monitor, you choose which sort of text you are adding when you first click.

- Click and type to add point text.

- Drag to create a text box and then type to add paragraph text inside the box.

Most of the options in the Essential Graphics panel apply to both types of text.

Adding point text

Now that you have been introduced to some of the main factors when modifying and designing a graphic, let's create a new one.

You'll create a new title to help promote a tourist destination.

1 Open the sequence 02 Cliff.

2 Position the Timeline playhead at the beginning of the sequence, and select the Type tool.

3 Click in the Program Monitor, and type **The Dead Sea**.

Premiere Pro adds a new graphic clip to the sequence in the Timeline panel on the next available video track. In this case, it's Video 2.

The settings you last used are applied to new titles when you create them.

If you clicked the white clouds in the background image before typing, it might be difficult to read the text.

4 Try changing the background video frame by dragging the Timeline playhead. Choose the background frame carefully when designing a title. Because video moves, you may find a title works at the start of a clip but not at the end.

5 Select the Selection tool by clicking it in the Tools panel. You won't be able to use a keyboard shortcut for the Selection tool because you're typing into a text bounding box. Handles appear on the text bounding box.

Choose the following settings in the Essential Graphics panel:

Font: Arial Bold   **Kerning:** 0
Font size: 83   **Leading:** 0
Tracking: 0   **Fill color:** White

In the Appearance options, enable the Fill only (deselect Stroke, Background, and Shadow). Try to match the example given here.

6 Try using the Selection tool to drag the corners and edges of the text bounding box. Notice that the Font Size, Width, and Height settings do not change. Instead, the Scale setting ⊞ in the Align and Transform section is adjusted.

By default, the height and width maintain the same relative scale. You can adjust the height and width separately by clicking Set Scale Lock 🔗.

Set Scale back to 100%, and make sure Set Scale Lock is selected.

7   Hover the pointer just outside a corner of the text box until a curved pointer appears. This allows you to rotate the text box. Drag to rotate the bounding box off its horizontal orientation.

The anchor point is the point around which objects will rotate and the single point that's referenced by position controls. When you adjust position settings, the position applies specifically to the anchor point, which itself has a position on the object. For many items it's the exact center of the object (which makes sense, particularly when rotating).

This is not the case with text objects. The default location of the anchor point for this left-aligned text is the lower-left corner of the text (not the box around the text). When you rotate the text, it doesn't pivot around the center but instead around that corner.

8   With the Selection tool still active, click the blue number for the Rotation setting ↻ in the Essential Graphics panel, type **45**, and press Return/Enter to manually set the angle to 45 degrees.

9   Click anywhere in the bounding box and drag the text and its bounding box toward the upper-right corner of the frame.

10 Disable the Video 1 track output by clicking the Toggle Track Output button 👁 in the Timeline panel.

11 Open the Program Monitor Settings menu, and choose Transparency Grid to enable it.

Now you can see the graphic against a transparency checkerboard, but it's almost impossible to read!

12 Make sure the text object is selected, go to the Appearance section of the Essential Graphics panel, and select the Stroke option to add an outline to the letters. Set the color to black, and set Stroke Width to 7.

Now it's easy to see the text, and you can be confident it will remain readable against a range of background colors. For more information about adding a stroke or a shadow to text, see "Text styles" later in this lesson.

The Text panel offers direct access to the contents of graphics added to a sequence.

▶ **Tip:** You can quickly open the Text panel by clicking the Show In Text Panel button at the lower-right corner of the Essential Graphics panel.

1 Open the Text panel. If it's not open already, you will find it in the Window menu.

2 Select the Graphics tab.

The thumbnail of only one graphic is displayed because all of the text you have added is part of one graphic clip.

3 Double-click the text to the right of the thumbnail to edit it directly. Try this now and watch the text update directly in the Program Monitor.

4 Use Undo to restore the original version of the text.

Adding paragraph text

● **Note:** If a title clip is selected, clicking to add new text or a shape will add to the existing clip. If no graphic clip is selected in the Timeline panel, a new clip will be created on the next available track above.

Although point text is flexible, you'll have more control over your layout using paragraph text. This option will automatically wrap the text onto the next line when it reaches the edge of the paragraph text box.

Continue working with the same graphic clip selected in the 02 Cliff sequence.

1 Select the Type tool **T**, and make sure the graphic clip is selected in the Timeline panel.

2 Drag in the Program Monitor to create a text box that fills the lower-left corner, with a gap toward the edges of the frame.

▶ **Tip:** A good way to avoid spelling mistakes is to copy and paste text from an approved script or email that has already been reviewed by your client or producer.

3 Start typing. Start entering names of participants who will be attending the tour. Use the names shown here or add your own. Press Return/Enter after each name for a new line.

Type at least one name with enough characters to go beyond the right edge of the text box. Unlike point text, paragraph (area) text remains within the confines of the bounding box you defined, and it wraps at the edges of the box onto the next line. If you add so much text that some won't fit in the text box, the extra letters won't be visible.

4   Use the Selection tool to change the size and shape of the bounding box to fit around the text a little better.

When you resize a text box, the text stays the same size, adjusting its position in the text box.

5   In the Essential Graphic panel, the Stroke Position menu sets whether a stroke is on the outside, center or inner edge. Change this to Center to give a sharper edge to the new paragraph text.

Each item has its own layer in the graphic, so there are now two layers displayed in the Essential Graphics panel. When selected, each item has its own controls.

Styling text

In addition to offering settings for fonts, position, and opacity, the Essential Graphics panel also allows you to apply a stroke and shadow to text or shapes in a graphic.

When you'd like to reuse a particular group of text settings, for example, to ensure all the lower-thirds in your video match, you don't have to manually re-enter the settings each time. Instead, you can save them as a *text style* (think of it as a preset look for text). You can then use the text style to apply all the settings at once.

After we refine the appearance of the graphics in our sequence a bit more, we'll save each appearance as a text style.

Changing a title's appearance

In the Appearance section of the Essential Graphics panel, there are three main options for improving the readability of text.

*   **Stroke:** An edge added to text. It helps to keep text legible over moving video or a complex background.

*   **Background:** A solid color that appears behind the letters, creating a controllable backdrop for the text.

- **Shadow:** A common addition to video text because it makes the text easier to read without being intrusive. Be sure to adjust the Blur of the shadow. Also, be sure to keep the angle of shadows identical for all titles in a project for consistency.

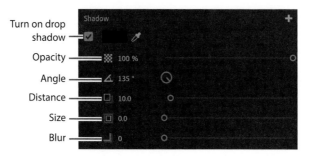

Turn on drop shadow
Opacity
Angle
Distance
Size
Blur

Just as with the text fill, you can assign any color to strokes, backgrounds, and shadows.

1 Enable the track output for Video 1.

2 Experiment with the options in the Essential Graphics panel to make the text more readable and add more color to the composition.

3 To set the color for the text in the upper right, select the text and use the Fill color eyedropper to select the orange rocks.

4 To set the color for the text in the lower left, select the text and use the Fill color eyedropper to select a pale blue from the sky around the clouds.

The colors in the rocks and clouds vary, so you may want to use the eyedropper to select an approximate color and then click the Fill color swatch to manually adjust the selection. Alternatively, keep clicking with the eyedropper until you have found a color in the image you like.

Try to match the appearance of the title in this example.

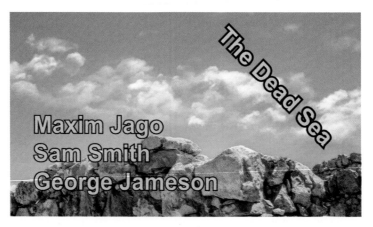

Saving Styles

If you create a text style you like, you can store it and reuse it in the project. A style describes the color, font, and appearance for text. You can use a style to change the appearance of a text object with a single click; all the properties of the text update to match the preset.

Let's create a style from the text you modified in the previous exercise.

1 Continuing to work on the same title, use the Selection tool to select the paragraph text in the lower-left corner.

2 In the Essential Graphics panel, open the Styles menu and choose Create Style.

The New Text Style dialog box opens.

3 Enter the name **Blue Bold Text**, and click OK.

The new style is added to the Styles menu in the Essential Graphics panel and appears in the Project panel.

Tip: You can copy styles from one open project to another. Plus, you can right-click a style in the Project panel and choose Export Text Styles to save it as a .prtext-style file that can be imported into other projects.

4 Select the other text in the upper-right corner and use the Styles menu to apply the Blue Bold Text style.

Any styles that are in the Project panel will appear on the list of available styles in the Essential Graphics panel. To remove a style, delete it from the Project panel.

Saving Source Graphics

So far, you have worked with a title that was already created in a sequence, edited one from the Project panel, and created a new one.

In most cases, Premiere Pro requires that items included in sequences also exist in the Project panel. Graphics created in Premiere Pro are an exception to this rule.

Earlier, you edited the Cloudscape Tracking title into the 01 Clouds current sequence. Open that sequence now, and from the Project panel, edit a second instance of the same title into the timeline on the Video 2 track. You may need to move the other version of the title out of the way to make space for the new copy.

Compare the two instances of the title clip. The changes you made to the title in the sequence, including adding text, have also been applied to the source clip in the Project panel. That's because the title is a *Source Graphic*.

You can convert any graphic to a Source Graphic by selecting it in the Timeline panel and choosing Graphics And Titles > Upgrade To Source Graphic.

A new graphic clip is added to the Project panel that you can share between multiple sequences or multiple projects.

Any graphic clips made from that Source Graphic, including the one you upgraded it from, are duplicates of each other. Any changes made to the text, style, or contents in any instance of a Source Graphic are reflected in all other instances of the same Source Graphic.

Source Graphics are useful when you expect to use the same graphic elements multiple times in a project. You might work on a multipart episodic show with standard opening titles, for example, or a documentary with the same lower-third design used to introduce every subject.

Being able to make adjustments to one item that updates everywhere can be a great time-saver.

Note: Titles have a default duration set in the user preferences, just like other single-frame media.

Working with shapes and logos

When creating title graphics, you'll likely need more than just words to build a complete graphic. Premiere Pro also offers the ability to create vector shapes as graphic elements. Many of the settings you adjusted when working with text also apply to shapes. You can also import completed graphics (like a logo) as a layer in a new graphic clip.

Creating a graphic or title in Adobe Photoshop

You can create graphics or titles for Premiere Pro in Adobe Photoshop. While Photoshop is known as the premier tool for modifying photos, it also has many capabilities for creating titles or logos for video projects. Photoshop offers several advanced options, advanced formatting (such as scientific notation), flexible layer styles, and even a spelling checker.

To create a new Photoshop document from inside Premiere Pro, follow these steps:

1 Choose File > New > Photoshop File.

2 The New Photoshop File dialog box appears, with settings based on your current sequence. Click OK.

3 Choose a location to store your new PSD file, name it, and click Save.

   Photoshop opens, ready for you to edit the file. The file has canvas guides for safe action and safe title zones (visible if you enable them in Photoshop). These guides won't appear in the finished image.

   ▶ **Tip:** If you have disabled canvas guides in the Photoshop View options, you can enable them by choosing View > Show > Canvas Guides.

4 Select the Horizontal Type tool by pressing the T key.

5 You can click to add point text or draw a text box for paragraph text. As in Premiere Pro, using a text box in Photoshop allows you to precisely control the layout of text.

6 Enter some text you'd like to use.

7 Adjust the font, color, and point size to taste using the controls in the Options bar across the top of the screen.

8 Click the Commit button ☑ (in the Options bar) to commit the text layer.

9 To add a drop shadow, choose Layer > Layer Style > Drop Shadow and adjust to suit.

When you're finished in Photoshop, you can save and close the file. It will already be in the Project panel in Premiere Pro, ready for you to edit into a sequence.

If you'd like to edit the title in Photoshop, right-click it in the Project panel or Timeline and choose Edit In Adobe Photoshop. When you save changes in Photoshop, the title updates automatically in Premiere Pro.

Creating shapes

If you've created shapes in graphics-editing software such as Photoshop or Adobe Illustrator, you'll find creating geometric objects in Premiere Pro similar.

You can use the Pen tool to click multiple points in the Program Monitor to create a unique shape.

You can also use the Rectangle tool, Ellipse tool, or Polygon tool. Access the Ellipse tool and Polygon tool in the Rectangle tool submenu. Using any of those tools, drag in the Program Monitor to create a new shape.

Try creating some shapes and adjusting their settings:

1 Open the sequence 03 Shapes.

Note: Until you quit Premiere Pro and start it again, new shapes will have the same appearance you last selected for a shape in the Essential Graphics panel. You can easily change the settings. New titles will have the same appearance you last selected for a title.

2 Select the Pen tool, and click multiple points in the Program Monitor to create a shape. Each time you click, the tool adds a new control point. Create something small and unique in the lower-left corner of the frame.

Complete the shape by clicking the first control point, and switch to the Selection tool.

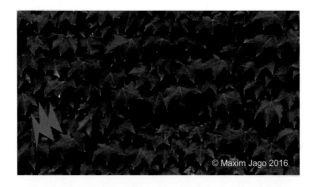

© Maxim Jago 2016

3 Try changing the fill color, adding a stroke, and changing the stroke color.

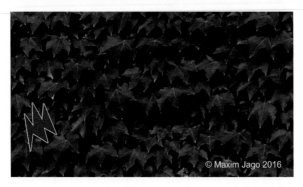

© Maxim Jago 2016

4   Create a new shape with the Pen tool, in the lower-right corner. This time, instead of just clicking, drag each time you click.

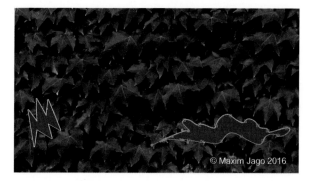

Dragging when you click creates control points with Bezier handles; these are the same handles you experimented with when setting up keyframes. These handles give you precise control over the shape you have created, allowing you to design more organic-looking shapes.

5   Select the Rectangle tool.

6   Drag to create rectangles in the Program Monitor. After you begin dragging, hold the Shift key to create squares.

7   Now click and hold the Rectangle tool in the Tools panel to select the Ellipse tool. Try drawing ellipses. The Shift key allows you to create perfect circles.

8   Click and hold the Ellipse tool in the Tools panel to select the Polygon tool. Try drawing a polygon, and then select the Selection tool.

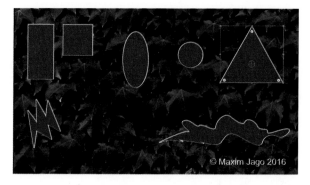

With a polygon selected, you can use the Corner Radius and Number Of Sides settings in the Align And Transform section of the Essential Graphics panel to change its appearance.

The Corner Radius setting can be changed for any polygon or rectangle. Using the Selection tool, drag the small circles  inside a shape to adjust the corner radius directly in the Program Monitor. Hold Option (macOS) or Alt (Windows) to adjust individual corners.

These kinds of random shapes may not win design awards, but they are the basic building blocks of some of the most common multilayer graphics.

You can use the Pen tool to adjust any selected shape. You can even click to add control points for more complex shapes. Try changing the selected shape using the Pen tool now.

9 If you want a clean slate, press Command+A (macOS) or Ctrl+A (Windows), and then press Fn+Delete (macOS) or Delete (Windows)—this is the Forward Delete key. You can also select layers in the Essential Graphics panel and delete them. For now, keep some shapes onscreen to work with later.

10 Experiment with the different shape options. Try overlapping them and using different colors, with different levels of opacity.

The layer positions of objects in the Essential Graphics panel set which objects appear in front, just as tracks do in the Timeline panel. You can drag objects to different positions on the list.

Adding a graphic

You can add image files to your graphic clips using common file formats, including vectors (AI, EPS) and still images (PSD, PNG, JPEG).

Let's try this with an existing graphic.

1 Open the sequence 04 Logo.

This is a simple sequence with space in the graphic for a logo.

Cloudscape

2 Using the Selection tool, select the "Add a logo" title clip in the sequence.

3 In the Essential Graphics panel, just below the layers area in the Edit tab, open the New Layer menu  and choose From File, or choose Graphics and Titles > New Layer > From File.

4 Browse to the file logo.ai in the Lessons/Assets/Graphics folder, and click Import (macOS) or Open (Windows).

5 With the Selection tool, drag the logo to position it where you want it in the title. Then adjust the size, opacity, rotation, or scale of the logo.

● **Note:** When resizing imported items in a graphic clip, scaling over 100% of the original item's image size will lead to a loss of quality because the result is displayed as pixels rather than as a vector image.

Masking with a layer

There's one further option in the Essential Graphics panel that deserves an explanation: Mask With Text.

This is best understood by trying it.

1 Open the sequence 05 Mask. This simple sequence has a slow-moving background clip and a graphic with one layer that is an imported image of some ivy. The background clip has a color adjustment and a blur to help separate it from the color and texture of the foreground clip.

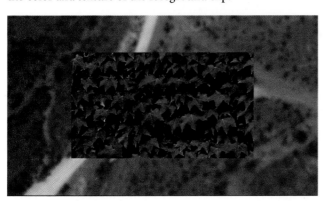

2 Position the Timeline playhead at the beginning of the sequence. Select the Graphic clip, and select the Type tool. Click in the Program Monitor, and type the word **IVY**, in all capital letters.

3 Switch to the Selection tool. Use the options in the Essential Graphics panel to expand the IVY text to fill the ivy clip area as closely as possible. Reposition the text with the Selection tool as needed to match this example.

Don't worry about the fill color or the stroke color—these will be ignored in the next step.

4 With the text item selected, scroll down in the Essential Graphics panel and select Mask With Text.

The Mask With Text option masks any layer inside a graphic, using the selected layer as the mask. This is similar to the masking you performed earlier using the Track Matte Key effect. The difference is that the effect is limited to the contents of the current graphic.

Using rulers and guides

There are several ways to arrange and align items in the Program Monitor. By default, you'll be able to move items freely in view, but, like the snapping option in the Timeline panel, there are also ways to snap items into position in the Program Monitor.

1 Open the 03 Shapes sequence you worked on earlier.

2 With the Selection tool, try moving the shapes around. They'll move freely and overlap based on their stacking order in the Essential Graphics panel.

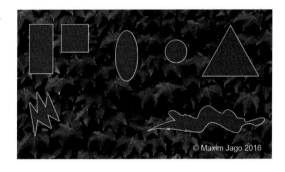
© Maxim Jago 2016

3 With the Program Monitor active, choose View > Snap In Program Monitor if it isn't already selected. Now as you drag items, lines appear showing alignment with other items or the center or edge of the Program Monitor. Any item you drag will also snap into alignment.

In this complex graphic, snapping can be a little overwhelming as there are just so many items.

Tip: If you find the Snap In Program Monitor option is unavailable, check you have the right panel active. The option is also available in the Program Monitor Settings menu.

4 Create a new graphic, with one shape, toward the end of the sequence, where the frame is clear again. Try dragging the graphic around the frame, and take note of the satisfying certainty when the shape snaps into position.

5 Make sure the Program Monitor is the active panel, with a blue outline, and choose View > Show Rulers. Rulers are not interactive, but they give you a reference for the next step.

6 Click the ruler at the top of the Program Monitor and drag down. This creates a guide that you can snap items to. As you drag, the pixel position is shown as a tool tip. You can drag multiple guides from either ruler.

Note: If you want to use specific guides as a long-term reference, you can lock them in position. Choose View > Lock Guides. Choose the option again to unlock the guides.

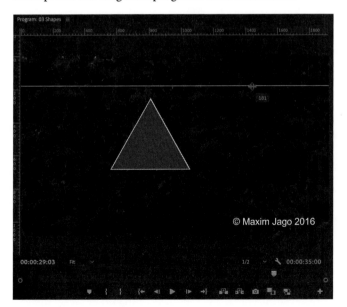
© Maxim Jago 2016

You can also right-click a guide and choose Edit Guide to assign a new color and specify a precise position.

You can show or hide rulers and guides by choosing them from the View menu. Guides are persistent: If you hide them and then show them again, they will be exactly where you left them.

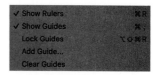

You can also use the View menu to clear any guides you have added.

In the Program Monitor, use the Button Editor ➕ to add buttons that let you select and deselect these options.

Making a title roll

You can make rolling text for opening and closing credits. In fact, you can apply a roll to any graphic, not just to text.

1   Open the 04 Logo sequence. Use the Program Monitor Settings menu to make sure the Transparency Grid is not active.

2   Position the Timeline panel playhead at the end of the sequence, just after the clip on the Video 1 track.

3   Using the Type tool, click in the Program Monitor to add point text.

4   Type several lines of text that you would like to use as a credit roll, pressing Return/Enter after each line.

For the purposes of this exercise, don't worry about the precise words.

It can be difficult to add many lines of text without constantly repositioning it. It's often easier to have the text ready in a document so you can copy and paste it into Premiere Pro.

5   When you have typed a few lines, use the Essential Graphics panel to format your text as desired.

6   Deselect the text layer (by clicking the background of the Program Monitor with the Selection tool). The Edit tab of the Essential Graphics panel will now show properties for the whole graphic, not just the text item you were typing.

7   In the Essential Graphics panel, select Roll to roll the title.

When you set a title to Roll, a scroll bar appears in the Program Monitor. Now, when you play through the clip, it will roll on and off the screen.

With the scroll bar in place, it's much easier to add more lines of text and navigate through a long title.

You have the following options:

- **Start Offscreen:** This sets whether the credit begins offscreen and rolls in or whether it begins where you positioned it in the Program Monitor. Combined with a Cross Dissolve effect, you could have your title fade up onscreen and roll off.

- **End Offscreen:** This indicates whether the credits roll completely off the screen or end on the screen. Combined with a Cross Dissolve effect, you could have your title roll onscreen and fade out.

- **Preroll:** This sets the amount of time to delay before the rolling motion begins.

- **Postroll:** This specifies the amount of time to play after the roll ends.

- **Ease In:** This specifies the number of frames at the beginning to gradually increase the speed of the roll from zero to full speed.

- **Ease Out:** This specifies the number of frames to slow down the speed of the roll at the end.

- **Soften:** This softens the edges of your rolling text.

If your credits begin or end offscreen, the Preroll, Postroll, and Ease options won't have much impact because the contents will be out of the frame.

When you trim a title to set the length, this sets the playback speed of a rolling title. A shorter title will roll faster than a long one because, one way or another, all of the contents of the title will be displayed in the duration you set for the clip.

8   Play through your rolling title.

Note: The Responsive Design options that were touched on earlier are for motion graphics with a precisely timed intro and outro. Use these time controls to prevent clip duration changes from retiming start and end animations.

Working with Motion Graphics templates

The Browse tab of the Essential Graphics panel includes many built-in template graphics you can add to your sequences. They are all customizable. Many of the presets include motion, so they are referred to as Motion Graphics templates (often abbreviated to MOGRTs).

You can add a Motion Graphics template to a sequence by dragging it onto a video track.

Motion Graphics templates can be created in Premiere Pro or Adobe After Effects, and there are differences in the templates each application creates.

- Motion Graphics templates created in Premiere Pro produce graphics that are completely editable.

- Motion Graphics templates created in After Effects can include more advanced design and complex animation. They also have restricted controls, set by the original designer to give flexibility while retaining the original core design.

The built-in templates are divided into categories. Drag a template directly into any sequence to add it.

Some templates may have a yellow font warning symbol 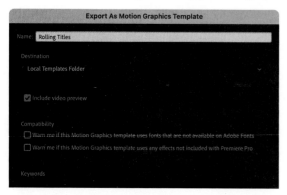. This indicates that the template uses a font not currently installed on your system.

If you use a template that includes fonts available on Adobe Fonts and you are online, Premiere Pro automatically downloads and installs the missing fonts. If in doubt, you can right-click a template in the Essential Graphics panel and choose Sync Missing Fonts.

If it's not possible to install a missing font automatically, you'll see a warning message advising you that the missing font can't be downloaded. The Resolve Fonts dialog box will appear, letting you know which fonts are missing.

The easiest way to resolve a missing font is to go online and add the template again. If that's not possible, you can choose another font in the Essential Graphics panel. You can also set a default replacement font in the Premiere Pro user preferences, in the Graphics section.

Experimenting with Motion Graphics templates is a great way to learn about what's possible when designing animated graphics. Add any template to a sequence and then explore the settings that have been used in the Essential Graphics panel.

Creating a custom Motion Graphics template

You can add your own custom graphics to the Browse tab of the Essential Graphics panel. Simply select a graphic clip in a sequence, and choose Graphics And Titles > Export As Motion Graphics Template.

Choose a name for the new template graphic, and choose a location from the Destination menu. You can add keywords to make the template easier to locate when searching by entering each keyword and pressing Return/Enter.

▶ **Tip:** You can quickly add multiple keywords, separating them with a comma (,) before pressing Return/Enter.

When you're happy with the settings, click OK. The new Motion Graphics template will automatically be added to the Browse tab of the Essential Graphics panel.

You can import an existing Motion Graphics template file on any computer by choosing Graphics And Titles > Install Motion Graphics Template or by clicking the button ⬛ in the lower-right corner of the Essential Graphics panel Browse tab.

This makes it easy to share your custom template titles or store them in a collection for future use.

Adding captions

There are two kinds of captions you might encounter when producing video for television broadcast and beyond: closed and open.

Closed captions are embedded in the video stream and can be enabled or hidden by the viewer. *Open* captions are always on-screen—and are described as "burned in."

The colorful onscreen captions that often accompany social media content are examples of open captions.

Premiere Pro allows you to work with either kind of caption in the same way. In fact, you can even convert one kind of caption file to another (though there are some limitations set by captions delivery standards).

Closed-caption files have a more limited range of colors and design features than open captions. This is because closed captions are actually generated and displayed by the viewer's TV, set-top box, or online viewing software, so display options are universal and fixed.

Using closed captions

Video content can be enjoyed by more people when it is accessible. It's a requirement for most broadcast television stations to add closed-captioning information that can be decoded by television sets. Visible captions are inserted into a video file and travel through supported formats to specific playback devices.

Adding closed-captioning information is relatively easy. You can work with a captions file or generate new captions in Premiere Pro.

Here's how to add captions to a sequence using an existing file.

1   Keeping the current project open, choose File > Open Project. Browse to the Lessons folder, and open Lesson 15_02.prproj.

2   Click the Lesson 15_02 Project panel to make it active, and save the project as **15_02 Working.prproj**.

3 If it's not displayed in the Timeline panel already, open the sequence Coach Interview.

4 Choose File > Import, and navigate to the Lessons/Assets/Video and Audio Files/ Interview folder. Import the file Coach Interview.srt. The DFXP, MCC, SCC, SRT, STL, and XML formats are all supported.

Premiere Pro adds the caption file to the bin as if it were a video clip, with a frame rate and duration.

5 Drag the closed-captions clip into the Timeline panel. The New Caption Track dialog appears.

There are different caption formats for different television systems:

- **Australian OP-47** is the Australian closed-captioning standard, used by Australian broadcast television networks.

- **CEA-608** (also known as Line 21) was the most commonly used standard for analog broadcast in the US and Canada.

- **CEA-708** is for digital broadcast in the US and Canada.

- **EBU Subtitle** is an older but popular subtitle type with broad compatibility.

- **Subtitle** is a newer subtitle type.

- **Teletext** is sometimes used in PAL countries.

Within each type there are multiple possible streams. For example, one stream might be English language, while another might be French. The settings displayed are correct, so click OK.

A new captions track is added to the sequence, with each part of the captions displayed as separate clips.

6   You can add multiple captions tracks to a sequence. You can enable output for one captions track at a time by clicking the Toggle Active Captions Track button .

Try toggling the captions output off and on now.

7   Play the sequence to see the captions.

Well, I've been doing this for 25 years.

You can trim caption clips to adjust their timing like any other kind of sequence clips.

After selecting one or more caption clips in a sequence, you can adjust their appearance by changing settings in the Essential Graphics panel.

You can also edit caption text directly in the Program Monitor by double-clicking it.

8   To make room for more captions in the next exercise, right-click the track header for the Subtitle captions track you just created and choose Delete Track.

Creating new captions

You can create your own closed captions automatically within Premiere Pro. There's even an option to automatically transcribe clips when you add them to a sequence.

You'll click to transcribe the current sequence, but to automatically transcribe all clips when they are added to a sequence, choose Premiere Pro > Settings > Transcription (macOS) or Edit > Preferences > Transcription (Windows), and select Automatically Transcribe Clips.

To automatically transcribe all clips when they are imported, choose Auto-Transcribe All Imported Clips from the Transcription Preferences menu, and click OK to close the Preferences dialog box. For now, click Cancel to leave the setting unchanged.

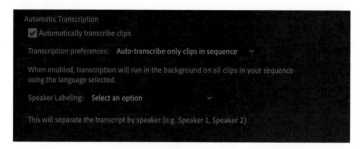

Let's transcribe the current sequence:

1 Open the Transcribe sequence. This is the same sequence but the clips have not been transcribed.

2 Open the Text panel and set it to the Transcript tab. If the Text panel isn't open already, you'll find it in the Window menu.

3 Click the blue Transcribe button. Premiere Pro transcribes the audio in the sequence.

The accuracy of the transcription depends in part on the quality of the original audio recording. If you find a word that should be replaced, double-click it in the Text panel and retype it.

● **Note:** By default, Premiere Pro will transcribe the first audio channel for clips with multiple channels. If you are working with multichannel audio clips, it may be helpful to check and configure the channels before transcribing. Select the clips, then right-click the selection and choose Modify > Audio Channels to access the settings, or press Shift+G.

4   Click the Create Captions button 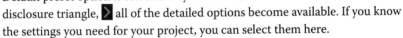 at the top of the Text panel. You may need to resize the panel to see the button.

The Create Captions dialog box opens.

There are several options available to configure the way captions will be displayed. Initially, the Subtitle Default preset option is selected. If you click the disclosure triangle, ❯ all of the detailed options become available. If you know the settings you need for your project, you can select them here.

Keeping the default settings, click Create Captions.

A new captions track is added to the sequence, much like the one you created when importing a caption file.

5   Play the sequence. The captions will update in the Text panel as the sequence plays.

You can use the Essential Graphics panel to change the appearance of captions. You can select more than one caption clip and changes made in the Essential Graphics panel will apply to all selected items.

Upgrading captions to graphics

The appearance options for captions are limited to ensure compatibility with players. If you'd like to get a little more creative with your captions, you can convert them to graphics.

To upgrade, select one or more caption clips and choose Graphics And Titles > Upgrade Caption To Graphic.

The selected captions will be removed from the Captions track and added as graphics to an empty video track.

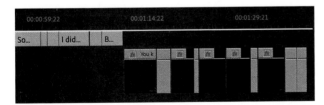

Now you'll have the full range of design features available in the Essential Graphics panel.

Closing multiple projects

You currently have two projects open at the same time. To close them both in a single step, choose File > Close All Projects. If you are invited to save a project, do so.

Review questions

1 What are the differences between point text and paragraph (or area) text?

2 Why display the title-safe zone?

3 How do you use the Rectangle tool to make a perfect square?

4 How do you apply a stroke or drop shadow?

5 What is the difference between kerning and tracking?

Review answers

1 You create point text by clicking in the Program Monitor with the Type tool. Its text box expands as you type. When you drag in the Program Monitor with the Type tool, you define a bounding box for paragraph text, and the characters remain within its confines. Changing the box's shape displays more or fewer characters.

2 Some TV sets cut off the edges of the picture. The amount lost varies from set to set. Keeping your text within the title-safe area ensures that viewers will see all your title. This is less of a problem with newer flat-screen TVs and isn't important for online video, but it's still a good idea to use the title-safe zone to frame your titles.

3 To create a perfect square, hold down the Shift key after you begin dragging as you draw using the Rectangle tool. You can create a perfect circle with the Ellipse tool in the same way.

4 To apply a stroke or drop shadow, select the text or object to edit, and enable the Stroke or Shadow options in the Essential Graphics panel.

5 Kerning adjusts the spacing between two characters. Tracking adjusts the spacing between multiple selected characters.

16 EXPORTING FRAMES, CLIPS, AND SEQUENCES

Lesson overview

In this lesson, you'll learn how to do the following:

- Make quick exports.
- Configure your exported video for a specific audience and medium.
- Export single frames.
- Create movie, image sequence, and audio files.
- Use Adobe Media Encoder.
- Upload to social media and Adobe Stock.
- Share projects with editors using other editing apps.

 This lesson will take about 90 minutes to complete. To get the lesson files used in this chapter, download them from the web page for this book at *peachpit.com/PremiereProCIB2024*. For more information, see "Accessing the lesson files and Web Edition" in the "Getting Started" section at the beginning of this book. Store the files on your computer in a convenient location.

One of the best things about editing video is the feeling you have when you can finally share it with your audience. Adobe Premiere Pro offers a wide range of export options. You can export to multiple high-level output formats using simplified Quick Export presets, using fully detailed settings, direct to social media, or even in batches via Adobe Media.

Starting the lesson

The most common form of media distribution is via digital files. Whether your completed project will be shown on a television, at the cinema, or on a computer or phone screen, you will usually deliver a file that has the particular specifications required for that medium.

● **Note:** To ensure that the tools function and the defaults are set exactly as described in this lesson, reset the Premiere Pro preferences by holding Option (macOS) or Alt (Windows) while launching the application and then clicking Continue in the Reset Options dialog box.

To create a file, you can export directly from Premiere Pro or use Adobe Media Encoder. Adobe Media Encoder is a stand-alone application (included with your Creative Cloud membership and installed alongside Premiere Pro automatically) that handles file exports in batches, so you can export in several formats simultaneously and process in the background while you work in other applications, including Premiere Pro and Adobe After Effects.

Making quick exports

Premiere Pro offers a Quick Export option that's perfect when you simply want to export a media file with settings that are appropriate for your current sequence or clip with the minimum number of clicks. You can produce several file types by choosing the appropriate preset.

Let's give Quick Export a try.

1 Open Lesson 16.prproj from the Lessons folder.

2 Save the project as **Lesson 16 Working.prproj**.

3 Switch to the Editing workspace, and reset the workspace to the saved layout.

4 If it's not already open, open the sequence Review Copy.

5 Click the Quick Export icon 📤 in the top-right corner of the Premiere Pro window to open the Quick Export dialog box.

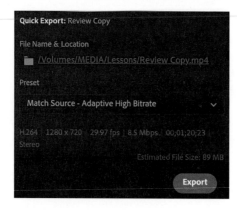

6 Use the Preset menu to choose Match Source – Adaptive High Bitrate. These settings automatically match the format of your sequence (or clip if you had selected one to export) and are encoded using the popular H.264 codec, which is perfect for uploading to social media or to streaming services.

There are also high quality 4K (Ultra High Definition), HD (High Definition), and SD (Standard Definition) presets available that will conform your export to a particular delivery standard.

A summary displays the settings you have chosen.

Note: Click the Preset menu and choose More Presets to see a full list of available presets.

7 The blue text showing the output name is actually a button that opens a Save As dialog box. You'll find the same type of text-as-a-button in Adobe Media Encoder. Click the blue text for the File Name & Location now. Create a folder named **Exports** in the Lessons folder. Browse into the new folder, name the file **Review Copy.mp4**, and click Save.

8 Click Export to create your new media file.

When encoding is completed successfully, a notification will appear in the lower-right corner of the Premiere Pro interface.

Understanding the full media export options

Whether you've completed a project or you just want to share an in-progress version for review, you have several export options.

- You can export to an appropriate file type, format, and codec for your chosen delivery medium.

- You can export a single frame or a series of frames.

- You can choose audio-only, video-only, or full audio/video output.

- Captions can be included, embedded in the output file, or stored in a separate file.

- Exported media can be reimported into the project automatically for easy reuse.

Beyond choosing an export format (frame size, frame rate, and so on), there are several other important options when exporting a file:

- You can choose to create files in a similar format and at the same visual quality and data rate as your original media, or you can compress them to a smaller size to make distribution easier.

Note: Whatever is selected when you export is what Premiere Pro will use as the new media file source. This can consist of clips, sequences, or parts of clips or sequences.

- You can transcode your media from one codec to another to make it easier to exchange with creative collaborators.

- You can set the frame size, frame rate, data rate, or audio and video codec and configuration if an existing preset doesn't fit your needs.

- You can apply a color lookup table (LUT) to assign a Look. You can also apply a video limiter, HDR-to-SDR conversion, and audio normalization.

- You can burn in timecode, name, or image overlays.

- You can upload an exported file directly to social media accounts, an FTP server, Adobe Stock, or your Creative Cloud Files folder.

Exporting single frames

Even while an edit is in progress, you may want to export a still frame to send to a team member or client for review. You might also want to export an image to use as the thumbnail of your video file when you post it to social media.

When you export a frame from the Source Monitor, Premiere Pro creates a still image that matches the resolution of the source video file.

When you export a frame from the Program Monitor, Premiere Pro creates a still image that matches the resolution of the sequence.

Let's give it a try.

1   Continue working with the sequence Review Copy. Position the Timeline play-head on a frame you want to export.

2   In the Program Monitor, click the Export Frame button ⬛ on the lower right. If you can't see the button, resize the Program Monitor.

> ● **Note:** If resizing the panel doesn't bring the button to light, it's possible that you removed it if you customized the Program Monitor buttons. You can select the Program Monitor or the Timeline panel and press Shift+E (macOS) or Shift+Ctrl+E (Windows) to export a frame.

3   In the Export Frame dialog box, enter a filename.

4   Choose a still-image format from the Format menu.

- **JPEG**, **PNG**, and **BMP** (Windows only) are universally readable. JPEG and PNG files are commonly used in website design.

- **TIFF**, **TGA**, and **PNG** are suitable for print and animation workflows.

- **DPX** is often used for digital cinema or color-grading workflows (fine color finishing).

- **OpenEXR** is used to store high dynamic range picture information.

5   Click the Browse button to choose the Exports folder you created earlier.

6   Select the Import Into Project option to add the new still image into your current project, and click OK.

The new still image is created, and a clip linked to it is added to the Project panel.

Note: If your video format uses non-square pixels, the resulting image file will appear to have a different aspect ratio. This is because still image formats have square pixels. Using Adobe Photoshop, you can resize the image horizontally and restore the original aspect ratio.

Note: In Windows, you can export to the BMP, DPX, GIF, JPEG, OpenEXR, PNG, TGA, and TIFF formats. In macOS, you can export to the DPX, JPEG, OpenEXR, PNG, TGA, and TIFF formats.

Note: If you export a TIFF file from Premiere Pro, the file will have a three-letter .tif file extension, rather than .tiff. Both are valid and work interchangeably.

Exporting a full quality media file

It can be useful to produce a pristine digital copy of your edited project that can be archived for future use. This is a self-contained, fully rendered output file from your sequence at the highest resolution and best quality possible. You can use a file of this kind as a source media file to produce other compressed output formats without opening the original project in Premiere Pro.

Though basing other copies on this source file technically means losing a tiny amount of quality (one digital generation), the loss is so minimal relative to the convenience and time-savings that many editors find it a worthwhile exchange.

In the next exercise, you'll learn about the various settings you can configure when exporting to a new media file. Premiere Pro can also automatically post to social media accounts, cloud storage, and an FTP (File Transfer Protocol) server (see "Uploading to social media," later in the lesson).

Once you have configured your output options appropriately, you'll be able to quickly export new files in just a couple of clicks.

Matching sequence settings

Ideally, the frame size, frame rate, and codec of a full-quality media file will match the sequence it's based on. It can seem like a lot of settings to think about when creating a new exported media file. Thankfully, Premiere Pro makes matching your sequence or original clip settings easy.

1 Continue working with the Review Copy sequence.

2 With the sequence selected in the Project panel or open in the Timeline panel, with that panel active (with a blue outline), click Export in the upper-left corner of the Application window, or choose File > Export > Media. You can also press Command+M (macOS) or Ctrl+M (Windows).

   Premiere Pro switches to Export mode.

● **Note:** In some cases, the Match Sequence Preview Settings option cannot produce an exact match of the original camera media. For example, XDCAM EX will write to an MPEG2 file. In most cases, the file written will have an identical format and closely match the data rate of the original sources.

3 You'll learn more about this mode later. For now, scroll down in the Preset menu and choose Match Sequence Preview Settings.

4 In the File Name box, enter **Review Copy - Match Previews**. (Don't worry about the file extension; Premiere Pro adds it automatically.)

5 Click the blue Location text. Browse to and choose the Exports folder you created earlier.

6 Review the Output information to check that the output format matches the sequence settings. In this case, you should be using DNxHD media at 29.97 fps. The Summary information is a quick, easy reference that helps you avoid minor errors that can have big consequences. If the Source and Output Summary settings match, it minimizes conversion, which helps maintain the quality of the final output.

● **Note:** The number in parentheses after the frame size in the export summary is the pixel aspect ratio.

When exporting a sequence, the sequence itself is the source in the Export dialog box—not the clips inside the sequence, because these will have already been conformed to the sequence settings.

7 Click the Export button to create a media file based on the sequence.

When the export is complete, Premiere Pro returns to Edit mode. You can switch between Import, Edit, and Export mode at any time.

Choosing the source range

You don't have to export a whole sequence. In fact, you'll commonly export only a selected part of your sequence for review.

Click to make the Timeline panel active; then click Export in the upper-left corner to switch to Export mode.

On the right side, above the output summary, you'll see a preview, with controls for making a partial selection for export.

If your source sequence or clip has In and Out points, they are automatically used to define the partial output. They are also displayed on the preview time ruler. You can override existing In and Out points by choosing Entire Source from the Range menu.

You can set new In and Out points by positioning the preview playhead and clicking the Set In Point and Set Out Point buttons or pressing I and O.

If you set new In and Out points, the Source Range menu updates to show Custom.

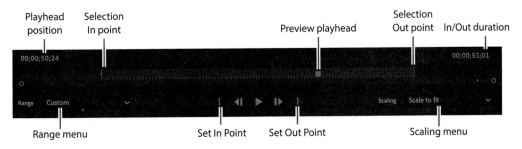

Configuring mismatched exported aspect ratios

Occasionally, you might need to export to an image format with a different aspect ratio than your sequence (or source clip). For example, you might export a 2.39:1 cinemascope aspect ratio sequence to a 16:9 widescreen HD or UHD aspect ratio video file. As another example, you might export a widescreen sequence to square video for social media delivery. In both cases, you might decide to crop, stretch, or scale the frame to fit the new aspect ratio. There are both creative and technical reasons for choosing any of these options, and it's easy to choose between them.

The Scaling menu lets you choose the way a mismatch between the source aspect ratio and the output settings is handled.

- **Scale To Fit:** The original aspect ratio will be maintained, and the frame will be scaled down to ensure the whole image can be seen within the new aspect ratio. This results in black areas at the top and bottom (letterboxing) or sides (pillarboxing), where there are gaps.

- **Scale To Fill:** The image will be scaled to ensure the frame is filled with no gaps. This results in cropping.

- **Stretch To Fill:** The image is stretched, changing its aspect ratio, so that it fits the new aspect ratio with no gaps and no cropping.

When you export a file with black bars at the top and bottom or sides, those bars become part of the file. These black pixels are sometimes desirable as it helps to ensure the image will be displayed with the correct aspect ratio within the delivered video.

Choosing another codec

When you export to a new media file, there are many settings available to define the output format and codec, audio encoding, metadata, effects, and more. The number of options can be overwhelming at first. The good news is that you will usually be able to choose settings based on a file delivery specification that is given to you.

In most cases, you will probably choose a preset and make just one or two adjustments (if any) to that preset before you click Export.

One of the most important choices you'll make is the output file's codec. Some camera capture formats (such as the H.264 MP4 files commonly produced by phones) are already heavily compressed, to save storage space. Using a higher-quality codec can help to preserve quality.

▶ **Tip:** Even if your original media is 8 bit, it is likely you will have been editing using higher-quality effects. The subtle results of color grading and adding graphics can be better captured in a 10-bit file than an 8-bit file.

Choose your preset and format, decide whether you'd like to export audio, video, or both by activating or deactivating those options 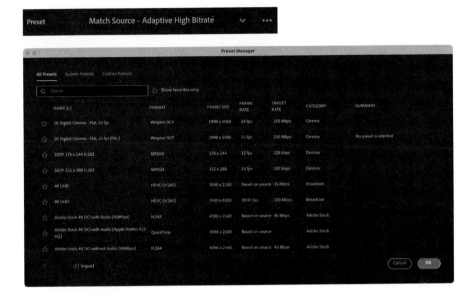, and then modify settings to suit. You can access groups of export settings by clicking a group heading.

1   With the Timeline panel active, press Command+M (macOS) or Ctrl+M (Windows) to switch to Export mode.

2   Next to the Preset menu, click the three dots for more options and choose More Presets.

| Preset | Match Source - Adaptive High Bitrate | ∨ | ••• |

| Preset Manager |

All Presets   System Presets   Custom Presets

| 🔍 Search | | ☆ Show favorites only | | | | |

NAME ≡↑	FORMAT	FRAME SIZE	FRAME RATE	TARGET RATE	CATEGORY	SUMMARY
☆ 2K Digital Cinema - Flat, 24 fps	Wraptor DCP	1998 x 1080	24 fps	250 Mbps	Cinema	
☆ 2K Digital Cinema - Flat, 25 fps (PAL)	Wraptor DCP	1998 x 1080	25 fps	250 Mbps	Cinema	No preset is selected.
☆ 3GPP 176 x 144 H.263	MPEG4	176 x 144	15 fps	128 kbps	Devices	
☆ 3GPP 352 x 288 H.263	MPEG4	352 x 288	15 fps	192 kbps	Devices	
☆ 4K UHD	HEVC (H.265)	3840 x 2160	Based on source	35 Mbps	Broadcast	
☆ 8K UHD	HEVC (H.265)	7680 x 4320	29.97 fps	120 Mbps	Broadcast	
☆ Adobe Stock 4K DCI with Audio (40Mbps)	H.264	4096 x 2160	Based on source	40 Mbps	Adobe Stock	
☆ Adobe Stock 4K DCI with Audio (Apple ProRes 422 HQ)	QuickTime	4096 x 2160	Based on source		Adobe Stock	
☆ Adobe Stock 4K DCI without Audio (40Mbps)	H.264	4096 x 2160	Based on source	40 Mbps	Adobe Stock	

⤓ Import   Cancel   OK

The Preset Manager offers many different presets you can use as a starting point for your configured export. To apply a preset, select it and click OK. For now, click Cancel.

3   Open the Format menu, and choose QuickTime.

A quick glance at the export summary on the right will tell you this format leads to an Apple QuickTime file with ProRes 422 HQ compression. This is a popular option for professional media delivery.

4   Enter the file name, **Review Copy QT**, and make sure the Location is set to your Exports folder.

Below the Format menu, you'll find a series of sections containing important additional options. Click a section name to view it.

Here's an overview:

• **Video:** The Video section allows you to set the video codec, frame size, frame rate, field order, and profile. The settings available are based on the preset you chose.

- **Audio:** The Audio section allows you to adjust the bit rate of the audio and, for some formats, the codec. The default settings are based on the preset you chose.

- **Captions:** If your sequence has captions, you can specify whether they are ignored, burned in (added to the visuals permanently), or exported as a separate file (referred to as a *sidecar file*).

- **Effects:** You can add a number of useful effects and overlays as you output your media (see these options in the section "Applying effects during export."

- **Metadata:** Specify the way metadata associated with your sequence or source clip will be handled, as well as the start timecode for the new media file.

- **General:** Choose whether you would like the new media file to be imported into your project and whether you would like to use sequence previews or proxy files as the source.

5 Click the Video section to open it. In the Video Codec menu, browse the available codecs.

   When you have finished browsing, choose Apple ProRes 422 HQ. This produces a high-quality file that many editors choose for final delivery.

6 At the bottom of the Basic Video Settings section, click the More button.

7 In the Depth menu, choose 16-bpc.

   If this menu is set to 8-bpc (the default), the video file will be rendered with only 8 bits per channel. With a Depth setting of 16-bpc, the full quality of the ProRes 422 HQ codec is used.

8 Click to expand the Audio section. In the Basic Audio Settings area, make sure 48000 Hz is chosen from the Sample Rate menu and 16 bit is chosen from the Sample Size menu. Click More, and in the Audio Channel Configuration area, make sure Stereo is chosen from the Output Channels menu.

   These audio options are common standards for professional media delivery.

9 Click Export at the lower-right corner to export the sequence and transcode it to a new media file.

Apple ProRes 422 HQ is a high-quality option for professional media delivery that produces relatively large media files.

The most popular delivery format and codec is MPEG4 (.mp4), using the H.264 codec. These media files are smaller than Apple ProRes 422 HQ files, so they are faster to upload to websites, and they produce acceptable quality for most online viewing purposes. You'll find built-in presets for YouTube and Vimeo in the Preset Manager.

● **Note:** The settings displayed in each section change depending on the format you choose.

● **Note:** ProRes is a professional codec that is supported natively by Adobe Creative Cloud applications. Like all codecs, it will play back only in media applications that support it.

● **Note:** If you're working with a professional format (such as MXF OP1a, DNxHD MXF OP1a, or QuickTime), you can export up to 32 channels of audio. To do so, the original sequence must be configured to use a multichannel mix track with the corresponding number of tracks.

Applying effects during export

At the time of export, you can apply visual effects, add information overlays, and make automated adjustments to the output file.

Here's an overview of the options on the Effects section:

- **Tone Mapping:** If you are working on a High Dynamic Range (HDR) sequence but exporting a Standard Dynamic Range (SDR) media file, use this option and select a Tone Mapping Method to automatically adjust the tones to fit the lower range.

- **Lumetri Look/LUT:** Choose from a list of built-in Lumetri Looks or browse to your own, allowing you to quickly apply a nuanced adjustment to the appearance of your output file. This is most commonly used when viewing recordings at the end of each day of production (the dailies).

- **SDR Conform:** If your sequence uses high dynamic range and you are delivering a standard dynamic range media file, you can make manual adjustments to the brightness and contrast using this effect.

- **Image Overlay:** Add a graphic, such as a company logo or network "bug," and position it on-screen. The graphic will be incorporated into the image (burned in).

- **Text Overlay:** Add a text overlay to the image. This is particularly useful as a watermark to protect your content or as a way to identify different versions.

- **Timecode Overlay:** Display timecode for your finished video file, making it easy for viewers without specialized editing software to note reference times for commenting purposes.

- **Time Tuner:** Specify a new duration or playback speed, up to +/–10%. This is achieved by applying subtle adjustments to periods of low action where the soundtrack is silent. Results vary depending on the media you are working with, so test different speeds to compare the end results. A continuous music soundtrack will interfere with the Time Tuner.

- **Video Limiter:** Although it's usually best to get your video levels right in the sequence, you can apply a limiter here too, to ensure your resulting file meets the required levels for broadcast television.

- **Loudness Normalization:** Use the Loudness scale to normalize audio levels in your output file. As with video levels, it's best to get this right in the sequence, but it can be reassuring to know your levels will be limited during export.

Working with Adobe Media Encoder

Adobe Media Encoder is a stand-alone application that you can run independently or launch from Premiere Pro. One advantage of using Media Encoder is that you can send an encoding job directly from Premiere Pro and then continue working on your edit as the encoding is processed. If your client asks to see your work before you finish editing, Media Encoder can produce the file in the background without interrupting your flow.

By default, Media Encoder pauses encoding when you play video in Premiere Pro to maximize playback performance. You can change this in the Premiere Pro Playback preferences.

Choosing a file format for export

AAC Audio
AIFF
Animated GIF
Apple ProRes MXF OP1a
AS-10
AS-11
DNxHR/DNxHD MXF OP1a
DPX
H.264
H.264 Blu-ray
HEVC (H.265)
JPEG
JPEG 2000 MXF OP1a
MP3
MPEG2
MPEG2 Blu-ray
MPEG2-DVD
MPEG4
MXF OP1a
OpenEXR
PNG
QuickTime
Targa
TIFF
Waveform Audio

It can be a challenge to know how to deliver your finished work. Ultimately, choosing delivery formats is a process of planning backward; find out how the file will be presented, and it's then usually straightforward to identify the best file type for the purpose. Often, clients will have a delivery specifications document to follow, making it easier to select the right options for encoding.

Premiere Pro and Adobe Media Encoder can export to many formats. In fact, Premiere Pro shares Adobe Media Encoder's Format options.

Let's take a look at some common scenarios and review which formats are typically used. There are few absolutes, but these should get you close to the desired output.

It's a good idea to test your output on a short section of your video before producing a full-length finished file. This will save you waiting for the complete version only to discover there is a better setting to choose.

* **Encoding for user-generated video sites:** The H.264 format includes presets for YouTube, Vimeo, Facebook, and Twitter in widescreen, SD, HD, and 4K.

* **Producing a DCP for theatrical distribution:** Choose the Wraptor DCP format and then pick 24 or 25 frames per second. If your sequence is 30 frames per second, choose 24 frames per second for output to a DCP. Settings are limited to ensure compatibility with standard DCI-compliant cinema-projection systems.

In general, the presets are proven and will work for your intended purpose.

Most presets are conservative and will deliver good results with the default settings, so you probably won't improve the quality by making adjustments.

Configuring the export

To export from Premiere Pro to Adobe Media Encoder, you'll need to queue the export. The first step is to use Export mode to make choices about the file you're going to export.

1 Continue working with the Review Copy sequence. Either select the sequence in the Project panel or have it open in the Timeline panel, with that panel active.

2 Choose File > Export > Media, or press Command+M (macOS) or Ctrl+M (Windows).

3 For this example, open the Preset menu and choose More Presets, or click the three dots next to the Preset menu and choose More Presets. Type **Vimeo** in the Search box; then select the Vimeo 720p HD preset and click OK.

   These settings match the frame size and frame rate of the sequence.

4 Click the File Name box and give the file a new name, **Social Media**. The location should already be set to your Exports folder. If not, set it now.

5 Check the summary information text to verify your choices.

Queuing the export

When you're ready to create your media file, you have a few more options to consider. These are some of the more advanced options available in Export mode. You may not decide to use any of these when exporting a particular sequence, or they may be central to your workflow. Either way, it's worth taking a moment to consider them before proceeding.

These are available whether you are exporting directly from Premiere Pro or queuing the export in Adobe Media Encoder.

- **Video > More > Use Maximum Render Quality:** If your sequence includes transformations like Scale, Position, or Rotation adjustments, or if you have used effects like the Warp Stablizer, consider selecting this option to produce the highest quality output possible. This option requires more RAM and can take longer to encode. This option is usually required only when working without GPU acceleration (in software-only mode) or when using non-GPU-accelerated effects.

- **Video > More > Render Alpha Channel Only:** Some post-production workflows require a separate grayscale file representing the alpha channel (the channel that defines opacity). This option produces that file, rather than a full-color version.

- **Video > More > Time Interpolation:** If your exported file will have a different frame rate than your sequence or source clip, this menu lets you specify the way the frame-rate change is rendered. The options are the same as those that apply when changing clip playback speed in a sequence.

- **Metadata > Set Start Timecode:** This allows you to specify a start timecode other than 00:00:00:00 for the newly created file. This is useful if you are working in a broadcast environment where a specific timecode start may be a delivery requirement.

- **General > Import Into Project:** This option automatically imports the newly created media file into your current project so you can review it or use it as new source footage.

- **General > Use Previews:** When you render effects, preview files are produced that look like your original footage combined with the effects. If you enable this option, the preview files will be used as the source for the new export. This can save a significant amount of time that would otherwise be spent rendering the effects again. The result might be lower quality, depending on the format of the sequence preview files (see Lesson 2, "Setting Up a Project").

  If you have configured your sequence previews to be very high quality and have rendered all effects already, this option can save an enormous amount of time when exporting—possibly 10x faster or more. If you have enough storage space, a good example of this workflow would be setting your previews to ProRes 422 HQ and then delivering a ProRes 422 HQ media file.

- **General > Use Proxies:** If you have created and/or attached proxies to your media to speed up previews, Premiere Pro will normally use the original media files for the purposes of exporting. If you select the Use Proxies option, the proxies will be used instead. This can speed up exporting in a similar way to the Use Preview option—though be warned that proxy video files are usually low quality to keep file sizes small.

Finally, there are these options to consider when exporting any kind of media file:

- **Send To Media Encoder:** Click the Send To Media Encoder button to send the file to Adobe Media Encoder,  which will open automatically, allowing you to continue working in Premiere Pro while the export takes place.

- **Export:** Select this option to export directly from the Export Settings dialog box rather than sending the file to the Adobe Media Encoder queue. This is a simpler workflow and usually a faster export, but you won't be able to edit in Premiere Pro until the export is complete.

1 For this exercise, click the Send To Media Encoder button to send the file to Adobe Media Encoder. Media Encoder should start automatically, with your media encoding tasks ready to go.

2 Media Encoder will not begin encoding automatically. To begin encoding, click the Start Queue button ▶ in the upper-right corner.

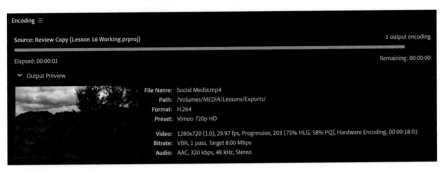

3 To add another item to the queue, choose more export settings in Premiere Pro and click the Send To Media Encoder button. Adobe Media Encoder will encode items in the order that they are added to the queue.

Exploring additional options in Adobe Media Encoder

Adobe Media Encoder brings a number of additional benefits. Although it involves a few extra steps beyond simply clicking the Export button in the Export Settings dialog box of Premiere Pro, the extra options are often worthwhile.

● **Note:** Adobe Media Encoder does not have to be used from Premiere Pro. You can launch Adobe Media Encoder on its own and browse inside Premiere Pro projects to choose items to transcode.

Here are some useful features:

- **Add files for encoding:** You can add files to Adobe Media Encoder by choosing File > Add Source. You can even drag files in from the Finder (macOS) or Windows Explorer (Windows). There's a Media Browser too, which you can use to locate items just as you would in Premiere Pro.

- **Import Premiere Pro sequences directly:** You can choose File > Add Premiere Pro Sequence to select a Premiere Pro project file and choose sequences to encode without ever launching Premiere Pro.

- **Render After Effects compositions directly:** You can import and encode compositions from Adobe After Effects by choosing File > Add After Effects Composition. Once again, you don't need to open Adobe After Effects.

- **Use a watch folder:** If you'd like to automate some encoding tasks, you can create watch folders by choosing File > Add Watch Folder and then assigning a preset to that watch folder. Watch folders exist in the Finder (macOS) or Windows Explorer (Windows) like any other folder. Provided Adobe Media Encoder is running, media files placed into the folder can be automatically encoded to the format specified in the preset.

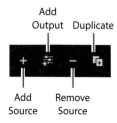

Add
Output Duplicate

Add   Remove
Source   Source

- **Modify a queue:** You can add, duplicate, or remove any encoding tasks using buttons at the top of the list.

- **Modify settings:** Once the encoding tasks are loaded into the queue, changing settings is easy; click the item's Format or Preset entry (in blue text), and the Export Settings dialog box appears.

When encoding has completed, you can quit Media Encoder.

Uploading to social media

Back in Premiere Pro, when encoding is complete, the next step is often to publish the video. In Export mode, you can pre-configure publishing settings to automatically upload your video when encoding is complete.

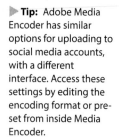

You will have noticed there are several output options displayed on the left side of the Export mode interface.

By default, the only enabled option is Media File, and these are the settings displayed in the middle of the interface. There are several other options that you can enable or disable at any time.

After selecting and activating a social media destination to display its settings, click Sign In beside the Publish heading in Settings to log into your account. You can configure media encoding and metadata settings, and Premiere Pro will upload the file automatically when it is created.

> **Tip:** Adobe Media Encoder has similar options for uploading to social media accounts, with a different interface. Access these settings by editing the encoding format or preset from inside Media Encoder.

The settings you choose are stored for future exports. This powerful feature is particularly useful: It allows you to preconfigure your social media upload settings and apply those settings to multiple future media uploads simply by activating an option.

If you click the three dots 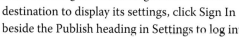 at the top of the list of output options, you'll find the option to add a media file destination. You can add multiple destinations, and each can have its own encoding settings.

All the activated output options are produced when you click Export. This means, in a single step, you can produce a full-quality exported media file, create a low-resolution small-file-size version for quick sharing and reviews, and upload to multiple social media accounts.

1 Click Edit to return to the Edit mode.

2 Make sure the Timeline panel is active, click Export at the top left of the interface.

3 Select and activate one of the social media output options to view its settings.

4 Click Sign In beside the Publish heading in Settings and to choose particular ways to deliver the file. For example, the YouTube output options allow you to specify a particular channel and/or playlist.

The menus populate automatically based on the account you have logged into.

5 When you are ready, click Edit to return to the Edit mode.

Each platform has its own delivery standards, though in many cases you can choose a high-quality source file and let the platform do the work of producing more highly compressed alternative versions from that file. Adobe Stock, for example, supports a range of video formats and codecs. If you produce a high-quality UHD (3840×2160) file, the server can handle the rest.

Exchanging projects with other editing applications

Collaboration is an essential part of post-production. Premiere Pro can both read and write project files and footage files that are compatible with many of the top editing and color-grading tools on the market. This makes it easier to share creative work, even if you and your collaborators are using different editing systems.

Premiere Pro supports EDLs (Edit Decision Lists), OMF (Open Media Framework), AAF (Advanced Authoring Format), ALE (Avid Log Exchange), and XML (Extended Markup Language) import and export.

If you're collaborating with an Avid Media Composer editor, you can use AAF as an intermediary, allowing the exchange of clip information, edited sequences, and some effects.

If you're collaborating with an Apple Final Cut Pro editor, you can use XML as an intermediary similarly.

It's straightforward to export an AAF or XML file from Premiere Pro; select a sequence you want to export, and either choose File > Export > AAF or choose File > Export > Final Cut Pro XML.

For more information about best practices when sharing creative work between applications, see *helpx.adobe.com/premiere-pro/using/exporting-projects-applications.html*.

Now that you have explored the export options, make sure you are in Edit mode, choose File > Close Project, and click Yes if you are invited to save.

Final practice

Congratulations! You have now learned how to import media; organize projects; create sequences; add, modify, and remove effects; mix audio; work with graphics and titles; and output to share your work with the world.

Now that you have completed this book, you may want to practice. To make this easier, the media files for a few productions have been combined in a single project file so you can explore the techniques you have learned.

These media files can be used only for personal practice and are not licensed for any form of distribution, including YouTube or any other online distribution, so please *do not upload* any of the clips or the results of any editing work you do with them. They are not for sharing with the public; they are just for you to practice with privately.

Trying out other workspaces

Throughout these lessons, you have worked in just a few of the available workspaces. Now that you have tried out several tools and explored many of the available panels, you may want to try out other workspaces.

All the available workspaces are listed in the Workspaces menu .

Consider starting with the Essentials workspace, which includes several panels you may find useful for different aspects of post-production.

Using practice media

The Final Practice.prproj project file, in the Lessons folder, contains original clips for a few productions that you can use to practice the editing techniques you have learned in this book:

- **Andrea Sweency NYC:** This is a short road-movie diary piece. Use the voice-over as a guide to practice combining 4K and HD footage in a single timeline. Experiment with panning and scanning in the 4K footage if you choose to use HD sequence settings.

- **Bike Race Multi-Camera:** This is simple multicamera footage. Experiment with live editing on a multicamera project.

- **Boston Snow:** This is a mixture of shots of Boston Common filmed in three resolutions. Use this media to experiment with Scale To Frame Size, Set To Frame Size, and keyframe controls to scale shots. Try using the Warp Stabilizer effect to lock one of the high-resolution clips and then scale up the clip and create a pan from one side to the other.

- **City Views:** This is a series of shots from the air and on land. Use these to experiment with image stabilization, color adjustment, and visual effects.

- **Desert:** Use the diverse colors to try color correction tools and combine the footage with music to produce a montage.

- **Interview:** This footage is useful for experimenting with the transcription and captioning tools. There are two camera angles for the same interview. You'll find an SRT file in the original media folder in case you want to practice importing captions.

- **Jolie's Garden:** This consists of atmospheric tableaux shot at 96 fps, set to play back at 24 fps, and filmed for a new feature film social media marketing campaign. Use these clips to experiment with the Lumetri Color panel Looks and speed change effects.

- **Laura in the Snow:** This is media for a commercial shot at 96 fps, set to play back at 24 fps. Use this footage to practice color correction and grading adjustments. Experiment with ramping slow motion and masking both the video and the effects you apply.

- **Music:** Use these music clips to practice creating an audio mix and editing visuals to music.

- **She:** This is a series of stylized, mostly slow-motion clips that will be useful for experimenting with speed changes and visual effects.

- **TAS:** This is footage from a short film, *The Ancestor Simulation*. Use this footage to try color grading and, as the footage is in two aspect ratios, mixing and matching the shots.

- **Theft Unexpected:** This is footage from an award-winning short film directed and edited by the author. Use this footage to experiment with trimming, and practice adjusting timing in simple dialogue to achieve different comic and dramatic results, changing the actors' performances.

- **Valley of Fire:** Try color adjustments to bring variation and visual interest, use speed changes to transform the experience of flying across a desert, and keyframe the rotating view to compensate for the movement and produce a static shot.

One of the best ways you can learn to edit with Premiere Pro is to create new projects of your own and explore new techniques. Non-linear editing means ongoing learning to continually improve your skills and expand your creativity.

Review questions

1 What's an easy way to export digital video if you want to create a self-contained file that can be played by most devices?

2 What social media-ready export options are available in Adobe Media Encoder?

3 What encoding format should you use when exporting a high-quality source file?

4 Must you wait for Adobe Media Encoder to finish processing its queue before working on a new Premiere Pro project?

Review answers

1 Click the Quick Export icon in the upper-right corner of the Premiere Pro interface.

2 There are built-in preset options for Vimeo, YouTube, X (formerly Twitter), and Facebook.

3 Use a format that supports high-quality codecs. A popular choice is QuickTime, which supports the ProRes codec. You could also choose DNxHR/DNxHD. It's important to check the required media specifications before exporting.

4 No. Adobe Media Encoder is a stand-alone application. You can work in other applications or even start a new Premiere Pro project while the render queue is processed.

INDEX